JAMES JOYCE AND PAUL L. LÉON: THE STORY OF A FRIENDSHIP REVISITED

Modernist Archives Series

From letters, journals, and notebooks to unpublished or out-of-print works, unfamiliar but important writings in translation and forgotten articles, Bloomsbury's Modernist Archives series makes available to researchers at all levels historical archival material that can reconfigure received views of Modernist literature and culture.

Annotated throughout and supported by extensive contextual essays by leading scholars, the Modernist Archives series is an essential resource for anyone with a serious interest in twentieth-century literature and culture.

Titles in Series

David Jones on Religion, Politics, and Culture
Edited by Thomas Berenato, Anne Price-Owen and Kathleen Henderson Staudt

David Jones's The Grail Mass and Other Works
Edited by Thomas Goldpaugh and Jamie Callison

Ezra Pound and Globe Magazine: The Complete Correspondence
Edited by Michael T. Davis and Cameron McWhirter

Ezra Pound's and Olga Rudge's The Blue Spill: A Manuscript Critical Edition
Edited by Mark Byron and Sophia Barnes

W. B. Yeats's Robartes-Aherne Writings
Wayne K. Chapman

Edith Ayrton Zangwill's The Call: A New Scholarly Edition
Edited by Stephanie Brown

Man into Woman: A Comparative Scholarly Edition
Edited by Pamela Caughie and Sabine Meyer

The Fifth Notebook of Dylan Thomas
Edited by John Goodby and Adrian Osbourne

Forthcoming Titles

The Correspondence of Ezra Pound and the Frobenius Institute, 1930–1959
Edited by Ronald Bush and Erik Tonning

James Joyce and Paul Léon, Paris (1936) © Boris Lipinski/Roger-Violle

JAMES JOYCE AND PAUL L. LÉON: THE STORY OF A FRIENDSHIP REVISITED

Edited by
Alexis Léon, Anna Maria Léon
and Luca Crispi

BLOOMSBURY ACADEMIC
LONDON • NEW YORK • OXFORD • NEW DELHI • SYDNEY

BLOOMSBURY ACADEMIC
Bloomsbury Publishing Plc
50 Bedford Square, London, WC1B 3DP, UK
1385 Broadway, New York, NY 10018, USA
29 Earlsfort Terrace, Dublin 2, Ireland

BLOOMSBURY, BLOOMSBURY ACADEMIC and the Diana logo are trademarks of Bloomsbury Publishing Plc

First published in Great Britain 2022
Paperback edition published 2024

Cover design: Rebecca Heselton
Cover image: Painters and Fishermen in Paris, 1930s. Photo © AGIP/ Bridgeman Images

A catalogue record for this book is available from the British Library.

A catalog record for this book is available from the Library of Congress.

ISBN: HB: 978-1-3501-3383-9
PB: 978-1-3503-5103-5
ePDF: 978-1-3501-3385-3
eBook: 978-1-3501-3384-6

Series: Modernist Archives

Typeset by RefineCatch Limited, Bungay, Suffolk

To find out more about our authors and books visit www.bloomsbury.com and sign up for our newsletters.

In memory of

Paul Leopold Léon
(1883–1942)

Elizabeth Lucie Léon
(1899–1972)

Alexis Léon
(1925–2018)

CONTENTS

LIST OF ILLUSTRATIONS

CHAPTER 6

LIST OF CONTRIBUTORS

Luca Crispi is Associate Professor of James Joyce Studies and Modernism in the School of English, Drama and Film at University College Dublin, Ireland. He co-curated the '*Ulysses*' at the National Library exhibition in 2004–5, where he first met the Léons. He has worked with Joyce's archives in various collections around the world for over twenty years. He is the author of *Joyce's Creative Process and the Construction of Characters in 'Ulysses': Becoming the Blooms* (Oxford University Press 2015) and is currently working on a monograph tentatively titled *Ulysses and Shakespeare and Company*.

Mary Gallagher is Professor of French and Francophone Studies at University College Dublin. She has published over one hundred critical studies in four main fields of research and reflection: academic ethics, postcolonial critique, translingualism and translation, and writing and global migration. Her book-length publications include *La Créolité de Saint-John Perse* (Gallimard 1998), *Soundings in French Caribbean Writing since 1950* (Oxford University Press 2002), *World Writing: Poetics, Ethics, Globalization* (University of Toronto Press 2008) and, most recently, the English translation and critical edition of Paul Morand's *Caribbean Winter* (Signal Books 2018). Her work on Paul Léon reflects her interest not just in translation, but also in migrant writing and in the ethics of transnational and transcontinental intellectual resistance.

Anna Maria Léon married Alexis Léon in Paris in 1979 and they were happy together for forty-three years. She encouraged this project from the start and ensured that this book would be published as a fitting tribute to her late husband and his family.

PREFACE

My name is Anna Maria M. Scala Léon (also known as Marilena) and I am the wife of Alexis L. Léon (who was also known as Alex). Alex and I married in Paris in 1979 and were together for forty-three years. I am very grateful for the life we shared. When I set about to write this preface, I was overwhelmed by the task – I had so many memories. For example, our trip to Montreux to visit the Nabokovs and Vladimir Nabokov asking Alex if we had set our wedding date. At that point in our relationship, we had not yet spoken about marriage. Mr Nabokov recalled when he would meet Alex's parents in Paris. As usual, I was a quiet listener, absorbing as much as I could from the interesting conversations.

Paul and Lucie came from two very prominent Russian Jewish families. They had lived in the two most important cities of the Russian Empire. Paul's family was from St Petersburg, while Lucie's was from Moscow. Elizabeth Lucie Ponizowsky (who was usually called Lucie) was the daughter of Amalia Wilenkin and Matthew Ponizowsky. Amalia died of the infamous Spanish flu that ravaged the world during the time of the Russian Revolution. Sasha Wilenkin, Amalia's brother, was executed during the Revolution. Russian history books now refer to him as a national hero. Lucie's father owned major textile factories in what are now Belarus and Poland. Matthew Ponizowsky managed to escape with Lucie, Genia and the twin sons James and Alexander. Thanks to the Nansen passports that they received from the Swedish Embassy, they made their way to England and settled in London with members of their extended family. Lucie's uncle Gregory Wilenkin had been attaché at the Russian embassies in the United States in Washington, DC, and in Tokyo, Japan.

Paul Leopold Léon was the youngest of Ida Rattner and Leopold Léon's six children, four girls and two boys. At her husband's death, Ida took over running the family's Grain Trading Company. They, too, managed to escape during the Russian Revolution with Nansen passports.

One of Paul's sisters, Henrietta, married a wealthy Russian antiquarian, V. Hirschmann Her portraits painted by Valentin Serov are now housed in the Tretyakov Gallery in Moscow. She often held chamber music concerts in their family home where Serge Koussevitzky (Director of the Boston Symphony Orchestra, who founded the Tanglewood Festival in Massachusetts) came to play. Henrietta and her husband took up residence in Paris, where they had an antique shop near the Élysée Palace. Paul worked in the antiques shop for a while.

At the beginning of their exile, Matthew Ponizowsky and his family took up residence in England at what was then the Kensington Gardens Hotel where they stayed for two years. They were certain that the Revolution would soon come to an end and that they would return to their homeland. Unfortunately, it wasn't to be. Having lived a very lavish lifestyle, their money started to dwindle and many members of the family had to look for some sort of employment. During their stay in London, and notwithstanding the opposition of her father, Paul and Lucie eloped and married at Kensington Town Hall.

The story goes that Lucie fell in love with Paul when she saw him dancing on the seashore in Finland where they first met.

Paul and Lucie went to live with Henrietta at 27, rue Casimir-Périer in the VIIth arrondissement. Henrietta and her husband rented the first-floor apartment, the same one in which the famous Russian-born French author of *Les malheurs de Sophie* (*Sophie's Misfortunes*), the Countess of Ségur, had lived half a century earlier. Several of Lucie's relatives also lived in Paris, though one of her twin brothers, Jim, lived in Brussels.

Alec was a very successful businessman and it is known that he had been a friend of Hazel and Peggy Guggenheim and Anaïs Nin. It was Nin who introduced Alec Ponizowsky to James Joyce, who was looking for someone to teach him Russian. Jim did not have the time and immediately thought of his brother-in-law, Paul Léon. That is how Paul and Joyce met. Joyce started visiting Paul at 27, rue Casimir-Périer, almost every day when he was in Paris. Paul was very much involved with Joyce, and Alex's mother, Lucie, who was the breadwinner in the Léon household, travelled frequently. Several languages were spoken in the Léon household, usually French and English, though at times Lucie and Paul spoke to each other in Russian. Alex was so upset that he could not understand what was being said that he persuaded his father to get him private Russian lessons.

The Léons, the Jolases and Joyces became close friends and enjoyed a fairly good life in Paris. Unfortunately, the Nazis put an end to all of that, but they all escaped from Paris, ending up in Saint-Gérand-le-Puy. During the day, while the adults were involved in their conversations, Alex would take his bicycle and explore the countryside. The Nazi occupation of France was a constant threat to them all. Paul wanted to return to Paris because he missed his books. Lucie needed to return to her post as a correspondent for the *New York Herald Tribune*, where her column 'Fashions in Paris' appeared regularly on Thursdays (under the pen name 'Lucie Noel'). Alex still had to pass his first-year exams for the Baccalaureate, which took two years to complete at that time. The Joyces were trying to get to Zurich and so, after a couple of months, the company disbanded.

Back in Paris, one day Paul met Samuel Beckett. Sam was very surprised to see him and asked what he was doing there. Paul replied that he was in Paris because Alex had to pass his exam. In the meantime, Joyce managed to reach Zurich, where he passed away on 13 January 1941. When Paul was informed that the landlord of the last apartment where the Joyces lived in Paris was putting the contents of the apartment up for auction, he made two trips there to recuperate, among other things, some documents that he knew were important. After Alex's father was taken prisoner and eventually sent to Silesia, Lucie decided that Alex could not stay in Paris any longer. So, with the help of Madame Francis Picabia, he became 'Alessandro Leone', took a train and, with the help of a '*passeur*', joined the Zone Libre and subsequently managed to join his grandfather and uncle Alec in Monte Carlo.

In Monte Carlo, he enjoyed playing tennis at the Country Club, and managed to get himself a job as a translator for the American troops stationed there. One day, he met a group of men and a couple of women arguing, one group speaking English, the other French. They were arguing about the cost of who knows what. Alex intervened showing off his language skills and was hired on the spot. That was the beginning of his work with the American Forces, which would take him to Frankfurt and would last for seven more years. When he completed his assignment with the US Army, Lucie convinced Alex to emigrate to the United States, which he did in 1956. His first job was with Brooks Brothers. The following year he was hired by Pepsi Cola, where he spent twenty-seven years in various capacities around the world. When Pepsi underwent a restructuring in

1979, Alex was fifty-five, and decided to accept Pepsi Cola's offer of early retirement. In September of the same year, my children, Marco and Barbara, and I moved from Rome to Paris and we settled in the apartment at 27, rue Casimir-Périer that Alex inherited in 1972 when his mother passed away. Marco and Barbara enrolled at the Italian Lycée in the nearby rue Sédillot.

We lived in Paris for four years. When we arrived, every drawer and cupboard was full of things, so, to make room for our own belongings, we filled up boxes that were eventually transferred to Bailly, a storage and moving company. The following year we were approached by the Irish broadcaster RTÉ who wanted to feature the Léon apartment in a documentary about James Joyce in Paris: *Is There One Who Understands Me?: The World of James Joyce*. Seán O'Mórdha, the director, came to visit us and asked Alex for permission, which of course he was happy to give. It was either 1980 or 1981. Maria Jolas and Philippe Soupault came to the apartment as they had done so many times before and the filming took place. They sat in the very room where Joyce, Paul and Soupault would meet around the table, which is now at the James Joyce Centre in Dublin, along with the famous chair in which Joyce liked to sit slumped over. The film won an Emmy Award for Best Documentary in 1982.

Soon after, we started the renovation work that the apartment badly needed, and we sent a lot more things to keep company with other things already in storage at Bailly. Alex kept looking for a new job, even though it was not easy at his age, but, with the help of former colleagues, he always managed to keep himself busy. In 1984, we moved to England to live in Oxfordshire, where Marco and Barbara attended the European School, Culham.

Alex was a wonderful husband and stepfather to my children. He never interfered but was always ready to help when asked. Marco and Barbara are happily married and are the proud parents of two sets of children, a boy and a girl each, all of whom are busy with their lives and careers.

A very intelligent man, Alex was also on the school's '*tableau d'honneur*' both at the Lycée Montaigne and the Lycée Louis Le Grand. He spoke a number of languages (French, Russian and English fluently, plus Italian, German, Spanish, Portuguese and some Serbo-Croatian).

At the end of a cruise that we took from St Petersburg to Moscow, he participated in a show that the guests on board organized to thank the entertainers for all they had done for their guests. Alex made a speech in Russian and explained that our trip was in homage to the memory of his parents who had fled Russia during the Revolution and had then settled in France. People cried and commented that they were very moved. They said it was like opening a book written by Pushkin, with a pure Russian language with no modern words. On the same trip we had the opportunity to visit the house where his mother lived before the Revolution; it is now the Afghan ambassador's residence in Moscow.

Alex never tried to portray himself as a Joycean. He always said that James Joyce happened to be his parent's friend and that usually entailed a lot of his father's time. In 2000, at a time when Alex was not working, while the first-floor apartment was rented, we took up temporary residence in the pied-à-terre on the sixth floor of 27, rue Casimir-Périer. For some time, I had been begging Alex to sort all the stuff we had in storage for so many years.

Every morning, Alex would don his worn Burberry raincoat and a pair of old shoes, and go to sort out our things at the storage facility. After discarding quite a lot, he put in the cellar things that should be looked at more carefully later. Finally, the time came for him to start looking at the boxes he had set aside. One afternoon, he came upstairs with a package wrapped in paper with something in Russian written on it that was held together with just a piece of string, and the rest is history. What a stroke of luck that he yielded to my insistence that he clean up the storage place. The package contained the magnificent collection of Joyce manuscripts that are now in the National Library of Ireland. As a joke, our friends often ask us if there is anything else in storage that needs to be sorted out.

Years later, chatting with Luca Crispi, we agreed that we should reissue Lucie's memoir and expand it. The Gotham Book Mart in New York was no longer in business and second-hand copies of Lucie's book were being sold on Amazon. Alex, Luca and I agreed that the expanded version of Lucie's book should concentrate on Paul, his background, his studies, his degree in Philosophy of Law and his work in Sociology. I believe we should consider Paul foremost a Jean-Jacques Rousseau and Benjamin Constant scholar.

Paul always felt that Joyce, although he had exiled himself from Ireland, had always had a longing for his country of origin. This explains Paul's decision to deposit the fifty manila folders that contained all the documents he had recovered from Joyce's flat after his death in the care of the Irish Legation in Paris, though with the caveat that they should not be made public for fifty years after Joyce's own untimely death. This collection is also in the National Library of Ireland.

As you will be able to read later in the book, during Paul's internment at the Drancy and Compiègne camps, Lucie and Paul were able to exchange smuggled correspondence thanks to someone the family referred to as '*Rayon de Soleil*', a social worker who helped them a great deal. Lucie also volunteered with the Red Cross to sort the packages that the families were authorized to send to the internees in such a way that they would comply with the rules. When we first read those letters, often written on tiny pieces of paper, Alex and I embraced and could not stop sobbing. After a good deal of thought, we agreed that this correspondence should be part of the expanded book, which was already underway, and that they eventually should be donated to the Holocaust Museum in Washington, DC.

Some of Alex's former colleagues have been kind enough to send me their memories of Alex, who sadly passed away on Friday, 29 June 2018, before this book could be finished. Ted Glover, who worked with Alex at Pepsi Cola, wrote that he vividly recalled two instances:

> Language skills ranked high among Alex's many talents. English was his third language, behind Russian and French, yet he routinely solved the London *Times* crossword puzzles. In addition, he was highly functional (if not fluent) in Spanish, Italian, Portuguese, German and Serbo-Croatian. In contrast, when I worked with Alex in London, I was a young marketing guy sent out from the corporate headquarters with no prior international experience and no language capabilities beyond the tattered remnants of my high school French.
>
> One day, our mutual boss approached us with the suggestion that we undertake a project together somewhere in Central Europe. I forget which country – possibly Poland or the Czech Republic. What I remember clearly is the expression of horror on Alex's face. His instant reaction: 'But Norman, we don't speak that language!' I burst out laughing and said in the kindest voice I could muster: 'Welcome to my world, Alex.'
>
> On another occasion, Alex and I were attending business meetings together in Paris. One night we had dinner at some lovely restaurant, for which Alex paid the bill. He

> then suggested that since the night was still young, we might want to go somewhere for after-dinner drinks, and specifically recommended the Crazy Horse Cabaret. Never having been there I quickly agreed. Since Alex had paid for dinner, I happily picked up the bar bill, which was roughly equal. But I remember thinking that it really didn't matter, because everything was on expense account anyway . . . until it wasn't. A week or two later, our boss came into my office, returned my expense report and said rather aggressively that the company wasn't going to pay for entertainment at the Crazy Horse Cabaret. I stammered and stuttered, mounting the best defence I could, based on the notion that our after-dinner drinks were simply an extension of dinner. Norman coolly replied that he'd approved Alex's expense report for dinner, but no way he was going to approve reimbursement of my bar bill at the Crazy Horse. With hindsight, that experience underscored Alex's street-smart side. I'd been outfoxed by a fox!

And Peter Riepenhausen wrote from Villeneuve Loubet, France:

> It is more than fifty years ago when I first met Alex at Pepsi and I worked closely with him during my entire time at Pepsi until I left in 1978. The best comment I can make is, that until both our retirement about twenty years later Alex was always one of the first to whom I went to obtain his advice or active help. I very much appreciated Alex's excellent education, his intelligence combined with outstanding objectivity. We often had very open discussions and even if we had different opinions Alex has always been absolutely loyal and I could trust his support.

Lennie Sassine wrote to say:

> Alex Léon was a good friend and dependable colleague for many years. Endowed with a sharp mind and fluent in both English and French, he easily fitted into any position he was assigned to. My own personal memory of Alex is as a connoisseur of wine and the most honest employee of the company. When charging a legitimate entertainment expense, he always deducted his own share of the expense – truly unique.
>
> Alex retired and elected to live in Florida with his beloved wife Marilena. He travelled very often to the UK, where he and his wife had family. I met with Alex, for the last time, during a trip to Oxford in 2006. We had an interesting conversation, both of us being retired, reminiscing about our experiences working for PepsiCo.
>
> We remained in touch, by phone and e-mail, until his untimely death.

I now leave you to discover the book that has been conceived to honour the memory of Paul and Lucie Léon. For my part, I also want to say: Alex, I am so sorry that you are not here with me . . .

ACKNOWLEDGEMENTS

Anna Maria Léon would like to sincerely thank Prof. David Llewelyn of David Llewelyn & Co LLC in Singapore, who has been a tower of strength. Alexis and I are forever grateful. To the memory of Peter Selley and his wife Juliet Dwek Selley. She would also like to thank Simon John, the photographer, for his collaboration and expertise. Many thanks to my friends Mrs L. D'Overbeck, Mrs Julie Dempsey, Mrs Karen Barash, Ms Peggy Frankston of the Holocaust Museum in Washington, DC to which Alexis and I have pledged to donate all the original letters and any other documents that may be of interest to them. Also Alex's Pepsi Cola colleagues who have gracefully contributed reminiscing the Pepsicoleros Happy Times. Last but least to all my family, especially my children, Marco and Barbara Betti-Berutto for their support and compassion showed during the completion of this work that lends a new perspective to the friendship of Paul Léon and James Joyce.

Luca Crispi would like to thank Colette O'Flaherty and the staff of the National Library of Ireland; Dr James Maynard and the staff of the Poetry Collection of the University Libraries, University at Buffalo, The State University of New York; as well as Marc Carlson and Milissa Burkart in the Department of Special Collections & University Archives, McFarlin Library, University of Tulsa. He is very grateful for the advice and support that Geert Lernout, Daniel Ferrer and Terence Killeen provided throughout. He also wants to thank Niels Caul for the editorial assistance he provided at the start and Ben Doyle and Laura Cope at Bloomsbury for their encouragement and support in getting this work into print, as well as Ben Harris, the copy-editor. This project has been part of the family for a long time, and Luca couldn't have completed it without Rita and Livia's patience and encouragement.

ABBREVIATIONS

BL	British Library
HCE	James Joyce, *Haveth Childers Everywhere* (Paris: Henry Babou and Jack Kahane; New York: The Fountain Press, 1930)
JJA	*The James Joyce Archive*, eds. Michael Groden et al., 63 volumes (New York: Garland, 1977–8); cited by volume and page number(s)
MS	Manuscript
NLI	National Library of Ireland
FW	James Joyce, *Finnegans Wake* (London: Faber & Faber, 1975)

CHAPTER ONE

Contexts

LUCA CRISPI

Paul Léon was James Joyce's closest friend and advisor in the last decade of his tragically short life. Joyce always believed in the forces of coincidence, and it seems that fate brought the two men together for the most challenging chapter of the writer's life, both personally and creatively. Without Paul's ever-devoted emotional and psychological support, his well-informed legal advice and his pragmatic financial counsel, Joyce would not have been able to manage the mounting challenges that he and his family faced in the 1930s. Furthermore, Joyce certainly could not have completed *Finnegans Wake* if Paul had not intervened to confront the obstacles that were preventing Joyce from 'finishing' his deliberately endless 'Work in Progress'. Lucie Léon summed it up best: 'Joyce needed a friend on whom he could depend for practical advice and spiritual consolation. My husband Paul, because of his interest in Joyce's work and his affection and deep sympathy for Joyce the man, became that friend.'[1]

While James Joyce is a world-renowned writer, whose works continue to engage readers and critics, and his life has been chronicled in Richard Ellmann's monumental biography, Paul Léon remains 'little known', as Maria Jolas put it over sixty years ago.[2] The aim of this volume is to shed light on their often-misunderstood friendship by returning to the voluminous archives that survive – thanks almost entirely to the courageous and tireless efforts of Paul himself. Chapter 2 makes available once again Lucie's memoir, *James Joyce and Paul L. Léon: The Story of a Friendship*, a personal and anecdotal account that was born out of the love she had for her husband, and the pride she always maintained for his work and legacy. Chapter 3 then tells the story of how the memoir came to be, starting life as a talk Lucie gave to an eager and enthusiastic meeting of the James Joyce Society at the Gotham Book Mart in New York City, and how it grew through many rewritings. It also captures the deepening friendship between two foundational Joyceans at the start of the so-called 'Joyce industry': Lucie Léon and John J. Slocum, the premier private collector of his generation (or any other to come for that matter), whose bibliography of Joyce's works is still the standard reference almost seventy years after it was first published.[3] Chapter 4 brings together Paul's writings on Joyce. They represent all we know about his critical engagement with Joyce's work and, more importantly, they capture his own perspective on his twelve-year friendship with Joyce. In Chapter 5, the longest in the book, we are publishing for the first time Paul's poignantly moving letters to Lucie during his internment in the Drancy and Compiègne camps from 21 August 1941 to 26 March 1942, prepared by Mary Gallagher both in the French original and in an English translation. The letters are an incomparable record of the slow but progressive decline of a man of letters when faced with the brutality of persecution by the Nazi forces and the physical and mental deprivation that they brought to bear on him. They vividly bring to life Paul's final months in his own voice, something that he would otherwise had been deprived of if his family had not preserved this invaluable collection and been willing to share it. It is impossible to read these final missives to his beloved wife without being moved to tears for the persecuted individuals and humanity in general during that dark period of world history. In the final chapter, Paul and Lucie's son, Alexis, recounts his own anecdotes about his family and their lives once they had been overtaken by Joyce's all-encompassing presence. It sums up the entire Léon family's enduring friendship with James Joyce and his family. As Lucie tells us, '[Joyce] was conscious of intruding into our lives and monopolizing the time of my husband, and often he would say to me, "Why don't you simply throw me out?" But I am certain he would have been very upset if we had taken such a suggestion seriously.'[4]

We hope that this volume will serve as a prompt to others to explore Paul Léon's life and writings so that we have a better sense of the man and his works.

PAUL LÉON: SCHOLAR, LAWYER, ADVISER, FAMILY MAN AND FRIEND

Paul Léopoldovitch Léon was born on 25 April 1893 in St Petersburg, Russia, the youngest child of Leopold Fedorovich Léon (1845–1902) and Ida Issodorovna Rattner (1863–1932).[1] His brothers and sisters were Henriette (1885–1970), Eugenia (known as Xénie or Genia; birth and death dates uncertain), Beatrice (1890–1950), Ekaterina (known as Catherine or Catia; 1891–1986), and Alexander (1891–1944). From the age of 10 Paul attended the city's principal German school, St Peter's, where he also became fluent in English, graduating with a Silver Medal in 1911. He visited London twice in 1912, staying there for three months.

Paul then went on to study in the Law Faculty at St Petersburg Imperial University, where he earned a first-class degree in 1915. As fate would have it, Paul spent the next year writing a thesis on 'Home Rule in Ireland', a subject that he and James Joyce would have been eager to discuss in the dozen or so years of their friendship.[2] Paul's doctoral studies were cut short when he was mobilized for active military service, volunteering in 1915 with the 334th Ibitsk Infantry Regiment. In April 1917 Paul enrolled in the Officer's Training Academy and was promoted to the rank of ensign in September. He then went to the Officer's Machine Gun Artillery Training school in Oranienbaum, just west of St Petersburg on the Gulf of Finland.

In January 1918 Paul returned to his studies at Moscow University, becoming an assistant lecturer in constitutional law. He worked on a dissertation on Mikhail Bakunin, entitled 'The Problem of the State in the Light of Anarchism' under the supervision of the noted Professors Paul I. Novgorodtzeff and S. A. Kotliarevsky. Paul's academic career ended abruptly when he, his family and so many others fled Russia following the Bolshevik Revolution in November 1918. Nonetheless, in 1925 he managed to have a portion of his dissertation published by Russian-language publishers in Prague and Germany. The Léons travelled to Finland and Sweden where they stayed for five months. It was here that he first met Elizabeth Lucie Ponizowsky.

The Léon family arrived in London in April 1919 and Paul quickly entered the intellectual circles there, collaborating with the distinguished Librarian at the London Library, Sir Charles Hagberg Wright (1893–1940), on a bibliographical study entitled 'Englishmen in Russia', and contributing to Wright's article on 'Herzen: The Founder of

Russian Liberalism' in *The Fortnightly Review* (November 1920). The Léons and Wrights remained friends as well as collaborators for many years, with Paul often providing bibliographical information about and locating books on Russian history and literature for Wright. In one of their letters, Wright thanked Paul for his contribution to another article entitled 'Bakounine' in *The Fortnightly Review* (May 1921), writing that Paul was responsible for 'the greater part of the work'.[3] Paul also prepared English translations of Russian articles for the *New Age* magazine in 1920.

Paul and Lucie married on 26 July 1920 in Kensington Town Hall, London. Two weeks later they moved to Paris, along with most of their extended families, settling in the city for the rest of their lives. To make ends meet, at first Paul worked in an antique shop owned and run by his brother-in-law, Wladimir Ossipovitch Hirschmann (1867–1936) and Henriette. Then Paul and Lucie's only son was born on 12 September 1925: they named him Alexis Leopold Alexander Léon. In 1926 and 1927 Paul obtained the required diplomas to pursue a Doctorate in Law in France, while at the same time contributing to journals in London and Paris, including his 'Une analyse russe d'Adolphe', which appeared in the *French Quarterly* in 1927, as well as several articles and reviews in the *Annales de la Société Jean Jacques Rousseau*. In fact, he was an active and well-respected member of this society in Geneva for the rest of his career.[4]

In 1928 Simon Kra publishers in Paris issued two of Paul's works in French. The first was his edited notes to Baronne Elisabeth de Nolde's 1905 translation of *Lettres de Madame de Staël á Benjamin Constant*, and the other was Paul's edition of the *Lettres de Nicolas II et de sa Mère*. Paul and Joyce became fast friends at the beginning of that same year. Lucie writes that from the start 'their daily program [was] already established. They were to see each other almost every day thereafter—days in which they worked together and days in which their selfless friendship was created.'[5] Although no letters between them survive before 1930, Joyce's manuscripts make it clear that their work together began in earnest in 1929, while Joyce was preparing his latest 'Work in Progress' fragment, *Haveth Childers Everywhere*, for press (see the following section for more information about Paul's contributions to that work). Beginning in November 1930, Joyce enlisted Paul, Eugene Jolas and Ivan Goll to review the French translation of *Anna Livia Plurabelle* that had initially been prepared by Samuel Beckett and Alfred Péron. Along with Philippe Soupault, Joyce met with Paul and Jolas in the Léon apartment in rue Casimir-Périer on Thursday afternoons. By mid-March Joyce was finally satisfied with the text, and then it appeared in the May issue of *La Nouvelle Revue Française*.[6]

At the same time, Paul began to take on more responsibilities in the management of Joyce's business dealings with his publishers in Paris, London, New York and around the world. Joyce also tasked Paul to be his intermediary with his agent (James B. Pinker & Sons) and his solicitor (Monro Saw & Co.), both of whom were based in London, and he assisted the Joyces as they managed the most basic aspects of their daily lives in Paris and abroad.[7] When away from Paris, Joyce and Paul kept in touch by means of letters and telegrams, but more often they simply spoke on the phone; this may explain why the surviving letters from Joyce to Paul are usually very brief and sometimes they are simply lists of instructions regarding the mass of correspondence he relied on Paul to reply to on his behalf. On the other hand, Paul's letters sometimes included puns and jokes, which Joyce tended to discourage. Joyce wrote: 'Anyhow as things are better better confine your letters to business.'[8] Most of Joyce's letters revolve around the same topics: difficulties with publishers, requests for money to be sent to him, instructions on paying bills, other errands Paul should run, his health, as well as the weather where he happened to be vacationing. This is a typical example from the Carlton Elite Hotel in Zurich in October 1934:

> Dear Léon: I hope you are better. We are not. Here's a cheque. Please pay Jung, Mrs Raphael (900 frcs, the rest in a week or so), whatever your expenses are and send me the usual by wire. I want that letter back from Goll or the expert's opinion. Please ring up [illegible name] and tell him the facts. From Mr Ver Hulst (who is anxious to have my MS) I want through you, Pinker or the Jolases some information as to 1) will he do the alphabet or not 2) did he send Mime to Faber, Budgen, and Goyert 3) will he pay Lucia the 5000 frs? Please cable Cerf preparing the reply. Has Lane managed for anyone to read the proof of *Ulysses* or is he supposed to be printing it? We got no suitable reply to our advert for flat here. My wife is against any return to Paris or set up of a flat there. If there any further news I shall let you know. Hope you are all well in no. 27.[9]

More generally, Joyce ended one very business-like letter by signing off: 'Thanking you for your trouble I confirm and sanction your doings on my behalf.'[10]

Besides taking care of all of Joyce's commissions, Paul continued to engage in his own scholarly pursuits throughout the 1930s. At the start of the decade, Rieder in Paris published Paul's monograph *Benjamin Constant*. Then, at its close (just as *Finnegans Wake* was finally being published), he collaborated with Nikolai Timacheff on a French translation of his *Introduction to the Sociology of Law*.[11] Paul was also Deputy Secretary General of the *Archives de Philosophie du Droit et de Sociologie Juridique* from 1930 until he resigned in 1940, during which time he published five major studies of Rousseau in its journal, where he also had other articles published, including 'Une doctrine relativiste et expérimentale de la souveraineté – H.-J. Laski' and 'Les idées sociales et politiques du guild-socialism', both in 1931.[12] The following year, they published his article 'Doctrines sociales et politiques du moyen âge (des origines au IXe siècle)'.[13] Busy as Paul was with his own intellectual pursuits, Joyce continued to rely on his friend and confidant to run innumerable errands for him both while he was in Paris and also when he was away on his working vacations across Europe. In 1931, they included having Paul write to Joyce's oculist in Zurich and telephone one friend to contact another. He also entrusted Paul to keep everyone updated on his itinerary, usually with a view to having them send advances and royalty payments as urgently as possible. Besides everything else Joyce expected Paul to do, his principal charge that year was to make sure that reluctant publishers returned Lucia Joyce's artwork. That year Joyce also signed a contract for the simultaneous publication of 'Work in Progress' in book form with Faber & Faber in London and the Viking Press in New York. At the time, no one could have predicted how onerous an ordeal getting *Finnegans Wake* into print would be for the writer and everyone else involved in this monumental endeavour. Over the next eight years Joyce had bursts of productive activity that were followed by prolonged periods of writer's block, especially when his creative and emotional energy was focused on his family as well as his own precarious health. As he became more preoccupied with Lucia's well-being, the mid-1930s were the most difficult years of Joyce's personal and professional life. To everyone concerned, it seemed that what turned out to be Joyce's final work would remain in progress forever.

In 1932 Paul took centre stage in the management of Joyce's publishing affairs when on the writer's behalf he began to pressure Sylvia Beach to publish yet another Shakespeare and Company impression of *Ulysses*. Given the impending publication of the book in

America, as well as her own financial and personal concerns, Beach rightly refused. Ultimately, a concerted effort by Joyce's circle of friends and admirers convinced Beach to give up her publishing rights and thus almost all her financial interest in the book. On 9 February, Paul introduced himself to T. S. Eliot in the following way: 'I am acting as lawyer for Mr Joyce in Paris and according to his wishes I am to inform you that I am in possession of a letter from Miss Beach containing a declaration annulling the contract which existed between her and Mr Joyce and a recognition of his ownership of the world rights for *Ulysses*.'[14] Once Shakespeare and Company was no longer the sole publisher of *Ulysses*, Paul worked tenaciously to ensure that Joyce's most lucrative work should be published in Europe, America and Britain.[15] In fact, even as the negotiations with Beach were ongoing, following Joyce's instructions, Léon singlehandedly arranged to have the Albatross Press issue a new continental edition of the book. As Joyce focused more of his time and energy on Lucia's welfare, Paul effectively took charge of Joyce's legal and financial negotiations with current and prospective publishers, often meeting with them in his apartment, reviewing contracts, offering advice both to the writer as well as to the publishers, and always ensuring that the author's advances and royalties were paid in full and as quickly as possible.

Given his legal training, Paul quickly became an expert in the complexities of international copyright laws, especially as they pertained to *Ulysses* and 'Work in Progress', much more so than Joyce's ineffective literary agents. As the Albatross/Odyssey Press edition of *Ulysses* was being readied for publication, Bennett Cerf of Random House instructed Paul on how to prepare a copy of *Ulysses* for seizure by the US Customs authorities by cramming it full of positive critical reviews. Joyce was always anxious for news about the court cases in America and relied on Paul to remain in constant contact with Cerf. From 1932 onwards, virtually everyone who wanted to reach Joyce came to realize that the best and often only way to do so was through Paul. It became quite routine for Paul to reply to correspondence addressed to Joyce. In fact, while there are many hundreds of letters from Paul to the various publishers, only a few dozen from Joyce survive. It was also due to Paul's strenuous activity on Joyce's behalf that Allen Lane of the Bodley Head signed a contract to publish *Ulysses* in England. In fact, rather than do what was expected of him as Joyce's agent, Pinker counselled Lane to travel to Paris to discuss the terms with Paul, even though both the publisher and the agent worked minutes away from one another in London. Nonetheless, Pinker certainly expected his usual 10% commission, just as Paul insisted on working on Joyce's behalf without payment. After a lengthy court battle, the Random House edition appeared in January 1934, while the English edition only appeared in October 1936.

In 1934, just as the *Archiv für Rechts- und Sozialphilosophie* published Paul's 'Le problème des sources du droit positif',[16] he was also negotiating the publication of Joyce's latest instalment of 'Work in Progress' with the Servire Press in The Hague. One of Joyce's primary motivations in allowing yet another fragment of his work to appear was to promote his daughter's artwork, which ended up being featured on the cover and also as the front initial and tailpiece of *The Mime of Mick, Nick and the Maggies* (see *FW* 210–59).[17] Besides dedicating so much of his time and effort to the management of the practical matters related to Joyce's works, Paul also became Joyce's closest friend and a bulwark against the mounting difficulties the entire Joyce family faced in the 1930s. As the years went on, Joyce increasingly withdrew from almost all personal, social and professional interactions, even with Harriet Shaw Weaver, his publisher, patron and most caring friend since 1914. At times Joyce simply stopped writing to Weaver at all. Therefore, she increasingly relied on Paul to keep her posted on what was happening with the Joyces, which he did tirelessly. Paul and Weaver worked together to solve the complex practical and emotional issues that Joyce and his family faced. It also often fell to Paul to ask Weaver to intervene with Joyce's solicitors so that he could draw upon the capital that she had bequeathed to him, against their more sensible advice not to do so. For almost a decade, Paul kept Weaver abreast of Joyce's health, work, shifting moods, and the family's always uncertain financial situation. Her concern for Joyce naturally extended to his daughter's health, treatments, happiness and, of course, her future. Paul's letters to Weaver chart the ups and downs of Lucia's condition and its psychological, emotional and material impact on the family, particularly the consequences that caring for her had on Joyce's ability to continue writing. In one letter after another, Weaver expressed her gratitude to Paul for keeping her informed, as well as for enjoining her to persist in her efforts to assist Joyce. She knew better than anyone else outside the Joyce family how important his presence was in the writer's life. On St Patrick's Day 1934, she wrote:

> I am greatly obliged to you for your long and very full letter and also for your suggestion that I should write direct and frankly to Mr Joyce. I have done so and shall be posting the letter today with this one. I think I should never have written to him had you not urged it, believing as I did that he still would not wish to hear from me. I have stressed the points that you suggested but greatly doubt whether the letter will carry anything at all the weight you think it may. If anyone has been a good and true friend to Mr Joyce it is yourself.[18]

Towards the end of the year, she confided her views about Joyce's state to Paul:

> I think too that you are right in your belief that constant alternations of hope and despair mean an altogether too nerve-racking strain for Mr Joyce with his extremely sensitive nature and that a definite verdict would be the best in the end for him, as also for Mrs Joyce who, you think, is now more able to bear it. All the same, one cannot expect them not to cling desperately to this last hope thrown out by the last doctor to see her, Dr Jung. In fact, I suppose they ought not entirely to give up hope while this last shred of it remains. But if only they would come away, leaving their daughter in the charge of Dr Jung while this last experiment is tried . . .
>
> And certainly the financial situation, in view of the bad outlook for the future, is very serious. Even large American royalties will soon melt away, and English ones (on Ulysses), Mr Joyce says, are to be reduced—if ever they do materialize. I imagine that Mr Joyce's Johannesburg stock must be rapidly approaching exhaustion point . . .
>
> PS I do not suppose Mr Joyce will write to me himself in his present state, so that if you would let me know any further definite news I should be very grateful.[19]

Although many other hurdles would still have to be overcome before *Finnegans Wake* finally appeared, Joyce finally began to make a real effort to finish the book in 1936. Lucie recounts her excitement when she delivered the manuscript of what would become Books I and III of *Finnegans Wake* to T. S. Eliot in London on Joyce's birthday that year.[20] At that juncture, Paul shared the writer's optimism that the book would be finished soon. In fact, Joyce continued to work steadily throughout 1936 and 1937, but the expectation that the book would appear on Joyce's father's birthday on 4 July 1938 proved to be unrealistic.

Meanwhile, Paul continued to regularly contribute critical reviews, often in *Politica*, the journal of the London School of Economics and Political Science, including one on R. W. and A. J. Carlyle's 1936 volume *A History of Medieval Political Theory in the*

West,[21] and another on W. I. Jennings's *Cabinet Government*.[22] His scholarly work also continued to be published. In 1937 his 'L'évolution de l'idée de la souveraineté avant Rousseau' appeared in *Archives de Philosophie du Droit et de Sociologie Juridique*.[23] Joyce must have realized the importance of Paul's intellectual engagements and was certainly aware of the extent to which his incessant demands on his friend took away from the time and effort Paul could devote to his own critical writings as well as to his family. Nonetheless, as usual, Joyce left the messy details of communicating with his publishers to Paul. While he was always there to advise on how best to proceed, there is no doubt that Paul was merely conveying Joyce's often ambivalent instructions in so many of the letters he wrote to Faber & Faber and the Viking Press. Paul recounted one particularly difficult charge that Joyce had given him at the start of 1938, just four months before Joyce wanted his still unnamed book published:

> I sent the other day under Mr Joyce's dictation an extremely curt and frank letter to Mr Eliot. Of course Mr Eliot diplomatically retired from the scene and handed the pen to one of the partners Mr Geoffrey Faber . . . Mr Joyce attaches so little importance to his letter that he has not even answered it yet but in point of fact it may involve an entire change of plans . . .[24]

When the publishers politely disabused Joyce of the idea of publishing in midsummer and pointed out the obvious but inconvenient fact that he still had not finished the book or even revealed its title, he decided to travel to Zurich. In mid-August Paul had a more positive report for Weaver:

> As you know it is now some eighteen months since he has been working on Work in Progress night and day and I am happy to say that the termination is not any more very distant. In fact I believe that the work will be finished by October [1938] . . . All this tremendous strain and work will of course tell on Mr Joyce's health. I fear a collapse when the work will be finished especially if the publishers raise difficulties as they are wont to.[25]

Paul's concerns about Joyce's health proved to be correct, as was his premonition that there would be difficulties getting *Finnegans Wake* published. Nonetheless, the next day he wrote another long letter to Weaver to say that he had just dined with the Joyces. He started with the facts, but at the end he confided one of the clearest statements of what he valued most about his friendship with Joyce:

> I found Mrs Joyce terribly depressed as she sees herself now separated by insurmountable obstacles from her second child. In fact I have never seen her as depressed as she was yesterday. As for Mr Joyce in spite of the three hours daily sleep he does not look badly and is aloof though not gay. His work is apparently his principal preoccupation as always, and he chooses it to hide whatever pain he may feel in his heart.

Then, Paul shared the good news that Joyce had arranged to get the Austrian writer Hermann Broch to England, and that he was busily writing letters to secure travel permits for several other Austrians who were trying to emigrate as well. He was clearly pleased to report that Joyce had undertaken all of this 'himself as I did not hear of it until it was done'. He also noted that Joyce's 'influence with the Foreign Office here in France must be considerable and I explain it by the fact that it is to a great extent manned by French men of letters'. Then Paul declared that Joyce's insistent efforts in these matters 'throws quite a new light on Mr Joyce's attitude'. He conceded:

> It is understandable perhaps that anyone who tries to grapple seriously with the many very serious problems, social, economic and political which harass the world today will deplore what may seem the purposeless triviality of his writings and the inconsequent wastefulness of certain of his habits and both these judgements may be very sound and matter of fact.

This shows that after almost a decade of hard work assisting Joyce with 'Work in Progress', Paul was still not fully convinced of its artistic merit, but he quickly qualified his overall judgement by adding that Joyce's actions as a person 'however are apparently not inconsistent with a very active intervention when appealed to on behalf of people who suffer the hardships and perils of the two new devouring idols [presumably fascism and communism]'. He concludes that 'this activity must reconcile us to an outward indifference which combines' with Joyce's 'exceptional qualities of the heart' and his tenacity to do whatever 'he can [to] be of help to a human being'.[26] This is precisely what Lucie underscores about their friendship as well: from first to last, Paul was always 'more interested in Joyce as a person'.[27]

Meanwhile, in September 1938, as Faber & Faber's printers were doing their best to contend with the unexpected technical difficulties caused by the marginal notes in Book II, Chapter 2, Joyce continued to write the finale of Book IV (and so of *Finnegans Wake*). Finally, on 13 November Joyce telegraphed Weaver to let her know that he had finally completed his 'Work in Progress'.[28] Unsurprisingly, just a month later, Joyce collapsed in the Bois de Boulogne due to years of overwork and stress. Paul let Weaver know that '[h]appily the collapse did not last—but of course he has not stopped working', as the doctor had advised. In fact, there was a lot more to be done to get the book into print. The number and kinds of additions and changes Joyce wanted made on the various settings of proofs were even greater than those for *Ulysses* seventeen years earlier.

Geert Lernout has described Paul as 'the one person without whom Joyce's last book would never have been finished at all'.[29] Still, as he was helping to prepare *Finnegans Wake* for publication, Paul confided to Weaver that he continued to have reservations about the book that he had an indispensable role in bringing into the world:

> [T]his makes me think and wonder how this work thousands and tens of thousands words of which have passed through my typewriter can with all their obvious triviality and to my mind often meaninglessness keep him in such suspense—in a moment when this triviality is standing in such gross relief on the background of the weighty and tragic events which surround us, are facing us or looming in the nearest future. However I cannot judge but still dread the [illegible word] it will be finished.[30]

We do not know whether Paul ever made the same critique of the book to the author himself, but soon enough the Léons as well as the Joyces would indeed have to face those 'weighty and tragic events'. In her memoir Lucie gives us an eyewitness account of Joyce and Paul's final weeks together in Saint-Gerand-le-Puy. It was during this time that the two friends reread *Finnegans Wake* together, carefully spotting errors that had crept in during the intense sessions when the writer and his press-ganged volunteers were working on the typescripts and proofs.

For many years, Joyce had also charged Paul with keeping track of and ultimately sending his manuscripts to Weaver in London for safekeeping and as an act of tribute. They form the bulk of her invaluable *Finnegans Wake* collection, which is now in the British Library. Then, after Joyce's death, with Paris occupied by the German Army, Paul performed another, final, even more significant act of personal and professional devotion. It would be hard to exaggerate the courage and dedication he showed in salvaging Joyce's books and manuscripts from the writer's last apartment at 34, rue des Vignes. If it were not for Paul's selfless act, what we know about Joyce's works and life would have been substantially diminished. In Chapter 2, Lucie recounts how she and Paul ensured that the Joyce family's possessions remained safe throughout the war, even as they themselves had to face its brutality head on. Paul was arrested by the Nazis in August 1941, and he recounted his agonizing stay in the French internment camps in letters to Lucie (see Chapter 5).

Throughout his life, Joyce was usually quite careless about whether he happened to keep his own correspondence. On the other hand, dedicated as always, Paul meticulously retained and sorted all the letters related to Joyce in his possession. He organized this mass of documents and entrusted them to Count O'Kelly, the Irish Special Counsellor of the Paris and Brussels Legations at the time, with the following note:

> Nineteen envelopes sealed containing private and business correspondence between James Joyce and Paul Léon in the years 1930–40 and the latter's correspondence business and otherwise, relating to Mr Joyce, his family and work. This is the property of Paul Léon, 27 rue Casimir, Paris. To be returned to him at his request. In case of death to be handed to Mr James Joyce. In case of both being dead to be deposited with the Public Library of Ireland or the British Museum to be made accessible for literary use fifty years after Mr Joyce's death; directions to be sought at present from Mr C. Curran and at any time agreement of Mr Joyce's family.[31]

Joyce died suddenly in Zurich on 13 January 1941, and Paul Léon was murdered by the Nazis on 4 April 1942. In accordance with Paul's wishes, the papers in the National Library of Ireland remained sealed until they were opened to the public for research purposes exactly fifty years to the day after his death.

After the war, Lucie and Maria Jolas spearheaded a Joyce exhibition at the famous La Hune Gallery, with many of the precious artefacts that Paul had rescued from the Joyce apartment.[32] Its goal was to put the entire collection up for auction to benefit Nora, Giorgio and Lucia Joyce. The collection was acquired by what is today the Poetry Collection of the University at Buffalo, where it became the foundation of their unrivalled Joyce archive.[33] It includes the 'Epiphanies', which are some of Joyce's earliest writings, several *Ulysses* drafts, all of the *Finnegans Wake* notebooks (which have been the foundation of so much recent scholarship on the book), the unbound copy of *Finnegans Wake* which Joyce and Paul corrected in Saint-Gerand-le-Puy, all that remains of Joyce's Paris library, copies of Joyce's books inscribed to his family, as well as the family portraits and almost all their surviving personal ephemera.

Throughout her life, Lucie kept the Léons' Joyce collection in the family apartment at 27, rue Casimir-Périer. Then Alexis and Anna Maria Léon sold the material to the McFarlin Library at the University of Tulsa in 1984.[34] It is a very personal collection, built around the gifts and photographs that Joyce gave Paul and Lucie over the many years of their friendship. It also includes their prized inscribed copies of Joyce's books; for example, there is a deluxe first edition of *Finnegans Wake* that reads: 'To | that Eurasian Knight | Paul Léon | with the thousand and | one thanks of that most | distressful writer | James Joyce | Paris | 4 May 1939'. Later, Maria Jolas gave Lucie a copy of Joyce's posthumous work *Pastimes* that she inscribed: 'To Lucie | the friend of Joyce | to whom all his | friends must always | be grateful | Paris, 1947'. Besides all of this, their single most significant memento are the corrected final page proofs of *Finnegans Wake*, most of which are covered in Paul's unmistakable handwriting.

In the preface to this volume, Anna Maria tells the story of how she encouraged Alexis to sort through the boxes of their belongings that had been in storage for decades. Among those boxes there was 'a package wrapped in paper with something in Russian written on it that was held together with just a piece of string'.[35] In it was the largest and most significant collection of Joyce's manuscripts to have surfaced in fifty years. It is now known as the 'Joyce 2002 Papers', and some of its highlights are Joyce's early 'Paris–Pola Commonplace Book', sixteen copybook drafts of *Ulysses*, as well as previously missing miscellaneous *Finnegans Wake* manuscripts. Together with the 'James Joyce/Paul Léon Collection' and the 'Papers of Paul and Lucie Léon', they make the National Library of Ireland the most significant and extensive Joyce collection in Europe. While Ireland did not repatriate Joyce's body from his final resting place beside Nora in the Fluntern Cemetery in Zurich, the Léon family has over two generations ensured that his writerly remains have finally come home.

ELIZABETH LUCIE PONIZOWSKY–LUCIE LÉON–LUCIE NOEL

Elizabeth Lucie Ponizowsky was born in Moscow on 4 December 1899, the eldest child of Amalia Wilenkin and Matthew (Mordukh or Metia) Ponizowsky Her mother was born in 1874 in St Petersburg, the second child of Rachel (1845–1921) and Abraam Markovich Wilenkin (1840–1924). In the aftermath of the Russian Revolution, Lucie's mother succumbed to the Spanish flu in Moscow in 1918. Lucie writes that her father (1873–1968) 'was one of the leading cotton manufacturers with great mills and branches all over Russia and a vast fortune'. Then the Revolution brought financial ruin and: 'Like the rest of the 3½ million, her family (and she) fled communism, succeeding to escape only at the end of 1918. Great loss of life was involved in the getting out.' The Ponizowskys and Wilinkens were thereby rendered stateless and forced to travel to Finland and Sweden on Nansen passports, which Lucie retained until she became a United States citizen on 9 May 1959. She used to enjoy telling her son that she had first seen his father dancing on a beach in Finland where she and her family had gone after fleeing Russia. The extended family then made their way to London, arriving there on 6 January 1919.

One of her maternal uncles, Gregory Wilenkin (1864–1930), had been a financial advisor to Tsar Nicholas II. He began working in the Ministry of Finance in 1895 and worked as a financial attaché for the Russian government in London, where he married Irma Sara Seligman (1871–1958) that same year, thereby connecting the Wilenkin family with a network of financial entrepreneurs in London and New York. In 1904 he was stationed in Washington, DC. Wilenkin then returned to London in 1913 and began to serve as honorary financial adviser to the Russian Embassy, which prompted the rest of the family to settle there, at least temporarily.

The Ponizowskys had lost virtually everything and Lucie writes that 'it was necessary to start from scratch. The first three years spent in London brought no solution', but she had nonetheless found the love of her life. Lucie and Paul Léon married on 26 July 1921 in Kensington Town Hall. Then most of the family decided to move to Paris, where they arrived on 16 August 1921. Four years later, on 12 September 1925, their only child, Alexis Leopold Alexander Léon, was born in Paris. According to Lucie's biographical notes, which she wrote in the third person when she returned to work as the fashion correspondent at the *International Herald Tribune* in November 1945,

> Life in Paris was cheaper at the time than in London; also it was possible to find work. Most Russian emigre wives and girls were either modelling clothes in the couture, waiting in restaurants, knitting, making hats, designing dresses and beautiful lingerie, selling their ware plus Chanel pearls, perfumes, silk stockings and artificial flowers. All Lucie Noel discovered was her innate taste for beautiful clothes, inherited from her mother who had always dressed at the Paris couturiers. Soon Lucie hit on the idea of helping American women pick their clothes in Paris, the hats and accessories. At the time Paris was cheap; they were buying madly.
>
> So from 1923 until 1935 Lucie piloted hundreds of Americans through the fashion labyrinths of Paris, making her first contacts with couturiers, also helping her compatriots with their wares.[1]

Building bridges between American buyers and French couturiers, Lucie worked with private clients, assisted buyers and residents to secure offices during the couturier season, and began writing fashion reports.[2] Helen Kastor Fleishmann was one of Lucie's many clients and they remained friends for almost twenty years. Helen came to Paris with her husband, Leon Fleischman, a vice president and Paris agent for the New York publisher Boni and Liveright. They divorced in 1929 and Helen subsequently married Giorgio Joyce in 1930. Lucie had twin brothers, Yakov (known as James or simply Jim) and Alexander (Alec), who were born on 26 December 1901, both of whom went to Cambridge; as well as a sister, Eugénie (1916–95). Alec Ponizowsky was a friend of Giorgio Joyce, gave his father Russian lessons, and ultimately introduced Paul Léon to James Joyce. Jim Ponizowsky and Paul were also close friends, but Lucie's brother died prematurely in Belgium on 31 December 1935.

That same year, Lucie was hired as the assistant to Selina York, the fashion editor on the European edition of the *New York Herald Tribune*. Lucie was then immediately given her own byline for both the paper's Paris and New York editions. The family thought it best that she not use her married name professionally, therefore she began to sign her columns as 'Lucie Noel' in 1935 and did so for the rest of her career. She remained a staff correspondent until 12 June 1940, when the European edition had to close down, just one day before German forces marched into Paris. The next day, Lucie, her husband and son 'were on the roads of France along with eight million other French, Belgians, and Alsatians, the roads that the Germans were strafing'. Lucie tells the story of how the Léons joined the Joyces in the summer of 1940 in Saint-Gerand-le-Puy in her memoir of the story of the friendship of Paul Léon and James Joyce (see Chapter 2).

Lucie described this period as 'marking time' before she returned to Paris and her fashion work at the *Herald Tribune* on 16 August, until the New York office asked her to cease work in October 1940.[3] According to the case history Lucie submitted to petition for United States citizenship, the Léons had 'returned to Paris because we had left everything behind and had no money and no clothes. On our return we lived off the sale of stamp collections, my husband's first editions, and much of our furniture'. In February 1941, the Gestapo first visited their home and they were 'denounced as pro-Allied spies'. Lucie recalled that they were 'dragged to their Gestapo Headquarters [on] Av Matignon, and after lengthy questioning [they] let us go. The Gestapo visits were repeated periodically, and every time it was worse. As we were completely innocent, my husband never had any political activity, we stayed in Paris, hoping it would blow over.'[4] Then, on

21 August 1941, Paul was 'arrested as a hostage and as a Jew by the Germans', along with numerous other Jewish lawyers, 'though [Paul] had never practiced law'. Of their return to Paris, she concluded that it 'was to prove a fatal step, one that never should have been undertaken'.[5]

The following day, Lucie joined the 'French Red Cross, services of Civil Internees (first aid to concentration camps)'. Then, 'as soon as the Germans permitted the distribution of food packages', she 'organized the collecting point and distribution to the camp, riding trucks almost daily'.[6] Paul recorded the tragic events of that period in his letters to Lucie from Drancy (see Chapter 5). In her biographical notes, Lucie recounted her endeavours:

> First as an official first aid worker, and later in a clandestine capacity, she penetrated into the camps, organized the official supply of packages the minute the Germans authorized this; later [Lucie] smuggled 'grapevine' correspondence and money to interned men at various camps, visited families, ran errands and generally made herself useful, in many desperate efforts to relieve their plight and save her husband. She also recalled, more pointedly, how she helped organize 'escapes' for marked men and their families, getting them over the line of demarcation. For a whole year she devoted her life to the persecuted, their families and the deported men.[7]

Then, on 12 December 1941, the 'Germans arrested 1,800 more Jews and moved 350 men to the camp of Royallieu, Compiègne. I transferred my services to that camp because my husband was among the 350. By that time I was going underground, and incognito. The Germans were starting to pick up the wives, children and families of arrested men. I continued to carry letters, money, and smuggle food packages whenever possible into the camp. The men were dying of starvation, cold and malnutrition.'[8]

Six months later, on 15 June 1941, one of Paul's students who was with 'the Resistance had seen my name on the potential lists due for arrest and deportation. He warned me, in the nick of time.' According to Lucie, 'The Germans came that night and every night for 6 months. I walked out of the house with a few belongings and led a precarious existence for 8 months, changing houses, addresses, moving continually and still trying to get my husband out and help the others too. This went on for 8 months, until December 27, 1941,'[9] during which time 'she hid, moving from place to place within Paris and with two long stops Compiègne'. Compounding her difficulties and despair, she 'clung to the hope offered by a "con woman" who, for sums of money and clothing, had convinced Lucie and ten other women that "she would bring them back to France". Lucie's typewriter, the few precious possessions, all naturally went that way. One and half million francs back in '42 was a tidy sum of money. This is what the woman had collected.'[10]

Meanwhile on 27 March 1941, Paul was 'deported from Compiègne to Silesia where he was murdered by the Nazis en route from Auschwitz to Birkenau, then nonexistent, on April 4, 1942'. Lucie was able to confirm this information in 1946,

> when the remainder of the 'convoi' returned to Paris. Five men returned from that train, out of a group of 1,200. We—my son and I—witnessed the deportation, which was a death march with all typical trimmings. We were able to say goodbye. The men left, singing the Marseillaise. We returned to Paris. A week later I shipped out my son clandestinely, through the Resistance, into the Free Zone. I had a brother living in Monte Carlo. Later he was to perish at the hands of the Germans [on 7 March 1943], as he was mixed up with British Intelligence. The day after my boy's departure, I had the Gestapo come for him and his bicycle at 6 a.m.

Finally, on 27 December 1942, 'there was nothing left for me to do but join my brother in Monte Carlo, Monaco',[11] so Lucie escaped to the Free Zone, but her troubles were far from over. She recalled: 'It took her four days to cross the line dividing Occupied and free French territory. In Monte Carlo, except for her immediate family and one or two friends, Lucie Noel lay very low.' For two years, she was 'completely destitute . . . Lack of food caused her to faint on the streets. At that time too, nothing, except Liberation, seemed to matter. She told her pupils that if ever they ran across any Americans they should mention her name. Food was becoming scarcer and scarcer as the days slipped into weeks. A black market existed but who could afford that? Certainly not Lucie.'[12] She and Alexis

> [l]ived there, concealed in a small room, at the flat of a workman until the American landings in August 1944. We had just 8,000 francs to live on per month and were practically starving. I gave English lessons to bridge the gap: from sheer despair—to a new lease on life—when we would be liberated. But as Monaco was not officially occupied and had a Casino, it was immediately 'off limits' for United States troops. One day, however, a group of Ordinance officers came over on a special assignment and needed an interpreter. Just what I had been waiting for.[13]

Then, finally, on 18 September, 'there was a ring at the doorbell of the flat she had emptied of all furniture belonging to part of the family. (In case the Germans should come for the furniture she had stored it all.) A fancy uniformed Monegasque policeman told her she was "wanted downstairs". But he would not tell who was asking for her.' She continued retelling her story:

> Expecting the worst—at that time she certainly was not registering quite normally—she picked up her handbag, gave the place one last look and with the words, 'Well, this is it, I guess,' followed the policeman.
>
> Sure enough a large khaki-coloured military car was waiting outside. Next to it stood a uniformed officer. He had to call her by her name, hold out his hand and explain before she realized or believed that the white star on the car meant that it was an American Army car, and that he was an American officer in combat dress.[14]

From 18 September 1944 to March 1945, Lucie served at the Ordinance Headquarters in Monte Carlo, Dijon, and then at the Ordinance Depot in Beaune. She was in charge of a team of twenty-four French volunteer clerks and typists and the liaison between civilians and the United States personnel. In March 1945, her outfit was transferred to Germany, but 'General de Gaulle at the very last minute issued orders that no French civilians were to enter Germany. He had decided it was too early and dangerous. Our contracts were pronounced void. Overnight I was without a job. But next day found I could be of use in the Signal Corps in Dijon, later transferred to Magasins Réunis, Nancy. I was placed in charge of the "Information-can-I-help-you table", which dealt with secret code . . . I used to work long hours, often taking night jobs at the special switch.'[15]

Meanwhile Alexis Léon, who 'had joined the American Forces in the South was "mopping up" in the Italian hills with the First Special Services Task Force'.[16] She notes: 'He was interpreter but spent part of the time in foxholes.'[17] By May 1945 he was working with the Supply and Procurement and had returned to the family's apartment at 27, rue Casimir-Perier in Paris. Alexis 'kept writing his mother, "There are plenty of jobs in Paris. Come home. All your friends are asking after you."'[18] By the end of the month, Lucie too was back in Paris where she 'resumed life in the old apartment. This had been saved for us by a French lady and her mother [the Perréons]. My husband fearing the worst had made it over to them in 1940. They, however, returned everything intact', and were still living with the Léons a decade later.[19] Lucie found work in 'a "Hush Hush" section of War Crimes doing a humdrum, tedious job of filling in the Wanted and Not Detained War Criminals forms. Never any good at figures—and numbers were given every criminal and were best memorized—she was getting depressed and morale was low.'

Meanwhile, the *Herald Tribune* in Paris had reopened in September 1944 and 'was going full blast, but nothing was further away, or more foreign at the time, to Lucie Noel's state of mind than fashion',[20] but two months later they asked her to take up her old post. 'After much hesitation, and much persuasion on the part of the Syndicate de la Couture (Press section was then headed by Lucien Lelong) I decided to do so. Lucien Lelong convinced [me] that my work was of aid to a national French industry. From then on I was once again regular staff correspondent, with the title of fashion editor for the European edition, and regular filing to the New York edition.'[21] Lucie wrote a column with her byline that appeared in the European and the New York editions every Thursday throughout the year as well as daily during the biannual Fashion Weeks in Paris. As she put it, 'As the fashion season develops, she covers everything from lace to leather, from High Fashion to French dime store operations, and from Haute Couture to Ready-to-Wear. Whether it's a story on winter sports, perfumes, hairdos, beauty products, makeup, furs or just a chic opening night or dinner, she keeps you informed, interested, and up-to-the minute.'[22] She was friends with and a confidante of many of the top designers, including Christian Dior, David Evins and Yves St. Laurent,[23] all of whom concurred that there was 'no better interpreter of their innermost thoughts. Inspiration can be found on either side of the Atlantic.'[24] She also served two terms as President of the Fashion Group de Paris.[25]

Lucie had a wide range of interests beyond fashion. She continued the Léon family's commitment to the memory of James Joyce, his work and family. Shortly after the war had ended, Joyce scholars began contacting her for information and insights. One of the first was Richard Kain, whose *Fabulous Voyager: James Joyce's 'Ulysses'* was published in 1947 by the University of Chicago Press. John J. Slocum followed and establish a life-long friendship with Lucie (see Chapter 3). In October 1948, Lucie travelled to the United States to renew and deepen her contacts in the fashion world, and she also presented a paper on her husband's friendship with the great Irish writer on 18 November at the James Joyce Society in the Gotham Book Mart, which became the basis of her memoir (see Chapter 2).

In the mid-1950s Lucie translated Boris Simon's *Les chiffoniers d'Emmaüs* that had recently been published by Éditions du Seuil in 1954. It is a biography of the Abbé Pierre (Henri Grouès, 1912–2007), a popular and well-respected Catholic priest who was member of the Resistance during World War II and deputy of the Mouvement Républicain Populaire. Lucie's work appeared under the title *Abbé Pierre and the Ragpickers of Emmaus* in 1955 (New York: P. J. Kennedy and Sons).[26] She continued to translate French works into English, working on Jean-François Six's *Vie de Charles de Foucauld* (Paris: Éditions du Seuil, 1962). Though she tried to have it published by Macmillan in New York, the translation never appeared.[27] In 1962, Lucie also wrote articles on such disparate topics as 'The Uncovering and Preserving of the Byzantine Mosaics', 'Contemporary Religious Architecture in France', as well as an article on Vladimir Nabokov to commemorate his seventieth birthday that appeared in the *Tri-quarterly* magazine in 1970.[28]

Meanwhile, Lucie was committed to becoming a United States citizen and filed her application on 16 February 1951. Although she tried, it became evident that she would not be able to fulfil the residency requirement and at the same time continue to cover the

French fashion scene for the *Herald Tribune* from Paris. Four years later, she was granted an immigration visa and arrived in New York on 1 September 1955. Then, with the vocal support of Emanuel Celler, the Representative of New York State and Chairman of the House Judiciary Committee, Lucie petitioned Congress in June 1956 for a waiver so that she could be granted permanent residence (H.R. 8181). Among others, she had letters of support from Eric Hawkins, Managing Editor, European edition of the *New York Herald Tribune*; from Lieutenant Colonel Shelton E. Lollis, United States Army; and also from John J. Slocum, Voice of America and former press attaché in the High Commission for Occupied Germany, Bonn. The bill was passed on 9 May 1959, making Lucie an American citizen 'because of her efforts on behalf of the Allied cause'.[29]

When the *New York Herald Tribune* was sold in 1961, Lucie was dismissed from the post she had held as fashion editor for over twenty years. She instituted proceedings against the dismissal and won the case four years later. Meanwhile, she continued to write articles on a wide variety of topics and was appointed fashion editor for the Associated Press in 1963. Elizabeth Lucie Léon (Noel) passed away on 29 April 1972 in Neuilly-sur-Seine at the age of 72. After the hardships of revolution and war as well as all the many good times she had lived through, she remained confident and resolute. In 1945 she wrote: 'Today she is happy that it happened that way.'[30]

PAUL LÉON AND JOYCE'S *HAVETH CHILDERS EVERYWHERE*

Only three of Paul's writings on Joyce's life and work survive. The first are his reflections on *Haveth Childers Everywhere*, the next are his notes on a memoir about his friend James Joyce that he expected to write, and the final document is a letter he wrote to Jean Paulhan shortly after Joyce's death.[1] He wrote the first in the summer of 1930 and the other two in the spring of 1941, and so they bookend the two friends' work and lives together. Lucie believed that her husband's fragmentary outline must 'have been a first effort to recapture the years of friendship' with Joyce. She concluded that Paul had written the sketch just a few months after Joyce's premature death and about a year before he himself was brutally murdered. She continued: 'I believe he started in this style and later, feeling it was not attuned to his wider appreciation of Joyce, changed the style.'[2] Paul's letter to Paulhan was his final effort to 'recapture the years of friendship' with Joyce. Although merely a sketch (Lucie calls it a 'resumé'), Paul's 'first effort' at recollecting how he worked with Joyce is of interest in its own right. One of the entries Paul made in this initial list of incidents in their friendship captures the sense of the urgency and commitment he felt the first time he was conscripted into the ranks of Joyce's beleaguered collaborators:

> The year 1929 seems to have been wiped from my memory. Maybe that year we started our morning strolls etc. etc. The end of '29 brought a call for help with *Haveth Childers Everywhere*. A large volume of *Encyclopedia Britannica*—reading of the study—research in common usage.[3]

Paul's thoughts returned to his plan to write his 'Recollections of Joyce' (among other projects he wanted to complete) on 28 November 1941, at a particularly difficult juncture during his internment in the Drancy camp.[4] Unfortunately, his premature death robbed his family and friends of the man, and posterity of a more complete account of his intimate friendship with James Joyce. Instead, Chapter 4 begins with what appears to be Paul's first (and possibly only) critical assessment of Joyce's work. It commemorates the recent publication of Joyce's *Haveth Childers Everywhere* in June 1930 by Henry Babou and Jack Kahane in Paris and by the Fountain Press in New York. Furthermore, Joyce's notebooks and his 'Work in Progress' manuscripts – as well as the letters and the recollections of his other friends (in their roles as Joyce's researchers and amanuenses) – can help us to recreate a fairly vivid picture of what it must have been like to be part of the workforce that the taxing writer assembled around him to prepare his newest 'Work in Progress' fragment for publication.

Paul noted that he met Joyce socially 'at the beginning of 1928',[5] but their work together on the various parts of what would become *Finnegans Wake* only began in 1929 at the earliest, just after Harry and Caresse Crosby's Black Sun Press had published Joyce's *Tales Told of Shem and Shaun*. A few months later, in November 1929, Joyce had Sylvia Beach contact James Wells, whose firm had published *Anna Livia Plurabelle* the previous year, offering him *Haveth Childers Everywhere*. On Joyce's instructions, she presented one of the clearest statements of the writer's rationale for his 'Work in Progress' fragments:

> The part of Mr. Joyce's 'WiP' in question is, like ALP and T. T. of S. and S.,[6] a fragment, the first of four fragments that Mr. Joyce designs to publish in this way before issuing the whole book in volume form. It is shorter than ALP but he wishes it to be printed in very large type and in big format on account of the subject matter, and with the appropriate preface of the kind I suggested.[7] On this later point he is very particular. The fragment itself is entrusted to the voice of the Viking father of Dublin City, and has been much amplified since it appeared in transition no. 15 . . . On account of the self-glorifying tone of old Earwicker, the format should be gaudy and aggressive, within artistic limits, as ALP was sober and unassuming.[8]

While the complicated negotiations about the publication of *Haveth Childers Everywhere* continued, at the start of 1930 Joyce enlisted the assistance of Paul and several others to help him construct the story of Humphrey Chimpden Earwicker, city builder. At the end of 1929, Joyce's eyesight was still good enough to allow him to revise the final pages of two different copies of *transition* 15 himself, from which a typescript was made, which he then also corrected and lightly revised.[9] Yet another typescript was prepared, and Joyce managed to continue to revise it himself, however minimally.[10] But, by the beginning of 1930, Joyce was physically unable to read and write sufficiently well to complete the piece he was working on, so he relied on his troupe of assistants – Paul, Lucia Joyce, Padraic Colum, Stuart Gilbert and Helen Fleischmann Joyce – to read to him, take notes and also write out the additions and changes that he wanted made to the text. As always, Joyce took inspiration from his notebooks as he continued to revise and amplify the text on several typescripts.

In an entry for 31 January 1930 in his posthumously published diary, Stuart Gilbert gives us an embittered sense of what the regime was like:

> At last J.J. has recommenced work on *Work in Progress*. The *de luxe* edition by ? soon to come out—about the old lady A.L.P., I think. Another about the City (H.C.E. building Dublin). Five volumes of the *Encyclopedia Britannica* on his sofa. He has made a list of 30 towns, New York, Vienna, Budapest, etc. Mrs Fleischmann has read out the articles on some of these. I 'finish' Vienna and read Christiania and Budapest, etc. Whenever I come to a name (of a street, suburb, park, etc.) I pause. J. thinks. If he can Anglicise the word, i.e. make a pun on it, Mrs F. records the name or its deformation in the notebook. Thus 'Slotspark' (I think) at Christiania becomes Sluts' park. He

> collects all queer names, in this way and will soon have a notebook full of them . . . He is curled on his sofa, while I struggle with Danish or Rumanian names, pondering puns.[11]

Although Gilbert conflates several events in his account, at least one of the notebooks that he refers to survives and it has been expertly edited by Geert Lernout, Vincent Deane and Daniel Ferrer.[12] While Joyce started off the note-taking himself, he then relied on whomever was available to continue with the work that needed to be done. The first task he asked Paul to do was to transcribe a passage that he wanted to include in the continuously evolving text of what would become *Haveth Childers Everywhere* and then the concluding part of Book III, Chapter 3 of *Finnegans Wake* (532.06–554). It reads:

> delivered them with frekandesias by the constant droppings from my smalls instalmonths while I totfortotlled titfortotalled up their farinadays for them on my slatoper's slate, with my chandner's chauk.[13]

This draft text is an excellent example of the complicated nature of Joyce's collaborative creative method at various times in the 1930s. First, Joyce had himself already noted 'Chandni Chauk' verbatim in the notebook.[14] According to the eleventh edition of the *Encyclopaedia Britannica*'s entry on the city from which Joyce took the note, this was the name of 'the principal street of Delhi, which was once supposed to be the richest street in the world'.[15] Fifty pages later, Joyce had Paul write out the above passage in the notebook, and by then the street name (meaning 'silver street') had been transformed into 'chandner's chauk'. Then, Joyce had another one of his collaborators add 'jacobeaters ^ and pottage bakes to the esausted: I delivered . . . chauk ^' to the then current typescript,[16] presumably when he did not have his notebook to hand. The ellipsis mark that Joyce had the amanuensis include between the first and last word of Paul's addition was a reminder to himself that this was the precise spot where he wanted it to be placed. Finally, it seems that when the subsequent typescript was being made Joyce dictated the insertion directly from the notebook, which is why it just appears as part of the text of *HCE* on the next typescript.[17] This is a quite typically long and convoluted story of how so many words, phrases, sentences and sometimes paragraphs became part of *Finnegans Wake*.[18]

Paul continued to assist Joyce by taking several pages of notes from the entries on 'Teheran' and 'Rangoon' in the *Encyclopaedia Britannica*.[19] As we saw from the entry on Delhi above, rather than making puns, most of the notes are (usually unexceptional) words and phrases taken verbatim from the source text, although sometimes there is already some wordplay evident in the elaboration of the notes. For example, on the one hand, the first word Joyce had Paul note was simply 'Elburz',[20] which is the name of a mountain range in the hinterlands of Tehran. Then, Paul was asked to note 'enceinte' ('pregnant' in French, though used in the sense of perimeter wall in the source text), which is the only word Joyce found of interest in this description of the city's architectural history in the encyclopedia entry:

> In 1869 Nasr-ud-din Shah decided upon enlarging the city; the old wall and towers were demolished, the ditch was filled up and used for building sites, and an **enceinte** consisting of a ditch and 58 unequal bastions according to Vauban's first system was constructed and completed in 1874.[21]

It is unlikely that most readers coming across 'the mightyevil roohms of enceint cartage' in *Haveth Childers Everywhere* or in *Finnegans Wake* would be able to discern the word's original, quite unusual, though mundane context.[22] On the other hand, further notes illustrate different aspects of Joyce's creative practices at work. Another fact about the history of Tehran in the encyclopedia reads: 'There are twelve gates, which are closed from two hours after sunset to an hour before sunrise.'[23] The first part of the note Joyce had Paul record was quite straightforward – 'sunset closure gate' – but then Joyce reconsidered the note's possibilities and had him write 'sunlay closure' just after it.[24] Interesting as this new formulation may have been, Joyce did not find a use for it in *Finnegans Wake*.

Paul and another amanuensis alternated the note-taking for another ten pages, but then Joyce relied on him once again to take notes on entries for other cities in the *Encyclopaedia Britannica*. Unsurprisingly, he returned to Dublin, and then moved halfway around the world to Rio de Janeiro – such are the possibilities in *Finnegans Wake*. Some of the notes on Joyce's own city are completely unremarkable, like 'Greater Dublin',[25] while others are more like the kind of punning Gilbert criticized. For example, Joyce had Paul note the name of the Dublin suburb 'Donnybrook', which the entry tells us is 'celebrated for its former fair'.[26] Reconsidering its possibilities, Joyce then had Paul write the name as 'Donkeybrook' just beside the earlier entry.[27] Joyce did find a place to include this note in *Haveth Childers Everywhere* and we find it in *Finnegans Wake* as 'to bray at by clownsillies in Donkeybrook Fair'.[28] Joyce showed a similar interest in noting specific words and phrases from the article on Rio de Janeiro, as well as a tendency to transform them as he thought best for his work. According to Gilbert, Rio was one of the entries he read aloud to Joyce and then the writer dictated what he wanted Paul to write in the notebook.[29] Almost twenty pages later, Joyce had Paul take notes from the encyclopedia entry on Paris, but (for whatever reasons) his current abode proved less interesting than Dublin, and so the notes on the city only take up two notebook pages. Paul then took a total of about ten pages of notes on London, but just less than half a page from the entry on Bristol, which is surprising given the city's ancient association with Dublin.

About halfway through the notebook, Joyce's interest in *Encyclopaedia Britannica* waned and he turned his attention to an eclectic range of books, including Reginald L. Hine's *The History of Hitchin*, which Lernout describes as

> a fascinating history of a small parish in Hertfordshire with a population, in 1921, of 12,829 . . . the most important reason for its presence [in the notebook and so in *Haveth Childers Everywhere* and *Finnegans Wake*] might be Hine's ambition to make one place the centre of the universe.[30]

On the other hand, Joyce also had Paul take notes from Seebohm Rowntree's groundbreaking sociological study, *Poverty: A Study of Town Life*, which Lernout describes as a 'very important source' among the books at the *Wake*.[31] Joyce had Paul take notes, from William Booth's highly influential tract, *In Darkest England, and the Way Out*, as well as, on the other hand, from Washington Irving's satirical *A History of New York from the Beginning of the World to the End of the Dutch Dynasty, by Diedrich Knickerbocker*.[32] Again, Lernout makes the telling point that

> it was almost inevitable that [Joyce] would come across Irving's spurious history of the founding and early years of New Amsterdam, the Dutch colony that would later become New York . . . The majority of the notes taken from this source deal either with Dutch words or names, or with New York place-names. Joyce may also have been attracted to this source because the book purports to offer the real and suppressed

history of New York, an originally Dutch colony, just as Dublin had been a Scandinavian settlement. Peter Stuyvesant as a founding father seems to have been an especially useful precursor of HCE.[33]

Once all the hard work was finally complete, Joyce wrote to Harriet Shaw Weaver on 18 March 1930:

> I finished the revision of the fragment for publication last night at seven, and, I suspect, my literary career at the same time . . . (the revision of this last fragment has been a frightful job, extending over two months day and night sometimes till one in the morning, with seven different people helping me to do seven different parts of the labour, but of course such a condition of affairs could not continue).[34]

But yet it did continue for the next nine years and the result was *Finnegans Wake*. All told Joyce and his associates compiled a bulky 220-page notebook in just a month and a half (from early February to mid-March 1930), and in total, Paul took notes on more of its pages than anyone else except Joyce. We also see a corresponding increase in the amount of responsibility Joyce placed in Paul to get *Haveth Childers Everywhere* into print, a precursor of evermore professional and personal responsibilities Paul would take on in the coming years. While a variety of friends helped Joyce revise the several typescripts that were made in early 1930, Paul's work is progressively more evident, especially in the typescript and instructions that were specifically prepared for the printers.[35] Describing this manuscript, Paul wrote to his niece: 'I have here the typescript of his new book which I am afraid is worth millions because all the alterations are done in my handwriting—had they have been done in his I am afraid nobody would have understood anything.'[36] In fact, given the large number of alterations that were made on some of those typescript pages, Paul himself also typed up a list of 'corrigenda' for the typescript, and marked the surviving exemplar at the end: 'This copy is for Mr Joyce.'[37] Then, finally, all of the emendations on the printer's proofs of *Haveth Childers Everywhere* are only in Paul Léon's capable hands. It is no wonder that he considered himself one of the best-informed readers of Joyce's newest work and set about writing one of its first critical responses (see Chapter 4). Lucie recounts an anecdote in her memoir that reveals precisely what Paul found so captivating about his collaboration with Joyce:

> Those who knew my husband well often wondered why anyone as self-sufficient as he was with serious interests and intellectual work of his own, should have been willing to devote so much time to Joyce. Frequently, when the question was put to Paul, he would answer:
>
> 'I am most interested in watching Joyce's process of creation. He has me look up words in various languages, and his mental process and the metamorphosis of language he indulges in are most fascinating to witness.'[38]

While Paul wrote the essay on *Haveth Childers Everywhere* at the start of their friendship, the reflections on Joyce that he recorded for posterity in the letter he wrote in May 1941 (also in Chapter 4) represent a dozen years of virtually daily contact with the man, during which he selflessly helped Joyce and his family cope with so many of the personal issues that they had to confront, as well as manage the writer's complex legal and financial affairs, all the while working with him to ready 'Work in Progress' to become *Finnegans Wake*. It was in this way that 'Paul gradually became Joyce's alter-ego and guardian in the practical details of every day life', as Lucie puts it so elegantly.[39]

FIGURE 1.1: Paul Léon as a young man, Russia (*c.* 1907) © The Léon Estate.

FIGURE 1.2: Paul Léon in uniform, Russia (*c.* 1917) © The Léon Estate.

FIGURE 1.3: Paul and Lucie Léon, Paris (1922) © The Léon Estate.

FIGURE 1.4: Paul and Lucie Léon, Paris (1922) © The Léon Estate.

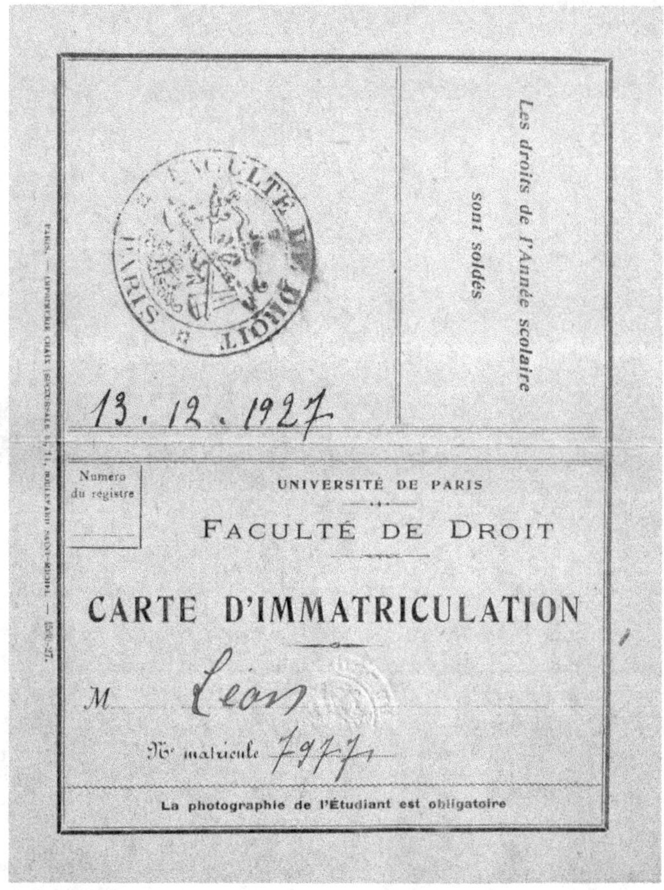

Les droits de l'Année scolaire sont soldés

FACULTÉ DE DROIT PARIS

13. 12. 1927

Numero du registre

UNIVERSITÉ DE PARIS

FACULTÉ DE DROIT

CARTE D'IMMATRICULATION

M Léon

N° matricule 7977

La photographie de l'Étudiant est obligatoire

Signature de l'Étudiant,

Le Secrétaire de la Faculté,

EXTRAIT

DU DÉCRET DU 21 JUILLET 1897 RELATIF AU RÉGIME SCOLAIRE ET DISCIPLINAIRE DES UNIVERSITÉS

ART. 6. — Toute carte est délivrée gratuitement à tout étudiant immatriculé. Elle ne vaut que pour l'**année scolaire**. Elle doit être renouvelée chaque année.

ART. 7. — Les cartes d'étudiant sont rigoureusement personnelles. Elles ne doivent pas être prêtées.

Toute infraction à cet article est punissable d'une des peines prévues à l'article 34 du décret susvisé.

FIGURE 1.5: Paul Léon, Student Registration Card, Faculté de Droit, Université de Paris (1927) © The Léon Estate.

Archives
de
Philosophie du droit
et de
Sociologie juridique

Extrait :

Paul-L. Léon

La notion de souveraineté dans la doctrine de Rousseau

CAHIER DOUBLE
HUITIEME ANNÉE
Nos 1-2 — 1938

RECUEIL SIREY
22, Rue Soufflot, Paris

FIGURE 1.6: *Archive de Philosophie du Droit*, Nos. 1–2 (1938) © The Léon Estate.

Léon, Paul Leopoldowitch

Son of Mr Leopold Léon and his wife née Rattner
born 25th April / 7th May 1898.

from 1903 to 1911 went to the Principal German School of St Peter, the course of which he finished with a silver medal

from 1911 - 1915 graduated at St Petersburg University faculty of law where he took a first class degree

from 1915 - 1918 ~~[illegible]~~ on active service in the Russian army
from 1915 - 1917 (April) volunteer in the 33rd infantry Regiment at Dorpat
1917 Paul's officers' training school
1st September promoted to the rank of ensign
1917 - 1918 (January) Officers' Machine gun training school of Oranienbaum

1918 After three months work attached to the Moscow University for preparation to the professorship of Constitutional Law sponsors Professors P. I. Novgorodtzeff and S. A. Kotliarevsky
Since November 1918 left Russia, lived for 5 months in Sweden

1919 April 1919 lived in England (London) where he ~~worked on~~ contributed to a bibliographical work on "Englishmen in Russia" with C. Hagberg Wright Esq and V. Polianoff Esq. till August 1920

1920 - 1925 in an Antique shop in Paris

1921 Married to Miss Elisabeth Ponizovsky

Began his studies of English since his 15th year and was in England twice in 1912 (three months) and in 1919 - 192[illegible] (15 months

Works. I Russian Home - Rule, an essay of legal analysis,
the Problem of the State in the light of anarchism
(Troudy Russkikh Ouchenykh vol. I)

II English Translation for the New Age (spring 1920)
contribution to the following articles:
A. Herzen, the founder of Russian Liberalism (Fortnightly Review)
M. Bakounine —"—
The spirit of Russia (XIXth cent. & after)
The failure of Russian intellectuals (Contemporary Review)
P. Chaadaev (Fortnightly Review)

FIGURE 1.7: Paul's Curriculum Vitae (*c*. 1926) © The Léon Estate.

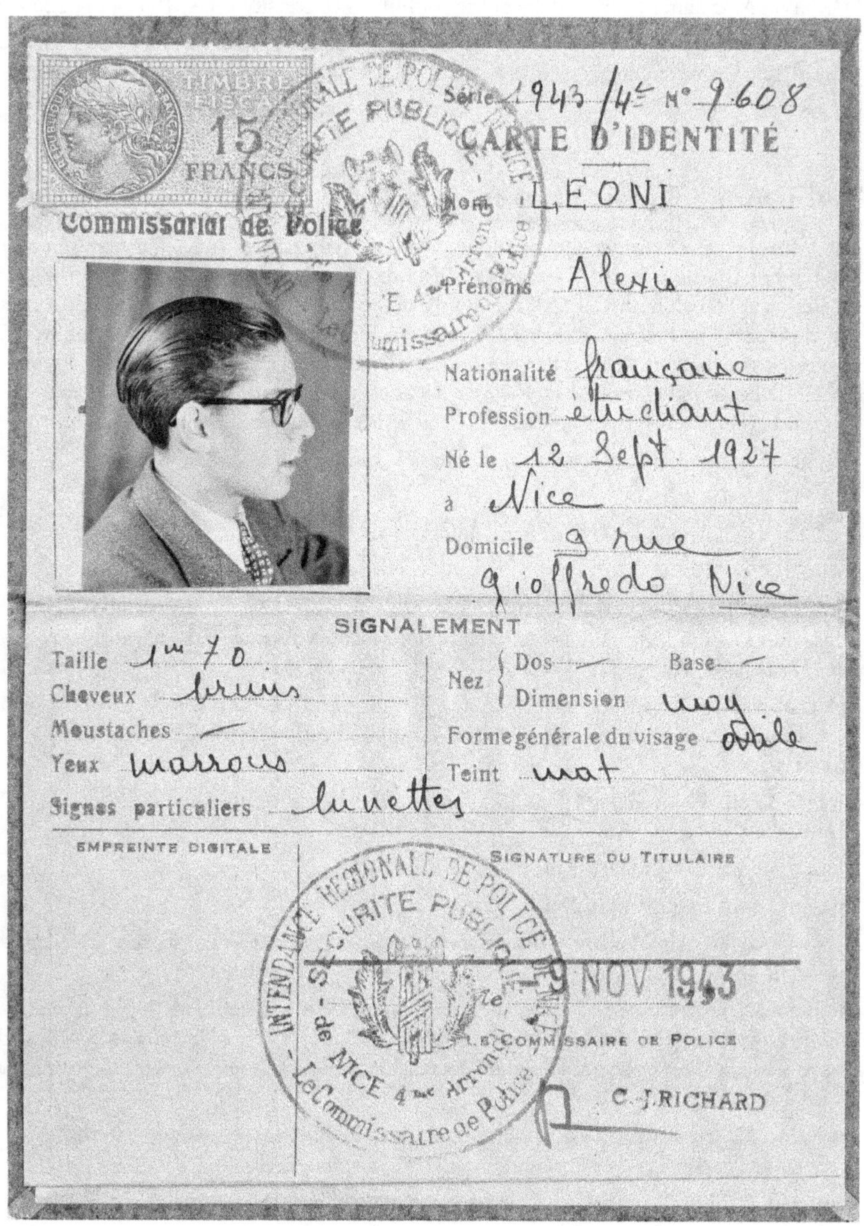

TIMBRE FISCAL
15 FRANCS
REPUBLIQUE FRANÇAISE
Commissariat de Police

Série 1943 /4e N° 9608
CARTE D'IDENTITÉ
Nom LEONI
Prénoms Alexis
Nationalité française
Profession étudiant
Né le 12 Sept 1927
à Nice
Domicile 9 rue Gioffredo Nice

SIGNALEMENT

Taille 1m 70
Cheveux bruns
Moustaches —
Yeux marrons
Nez: Dos — Base — Dimension moy
Forme générale du visage ovale
Teint mat
Signes particuliers lunettes

EMPREINTE DIGITALE
SIGNATURE DU TITULAIRE

INTENDANCE REGIONALE DE POLICE DE NICE – SECURITE PUBLIQUE – NICE 4ème Arrondt – Le Commissaire de Police

9 NOV 1943
LE COMMISSAIRE DE POLICE
C. J. RICHARD

FIGURE 1.8: Alexis Leoni Carte d'Identité (1943) © The Léon Estate.

NOTES

1. Chapter 2, p. 36.
2. Maria Jolas, 'The Little Known Paul Léon', *A James Joyce Miscellany, Second Series*, edited by Marvin Magalaner (Carbondale: Southern Illinois University Press, 1959), pp. 225–33.
3. John J. Slocum and Herbert Cahoon, *A Bibliography of James Joyce, 1882—1941* (New Haven: Yale University Press, 1953).
4. Chapter 2, p. 39.

Paul Léon: Scholar, Lawyer, Adviser, Family Man and Friend

1. The facts of Paul Léon's life here are drawn from two curriculum vitae. The first is in his hand in English (now in the Léon family collection; see Illustration 1.7). The other is a typescript in French in the NLI's 'Papers of Paul and Lucie Léon' collection (MS 36,918/9). It was prepared by Lucie in March 1957 as part of her application for a subvention from the Centre Nationale de la Recherche Scientifique (CNRS) for the publication of a posthumous work titled *Le Pensée juridique et politique de Jean-Jacques Rousseau* that would have brought together several of Paul's unpublished writings. The book was never published.
2. Fragments of the thesis survive in Paul's hand in Russian (NLI MS 36,922).
3. NLI MS 36,919.
4. See Chapter 2, Appendix H for their tribute to Paul.
5. Chapter 2, p. 36.
6. 'Anna Livia Plurabelle', translated by Samuel Beckett, Alfred Perron, Ivan Goll, Eugene Jolas, Paul L. Léon, Adrienne Monnier and Philippe Soupault, with the author, *La Nouvelle Revue Française*, Vol. xix, No. 212 (May 1931): 633–46.
7. The thousands of letters between Joyce and Léon in the NLI – and who knows how many more have not survived – attest to Paul's constant dedication to Joyce's professional and private affairs.
8. Joyce to Léon, 6 November 1934; NLI. Unless otherwise indicated, the correspondence is unpublished.
9. Joyce to Léon; 20 October 1934; NLI.
10. Joyce to Léon; 21 July 1936; NLI.
11. Nikolaj Sergeevi Timašev, *Introduction à la sociologie juridique, version française d'après le manuscrit anglais*, translated with Paul L. Léon (Paris: A. Pedone, 1939).
12. Paul Léon, 'Une doctrine relativiste et expérimentale de la souveraineté – H.-J. Laski', *Archives de Philosophie du Droit et de Sociologie Juridique*, Nos. 1–2, 1931: 231–40; and 'Les idées sociales et politiques du guild-socialism', *Archives de Philosophie du Droit et de Sociologie Juridique*, Nos. 3–4, 1931.
13. Paul Léon, 'Doctrines sociales et politiques du moyen âge (des origines au IXe siècle)', *Archives de Philosophie du Droit et de Sociologie Juridique*, Nos. 3–4, 1932: 247–67.
14. Léon to T. S. Eliot, 9 February 1932; NLI.
15. For a fuller account of Paul's efforts to get *Ulysses* published outside of Paris, see Luca Crispi, '*Ulysses* in the Marketplace: 1932', *Joyce Studies Annual* (2012): 29–65.
16. Paul Léon, 'Le problème des sources du droit positif', *Archiv für Rechts- und Sozialphilosophie*, Vol. 28, No. 4, 1934.
17. For further information, see Luca Crispi, 'Paul Léon and the Publication *of The Mime of Mick, Nick and the Maggies*', *Joyce Studies Annual* (2019): 125–61.

18. Weaver to Léon, 17 March 1934; NLI.
19. Weaver to Léon, 5 October 1934; NLI.
20. Chapter 2, Appendix A.
21. R. W. and A. J. Carlyle, *A History of Medieval Political Theory in the West*, Vol. IV (Edinburgh and London: Blackwood, 1936).
22. Paul Léon, review, W. I. Jennings, *Cabinet Government* (Cambridge: Cambridge University Press, 1936) in *Politica* (June 1937): 398–402.
23. Paul Léon, 'L'évolution de l'idée de la souveraineté avant Rousseau', *Archives de Philosophie du Droit et de Sociologie Juridique*, Nos. 3–4, 1937.
24. Léon to Weaver, 2 February 1938: NLI.
25. Léon to Weaver, 17 August 1938; NLI.
26. Léon to Weaver, 18 August 1938; NLI.
27. See Chapter 2, p. 36.
28. Léon to Weaver, 14 December 1938; NLI.
29. Geert Lernout, 'Finishing a Book Without Title: The Final Years of "Work in Progress"', *Joyce Studies Annual* (2013): 3–32 (30).
30. Léon to Weaver, 14 December 1938; NLI.
31. Quoted in Catherine Fahy, *The James Joyce–Paul Léon Papers in the National Library of Ireland* (Dublin: National Library of Ireland, 1992), p. v.
32. See Chapter 3 for more information about the preparations for the La Hune exhibition and its sale of Joyceana.
33. See Peter Spielberg's *James Joyce's Manuscripts & Letters at the University of Buffalo: A Catalogue* (Buffalo: University of Buffalo, 1962), as well as my revised catalogue, which is available on the Poetry Collection's website.
34. For more information about it, see *The Paul and Lucie Léon/James Joyce Collection* (Tulsa: University of Tulsa, 1985).
35. Preface, p. xvi.

Elizabeth Lucie Ponizowsky – Lucie Léon – Lucie Noel

1. Lucie Noel, 'Lucie Noel's Biographical Notes', NLI MS 36,915, pp. 3–4. Hereafter cited as 'Biographical Notes'.
2. Elizabeth Lucie Léon (also known as Lucie Noel), 'Case History' in *United States Congressional Serial Set*, Vol. 11904, for the 84th Congress, 2nd Session, House of Representatives (Report 2528), 28 June 1956, p. 6. Hereafter cited as 'Case History'.
3. Noel, 'Biographical Notes', p. 4.
4. Noel, 'Case History', p. 6.
5. Noel, 'Biographical Notes', p. 5.
6. Noel, 'Case History', p. 6.
7. Noel, 'Biographical Notes', p. 5.
8. Noel, 'Case History', pp. 6–7.
9. Noel, 'Case History', p. 7.
10. Noel, 'Biographical Notes', pp. 5–6.
11. Noel, 'Case History', p. 7.

12. Noel, 'Biographical Notes', pp. 6–7.
13. Noel, 'Case History', p. 7.
14. Noel, 'Biographical Notes', p. 7.
15. Noel, 'Case History', pp. 7–8.
16. Noel, 'Biographical Notes', p. 8.
17. Noel, 'Case History', p. 8.
18. Noel, 'Biographical Notes', p. 8.
19. Noel, 'Case History', p. 8.
20. Noel, 'Biographical Notes', p. 8.
21. Noel, 'Case History', p. 8.
22. Noel, 'Biographical Notes', p. 1.
23. See the clippings of some of her work as well as the related correspondence that she preserved in NLI MS 36,908–11.
24. Noel, 'Biographical Notes', p. 1.
25. Noel, 'Biographical Notes', p. 2.
26. Drafts and correspondence related to the translation and publication can be found in NLI MS 36,911.
27. Drafts of the unpublished translation can be found in NLI MS 36,912.
28. In January 1939, Vladimir Nabokov, a friend of Alec Ponizowsky, asked Lucie to work with him on *The Real Life of Sebastian Knight*, his first novel in English. Lucie and Paul Léon introduced Nabokov to James Joyce.
29. Quoted in Peter Kenny (compiler), 'Collection List no. 70: Papers of Paul and Lucie Léon' (Dublin: National Library of Ireland, n.d. [2005]), p. 4.
30. Noel, 'Biographical Notes', p. 9.

Paul Léon and *Haveth Childers Everywhere*

1. Lucie transcribed Paul's notes in her memoir (Chapter 2, Appendix I) and his two other works on Joyce can be found in Chapter 4.
2. See Chapter 2, Appendix I.
3. Chapter 2, Appendix I.
4. This is letter no. [29] in Chapter 5.
5. Chapter 2, Appendix I.
6. That is, *Anna Livia Plurabelle* and *Tales Told of Shem and Shaun*.
7. In a previous letter, on 18 October 1929 (James Joyce Collection; Buffalo MS XII, no. 10), Beach informed Wells: 'Joyce wishes the preface to be written by a town planner or city historian such as the Rowntrees, Cadburys and Lord Leverhulmes in England, or the architect Le Corbusier, rather than a man of letters.' Ultimately, the book appeared without an introduction.
8. Sylvia Beach to James R. Wells, The Fountain Press, 522 Fifth Avenue, New York; 14 November 1929; Correspondence from Sylvia Beach & Shakespeare and Company (James Joyce Collection; Buffalo MS XII, no. 11).
9. The manuscript is BL MS 47484b, ff. 347–50; see *JJA* 59:55–62.
10. This manuscript is Buffalo MS VI.E.1; see *JJA* 59: 71–84.

11. Stuart Gilbert, *Reflections on James Joyce: Stuart Gilbert's Paris Journal*, edited by Thomas F. Staley and Randolph Lewis (Austin: University of Texas Press, 1993), pp. 20–1.
12. The notebook is Buffalo MS VI.B.29, which has been reproduced in black-and-white, high-contrast photo-facsimile as Vol. 59 in the *JJA*, and edited in full as Vincent Deane, Daniel Ferrer and Geert Lernout, *The Finnegans Wake Notebooks at Buffalo: VI.B.29*, with an Introduction by Geert Lernout (Turnhout: Brepols, 2001); hereafter cited as *FWNB: VI.B.29*, by notebook page and entry.
13. *FWNB: VI.B.29*, p. 65(a).
14. *FWNB: VI.B.29*, p. 14(b).
15. *Encyclopædia Britannica*, 11th edn (1911), 'Delhi', p. 955b; hereafter cited in abbreviated form as *EB*, entry title, page and column.
16. Ellipses in the original; BL MS 47484b, f. 394; see *JJA* 59:116. The additions are signalled with matched sets of nested caret marks (^ added text ^).
17. Bl MS 47484b, f. 373; see *JJA* 59:140 and *FW* 542.31–4.
18. See *FW* 542.31–5.
19. *FWNB: VI.B.29*, p. 66(a)–67(h).
20. *FWNB: VI.B.29*, p. 66(a); *EB*, 'Teheran', p. 506b.
21. *FWNB: VI.B.29*, p. 66(b); *EB*, 'Teheran', p. 506b.
22. *HCE*, p. 25; *FW* 538.12.
23. *EB*, 'Teheran', p. 506c.
24. *FWNB: VI.B.29*, p. 65(c).
25. *FWNB: VI.B.29*, p. 77(c).
26. *EB*, 'Dublin', p. 620d.
27. *FWNB: VI.B.29*, p. 78(m).
28. *FW* 537.35–6; see BL MS 47484b, f. 406; *JJA* 59:129.
29. Gilbert, *Reflections on James Joyce*, pp. 26–7; entry for 28 April 1930.
30. Reginald L. Hine, *The History of Hitchin*, 2 vols. (London: George Allen & Unwin, 1927 and 1929); *FWNB: VI.B.29*, p. 8.
31. Seebohm Rowntree, *Poverty: A Study of Town Life* (London: Longmans, Green & Co., 1922); *FWNB: VI.B.29*, p. 9.
32. Washington Irving, *A History of New York* (New York: Doubleday, Doran & Co., 1928). See Mikio Fuse et al., 'Emendations to the Transcription of *Finnegans Wake* Notebook VI.B.29', *Genetic Joyce Studies*, Issue 3 (Spring 2003).
33. *FWNB: VI.B.29*, pp. 9–10.
34. 18 March 1930; James Joyce, *Selected Letters of James Joyce*, edited by Richard Ellmann (London: Faber, 1975), pp. 346, 350.
35. Paul also confided to his niece: 'Now as to his work it might be sheer nonsense, and I am careful telling him my opinion every evening after work' (Chapter 2, p. 54).
36. Chapter 2, p. 54.
37. BL MS 47484b, fs. 459–60; *JJA* 59:206–7.
38. Chapter 2, p. 35.
39. Chapter 2, p. 55.

CHAPTER TWO

James Joyce and Paul Léon: The Story of a Friendship

LUCIE NOEL*

A Proceeding of the James Joyce Society

Delivered in Part at the Meeting of November 18, 1948.

The Gotham Book Mart, New York

FOREWORD

In these pages I have tried to erect a memorial, building it stone by stone, to a human relationship. I have laid the stones painstakingly, painfully, lovingly, assailed by a gamut of emotions ranging from grief and sadness to at times almost burlesque laughter. I have tried to pay homage to the friendship between James Joyce and Paul Léon, and I have tried to recapture the atmosphere and mood of the twelve years we spent together.

Nine years have passed since Joyce and my husband parted for the last time. Although each lived an intense life of his own, with separate intellectual interests and pursuits, their meetings were so frequent and their friendship so profound and sincere that it is difficult for me to look back on those years without evoking the figure of our friend James Joyce.

My husband's understanding of Joyce, as a man and as an artist, and his devotion to him were of a quality that only war and death can end. We shared many joys and sorrows, enjoying carefree days and living through tragic times, forerunners of still darker years to come. James Joyce was spared these latter. My husband was not spared.

I can only call these pages *The Story of a Friendship*, and it is to this remarkable and touching friendship that I humbly dedicate these memories.

LUCIE NOEL

New York, December, 1948
Paris, March, 1949

ACKNOWLEDGEMENTS

The following pages are an extension of a paper which I read before the James Joyce Society in New York on November 18, 1948, at the Gotham Book Mart.[1]

I wish first to thank Frances Stelloff for her gracious co-operation and rare understanding on that evening, and John Slocum for placing at my disposal his magnificent library of Joyceana and for helping me to recapture thereby the Joyce mood.[2]

On my return to Paris new material became available. Dates, events and places had to be checked. I am grateful to Eugene and Maria Jolas,[3] to Henriette Hirschmann and to Stuart and Moune Gilbert for helping me situate some of them correctly;[4] to Olga Howe, my husband's niece, for contributing a most valuable letter;[5] to Alexander Troubnikoff [6] for material on Joyce's visit to Lausanne; and to Serge Kaminsky,[7] with whom my husband frequently discussed his own reactions to Joyce's creative process.

I am also deeply indebted to those friends who have helped me prepare the manuscript for printing, to Scott Conkling for his unstinting devotion, to Anne Cottrell for her editorial advice, and Roy McMullen, whose experienced eye has been invaluable.

LUCIE NOEL

New York, December, 1948
Paris, March, 1949

I

James Joyce and Paul Léon met in 1928. It was the beginning of a friendship that was to last twelve years and would have certainly continued indefinitely had they lived. Joyce was forty-seven years old and my husband was thirty-five at the time of their first meeting. But differences in age and early background did not prove a barrier to their understand of each other.

They met through my brother Alec,[8] who had been giving Joyce Russian lessons after meeting him at the home of an American friend who later married Joyce's son Giorgio.[9] Knowing the interests of both men, my brother arranged a meeting. I was in England at the time, and received a letter from my husband.

"Wait until you see him," he wrote.

I returned to Paris to find their daily program already established. They were to see each other almost every day thereafter—days in which they worked together and days in which their selfless friendship was created.

My husband Paul was a man of many interests. He was Russian, and an exile, as was Joyce, from his country. He had escaped from the Bolsheviks in 1918 after having fought as a volunteer enlisted man in the war. He was a scholar with a knowledge of Greek and Latin, and a professor of philosophy and sociology. His special studies were Rousseau and Benjamin Constant. He was secretary of the journal, *International Archives of Sociology* and was active too in the Society of Sociologists and Philosophers.[10]

He fully appreciated Joyce's achievement as a writer, defending it tooth and nail when the occasion arose, but he was more interested in Joyce as a person. Joyce's capacity of getting himself involved in complications with editors and publishers is well known. Everyone knows, too, how unfortunate Joyce often was in the people he trusted. A special flock of Eumenides seemed to plague his day-by-day existence.[11] In addition to financial and business troubles, he had family worries—the sickness of his daughter, the death of his father—and he was partially blind.[12]

Joyce needed a friend on whom he could depend for practical advice and spiritual consolation. My husband Paul, because of his interest in Joyce's work and his affection and deep sympathy for Joyce the man, became that friend. He transcribed and corrected manuscripts, read aloud to Joyce, took care of business and personal mail, and saw to contracts with publishers.[13] During the 1930s he assumed many burdens which might have prevented Joyce from getting on with his principal job.

But Paul Léon also provided the stimulus of a classically-educated mind and a cultural background quite different from that of Joyce. My husband was a man of the world in the best sense; his mind worked with a precision and an independent brilliance which made him impatient with mediocrity and quick to perceive the genius of Joyce.

He very much resented being called—as he often was—Joyce's "paid secretary," Joyce's "lawyer," Joyce's "manager," or Joyce's agent."[14] But since it was often impossible to reach Joyce without going through Paul, those titles were bound to arise in people's minds. Paul was there to handle every situation, to smooth over all sorts of misunderstandings, to protect Joyce from gate-crashers and intruders.

Those who knew my husband well often wondered why anyone as self-sufficient as he was, with serious interests and intellectual work of his own, should have been willing to devote so much time to Joyce. Frequently, when the question was put to Paul, he would answer:

"I am most interested in watching Joyce's process of creation. He has me look up words in various languages, and his mental process and the metamorphosis of language he indulges in are most fascinating to witness."

Joyce willingly would have paid Paul a regular salary. But my husband had an aversion to accepting a salary which he explained thus: "By not accepting a salary I retain my complete independence. This way, the day I do not feel like seeing Joyce I do not have to do so." But I never saw the day when Paul would refuse to see him.

He claimed further that—without a salary—his judgement was free and he could tell Joyce what was on his mind if he felt like doing so. And they did have a few arguments. My husband would brood and take to playing solitaire. For two days I could tell something was bothering him. To my questions he would say:

"The old man is acting like a child. I think I will have to tell him so."

An argument would usually start with Paul saying: "Sir, (they were always quite formal with each other) I think you are quite wrong . . . I want to scold you . . . I think you are making an error . . .."

If this occurred in the house, I would leave the room as quickly as possible. But these spats were never very serious nor very stormy. Everyone would look gloomy, and Paul most of all, during the aftermath of a quarrel, but soon all would be well and the old routine would start up again. And the two familiar taps on the door around noon or after six would bring a sigh of relief from my husband and a smile from everyone. Andrée, our little maid, would open the door beaming—

"C'est Monsieur Joyce, Monsieur."

To the period around 1933 to 1936 belongs the following anecdote recalled by Padraic Colum,[15] who was a close friend of Joyce:

"One day, I went over to Joyce's place to find him depressed and upset.

"'What's wrong, Joyce?' I said, "What's the matter?"

"'It's Léon," Joyce replied, "he won't speak to me."

"'Why, whatever have you done?" said I.

"'It isn't so much what I've done, as what I've said. You know I said something about the Pope. Well, Léon strongly disapproves of it. . . . Now Colum, you are an Irishman and an Irish Catholic. *You know* what I have written. You don't think it so terrible, do you? Then why is Léon so upset about it?'"[16]

My husband was as aware as was Joyce of the latter's mission in the field of experimental letters—that no one had ever written a *Finnegans Wake*. But one day I overheard him say to Joyce:

"Sir, this may be genius, this may be art, I grant you all that, but please don't ask me to understand it."

When he would tease Joyce in this way about "Finnegan," Joyce would accuse him of not taking his mental acrobatics seriously enough. But Paul, whose memory was brilliant, could quote entire paragraphs of Joyce's work, and correct offhand any misquotations he might read or hear.

Nearly every day, at a quarter to one or around six o'clock there would be those two light taps on the door of our apartment at 27 Rue Casimir-Périer, and the maid would usher Joyce into our living room. "Is he there?" would be his first question. And if my husband were at home, they would begin pouring over proofs again, or else wander off to the corner bistro for an apéritif and a chat. Or they might discuss some current problem, Finnish royalties or the health of Joyce's daughter Lucia.[17]

Joyce would be wearing a dark suit, brown or blue. He was slighter than my husband, and when we first met him was very slender. Later he became painfully thin. There were times when he seemed to gain a little weight, but generally speaking he was a thin man. He always wore his famous double-lens glasses, without which I never saw him except for the moments when he would take them off to polish them with a silk handkerchief. That, I suppose, is why his death mask looks so strange and unfamiliar to me.[18]

If my husband happened to be out, I would keep Joyce company. Sometimes he would talk to our son Alexis, if the latter had finished his homework. Joyce had a charming manner with children. They loved him. He talked to them as if they were grown-ups. His manner was always gentle anyway, but with children in particular he made a point of being simple and serious, and if he chose to be gay, he never talked down to them.

If he were in the mood we would play the phonograph. He liked gay French songs and comic English ones. He laughed at *Madame la Marquise* and *V'la les Pompiers*,[19] and got quite hilarious over the jail-song *Eleven More Years and Ten More Days*.[20] We also played Irish records, McCormack and Sullivan arias,[21] but to these I shall return later.

Joyce's eyesight was very poor even in those early years of our friendship. I can recall him groping for a tumbler of water on the table and not finding it. He was treated by Professor Alfred Vogt of Zurich,[22] one of the world's best oculists, and there were times of great improvement, but the improvement did not last. Joyce told me once around 1932 that he had undergone something like seventeen operations, and all without anaesthetic.[23]

One day when we were all sitting in our living room he suddenly exclaimed: "Mrs. Léon, are you not wearing a white blouse? I believe I can see something white." This seemed to all of us an event of tremendous importance, and we were all moved by the hope that Joyce's eyes were getting better. He claimed he saw better with the artificial pupil than with the "well eye."[24]

But at the end of every visit to our place some one would always guide him downstairs and see that he found a taxi. Paul usually did this, and would often take him all the way home.

Paul often read aloud to him—Newman, Dean Inge, Duns Scotus, Ibsen, Dickens. One of his favourite characters was Mr. Micawber.[25] There is a character in *Martin Chuzzlewit* Joyce used to say reminded him of my husband because of his gaiety and good nature.[26] *Ghosts* meant a great deal to Joyce, I am not sure why.[27] They discussed Nora's character in the *Doll's House*; and Joyce liked to hear Paul talk about the people in Gogol's *Dead Souls*. He also was interested in *When We Dead Awaken*, *The Master Builder*, *War and Peace*, and *Dostoievsky*. My husband was a great admirer of Anatole France but they agreed that *Madame Bovary* and *Anna Karenina* were the two great novels. I was sometimes under the impression that Joyce did not approve of his predecessors' way of writing, but that he admitted their greatness and significance.

I have heard them thrashing out Anatole France's *Penguin Island*, its amazing satirical approach applicable to life today.[28]

When Paul spoke to me in Russian and mentioned Joyce, he frequently referred to him affectionately as the "old man," in the same spirit with which a junior officer will refer to his colonel as the "old man." Joyce often repeated Russian words for their musical sound and asked to have them explained to him. He knew that *starik* meant "old man," and was irritated by what he considered a reflection on his age. On several occasions he said to me:

"Mrs. Léon, will you please ask Léon not to call me *starik. I am not old.*"

He was a man of infinite tact. He was conscious of intruding into our lives and monopolizing the time of my husband, and often he would say to me, "Why don't you simply throw me out?" But I am certain he would have been very upset if we had taken such a suggestion seriously. And so nearly every morning would start with a telephone call: "Good morning, this is Joyce. Is he there?" And then the morning's mail and the day's program would be discussed.

Joyce had many hours of despair, and there was little anyone could do to help him at such times. He was very much a family man, a devoted husband, a good father, and a loyal son. To his nostalgia for Ireland was added the pain of being separated from his father. The death of his father was a severe blow for him, but it was softened by the birth of his grandson Stephen:

Of the dark past
A child is born
With joy and grief
My heart is torn[29]

One day I asked Paul if Joyce had not at last succeeded in accumulating enough money to be able to live peacefully, to work and not worry about his immediate future. Paul's answer was definite: "Joyce has spent three quarters of his income on doctors, sanatoriums and cures for Lucia." Few people except Joyce's closest friends knew the depth of his anguish over his daughter, the haunting anxiety which never left him. Here was the answer. This was the great cross he bore in life.

During all this distressing period, which extended over the last eight years of Joyce's life and is still going on, Maria Jolas demonstrated the exceptional quality of her devotion to both Joyce and his daughter. Whenever a personal crisis arose he knew he could turn to my husband and to Mrs Jolas for advice and help. For a literary crisis he turned to Paul and Gene Jolas and frequently to Stuart Gilbert. The Jolases, as most people know, published serially from 1927 to 1938 the greater part of *Work in Progress*, (*Finnegans Wake*) in their avant-garde magazine "transition."

Some of our most memorable evenings were those spent in the Jolas home in Neuilly.[30] Maria Jolas is a fine musician with a beautiful contralto voice, and she and Joyce, who had a mellow Irish tenor, and his son Giorgio, who had a deep baritone which later developed into a fine bass,[31] would provide the evening's entertainment. Each of them would sing in turn, and then often in duets or trios. Joyce loved early Italian music and bel canto, and he also liked to sing early Elizabethan songs and Purcell.[32] He and Mrs. Jolas would sing a duet from *Il Trovatore*,[33] and I remember, too, that he sang a song of his own, of which he had written both the words and music, which was particularly lovely. It is called *Bid Adieu*, and Edmund Pendleton has now arranged the music, after Joyce's script.[34]

Giorgio Joyce, whose Italian repertoire was quite important, would render the *Figaro* solos, Tosti's *Donna Vorrei Morir* and *Amaryllis,* and Franz's *Friedhof*, which Joyce particularly enjoyed.[35]

But what we liked best was to get Joyce in the Irish mood. Then he would sing the melodies of his beloved country, rendering them with more feeling and charm than I have ever heard. He often told us that in youth he had sung in the same church choir as John McCormack and that "our voices were so alike, they could not tell us apart at the time." Mrs Joyce corroborated this statement, and my own feeling, based on a favourite record of McCormack singing *None but the Lonely Heart*,[36] was that Joyce's voice, though untrained, did have an extraordinary mellowness and was softer in quality that that of McCormack.

At the Jolases on these evenings so filled with beauty and music, my husband would seat himself at the piano at about one in the morning and give us Chopin and his idea of Rimsky-Korsakow's *Scheherazade*, and then wind up with his repertoire of gypsy music.[37]

Joyce was a very formal person, and always Mr. Joyce to us. He did once or twice suggest that we call each other by our first names, but nothing ever came of it because Paul was just as formal as he was. But there was nothing he enjoyed more than an informal celebration. His amazing memory never failed him on birthdays, anniversaries, and holidays.

Christmas was usually marked by grand party at his own home or at the home of his son and daughter-in-law Helen. Thanksgiving was nearly always celebrated at the Jolases, with due pomp and circumstance, since Mrs. Jolas is a Southerner. Sweet potatoes, pumpkin pie, turkey, and trimmings were served in traditional style. The Joyces were the guests of honor.

The reader is doubtless familiar with the most literary of these occasions—when the turkey lost its liver "and met with foul disaster in the Place St. Augustin" while being delivered to the Jolas home. Joyce immortalized the event and the turkey—with a rollicking ballad entitled *La Dinde Aux Comeallyous* (1937). This was published under the title *Pastimes* in 1941.[38]

At these parties the spirits of the guests rose as the hours grew smaller, and Joyce would finally indulge in an indescribable Irish jig which delighted everyone far beyond the quality of capers. He looked rather like a Polichinelle practicing high jinks,[39] and to us it meant that for a moment he was forgetting his worries and was able to relax with his friends.

And of course he never forgot St. Patrick's Day. Nothing would please him more than a sprig of shamrock which he could wear in his lapel. Once in spite of finding myself in London on that date, I airmailed him a whole pot of shamrock, and he was quite delighted.

On December 13, his daughter Lucia's feast day, he always burnt a candle.[40] During the years she was so sick he kept up this custom and always sent her gifts.

Joyce's gifts were often in the nature of a pun. He liked to play on Paul's name "Léon," and once sent us a large Copenhagen porcelain lion. This "lion theme" would also frequently appear on postcards which Joyce would send me when he and Paul were away together. I have one about the Lion of St. Mark's, and one from Lausanne, where they went one summer: "Léon is at his fourth bath and turning a delicious Nubian."

I think, however, that the most subtle of these "pun gifts" was a blue and white striped necktie which Joyce gave my husband—for Easter, if I recall correctly.[41] The blue was the shade of the Liffey and also matched the jacket of the first edition of *Ulysses*, and of course blue and white are the colors of Greece. I like to think of them as Joyce's colors.

Despite his poor eyesight, it always seemed to me that Joyce was very conscious of color. I remember his asking me in the early years of our friendship to name colors, their shades and ranges. We talked of the rainbow and of prisms, and he made notes. I asked him why he wanted all that information, and he told me that in *Ulysses* he had made use of children's games and that now, in *Work in Progress*, he intended to use colors.[42]

The nature of Joyce's work made proof-reading and translation extremely difficult. Philippe Soupault, in his little book *Souvenirs de James Joyce*,[43] in the chapter entitled "Anna Livia Plurabelle, translations of Fragments,"[44] describes some proof-reading which took place in our apartment:

"The translation of the "Fragments of Anna Livia Plurabelle" was tackled in the following way. A first trial translation was submitted by Samuel Beckett, Irish lecturer at the Ecole Normale. He had been aided in this undertaking by Alfred Perron, B.A., who had spent one year in Dublin. The revising of this version, under the direction of the author, was made by Paul Léon, Eugene Jolas and Ivan Goll.

"At the end of November, 1930, we met, Mr. Joyce, Paul L. Léon and myself, in the Rue Casimir-Périer at the home of our friend Léon. We had selected Thursday for the day of our meetings. At 2:30 Mr. Joyce arrived and immediately we started work. We installed ourselves at a large round mahogany table.[45] Mr. Joyce settled down in an armchair and smoked Maryland cigarettes. Mr. Léon read aloud the English text and I followed immediately with the revised French version. Paul Léon then picked out a sentence in the English text, I read a sentence, and we discussed it. In accordance with Mr. Joyce we rejected all that appeared to contradict the rhythm, the sense of the metamorphosis of the words, and we tried in our turn to suggest a translation. Mr. Joyce exposed us to the difficulties; together by common accord we sought for the equivalent. There would be a sentence which would ring with better rhythm, a word which would appear more forceful.

"'Just a moment,' Mr. Joyce would say to stop us. We concentrated and suddenly Mr. Joyce, Paul Léon or myself would discover precisely that which we had been seeking. These sessions lasted for three hours.

"Fifteen sessions proved necessary to complete our task."

One afternoon during this period I came home from calling at the school for my son Alexis, who was then six years old. We opened the living room door, and there the familiar group was—hard at work on *Anna Livia*. Before anyone could move Alexis cried in a child's clear tones: "Look, Mummy, Daddy must be giving Mr. Joyce an English lesson."

The proof-reading of *Finnegans Wake* was the most hectic of all. Mrs. Jolas in Neuilly, Stuart Gilbert on the Ile St. Louis, Joyce in the Rue Edmond Valentin,[46] and my husband were all working against time. They were in a continual whirl, either rushing to exchange and check sections of copy or bringing corrected proof over to our place where a secretary was taking dictation. My husband was supervising her work, giving her new instructions and making new corrections. (It is possibly of interest that she knew hardly any English.) Paul would also fly over to the Joyce apartment for more corrected galley proofs. Joyce himself was continually revising and making last-minute corrections. The telephone was going all day, calling London, the printers, Pinker, the agent . . . and all this because Joyce's friends and Joyce himself were determined to get out the first edition on February 2, his birthday.

About three days before the "fatal date" Paul arrived home from Joyce's late for lunch. On entering the living room he suddenly grabbed his head and cried "My God." He had left a large part of the corrected final proofs of Finnegan in the taxi. He rushed back down the stairs, but the taxi was gone.

He jumped into another cab and went back to the Joyce apartment. Although the calamity meant that more than a month of hard work had been lost, Joyce had no reproaches. He seemed to take it as the usual sort of bad luck. There were copies of the manuscript, of course, but no corrected proof, and Paul was frightfully upset. He called London to warn Pinkers and to ask the printer for more galley proof, and then told the bad news to the other people who had been working in Paris.

Naturally, those concerned were in something of a state. But the work continued. All we could do was to bank on the honesty of the driver, and we were encouraged by the fact that if anyone did find the package these proofs of "Finnegan" could not possibly mean anything to him. And lo and behold, two days later there was a ring at the door, and there stood a fat cab driver with the package.[47]

And so *Finnegans Wake* appeared on time, an advance copy arriving from London on Joyce's birthday, and there was a celebration at the home of Mr. and Mrs. Giorgio Joyce.

At one time our apartment had been occupied by the Comtesse de Segur, whose *Malheurs de Sophie* and *Petites Filles Modeles* are still as popular with French children as is *Little Women* with young Americans.[48] We often wondered during those final days of work on Joyce's epic what the Comtesse would have thought of the progress made by literature. Paul thought she was "turning somersaults in her grave," for it was just possible that Anna Livia was being presented to the world in the very room where Sophie and her little cousins, Second Empire paragons, were born.

Joyce was a great theatre-goer, but he disliked going alone, and Mrs. Joyce was not always available, particularly if he wished to see something in the afternoon, which was frequently the case. So he was often accompanied by the Jolases, the Gilberts, the Giorgio Joyces or by my husband. Paul was not always enthusiastic, for it sometimes seemed to him that Joyce's selections were prompted by some mysterious reason which had little to do with the quality of the play. But they saw many plays together—Moliere, Racine, Ibsen, and *Les Corbeaux* several times.[49] Joyce appreciated good acting, and I confess I enjoyed his choices even though we often had to sit right up front because of his poor eyes. We saw d'Annunzio's *Citta Morta* sometime around 1932, with the old Italian actor Ermete Zaccone and Joyce's enthusiasm for his performance impressed me.[50]

He enjoyed good light music, too. We saw the French operetta *La Fille de Madame Angot*, which I had not heard before, but he knew all the gay songs and Ange Pitou was one of his favorite characters. The action took place in the Palais Royal, and the costumes were of the Directoire period.[51] Joyce asked me to describe them to him and I remember that they were crude in a small music-hall way, but true in style and feeling, with loud colors and the most made of the slashed sheath with its very low-cut decolletage.

I was his "seeing eye" on a more difficult occasion in 1935 or 1936, when he took me to see a film in the Rue de Clichy which had been causing some comment. He had tried to get Paul to go, but my husband said the idea bored him. The movie was Extase, in which Hedy Lamarr ran around the countryside perfectly beautiful and quite nude.[52] There was also a very realistic love scene between horses. The picture was quite erotic and I was quite embarrassed, because I had to explain much of the action to Joyce and keep up with the subtitles as well. At that time his eyesight was really bad, and every few minutes he would ask, "What are they doing now?" I would try to tell him in as general a way as I could, and he would say "I see," obviously amused by my fumbling explanation. But we both thought it was a very fine picture.

Opera, however, was Joyce's greatest delight. I went once with him to hear *Lucia di Lammermoor*,[53] which he knew thoroughly and which moved him especially because it reminded him of his daughter Lucia, as did another Opera which he had seen and liked in Italy—*La Somnambula*.[54] But it was really John Sullivan, the Irish tenor, who was for years the focus of his musical interest.

Sullivan looked like a prize-fighter and had a great big voice which seemed to me to be more baritone than tenor robusto. He had sung in many roles in many cities, but Joyce admired him especially in *Wilhelm Tell* and *Aida*.[55] He thought Sullivan's voice and Sullivan's acting were both wonderful, and this notion was the cause of endless discussions with Paul, who considered Chaliapin the greatest singer and impersonator of the time.[56] I forget exactly why Joyce thought Sullivan was superior, but I recall he also thought Chaliapin was inferior to the Russian basso Zaporojetz,[57] who sang in the Russian Church choir, and really beautifully on Maundy Thursday. Every year during Passion Week Paul and Joyce would go to hear Zaporojetz, and I am told that Joyce often dropped into the church on other days when he knew he could listen to the basso.

One evening in 1936 Joyce invited us to the opera for a gala event. Sullivan was to sing *Wilhelm Tell*. Paul had heard him in *Tell* several times with Joyce, and so had Joyce's family and the Jolases and the Gilberts, and I certainly had no particular desire to go. But Mrs. Joyce had joined in the invitation, there were to be just the four of us, so we had to face it.

Years of life in Italy had made Joyce very opera conscious, and he looked marvelous that night in his flowing satin-lined opera cloak, with his silk hat set a trifle askew on his head. He carried the monogrammed ivory-tipped evening cane which he reserved for special occasions.[58] Paul disliked wearing evening dress, but he had made a special effort, because he knew it would make Joyce happy.

No one was at all excited about *Wilhelm Tell* except Joyce. The opera developed at its usual pace until Sullivan had finished his famous solo, when there was some applause. But Joyce clapped the loudest of all, and suddenly, jumping from his seat and waving his arms in the best Scala style, shouted:

"Bravo Sullivan et merde pour Lauri Volpi!"

There was a second of silence, and then howls of joy from the audience. We couldn't get Paul to stop laughing, for he knew that Joyce honestly felt that Volpi—who was singing in Paris at the time, although not, thank heaven, at the opera that night—was stealing the glory of Sullivan.[59]

We went over to the Café de la Paix after the performance to recover from the excitement, and Sullivan—full of his succès de scandale—came over and later joined us, drinking a demi-blonde like any ordinary mortal.[60] But the incident did not end there. The morning papers picked it up, and all the next day people were calling us to find out whether he "had really said it." "C'est vrai, tout ça? C'est merveilleux . . . ."

Joyce provided us with some Sullivan records, hoping we would end up liking them. (I still have them, for although the Germans helped themselves to many of our records, they left Sullivan's alone.) *Wilhelm Tell* and *Celeste Aida* on the phonograph made even more noise than Sullivan did on stage, and we played them exclusively for Joyce. He would sit drinking in "the voice" from the depths of a huge, dilapidated leather armchair which we kept around the house because I liked it and because Joyce regarded it as "the only comfortable chair in the house." But its springs were on the verge of giving way and Paul warned him constantly: "Sir, one day you will be on the floor." And one day, listening to Sullivan, he was, looking like a marionette with his bony knees under his chin, and shaking with laughter.

In February, 1931, I made a trip to the States, and before I left my husband said to me; "the old man wants to ask you to do him a favor." The "favor" turned out to be a démarche. I was to submit to the management of the Metropolitan Opera a list of the operas Sullivan had performed in Europe plus a general account of his ability. Joyce felt that the Met would be interested and perhaps introduce Sullivan to the American public.

I was rather doubtful, but I began working on the Project shortly after my arrival in New York, for we knew that it really meant a great deal to Joyce. I succeeded in getting an interview with Edward Ziegler, one of the directors of the Metropolitan,[61] and he listened politely and patiently to my somewhat complicated and confused story. "Sullivan has not been appreciated by the world at large," I told him. "His magnificent voice is almost unknown to the general public. Take Gigli,[62] Volpi, and others, who Mr. Joyce claims are not a patch on Sullivan . . .."

Mr. Ziegler listened for a while, and then said evenly: "But we know all about Mr. John Sullivan. He has sung here before." And that was that. Mr. Sullivan was known all about, and I folded away Joyce's list of his achievements and retired with apologies.

On my return to Paris, Joyce heard my story with a mixture of regret and amusement. To mark the occasion he wrote in my memory book: "Oh, tell me all about Mr. Ziegler. I want to hear all about Mr. Ziegler. Well, you all know Mr. Ziegler. . ."—quoting his "Anna Livia." ("Oh, tell me all about Ana Livia. I want to hear all about Anna Livia. Well, you all know Anna Livia. . .").

Paul and Joyce went for daily strolls together. In the morning they would "do errands" and frequently go to Lloyds Bank,[63] where Joyce had his account, and then pick me up around noon at Weber's Café.[64] Weber's in those days was a convenient and central meeting place. We would linger on the terrace for an aperitif if the weather were fine, and Joyce would often order un quart de Vichy.

Paul and Joyce made a strange sight sailing down the Rue Royale arm in arm, Joyce looking skywards, his hat on the side of his head, and Paul with his scholar's stoop—his bearing was poor despite his three and a half years of active duty in the war. Philippe Soupault used to call them "l'aveugle et le paralytique."[65] But they were contented to be together and appeared to be braving the world.

My husband had asthma, and about once a year he would have a severe attack. It usually started with a bad cold, and then bronchitis would set in. Paul would have to go to bed and treat himself with hot tea, cognac and lemon, and adrenalin drops if the asthma got bad. This would usually relieve him, but it would upset his routine with Joyce, for the latter had to be particularly careful about any possible infection of cold or grippe, lest it affect his "well eye."

But if Paul's sickness lasted more than two or three days Joyce would "brave fate" and come over for a visit anyway. He would install himself in a comfortable and safe chair in the living room, with the French doors leading to the bedroom wide open, and carry on a conversation under the pretense that he was not really in the sick room—despite Paul's protests that this was "cheating God."

Joyce liked writing inscriptions, and they were usually in green ink. A basket of fruit sent during one of Paul's asthma spells bore the message: "Hope this fruit is acceptable to your invalidship. J. J." An edition of *Finnegans Wake* is dedicated

"To that Eurasian Knight, Paul Léon,
with the Thousand and one thanks
of that most distressful writer,
James Joyce.
Paris, May 4th, 1939"[66]

A deluxe edition of Byron's *Don Juan*, a birthday gift, is inscribed:

"Don Leone, a pranzar teco
non m'invitasti, ma son venuto"
(signed) Il Commendatore
April 21st Chez Chauland

This was an allusion to the fact that my husband was to meet a lovely lady and had not asked Joyce to come too. Chauland is a good little restaurant near the Invalides which we frequented for a number of years.[67] It was located about half way between the Joyces' place, when they lived near the Avenue Bosquet,[68] and our apartment. Paul and Joyce often met there; the bar was never crowded, and they were known there and felt at ease.

Joyce was a dapper dresser with a liking for fads. Most people have heard of his white linen coats and the red one he liked to wear for working at home. Usually, however, he wore a dark suit, and his eccentricity would appear in only in his tapestry wool vest, which was embroidered with hunting scenes and had once been worn by his grandfather.[69] When dining informally at his son's home or at the Jolases he often wore a dark velvet jacket which was most becoming. This is the one he is wearing in the series of Lipnitzki photographs I have.[70]

I have said that Paul was there to protect Joyce from intruders. This he did to the best of his ability, but in the process there were some entertaining incidents. People often wrote to him for literary advice—just a few months ago an American girl who had heard that I knew Joyce wrote to ask me what Joyce's advice on her novel would have been. One day Joyce arrived at our place brandishing an embroidered tea-cloth which had come all the way from India. He explained that an Anglo-Indian lady was about to give a tea party. She had read and admired him, and she was humbly requesting him to sign the tea-cloth in one corner. This would be, she felt sure, an added attraction for her "tiffin at home."[71]

One day I came home to find Paul disturbed and annoyed by a letter he had received from a young man who was the secretary of a literary society. The members of this group called themselves "The Friends of 1914,"[72] although their organization had nothing to do with the war. But it certainly marked an era in French letters.

What annoyed my husband was not the young man, who seemed harmless enough, but the fact that the society inspired by the whim of a very fashionable woman, planned to stage an evening dedicated to Joyce. The Honorable Lady—for she was titled—was evidently out to prove that she had literary and intellectual interests. All in all, it was the sort of project Joyce despised, for he shunned the limelight and had no patience with chichi.

But Paul invited the young man to lunch. He proved to be intelligent, reminded me somewhat of Soupault, and appeared very much aware of his intrusion. He explained that the lady in question wished to meet Joyce and that at the meeting of the society she intended to give her impressions of *Ulysses*.

"I am afraid," Paul replied, "meeting Joyce will be very difficult to arrange. He is not too well just now. Also, he is hard at work and cannot be disturbed. But tell us about the rest of the program . . .."

The rest was interesting. The Hon. Lady was to sit on the platform next to Joyce, and would open the meeting. Then Edouard Dujardin, the author of *Les Lauriers Sont Coupés*, which was supposed to have influenced Joyce's stream-of-consciousness technique, was to speak on his own work and express his satisfaction at seeing it further developed by Joyce. Then Louis Gillet, of the Académie Francaise, was to make a speech. Gillet, a most conservative person, was a complete contrast to Joyce in mind and character, but after years of opposition to the latter's work he had acknowledged its merit publishing his acknowledgement in the *Revue des Deux Mondes*. Joyce often recalled Gillet's protests (I also remember his telling of similar objections from Sir Edmund Gosse) and I knew he would relish this triumph over French conventional opinion.[73]

Rachel Berendt, the actress, was to give a reading of "Fragments of Work in Progress," and Léon-Paul Fargue, the poet, was scheduled for an address. Fargue had also experimented with language—his last book, *Haute Solitude*, is an excellent example of his research—he was a friend of ours and of Joyce, and we knew that his admiration for Joyce's work would produce a fine tribute.[74]

So that afternoon Paul went over to see Joyce about the matter. Just as he entered the living room there was a ring at the door, and in sailed the beauteous Hon. Lady, followed by a photographer—both unexpected and unannounced. She wished to be photographed with Joyce. Then there was another ring at the door, and Gene Jolas appeared.

"This is wonderful," said Joyce, "we can have a family group." Despite the lady's protests he seated everyone in a row, and then the concierge appeared at the door with the mail.

"Fine," said Joyce, and drew the buxom concierge into the picture. By the time the ceremony was over everyone except the lady was slightly hysterical, but she proceeded to cross-examine Joyce. "When were you last in Edinburgh?" was one of her first questions.

Léon Bailby, editor of *Le Jour*, published the picture a couple of days later.[75] Everyone except Joyce and the lady had been cut off, from the waist up.

The evening of the meeting, the lady, elegantly dressed and unabashed, walked onto the platform, seated herself beside Joyce and opened the session. Her story went something like this: In the summer she sailed the sunny blue waters of the Aegean in her yacht, and "I never lie in my deck chair without a copy of *Ulysses* by my side . . . ." We were all under the impression that she was confusing Homer and Joyce, but she might have made a worse compliment.

Rachel Berendt's rendering of *Anna Livia* was excellent, and the rest of the program turned out to be a valuable contribution to Joyce's struggle for recognition.

The years were packed with incidents and people—people who were usually to be found sitting in one of our favorite cafes. There were Herbert Gorman, who for many years had worked on a biography of Joyce; Stuart Gilbert, author of *James Joyce's Ulysses*; Frank Budgen, an old friend from London and the author of *The Making of Ulysses*; the William Birds,[76] the Padraic Colums, and of course the Jolases. I can recall the Sweeneys at the Joyce home or at Fouquet's, and en passant young Lord Carlow, who published *Storiella*.[77] There were many others, but some of them I did not know, for they belonged to an earlier period, before we knew Joyce. I usually think of that time as the "Closerie des Lilas epoch." That famous café near the Observatoire was a landmark in the first postwar period and became the meeting place of the literati of the Left Bank. Valéry Larbaud and Ezra Pound in their relations with Joyce belong to that era.[78]

Later, during the years when we first knew Joyce, he was taking his meals at the Deux Trianons, in the Boulevard Montparnasse, opposite the terminal, and he used to spend many evenings there.[79] We sometimes joined the Joyces there for dinner, and it always distressed me to see what a poor eater he was. He would say, "Go on with your dinner, don't mind me," and then sit and pick at his food. I cannot recall what those meals were which he barely touched, but I do remember that he liked string beans cooked French style.

Then it was Chez Francis in the Place de l'Alma for which he and his circle developed a liking.[80] Some of the old waiters are still there, and enjoy reminiscing about the days when Joyce, Paul and the Jolases used to meet there.

Waiters, taxi-drivers, sommeliers—the garçon attached to the wine cellar to be found in every good French restaurant—always loved Joyce. He had a way with them. He knew their family histories, from what part of France they had come, and all about their children. And if a French or Italian waiter feels that a client is *sympathique,* it will not take long for him to tell you his whole life history.

At the Deux Trianons there was Norbert, at the Chez Francis there were Albert, and Xavier, an Alsatian. Albert is still there, remembering everyone and everything, and greets me effusively whenever I stop by. At Fouquet's for many years there was a solemn maître d'hotel who liked to pompously usher Joyce and his party always to the same table along the wall against the huge mirrors in the cafe downstairs. I believe his name was Celestin.

The Café de la Paix was an old favorite, particularly after an evening at the Opera—with or without Sullivan—and Joyce never really stopped going there. But Fouquet's finally replaced it as a regular meeting place. Joyce liked to bring a party of friends to Fouquet's after a play or a concert, and Paul liked to join them at those late hours. He would get there at eleven, and if he were the first to arrive he would order his favorite mixed grill while he waited.

Ending the day in a café is a tradition in France, and Joyce liked to wind up a day of hard work with a small carafe of vin ordinaire, which he preferred when he was not ordering wine for dinner. I recall also that he was partial to Alstatian wines in their tall, thin necked bottles, Traminer and Riesling in particular. From time to time he would listen to Paul's advice and order champagne nature, the dry white wine which can be served through the entire meal—which might often start with oysters. And he was very fond of Neuchatel, the Swiss wine which as you fill your glass forms a star on the golden surface.

We often stayed in Fouquet's quite late, often much too late. At one o'clock Mrs. Joyce would start: "Now, Jim, come along. We are going home . . ." and finally after some delay he would have to obey and the party would break up. Goodbyes were said. The Jolas's would go Neuilly-way. The other guests, whoever they might be, their way, and the Joyce's and we would get a taxi. With his usual gentle consideration for our pocketbooks, Joyce would drop us home first, though sometimes after some argument we would insist on dropping the Joyce's at their door.

Alexander Troubnikoff, a close friend of ours, and an authority on Dutch and Italian art, a writer and an epicurean, once accompanied my husband on a trip to Lausanne, where Paul was to meet the Joyces. I believe this was in 1937.[81] Troubnikoff was asked to reserve a table for four at the Lausanne terminal restaurant. As in many European towns, the railroad station was a popular meeting place. The townspeople like meeting the trains, seeing who is arriving and who is leaving. That night there was an orchestra playing light music which went well with the frescos of Swiss rural scenes—including vineyards. The party was on time, Joyce arriving in a carriage, and the only problem was the choice of wines. Joyce finally suggested that they consult the fresco vineyards, and they eventually decided to order three decimas of each of the twenty-odd crus represented on the wall. By the time they got through it amounted to about two bottles a piece, and Troubnikoff says the party broke up very late indeed.

On the many occasions we had Joyce to lunch or dinner Paul never forgot the Neuchatel. We used to buy it a small restaurant, the Helvetia, in the Rue de Medicis. It is opposite the Luxembourg gardens and the only place in Paris where that particular wine could be found. One day in 1938 he got a letter from the Swiss Legion asking him to get from Joyce the exact reason for his preferring Neuchatel to any other white wine. They were eager to use the reply in their publicity—but they didn't get one.

Troubnikoff has also reminded me of Joyce's fancy for the various makes of candy to be found in almost every region of France. He was amused by the play on words in les verités de Monsieur de la Palice, a local bon-bon, and he liked nougat from the Monthelimar, Montargis pralinés, and Bar-le-Duc jelly.[82] One year Troubnikoff introduced him to Russian Lenten sugar, refined in a special way according to Orthodox custom. After our exodus from Paris in 1940 Joyce cheered me up one day with a box of Aix-en-Provence caliçons, made of almond paste glazed in coated sugar and pistachio.

Sometime in 1934 or 1935 Joyce had his first bad attack of what we came to call his "pains of the stomach." He was quite sick. I was in England at the time, and Paul wrote me about it. The attack came on while he was at our place, and my husband called Mrs. Joyce, their family doctor, and our own. Both doctors diagnosed "nervous cramps," and put Joyce to bed for a week. He was given a diet which he more or less followed and eventually the pains subsided.

That Joyce was suffering from something more serious than "nervous cramps" never occurred to any of us. My brother Alec was being treated for chronic duodenal ulcers,[83] and Joyce frequently compared symptoms with him, as he did also with Mrs. Stuart Gilbert, who suffered from the same ailment. But he always insisted that he merely had "nervous cramps," and one day I discovered him drinking a horrible apéritif called Fernet Branca.[84] He made me taste it and I told him it was worse than medicine, but he insisted that it "soothed the pains." I recall one evening when Paul made me buy some Fernet Branca instead of Neuchatel for a dinner for Joyce, and Joyce was very pleased. But after several months he gave up the aperitif and went back to his vin ordinaire—a fatal error in my opinion.

Joyce's poor appetite usually made him something of a problem for his hostess, although Maria Jolas claims he sometimes ate well, and I have seen him enjoy his Thanksgiving dinner at the Jolases or at his daughter-in-law Helen's house. And he undoubtedly appreciated Mrs. Joyce's home cooking—especially the delicious cakes she made. They were a feature of those dismal afternoons at the small hotel in St. Gerand-le-Puy after our departure from Paris, when Mrs. Joyce served tea religiously every afternoon.

It must be extremely hard to be the wife of a great man in any case, but to be the wife of a semi-blind writer must be doubly difficult. I can say with all sincerity that I do not believe James Joyce could have coped with all the difficulties of daily life had it not been for the great devotion and courage of his wife Nora. Their's was a constant companionship based on love and congenial understanding. Anyone who knew Mr. and Mrs. Joyce realized that no important move would be made one without the other. Unless one had seen them together one would not realize how much James Joyce depended on his wife Nora. In all the blows that fate dealt Joyce and his family, through all the trials and tribulations, they remained devotedly together.[85]

I have often wondered: Have I ever seen Joyce really happy? The answer is no, because I never saw him completely free from care and worry. But I have seen him relaxed, during the times when all went well with his family and the news of his daughter's illness was less tragic.

Water seemed to exercise over him a real fascination, and I think he was most relaxed when he was near the sea or a river.[86] I remember him lying flat on the pebbles on the beach at Dieppe, listening to the tide come in. That was in September, 1938, when the Joyce's invited me down to the beach because I had been ill. We were caught by Munich and had to rush back to Paris because Joyce was afraid of being cut off "by events" from his daughter, then in a nursing home in the Paris suburb of Ivry.[87]

I recall him, too, listening to the sound of a river—a French river and not his beloved Liffey. The Loire in all its majesty flows through the little town of Beaugency, where we had been going for many years and where we finally succeeded in luring the Joyces.[88] He would sit or lie on the grass banks up near the old bridge where he could hear the rush of the current, and sometimes he would wander further down-stream to listen, where the water and the elms and crooked willows in the soft light always made me think of the washerwoman's scene in *Anna Livia*.[89]

Time and coincidence had much to do with Joyce's Weltanschauung: he liked to remind us that he and James Stephens were born in Dublin in the same year, on the same day, at the same hour.[90] And February 2, his birthday, was always a great event, with a celebration at some one's home or in a favorite cafe.

Often held up with cable deadlines and work on the *New York Herald Tribune*,[91] I would arrive last and latest of all at Fouquet's or wherever the party was being held. On one such occasion, Mr. Joyce maliciously remarked (with a definite intention of amusing his guests) alluding to me:

"The only one of us who earns an honest living."

The years passed by and these birthday celebrations and anniversaries had long since become an institution.

But time was fast running out. Time, one of the main elements in all of Joyce's writings, was as relentless and mysterious as ever. None of us could foretell this, nor could any of us at that moment foresee the future, so dark were the storm clouds gathering over Europe.

February 2, 1941, was the first time his birthday came around after his death. We were back in Occupied France, in Paris.[92] Our group had scattered; Mrs. Joyce was in Switzerland with her son Giorgio and Stephen, the grandson; the Jolases and the Birds were back in the States, the Gilberts in Dax in Free France, and Soupault in Algiers. Cut off from the outside world with us in Paris were Sam Beckett, a friend for whom Joyce had a great regard, and Léon-Paul Fargue.

Fargue's gallic wit and charm compensated for the fact that, in contrast to Joyce, he had absolutely no idea of time, and was usually two hours late for an appointment or meal. Those who knew Paris and the Left Bank in the twenties and thirties will like to recall Fargue in his wide-brimmed felt hat wandering from table to table at Lipp's around ten every evening.

We asked Beckett, Fargue, and Madame Cheriane, who later married Fargue, to come over to our apartment and share our dinner in memory of Joyce's birthday. Those were the lean years when "rootabagas" were part of the daily menu and when the bread was black and awful.[93] But we managed to concoct what was a magnificent meal for the times. Paul bought some smoked eels at the Russian fishmongers, I found some coquilles St. Jacques which I scraped and cooked mariniere in herbs, and the poultrywoman in our market street let us have two small pheasants—pintades.

Fargue arrived only one hour late, and the evening progressed in extraordinary spiritual communion. As I look back it seems to me that there was no war that night in Paris, no German occupation, and that Joyce's gentle spirit was there in the room where he had spent so many hours talking with Paul. Each of us had recollections of our friend to contribute, and sometimes we would all remember the same incident together. Late in the evening we played the two *Anna Livia* records Joyce made, and the sound of his dear familiar voice was almost more than we could stand.[94]

Acutely and painfully it made us realize all we had lost. First of all our friend, James Joyce. And next, the entire former pattern of our lives. It had been swept away by a cyclone. And for us it was but the prelude to still darker days and of a more tragic period.

II

In June, 1940, we were all stranded together in a little village in the center of France, St. Gérand-le-Puy, in the heart of Allier. We gathered around Mrs. Jolas, who had moved her Ecole Bilingue from Neuilly to a chateau in the Allier during the period of the "phony war." The fall of France had caught her there with about fifty American and French children under her care, and no money, no news of their parents, no protection against the Germans except courage and a large American flag.

Families became separated during the exodus from Paris, and we straggled in one by one. I arrived on June 16th,[1] and Paul came in the next day in a donkey cart. "The Lord Jesus Christ rode into Jerusalem on a donkey," he cried as we rushed to meet him. "But he wore a white robe and his path was strewn with flowers," we reminded him, "and it was a white ass, anyway, and you had better have a bath."[2]

Before the line of demarcation was drawn a German motorized unit overran the village, but the soldiers didn't molest anyone, and did not search the Jolas chateau school.

This was just as well. Mrs. Jolas had offered hospitality to numbers of friends from Paris, friends of friends, and about fifty unknown refugees who had no more idea for where they were bound than the rest of the human tidal wave fleeing before the Germans, across Luxembourg, the Ardennes, Belgium, and France. All they did was to buy all the toothbrushes, shaving equipment, and underwear they could find.

The Joyces had been in St. Gérand for some time, visiting Mrs. Jolas, and were installed in a flat in the village when we arrived.[3] We moved into Mrs. Jolas's "annexe for boys," which was really a small hotel, called as in every French town the Hotel du Commerce. The boys were moved to a nearby farm, and the Joyces joined us in the hotel on July 1st. The place was not uncomfortable; we had to sleep on army cots, but we had an enormous kitchen to ourselves.

In the evenings we would all go down to the main dining room and spend an hour listening to the news—what there was—on a ramshackle old radio. Joyce, previously not much interested in world affairs, was as eager as we were to hear something, but there was little that was good. I remember arriving late on one occasion and asking him in a whisper if there was "anything."

"Yes," he said, "things seem a little better." But I soon found he was alluding to a couple of German ships that had struck mines. In our helplessness we tried to make the most of any news we got.

Joyce was especially interested in Eire's attitude toward Britain, and listened attentively when De Valera spoke on the radio. I have been told that the Eire Legation offered Joyce a passport after the war started, but that he refused. Having benefitted all his life by a British passport, he felt that it would be undignified to give it up at such a time.[4] In spite of the difficulties he had had with the British government over his publications,[5] he had to act according to his ideas of loyalty and fair play. Loyalty and dignity were, I think, two of his chief characteristics, and they were matched by his gentle manner—a manner which made even the hail-fellow types who knew him treat him with a certain deference.

The line of demarcation was finally drawn at Moulins, thirty kilometers from St. Gérand, and we found ourselves automatically in Unoccupied France. Our lives settled down into a monotonous period of waiting without much hope. The calamity of France seemed complete, and none of us could see ahead clearly enough to make any plans. We were all too stunned. We were marking time.[6]

Mrs. Jolas had to move back into the Hotel du Commerce, and we found a room on a farm not far from the village. The Joyces stayed on at the hotel through July and August, but every morning around eleven Joyce would walk over to our farm to get Paul. I can still see him arriving on those summer mornings, rapping on the fence with his cane to let us know he was there. "Le voilà," Paul would say, hurrying out to meet him. Sometimes he would sit in the garden, and I remember him watching me hang out the meager washing, or sitting with me while I minded an American child whose parents were packing to go home. I had the impression that the presence of the child seemed to him a reassuring and normal thing in our upset lives.

But more often he and Paul would stroll together, arm in arm, down the Lyons highway. They found a tree which had been felled in a convenient position, and they spent a good deal of time sitting there—sometimes talking, but often in silence. We all felt that our particular dramas were being submerged in the general tragedy. Paul spoke of "writing Petain a letter,"[7] a scornful letter, "after it's all over."

I was constantly going into Vichy, which was not far away, trying to get a permit to go back to Paris. We had left all we had there, and our funds had dwindled to nothing, so to return seemed to be the only thing to do. The couture had reopened, and my *Herald Tribune* job was apparently still available. If the job gave out—as it did, of course, in two months—we knew we could raise money by selling our books.

Joyce also was hard up for pocket money, although his account at Lloyds Bank still showed a balance of I believe about six thousand francs. One day he gave me a small check to cash for him at the bank in Vichy. It was only for something like six hundred francs, but then money was still worth something in France. I took his identity card with me, and explained at some length to the director of the bank how hard it was for an invalid like Joyce to get around under the existing conditions. But the director refused to believe that the check had really been signed by James Joyce the writer. I tried to have him telephone the village for confirmation, but he refused, and finally I called his attention to the green ink on the check, explaining that this was "typical" of Joyce.[8] That seemed to make the director even more suspicious, and so I abandoned the project—convinced the man was a collaborator.

I saw Joyce for the last time on August 16, 1940, when, having obtained a permit for myself, I left for Paris. He came down to the bus-stop to see me off, and as we kissed goodbye I said to him:

"Mr. Joyce, do you think this is *ever* going to end?"

I can still hear his reply. It was like a sigh.

"Och, Mrs. Léon, I don't know."

Paul took me to the train in Vichy, begging me to attend to his permit immediately. He was longing to be home among his books. The Joyces were planning to go to Switzerland, he had no warm clothes—it all seemed reasonable at the time. It was only later that we realized what a mistake we had made returning to Paris. My husband came back on September 4, leaving the Joyces alone in the village, for Maria Jolas had returned to the States with her two daughters.[9] Paul never saw Joyce again.

The first thing he did on his return to Paris was to resign as secretary of the Archives of Philosophy.[10] Already everything was under German control. The letter of resignation Paul wrote was restrained, dignified, and, I thought, remarkable, but professor Lefur merely acknowledged it as though it were a bill.[11]

The next things to be attended to were Joyce's affairs. Paul put all the important papers and documents in a large brown suitcase. Then he took all of his and Joyce's private correspondence over the years of their friendship and put it in a large brown envelope on which he wrote:

> Private correspondence between James Joyce and Paul Léon. In the event of my death I bequeath these letters to the Dublin library.[12] They are not to be opened before fifty years from now (1990). Only the immediate family of James Joyce and his literary executors may have access to these letters, when necessary.

He took the envelope personally to Count O'Kelly,[13] then head of the Irish Legation in Paris, and asked him to place them in the Dublin Library.

I am aware of the many rumors that have been circulated regarding this correspondence between my husband and Joyce. Paul wished the letters to be kept private because he felt that Joyce wanted it that way, since most of them are discussions of financial matters and such family concerns as the illness of Lucia Joyce.[14] The idea back [then] of sending them to the Dublin Library was, of course, to get them away from the Germans, but I found out much later, through an article by Miss Kathleen Fitzpatrick, correspondent for the *Irish Times*, that the actual transfer to Dublin did not occur until 1946. The letters are now in the library there, however.

Joyce died in Zurich on January 13, 1941, from peritonitis caused by a perforated ulcer. We got the news in a painfully indirect way. Downstairs in our apartment house there is a little shop where two young women do mending. For many years Joyce had been a familiar figure to them, as he was to everyone in our quarter. They saw Alexis go by on his way home from school, and called him in to tell him they had been listening to Radio-Lausanne[15]—as did most of the self-respecting French at that time—and that the death of Joyce had been announced from Zurich.

That evening Paul went as usual to buy his two packs of cigarettes at the bistro on the corner of the Rue de Bourgogne where he and Joyce had gone daily for so many years. Madame Lapeyre, the gérante [manager], burst into tears when she saw my husband; she had heard the news. "What a calamity, Monsieur—all because of this terrible war." Firmin, the garçon, who has served them for years, stopped waiting on his clients and gathered around with the others to find out how it happened.

Paul was so shattered that for days he could not bring himself to speak of Joyce. Jean Paulhan, then publisher of the *Nouvelle Revue Francaise*, approached him for an article, which would appear in the Free Zone, but he refused to write anything. We all tried in vain for two weeks to persuade him to write *something*, and then suddenly he told me he had decided to write just a letter to Paulhan, in which he would "speak of Joyce." But he would just sign it with three asterisks, for he felt that the Germans might hear about it and pry into our lives. He wrote the letter and took it to Paulhan. The next day we heard that Paulhan had been arrested by the Germans along with other French intellectuals.[16]

Meanwhile the sad work of winding up Joyce's affairs had to be undertaken. The owner of the Joyce flat in the Rue des Vignes in Passy was demanding the rent,[17] which of course had been overdue for several months. Paul pleaded with him to wait until the end of the war, but the only reply was a threat to seize everything in the apartment, which was just about everything the Joyces had left in Paris.

The climax was the announcement that an auction was to take place. My brother Alec arrived in Paris about this time on a clandestine trip from the Free Zone, and since he was the only one of us who could help financially, Paul told him about the danger hanging over the Joyce possessions.[18] Alec returned to Free France and that week sent us a message asking us to buy back the best things and explaining he could place at our disposal twenty or twenty-five thousand francs, which at that time meant about six or seven hundred dollars.[19]

Early on the morning of March 7, 1941, Paul and I, with heavy hearts, went over to the Salle Drouot, where the auction was to place. We looked over the "lots" which were arranged pell-mell in large baskets, and then at the other people in the room. Their faces seemed to me to be as sharp as battle-axes, but it soon became apparent that they were more interested in the household articles than in such things as first editions, and Paul had the advantage of knowing the value of every book important enough to bid for the with funds Alec had supplied.

He was able to buy back all that he considered worthwhile with the exception of one book. This was a copy of *Pomes Penyeach* with original lettrines by Lucia Joyce.[20] A Rue de Seine bookseller went up to five thousand francs and made it clear that he was ready to go higher. Paul was very distressed. He knew who that man was, and told me his name. But I have forgotten it, and I do not think that after all these years I would recognize the man—all I can remember is that he was blond and fat.

It was most painful to me to see the Joyce family belongings go under the hammer, and I bought back a whole trunkful of linen and odds and ends which I thought Mrs. Joyce might want to keep. Paul for once was more business-like than I was, and warned me against being sentimental and wasting our money on trifles. But among other things I got Joyce's tooled leather writing pad and his paper knife, and I sent Mrs. Joyce what I could via Alec and the Free Zone.

Paul also rescued many things from the Joyce apartment, at great risk to himself.[21] At that time during German occupation, one was at the mercy of a chance informer or of the least indiscretion. The danger lay first in the concierge, but he gave her two hundred francs and told her he was getting some of his own things he had left there and he would be back again, since if the proprietor had found out he was after Joyce's things there would have been the devil to pay.[22] The second danger was that of being caught by a German patrol, who were always suspicious of anyone in the street with a pushcart.

Paul and a handy-man we sometimes employed made two trips with a pushcart, and it was only later I realized how distasteful entering somebody else's home and rummaging through private possessions had been to my husband. He told me he hoped he had saved everything of importance, and I suggested that he go once more and make sure. Paul looked at me steadily and said very gently, "Do you realize what you are saying?"

Many of the Joyce belongings were put in the care of a lawyer, and some of the more personal things we left with a friend. We made a complete, detailed list of everything,[23] and by various channels Mrs. Joyce eventually got everything back after the war was over.

In 1942 there was still the suitcase with important Joyce papers in our apartment. I knew I would have to get rid of that and quickly too. Prior to my husband's arrest we had had the Gestapo three times. If they ever came again, they might find the papers, contracts, etc., and seize them. For some queer reason though, we had two thorough searches and they had not found them. We had hardly given those papers a thought.

By that time they were beginning to pick up wives and dependents of arrested men. I might have to go underground any minute, or more likely be arrested and disappear.

At that time the Swiss Legation right nearby were protecting British interests. Mr. Joyce carried a British passport. I called there and begged them to place the suitcase in storage until the family or I would claim it at the end of the war. I even suggested their placing it in the cellars if they had no room elsewhere. They assured me politely enough that all was filled, that they had no room anywhere, and that they absolutely could not take it. So in despair I finally took it over to Maître Gervais, the lawyers, where, due to his kindness, everything else was stored. As far as possible I felt it might have been better to store these papers and contracts separately from the rest, in case the Germans ever discovered the bulk of books. (But happily after all these years everything was recovered intact. Mrs. Joyce and her son, Mrs. Jolas and myself have been over and through all the things. The papers too were all intact, but I must have brought the suitcase home again at the time. Today the books are all listed, sorted, covered in blue paper wrappings, and catalogued. This work took two librarians over five weeks, which may give the reader some idea of the quantity and detail involved in the rescued property.[24]

My husband was arrested by the Gestapo on August 21, 1941, and the last incident in the story of his rescue of Joyce's books took place six months later.

One morning in February, 1942, I was dusting the books in our living room—even in times of stress such everyday gestures persist. At that moment Paul was being starved and frozen in a camp near Compiegne.[25] In my desperate efforts to save him I had entered the Relief Section of the French Red Cross and was doing clandestine work at the same time.[26]

There was a ring at the door and two men came in, both civilians. One was French, tall and swarthy. He wore a Basque beret, and produced the tricolor-barred card of the Vichy militia. The other, shorter and wearing brown civilian clothes, turned up his lapel to show me his Gestapo insignia and said "Polizei."

"Well," I thought, "this is it." But no, they wanted to see my husband. I exploded:

"Don't you know that you arrested him six months ago? Don't you know they are starving him to death in Compiegne?"

"No, we did not know. In that case we must see his wife."

"I am his wife. Please come in." They came on into the living room.

"How can you *not know* my husband was arrested?" I repeated, beginning to feel that this couple were not going to be so bad as the ones I had dealt with previously.

"Because we come from a different section," replied the German, and he started to question me.

"What did your husband do?" I can still hear his persuasive tone—"Was tat Ihr Mann denn eigentlich?"[27]

"My husband was a scholar, a philosopher, an homme de lettres. He was *never* interested in politics of any kind."

"For whom did he work?"

"For no one. He worked for himself. At home. On Rousseau, on Benjamin Constant. On his philosophy. And for the Archives of Philosophy before the war."

"But he worked for some one else too." "Jemanden andern auch" still rings in my memory.

The Frenchman was prowling around the room, examining family photographs on the walls Suddenly he cried:

"This uniform. What is it? A Russian officer? The medals?"

"That," I answered, "is a Russian uniform from before the Revolution. My mother's youngest brother. He was a hero in the first world war. Those medals are St. George's Crosses. He was shot by the Bolsheviks in 1918. . . ."[28]

"The other one over there?"

"My eldest uncle. A diplomat in Washington."[29]

He pounced: "And *that*? Is that your husband?"

"That" was Joyce's photograph, which always hung and still hangs on our living room wall.

"No, no, that is the Irish poet and writer James Joyce."

"Where is he?" both cried.

"He has been *dead* for over a year. Have you never heard of him?"

"Where did he die?"

"In Zurich."

"That is what I mean," the German cried triumphantly. "That is the man your husband worked for."

My nerves were giving way. "It's a lie," I shouted. "He never worked for him, he worked *with* him. He was his *friend*—can't you understand the difference?"

There was a moment's silence, and then the Gestapo man said quietly: "That is why we have come (Darum sind wir hier gekommen.) For first editions. We know you must have some. Nicht war?"

I was ready to laugh, I was so relieved. "But of course we must have some. But why? Are you interested in Joyce, in *Ulysses*?"

"Aber nein. Weil das Wert hat. Because they are of value." He spoke patiently, as if he were explaining something to a child. Suddenly it all became ludicrously simple. They were starving and murdering men, but they *wanted first editions.*

I got down on my knees and began going through the bottom shelf of books. Then my heart almost stopped. We had no books left by Joyce; Paul had distributed them around to friends for the duration. The Germans must not find them. I grabbed Frank Budgen's "Making of Ulysses."

"Here you are. Voilà." I produced a couple more books on Joyce. "A wonderful critique it explains everything. . .."

"By Joyce. Not on Joyce. Verstanden?"

"Oh," I said, "my husband must have sold the other books by Joyce. You see we had to live when we returned. I did not understand."

"Where can we find them?"

"At the Salle Drouot. There has been an auction." And I told them that the Joyce's landlord sold everything—alles, alles—for the rent. They took down everything, including the address of the Salle Drouot, and departed satisfied on what I hoped was a wild goose chase.

The Gestapo man also took down the details of Paul's case and said he would look into it and help to get him freed. I promised to find some Joyce first editions for him if he were successful, but I never heard from him again and never saw him again, though I tried to find him.

III

It was, I suppose, inherent in the day-by-day relationship between Joyce and my husband that the latter should seldom have made any generalizations about the value of his friend's writing. What he had to say came out in private discussions of details with Joyce himself, and perhaps in the private correspondence which is now in the Dublin library.[1] His attitude, however, is indicated in the following letter to his niece, Mrs. Olga Howe, written May 23, 1930:[2]

My dear Olga,

Many thanks for your quickly sent note—so short and so sweet enclosing the Bystander's opinion of Joyce. It might be he is right on the whole except for one or two things. I read an article on "Joyce working" in some American paper to which he seems to refer in which all the details of how, where and when he works were given: white cloths, red pencil, huge sheets of paper—I am glad to say I have never seen him working if that description is correct. Besides I have here the typescript of his new book which I am afraid is worth millions because all the alterations are done in my handwriting—had they been done in his I am afraid nobody would have understood anything.[3] This brings me to "his" almost accusation of his not being blind yet. I am afraid and sorry indeed that this accusation is untrue but from what I hear from Zurich the latest news is that he might be losing one of his eyes completely. (This information is for your personal use only as the operation he has just undergone was not as successful as expected.[4]) Anyhow he did not see anything with that eye, the loss would thus mean not much materially except the nervous shock which I expect will prevent him from writing anything further. As to his "good" eye it has a secondary cataract[5]—so judge for yourself. The last thing he wrote before going to Zurich was the inscription in your book.

Now as to his work it might be sheer nonsense, and I am careful telling him my opinion every evening after work. Though I seem to share the opinion of the reviewer in as far as I do not understand anything at all about it I still think some theory can be worked out. At present my latest based on "ipsissima verba" is approximately as follows: When St. Patrick went to baptise Ireland he found some difficulty to explain the sense of the Holy Trinity when suddenly his eyes fell on the ground where he saw a most commonplace flower, trodden by the people, dirtied by the animals which had a three-leaf forming a single one. He took it and showed it to the people who shouted: Credimus, Credimus!

Now does not every word we use represent a Trinity: it has a sense, a sound, a power to evoke pictures. One does not feel it as rule unless "something goes wrong" i.e. either the sense is stupid, or the picture obsolete, or the sound false. Would it not be possible to write a book where all these three elements of literature are segregated and dissociated? A device can be used, a most commonplace banal device to prove it: a pun. Hence in the description of the river Liffey there are in the text the names of 600 rivers and in the description of Dublin, some 500 names of places, cities, lord mayors etc. etc. Naturally all this was known before, but the adjustment done by great authors was done unconsciously, I wonder is there anything wrong in attempting to make this process of reconstruction of the LOGOS conscious?

Now the last part is the Obscenity. A thing I have been unable to swallow myself until I discovered that it was a peculiarly Anglo-Saxon pruderie that made him apply this device.

To all my objections he answered—"it is not my fault that God has made the same organs to serve two purposes." Hence the basis of Anglo-Saxon pruderie is apparent: people do not do certain things in public because they could be mistaken for something else. Such argument naturally is beyond me, as I would any day any time rather do what I call "deliver a cake" in public than conjugate the verb which sounds very much like "fortification" but has nothing whatever to do with it. Why, I do not know exactly, but the theory that I could disclose would be too long to dwell upon right now.

This is altogether enough—I am afraid too much, even for what it is worth—so I am taking the stand when I read:

"But I waged love on her and spoiled her undines"[6]

that it is good to remind people that while their heads touch heaven their feet are often in the mud. It happens so often.

If you know Dickson of the *Contemporary* will you kindly tell him that he is an uneducated ass. On your father's request I wired him and wrote a letter besides the information I gave him I put two questions to him. Never a reply. One of the questions was—has he been responsible for the *Fortnightly* ever since Courtney died?[7]

Again many thanks for the prompt reply. I hope Lucy will get her visa today as she was so very keen on crossing the channel tomorrow. However there is no reply yet at the consulate.

Very affectionately and unclishly yours

PAUL[8]

The above letter was written, it will be noticed, less than two years after my husband met Joyce; in the course of the next ten years Paul became less diffident in his championing of Joyce's work. But he was always, as I have already indicated, more interested in the person than in the artist, and I think the following excerpts from his letters to me may help suggest the quality of their friendship—the way in which Paul gradually became Joyce's alter-ego and guardian in the practical details of every day life:[9]

January 1, 1929. . . . In spite of my trying to lead an almost hermit-like existence I find it difficult as people seem to insist on seeing each other, eventually on seeing me. . . . Both on Dec. 26 and yesterday Dec. 31 I visited the Joyces. I like them both more than I can say. We made friends with Papa Joyce—he is enthusiastic about some tenor and I think he wants to take me to the Opera on the 13th to see the "Huguenots."[10] I think to know them better will be a distinct pleasure.

January 12, 1930. . . . Will you please explain to Olga that Ulysses was 25 and not 90—and therefore she can send me two copies of Anna Livia Plurabelle—Faber and Faber.[11]

February 25, 1931. . . . Tomorrow Soupault and Joyce are to work here.[12]

February 18, 1931 cable to New York: SULLIVANS REPERTOIRE GONE LONG AGO. JOYCE EVENING THURSDAY.

March 10, 1931. . . . Joyce lunched here with Katia (Paul's sister) and Jim's friends (my brother Jim). . . . He wanted to lunch alone with me. We talked him into staying. . . . Everyone talked so much. He tried to chime in and was interrupted. No one gave him a chance. On leaving he said: "Next time I will not say a word." On Sunday he and I went to hear Massenets "Werther" at Trianon Lyrique.[13]

March 17, 1931. . . . and am going to Miss Beach, dinner in honor of St. Patrick this evening. Patrick as you can imagine being represented by Joyce.[14]

November 26, 1933. . . . Had dinner last night with the old Joyces but was home by twelve and did not drink much.[15]

November 30, 1933. . . . Two calls from Geneva and two from London. The old man wanted to return alone but changed his mind later. Miss Weaver is leaving for a vacation. What will be God only knows.[16]

September 3, 1935. . . . Joyce fell ill on Saturday and yesterday they left for Fontainebleau.[17] They insist I should join them but I have not decided yet.

September 6, 1934. . . . From Joyce a tragic letter. Am forwarding it to you. If you can do so, write him a few lines—Hotel de la Paix, Geneva.[18]

September 6, 1935. . . . Went to Fontainebleau with the Hagberg-Wrights. I think Lady Wright was disappointed because Joyce was not nude and did not wear roses in his hair. (Sir Charles Wright was the secretary of the London Library and close friend of ours.)[19]

August 18, 1936. . . . The Joyces left this morning for Liege en route for Copenhagen.[20] Will they get there?

March 30, 1937. . . . Spent evening at Fouquet's.

August 25, 1937. . . . Just had a telegram that Joyce is sick. Will cable him funds and expect a reply.[21]

August 14, 1938. . . . Joyce wants me to go to Lausanne, leaving the 18th. I would stay ten-twelve days. Will only go if I can bathe and lie in the sun.[22]

August 16, 1938. . . . Will be back from Lausanne on the 29th. Like last year hope to get a good tan in ten days.[23]

August 18, 1938. . . . You see I am still here (in Paris). But as soon as Joyce's money arrives we will leave. I am not too keen on Lausanne and am trying to persuade them to pick another spot, so far unsuccessfully. 6 p.m. The bank has just phoned. Money arrived. Will cable hotel address from Lausanne. We are leaving Sunday.

August 19, 1938. . . . Have succeeded in dissuading them from going to Lausanne and now they are hesitating between Le Touquet and Dieppe. We will probably leave for Dieppe tomorrow morning.

August 20, 1938. . . . All is changed again. Tomorrow morning we leave for Lausanne.[24] Have my ticket and visa. Had to buy a new hat and new shoes.

My husband disliked leaving his own home, and the above letters show how much of an event even a short trip was for him. Joyce's insistence on going to Lausanne is explained by the fact that his daughter Lucia was being treated near there at the time.

During Paul's in internment in Drancy and Compiègne camps we kept up a clandestine correspondence, and the following letters from Drancy reveal how often Joyce was in my husband's thoughts.[25]

November 28, 1941.[26] . . . I am obsessed by the idea they may be keeping us here for the winter. How I would love to be home, near you, able to go on with my work. . . . This may be just another illusion, but there are five things I want to do. First of all revise Ulysses with Beckett, then write my memoirs on Joyce, next finish Constant, continue Rousseau, and finish my book on Rousseau.[27] That, besides all the rest, I can hope to do.

November 29, 1941.[28] . . . Curious this constant urge to write you, the sudden strength to formulate a thought or two and immediately lose the thread . . . To fall back into the night, to think of the night, and the feeling of hunger and the fascination of the thought of a food package. Maybe one tomorrow? How I would love to be home, Thursday at the latest. But my head falls not from slumber but from torpor . . . "My ho head halls. . ."[29] That is from Anna Livia—and it echoes like a hollow bell. . . Au revoir for the moment.

December 6, 1941.[30] . . . Just in case I forget. The thirteenth is Saint Lucie. Would you ask Beckett to send something to Lucia Joyce and give him 200-250 francs—in memory of her father.

This is the last reference to Joyce. In the spring Paul was moved to Silesia and murdered by the Germans, presumably on April 4, 1942.

The facts I have described in these pages came from my memories. They are all the more precious to me because they spell that "sweetness of life" which was Paris in the odd twenty years the French know as l'entre deux guerres.

Looking back, these years between two wars, in spite of daily dramas and worries, had a peculiar charm of their own. A charm which both Paul Léon and James Joyce admitted could only be found in Paris as long as one could not live in one's own country. Strangely enough death came to both of them away from France. Exile was forced on both of them by war.

People often wonder whether Joyce would have written anything else. Some claim he was vidé (burnt out). Others feel he was contemplating an epic on the ocean, a continuation of Anna Livia.

To Paul he said: "Wait until Finnegan awakes. . ."

Appendix A

Eliot and Joyce

In 1936 I was entrusted with the manuscript of *Work in Progress* and instructed to give it to T. S. Eliot in London. I worried all the way over, fearing there would be an accident, that the ship would sink. If I had been carrying top secret documents for the state I could not have been more anxious. But everything went well, and Eliot wrote in my album: "to Madame Paul Léon, in memory of a brief visit to London as Ambassador extra-ordinary and Minister plenipotentiary with *Work in Progress.* 14/July 1936."[1]

Appendix B

The Old Man and 100 FRCS

When Joyce found himself stranded in the little village to which Mrs. Jolas had moved her school during the war,[2] France had fallen and we were all converged there together. By the time the anniversary of his father's birthday came around we had just returned to Paris.[3] Joyce found himself at a loss, because there was the annual gesture of the hundred francs—a gesture he had never missed. He asked everyone he could find whether they might not be going to Paris, because he wanted to entrust one hundred francs to them to give to a poor old man with a beard in memory of his father.[4]

Appendix C

Souvenir De Joyce

When Jean Paulhan was arrested we thought that was the end of Paul's "letter" to him about Joyce.[5] It was only much later that I learned it did actually appear in print. At the end of 1942 I escaped from the Occupied Zone and made my way to Monaco, which was presumably neutral territory, although it did not remain so for long.[6] One night in 1943 two friends of mine, a French publisher and his wife, called me and asked me to come over for tea the next day. One could not say much over the telephone. When I arrived at their apartment they presented me with a copy of the June issue of *Poesie '42,* edited by Pierre Seghers.[7] There was Paul's letter entitled "Souvenir de Joyce" and signed with an "L" instead of the asterisks he had used. I have translated it, and with Seghers' permission it has appeared in *A James Joyce Yearbook* which Mrs. Jolas has published in her husband's Transition Press.

Appendix D

Sale of Joyce's Property

Actually the owner of the Joyce apartment had no legal right to touch the Joyce flat and belongings because Joyce and his family were holders of British passports. But during Occupation such things did occur, just as it happened in the case of the Jolas's losing all of their personal belongings and furniture in Neuilly. Their passports were American.

Appendix E

Fargue, Jamaty and Lefur Letters

Our impression of the latter's meanness and cowardice which by that time people were openly discussing was confirmed later. When my husband had been arrested by the Germans I went to see Lefur to ask him for a letter proving my husband's moral integrity and that he was absolutely non-political. Lefur was very cold, very wary, and he told me I could use the letter acknowledging my husband's resignation (the "receipt") if I wished. Obviously he was afraid of compromising himself defending a Jew. I walked from the room without shaking hands with him, promising myself I would have it out with him after the war. But he died, I believe within a year.[8] On the advice of friends I had compiled a file consisting of letters from friends whose names I hoped would have some influence with the Germans. Two were outstanding: the first from our friend the writer Léon Paul-Fargue; the second from George Jamaty, chief of the Secretariat of the Ministry of National Education.

Fargue's letter: In the widest circles, literary, scientific as well as social, where many years ago I met Paul Léon, I can state he was loved by all for his straightforward character as much as for his vast culture and awareness. Until I believe 1940 he was the managing secretary of the Archives of Philosophy of Law to which he contributed work of importance.

Paul Léon 's friendship is very precious to me and I will always be his friend, convinced as I am that he is a victim of error. *To be noted* and known by all he is a convinced anti-Communist.

(Signed) Léon-Paul Fargue
of the Académie Mallarmé
Commander of the Legion of Honor

Jamaty's letter: Neighbor of M. Paul Léon who resides as I do at 27 rue Casimir-Perier, Paris 7e, I have known and appreciated him for the past few years. A man of great dignity he is at the same time a man of letters and writer of merit. Author of works and studies of *Benjamin Constant*, *Jean Jacques Rousseau*, *Letters of Nicholas II to his Mother* he is also a regular contributor to the legal reviews.

The interest he takes in questions of philosophy and particularly in philosophy of law has brought him into contact with myself on several occasions. This has permitted me to further increase my esteem for him.

(signed) Georges Jamaty
Chief of the Secretarial Bureau
of National Education

Appendix F

Joyce and Paul Léon

On my recent visit to the States Maria Jolas sent me the July copy of *Critique*, No. 26, edited by Georges Bataille.[9] This magazine reached me a few days before the reading of the Joyce paper at the James Joyce Society on November 18, 1948.

Critique, which is dedicated to modern French and English publications, contained an essay by Eugene Jolas on Joseph Campbell's and Henry Morton Robinson's *A Skeleton Key to Finnegans Wake.*[10] In his essay Jolas describes some of the incidents I have already mentioned, as the proof-reading of Anna Livia, the race to get it out by Joyce's birthday. He also tells of our exodus from Paris in 1940 and says that "the arrival in the same village as his friend and collaborator Paul Léon has inspired Joyce to take up his *Finnegans Wake* and that it was during the stirring months of the fall of France that they re-read and corrected errata that had slipped into the first edition. A word here or there. And they went over punctuation too . . .[11] Paul Léon who left for Paris in September 1940 was to die 'in deportation' in 1942. After numerous painful demarches Joyce and his family managed to reach Switzerland, in December 1940. It was in the town of Zurich where he had already spent the war of 1914–18 that Joyce died, on Jan. 13th 1941, as the result of a grave operation."

Eugene Jolas ends his extensive sixteen page Analysis of the *Skeleton Key* with the following:

"*Finnegans Wake* is simultaneously the Requiem of a civilisation and the announcement of a new era. James Joyce with a poet's gift of prophecy heralds the atomic age in the repeated Thunder Theme with stems from Vico. The fearful crash of the bomb at Hiroshima was heard in advance by Joyce, who however did not despair of mankind."

Appendix G

Christ and Drancy

My husband was not easily shocked but religious irreverence annoyed him profoundly. Joyce knew this and that is what had upset him. My husband had the greatest respect for other people's creeds and the greatest reverence for Christianity. Though born a Jew he was deeply religious in a Christian sense. Fully acquainted with the dogmas of the Catholic Church he was particularly cognizant of the rites of the Orthodox cult as well as the Protestant religion.

He was deeply conscious of the teachings of Christ and I can truly say practiced them in life. The Gospels were literally his livre de chevet, he read them nightly before going to sleep and his knowledge and understanding of them were profound and sincere.

If he had not adopted the outward signs of Christianity, I am certain he was prompted by a feeling of "dignity" preventing him from doing so. This is frequent in many Jews believing in Christianity. He felt that during his lifetime it would have been misinterpreted. Besides there was the conviction that a man is free to worship as he chooses. Also in the old days in St. Petersburg, socially there was no antisemitism. It existed politically, but certainly never affected the lives and moral tranquility of my husband's circle.

During the terrible first months of Paul's internment in the camp of Drancy, starved, frozen, and maltreated as he was, he wrote me begging me to send him his Gospels which he had left by his bedside the morning of his arrest.[12] I tried every way I knew to get them through to the camp. German regulations, the guards, and French militia permitted no books, not even the Bible. Several times I met with failure. I was afraid to smuggle them into the camp lest the two books he had asked for should be seized or lost.

One book was the New Testament in Greek. With this in his pocket he left Russia in 1918. The other was Guillaume Bude's *Evangiles*.[13]

I was desperate and in my despair went to see my friend, the Russia priest Father Cyprien K. I told him how miserably I had failed. I told him all it meant to Paul. But I did not have to say very much. For when he had heard my story he said: "I will try and manage this for you."

"You!" I exclaimed. I could hardly believe my ears. For those were the days when darkness had descended. Persecution of the Jews had reached an all time peak. One expected nothing from anyone. But suddenly it seemed to me that a bright light had illuminated the night.

We made plans. Next morning I was to fetch him at his Church at ten o'clock. We would take the bus to Drancy, the famous "51" which was jammed to capacity every time. There we would try and persuade the guards to let Books through.

Next day after a bumpy forty-five minute ride to this sordid distant suburb we alighted at the crossroads leading to the camp. French guards were guarding the crossroads. German patrols were parading up and down the avenue leading to the camp and the road running along its side. I was laden with a large red quilt destined to a friend of Paul's, Maitre Albert Ullmo, a lawyer.[14] He had also been taken as hostage being one of the fifty lawyers seized on Aug. 21. My husband was included in their numbers, though he was not French and never practiced at the bar. I had taken Mme. Ullmo under my wing, for he was a widower and his mother-in-law, the only kin he had, was eighty-three. The poor old lady had not been able to get his quilt to the camp in time. They had been authorized the week before, for the men were dying of cold. I hoped they would let it pass.

We must have made a strange couple, Father Cyprien and myself. I was wearing my Red Cross veil and uniform, and Father Cyprien his priest's vestments. The first guards stopped us and would not let me pass. I had not brought a special card entitling the delivery of a package to the camp. They said the one I showed was no longer valid. I looked hopelessly at Father Cyprien. Outwardly he appeared confident. If he felt any emotion his face did not betray it. He had told them he was a priest. Unwillingly they agreed he could pass. "I will wait for you in the café" I said.

He walked with me to the corner bistro which was a sort of clandestine meeting place of friends and relatives of the interned men. But it was mainly filled with a noisy crowd of workers and workers' wives drinking apéritifs and beer, I knew that café well indeed. Almost daily for weeks I had been trying to persuade the patron to contact a policeman so that I could get letters or packages into the camp. Such things were constantly being done, but I had had no luck. Maybe they feared they were too close to the camp. One wall of one of the camp buildings overlooked the street and from the café windows you could see the prisoners. They had their faces glued to the windows and when they saw you looking they would make desperate signs begging for food, pointing to their mouths. Several women sat in the café armed with field glasses and binoculars trying to find their men. At that time about five thousand were interned there and the figures fluctuated between four and eight. Finally the French militia "got wise" and the rumor flew around that any man or woman caught wandering around the camp would be arrested. I immediately went into my oldest civilian clothes and, hoping to be taken for one of the Drancy population, even wore an old kitchen apron and carried a marketing bag on the street. To solve the problem the Germans blued their windows over, soi-disant as an air-raid precaution. Father Cyprien left me sitting in the café.

"You will pray," he said. "Pray to the Blessed Virgin. She will understand."

Why should I pretend I did not pray. I prayed as earnestly as I have ever prayed in my life. At the time it seemed all that mattered once we were so helpless before brute force.

I implored the Virgin Mary: "Have mercy. Blessed Mother of God. I implore thee for the sake of Thy Son Who died on the Cross, have pity on these poor men. They are innocent of any crime. To them, receiving the Gospels means everything. It will bring them peace and solace. The teaching of Thy Son Jesus Christ will give them courage and strength to face their torturers and tormentors. Holy Virgin I implore Thee, in the name of Thy beloved Son, have mercy. . ."

And I prayed to God: "Oh my Lord God. I beg and implore Thee have mercy on us and permit this thing to come to pass. Let Father Cyprien succeed in his sacred mission."

To Jesus Christ I could only pray: "You knowest what suffering is, have pity. . ."

At last through the glass door of the café, in the distance, I saw the familiar figure of Father Cyprien approaching. His gait was energetic, his flowing locks and his robes blowing the November gale. He appeared triumphant. Finally he entered. My face was streaming with tears. I did not care. I could hardly speak.

"Well?" was all I could say.

He was beaming. His great eyes were luminous with faith and confidence. "I have succeeded" he said in low tones. We knew we must not attract attention. It was difficult not to do so. But the people were still milling around the bar and the noise drowned everything.

"How did you do it?" I could only whisper.

Father Cyprien smiled. Then he said, "I prayed all the time. At first I believe they thought I was a Rabbi. The guards at the gate. Luckily today they were all French. So I unbuttoned the collar of my coat—like this—and showed them the Cross. They changed their tune immediately."

"But what did you tell them," I asked anxiously.

"I first spoke to a soldier and it was no good. So I told him to go and get his captain. That is when I had to show him the Cross. I told him it was very urgent. When his Captain arrived on the scene—this was in the guardhouse inside the gates—I said to him:

"Mon Capitaine, you are a French man and probably a Catholic?" He told me he was. I next said to him: "I have come to you to ask you to grant the wish of one of your internees. You will not, I am sure, refuse the wish of a dying man. Neither you nor I know what awaits him. Maybe he is a dying man. He asked for the Gospels. You will not refuse that?"

"No books are authorized at all, not even the Bible," the man started to declaim. With a gesture of the hand which I know so well, Father Cyprien stopped him.

"You say you are a Catholic. My religion, the Russian Orthodox creed, is a Christian religion too, and very much the same as yours. As a Christian you cannot refuse what I ask. *Remember this may be the wish of a dying man.*"

Suddenly the Captain said: "Very well, Father. Your prisoner will have the books within two hours. You have my word."

Next day I had word through a clandestine channel. Paul received both books within two hours, as the Captain had promised.

Weak, sick and starving as he was, he read the Gospels aloud to the other men. There are no words I can find to describe all it meant to them. But a few who were liberated by a miraculous fluke at the beginning of December came to see me and told me. Others wrote. Christ had suffered in both the spirit and the flesh. They were suffering martyrdom too. And they knew not what awaited them further. The shining glory of His example was a consolation and comfort to them. Late in November Paul wrote: "Merci, Merci. This has restored our Faith. But how close I feel to the Sermon of the Mount."[15]

Appendix H

Journal De Genève. Mercredi, 6 Avril 1949

Paul L. Léon, Rousseauiste Fervent

Quand je me rendis a Paris en 1936, Bernard Bouvier me dit: "Vous irez voir Paul Léon et vous lui exprimerez notre reconnaissance pour sa collaboration aux *Annales*.

Cet éminent spécialiste de la pensée de Jean-Jacques était en effet depuis quelques années un fidèle correspondant de la publication de la Societé Rousseau a Genève, et il le demeura tant que cela lui fut possible.

Depuis pluisieurs années, Paul Léon n'est plus. Son long silence nous inquiétait, mais nous ne soupçonnions pas la terrible realité. Un ami commun, de passage en Suisse, ancien sous-conservateur du Musée de l'Ermitage a Saint-Petersbourg, qui a décrit sous le pseudonyme Trofimoff[16] ces ouvrages pleins de charme: *Ciels et Paysages de France* et tout récemment: *Au Jardin des Muses Françaises*, nous l'a revelée: l'inoffensif érudite, dont le seul crime etait de ne pas appartenir a la race aryenne est tombé, victime de la barbarie hitlérienne. Sa femme vient de nous le confirmer.

"Nous l'avons vu partir. Il a été deporté de Compiègne le 27 mars 1942 'vers une destination inconnue' et l'on presume qu'il a été assassiné le 4 avril, huit jours après son arrivée. . . . Ils étaient 1200 au depart. Sept en sont revenus. L'un d'eux a été a coté de mon mari quand les SS l'ont abattu. Je n'ai eu ces details que bien après la Libération—et qu'ils faisaient le trajet d'Auschwitz-Birkenau a pied. Et qu'ils avaient été deportés en Silesie. Moi-meme êtant a la Croix Rouge Francaise j'ai echappé par miracle. . . .."

Fils d'un grand exportateur en cereales de Saint Petersbourg, emigré avec un passeport Nansen,[17] Paul-Léon était devenue sécretaire de rédaction de la *Revue de la Philosophie du Droit*. Il est l'auteur d'Etudes pénétrantes sur le *Contrat Social* et sur *l'Idée de volonté générale chez J.-J. Rousseau*. Il était un des meilleurs connaisseurs de Jean-Jacques sous l'aspect qui a le plus contribué a faire de lui le Citoyen de Genève. La mort de Paul-Léon est une perte sensible pour les études scientifiques concernant le rayonnement de notre ville dans le domaine de l'esprit. Paul-Léon s'était également fait connaitre par la publication avec Rudler d'une correspondance inédite de Benjamin Constant et par une biographie de *Benjamin Constant* avec soixante planches hors texte dont beaucoup interessent notre pays.

Léon nous recevait dans son appartement de la Rive Gauche aux parois tapissés de livres de et sur Rousseau, plein de bienveillance pour tous ceux qui s'intéressaient aux questions littéraires ou de la pensée. Nous l'écoutions toujours avec profit. . . .

Mme. P. Léon conserve pieusement toute la partie inédite de l'oeuvre de son mari: vingt-trois chapitres sur Rousseau et tout ce qu'il a fait sur Benjamin Constant. Souhaitons que cet immense travail trouve bientot un interprete qui comme le Genevois Etienne Dumont l'avait fait pour Jeremias Bentham, nous donne le privilège de lire de nouveaux livres de Paul-Léon sur Rousseau.

Paul-Emile Schatzmann[18]

Appendix I

Fragment of a Letter

The fragment opposite was found in August 1949 in a folder belonging to Paul L. Léon.[19] The folder contained letters and business papers pertaining to Joyce, current affairs, etc. The original is in French, probably dated May 1941.

Written in Paul's own hand, in pen and ink, it would seem that it may have been a first effort to recapture the years of friendship, degenerating into jotted down dates and events after Joyce's death on request of Paulhan, then bringing out a magazine in Free France. Paulhan had asked Paul for something on Joyce. I believe he started in this style and later, feeling it was not attuned to his wider appreciation of Joyce, changed the style of writing and finally produced *Souvenir de Joyce*, which has appeared in Maria Jolas's *James Joyce Yearbook* (1949).[20]

However this confirms facts and dates found in this volume and is of interest for that reason, besides being a resumé by Paul himself.

"Soon after my marriage in 1921, through a relative of my wife Miss G.[21] I made the acquaintance of a young American couple who had come to settle in Paris, L. and H.F.[22] Ulysses had been published and people were discussing it a great deal. I did not read it, but my wife studied it consciencioushly. Several years later, family difficulties separated L. and H. and Joyce's son became friendly with H. It was this that caused me to be invited to meet J.J. at the beginning of 1928. (At that time my brother-in-law [Alec] was giving Joyce Russian lessons). Joyce was publishing *Tales told by* [*sic*] *Shem and Shaun*.[23] (rather banal conversation—разговоръ—ἀλώπηξ—Fuchs. A little later a phone call from H. how should one translate the word *whore* into Russian—refusal.) I forget the exact

FIGURE 2.1: Paul and Lucie Léon, Paris (1922) © The Léon Estate.

FIGURE 2.2: Lucie and Alexis Léon (1929) © The Léon Estate.

continuation of events, but a little later I am invited to spend New Year's Eve[24] at the Joyce's in Square Robiac,[25] where I had already met the son and daughter. The year 1929 seems to have been wiped from my memory. Maybe that year we started out morning strolls etc. etc. The end of '29 brought a call for help with *Haveth Childers Everywhere*. A large volume of *Encyclopedia Britannica*—reading of the study—research in common usage.[26] "Putzandow Cais" [?] Regular work and walks. Joyce's departure for consultations with his oculist, Pagenstecher in Wiesbaden. Parallel story of Sullivan. Work in the evenings before supper. Parution of *Haveth Childers*.[27] End 1930: histoire Beach-Monnier. Breaking of the contract with Beach.[28]

Champ-de-Mars—We are speeding in a taxi. A good bottle of white wine—Promenades au Bois—"olos cycmus."

NOTES

* The text of Lucie's memoir is reproduced here as first published.

PART I

1. Several revised typescript drafts of Lucie's talk survive in the NLI (MSS 36,932/18 and 36,932/22) as well as in the Léon family collection.
2. In 1920 Frances Steloff (1887–1989) founded the Gotham Book Mart in New York City. It was the home of the James Joyce Society, which was established in February 1947, with John Slocum as its first president and Steloff as its first treasurer. It only closed its doors in 2006. The Slocum Joyce collection (GEN MSS 112) is in the Beinecke Library of Yale University and formed the basis of his and Herbert Cahoon's *A Bibliography of James Joyce, 1882–1941* (New Haven: Yale University Press, 1953). Chapter 3 recounts the story of Lucie's talk at the Gotham Book Mart and its transformation into her memoir of Paul and Joyce's friendship. Chapter 6 is a transcript of a talk that Alexis Léon gave at the Gotham Book Mart to mark the fiftieth anniversary of his mother's talk.
3. Eugene Jolas (1894–1952) was a journalist, writer, translator and literary critic. After leaving the *Chicago Tribune in Paris*, he co-founded *transition* magazine in 1927 with Elliot Paul (1891–1958), an American journalist and author, together with his wife, Maria McDonald Jolas (1893–1987), who was a translator and an international peace activist. It would be difficult to exaggerate the importance of the Jolases' friendship and dedication to James Joyce, his family and his legacy.
4. Henriette (née Léon) Hirschmann (1885–1970) was Paul's eldest sister. Some of the papers pertaining to Wladimir and Henriette Hirschmann are in the NLI (MS 36,930). Stuart Gilbert (1883–1969) was a British critic, translator and friend of James and Nora Joyce. Besides co-translating *Ulysses* into French (Paris: La Maison des Amis des Livres, Adrienne Monnier, 1929), he also wrote *James Joyce: Ulysses* (London: Faber & Faber; New York: Alfred A. Knopf, 1930), one of the first and most influential early critical books on the novel. He married Moune (Marie Agnès Mathilde) Douin (1919–85), who was also a close friend of the Joyces.
5. Olga Howe was presumably the daughter of Paul's other sister Genia Polaikóv (née Léon).
6. Lucie recounts an amusing anecdote of Paul and Joyce's trip to Lausanne as told to her by Alexander Troubnikoff; see pp. 47–8.
7. Kaminsky and Father Serge are mentioned in Paul's letters from Drancy in September and October 1941 (see Chapter 5, Letters [12], [15] and [48]).

8. Alexander (Alec) Ponizowsky (1902–44) was one of Lucie's brothers. He had a degree in economics from Cambridge and moved in the crowd around Hazel and Peggy Guggenheim in Paris in the 1930s. He was very briefly engaged to Lucia Joyce in 1932. Alec provided Paul with the funds to bid on the remaining books and manuscripts from the Joyces' apartment at the Salle Drouot auction on 7 March 1941. Alexis and then Lucie joined Alec in Monaco after they escaped Paris. Lucie discusses this period in her biographical notes (see Chapter 1, p. 15).
9. The mutual friend was Helen Kastor Fleishmann (1884–1963), one of Lucie's many American couture clients in Paris. She married Giorgio Joyce (1905–76) on 10 December 1930 and they had only one son, Stephen James Joyce (1932–2020).
10. Paul was Assistant Secretary-General of the Archives de Philosophie du Droit et de Sociologie Juridique from 1930 until he resigned in 1940. He contributed a variety of papers to the *Archives* including a number of studies on Rousseau (see Figure 1.7).
11. The Eumenides (Erinyes) are the Furies or Greek deities of vengeance.
12. James Joyce's daughter was Lucia Joyce (1907–82) and his father was John Stanislaus Joyce (1849–1931).
13. The sheer volume of correspondence Paul undertook for Joyce over a dozen years is evident in the several thousand letters in the James Joyce/Paul Léon Collection in the NLI.
14. Joyce never paid Paul a salary of any kind for all the many years of work he did for him. However ineffective they proved to be, Joyce's literary agents in London and New York were Eric and Ralph Pinker. Paul also advised Joyce on various legal matters, especially in his negotiations with publishers around the world. Fred Monro of Monro Saw & Co. provided legal and financial advice and managed Joyce's investments in London.
15. Padraic Colum (1881–1972) was a versatile writer and a leading figure of the Irish Literary Revival. Along with Constantine Curran (1883–1972), he was one of the few friends from Dublin with whom Joyce remained close throughout his life. Padraic and Mary Colum (1884–1957) have left a sympathetic portrait of the writer: *Our Friend James Joyce* (Garden City: Doubleday, 1958). Colum was the second president of the James Joyce Society.
16. Author's note: Joyce was implying that if Colum, an Irish Catholic, was not shocked, he was amazed that Paul, a Jew, should be.
17. Much as it would have pleased Joyce to have his works translated into Finnish, especially as he was busy with *Finnegans Wake*, the earliest Finnish translation of any of his works was *A Portrait of the Artist as a Young Man* (Helsinki: Kustannusosakeyhtio Tammi), which appeared in 1946 (see Slocum and Cahoon, *Bibliography*, p. 110; item D10). It may be that Lucie is recalling that Paul and Joyce discussed the several Czech translations that were being published in the early 1930s.
18. On the day of James Joyce's death in Zurich on 13 January 1941, Nora Joyce commissioned the Swiss sculptor Paul Speck (1896–1966) to cast a death mask of her husband. Two original copies are known to survive; one is in the Zurich James Joyce Foundation, while the other is in the James Joyce Museum in Sandycove, Dublin.
19. 'Tout va très bien, madame la marquise' was a popular song in 1935, with lyrics and music by Paul Misraki. 'All is well Madame la Marquise' has become a proverbial expression for an attitude of blindness in the face of a desperate situation and a clumsy attempt to hide the reality of it.'Au feu les pompiers' was an amusing French children's song.
20. 'Eleven More Years and Ten More Days' was written by Fred Hall and Arthur Fields. It was first released by Lone Star Ranger (John I. White) in 1930.
21. Count John McCormack (1884–1945) was a celebrated Irish tenor who had known Joyce in Dublin in 1904. McCormack urged Joyce to enter the Feis Ceoil that year, where Joyce

was awarded the Bronze Medal. Joyce championed the career of the Cork-born opera singer John O'Sullivan (1877–1955) in the 1930s.

22. Professor Alfred Vogt (1879–1943) was one of Switzerland's foremost ophthalmologists. In 1923 he was Director of the University Clinic of Ophthalmology in Zurich and full professor at the University of Zurich. Joyce began consulting Vogt in April 1930.
23. Joyce gave varying accounts of the number of eye operations he underwent to different people over the decades.
24. Joyce was known to refer to his right eye as his 'good' one.
25. Wilkins Micawber is an optimistic character in Charles Dickens's 1850 novel *David Copperfield*.
26. Possibly, Joyce had in mind Mark Tapley, the always cheerful character in Charles Dickens's *Martin Chuzzlewit* (1842–4).
27. Henrik Ibsen's (1828–1906) play *Ghosts* was first performed in 1882, the year of Joyce's birth. The Norwegian dramatist was one of several major influences on all of Joyce's works, which he signalled as early as his lecture before the University College's Literary and Historical Society on 20 January 1900.
28. Ibsen's *A Doll's House* premiered at the Royal Theatre in Copenhagen, Denmark, on 21 December 1879. Nikolai Vasilyevich Gogol's (1809–1852) *Dead Souls* was first published in Moscow in 1842. Leo Tolstoy's (1828–1910) *War and Peace* was published in 1869. Fyodor Dostoevsky (1821–81) was one of the most influential Russian writers of the nineteenth century. *When We Dead Awaken* (1899) and *The Master Builder* (1892) are both plays by Henrik Ibsen. Gustave Flaubert's (1821–80) *Madame Bovary* (1857) and Tolstoy's *Anna Karenina* (1878) were major influences on *Ulysses*. Anatole France's (1844–1924) *L'Île des Pingouins* was published in 1908.
29. This is the first stanza of Joyce's poem '*Ecce Puer*', which was originally published in 1932. Joyce wrote it to mourn the recent death of his father and to mark the birth of his grandson.
30. Neuilly is an affluent suburb just west of Paris.
31. Giorgio Joyce had an operation to stabilize his voice in May 1936 which caused it to shift from bass to baritone.
32. In the early months of 1903 Joyce spent his days in the Bibliothèque Nationale reading Ben Jonson (1572–1637) and then transcribed some of his songs in his Paris–Pola Commonplace Book (NLI MS 36,639/02). We read about Stephen Dedalus's interest in Elizabethan song in *A Portrait*. Henry Purcell (1659–95) was an English Baroque composer.
33. The Italian opera composer Giuseppe Verdi's (1813–1901) 'Il trovatore' premiered in Rome in 1853.
34. Written as early as 1904, Poem IX in *Chamber Music* (London: Elkin Mathews, 1907), *Bid adieu*, was published in 1949, subtitled 'Words and Air by James Joyce. Musical Setting by Edmund Pendleton' (Paris, Ars Musica).
35. Wolfgang Amadeus Mozart (1756–91) composed his 'The Marriage of Figaro' in 1786. Francesco Paolo Tosti's (1846–1916) 'Donna, vorrei morir' was published in 1879. Presumably Lucie is referring to the Austro-Hungarian composer Franz Lehár (1870–1948).
36. Pyotr Ilyich Tchaikovsky (1840–93) composed 'None but the Lonely Heart' in 1869.
37. Nikolai Rimsky-Korsakov (1844–1908) composed *Scheherazade* in 1888.
38. Joyce's piece is a parody of *La Dame aux Camélias*, the romantic novel by Alexandre Dumas *fils* (1824–95). *Pastimes* was a commemorative volume published by the Joyce

Memorial Fund Committee in May 1941. It included a facsimile of Joyce's manuscript version of 'Come-all-ye', signed and dated 'Thanksgiving Day 1937'.

39. Frank Budgen memorably recounts Joyce's eccentric mode of dance decades earlier in Zurich: see *James Joyce and the Making of 'Ulysses'* (Oxford: Oxford University Press, 1972), pp. 194–5. Pulcinella is a classic Neapolitan *commedia dell'arte* character.
40. Saint Lucia, Lucia of Syracuse (283–304 CE), was a Christian martyr who is the patron saint of the blind.
41. Some but not all of these gifts and correspondence are in the Paul and Lucie Léon/James Joyce Collection in the McFarlin Library, University at Tulsa. On the subject of his love of sunbathing while travelling with Joyce, see Paul's letters to Lucie of 14 and 16 August 1938 (p. 58).
42. The 'Children's Games' chapter became Book II, Chapter 1 of *Finnegans Wake*, an early version of which was published in *transition* 22 in February 1933.
43. Philippe Soupault, *Souvenirs de James Joyce* (Algiers: Éditions Edmond Charlot, 1943), p. 24.
44. The 'Anna Livia Plurabelle' chapter is Book I, Chapter 8 of *Finnegans Wake*. This French translation appeared in *La Nouvelle Revue Française*, Vol. xix, No. 212 (1931): 633–46.
45. The Léons' 'large round mahogany table' is currently on display at the James Joyce Centre in Dublin.
46. The Joyces lived at 7, rue Edmond Valentin from February 1935 to mid-April 1939.
47. Paul recounts some of the difficulties involved in getting *Finnegans Wake* published in his 'Souvenir de Joyce' in Chapter 4.
48. The Russian-born Sophie Rostopchine, Countess of Ségur (1799–1874) wrote several very popular children's books. There is a plaque in her honour affixed to 27, rue Casimir-Périer.
49. Henry François Becque's (1837–99) *Les Corbeaux* premiered at the Comédie-Française in 1882.
50. Joyce's interest in Gabriele D'Annunzio's (1863–1938) *Citta Morta* dates back at least to 1900 when he saw a production of the play with Eleanora Duse in Dublin. Ermete Zaccone (1857–1948) was a versatile Italian stage and film actor.
51. The comic opera *La fille de Madame Angot* premiered in 1872 in Brussels and became an international success.
52. The controversial Czech film 'Extase' was directed by Gustav Machatý in 1933.
53. Gaetano Donizetti's (1797–1848) *Lucia di Lammermoor* premiered in Naples in 1835.
54. Vincenzo Bellini's (1801–35) *La sonnambula* (1831) features in the 'Sirens' episode of *Ulysses*.
55. Gioachino Rossini's (1792–1868) *Guillaume Tell* and Giuseppe Verdi's (1813–1901) *Aida*.
56. Feodor Ivanovich Chaliapin (1873–1938) was a Russian opera singer.
57. Capiton Zaporojetz (1880–1937) was a member of the Russian Private Opera in Paris in the 1920s and 30s.
58. Joyce's monogrammed, ivory-tipped evening cane is now in Poetry Collection of the University at Buffalo.
59. Giacomo Lauri-Volpi (1892–1979) was a much-admired Italian tenor. At Joyce's behest, Paul recounted the events that night in a letter to Frank Budgen (see Budgen, *Making of 'Ulysses'*, pp. 362–3).
60. Founded in 1862, the famous Café de la Paix is still located at 5, place de l'Opéra in the IXth arrondissement of Paris. A demi-blonde is a small (250 ml) glass of lager.

61. In the 1930s Edward Ziegler (1870–1947) was the assistant general manager of the Metropolitan Opera.
62. Italian opera singer Beniamino Gigli (1890 –1957) is generally considered to be one of the greatest tenors of his generation.
63. Like Sylvia Beach, Joyce kept a current account at Lloyds bank throughout his two decades in Paris.
64. Founded in 1899, Weber's Café at 21, rue Royale was a meeting place of writers, artists and journalists until it closed in 1961.
65. That is, 'the blind and the lame' in English.
66. The inscribed copy of *Finnegans Wake* with the note is in the Léon /Joyce Collection in Special Collections, McFarlin Library, University of Tulsa.
67. Chauland was located at 107, rue de l'Université.
68. They frequented the restaurant when the Joyces lived at 7, rue Edmond Valentin.
69. The waistcoat is on display in the Joyce Tower and Museum in Sandycove, Dún Laoghaire, Dublin.
70. These treasured photos are also in the Léon collection in McFarlin Library. See Frontispiece.
71. Tiffin refers to a light tea-time meal.
72. Richard Ellmann recounts the story of the Honourable Mrs Fellowes and her group 'Les Amis de 1914', *James Joyce* (Oxford: Oxford University Press, 1982) p. 668.
73. Joyce and Édouard Dujardin (1861–1949) were friends for over two decades. Similarly, once they became friends, Joyce and Louis Gillet (1876–1943) remained close throughout the 1930s. See his 'Du côté de chez Joyce', *Revue des deux mondes* 28 (August 1925), and then his 'M. James Joyce et son nouveau roman', *Revue des deux mondes* 84 (15 August 1931). Prompted by W. B. Yeats, Sir Edmund Gosse (1849–1928) helped to secure a grant for Joyce from the Royal Literary Fund in 1915.
74. Rachel Berendt (Marie Monique Arkell) was a well-known French actress (1893–1957). Léon-Paul Fargue (1876–1947) was part of the Joyce circle at Sylvia Beach's Shakespeare and Company. His *Haute Solitude* was published by Emile Paul Freres in 1941.
75. Léon Bailby (1867–1954) was a prominent French journalist who founded *Le Jour* in October 1933.
76. With Joyce's active participation, the American journalist Herbert S. Gorman (1893–1954) wrote the first biography of the writer in 1924, *James Joyce: His First Forty Years* (New York: B. W. Huebsch), which he subsequently expanded in his *James Joyce* (New York and Toronto: Farrar & Rinehart, 1939). The artist Frank Budgen (1882–1971) was Joyce's close friend in Zurich. William Bird (1888–1963) founded the Three Mountains Press in Paris in 1922 and published important books by Ezra Pound, Ernest Hemingway, William Carlos Williams and Robert McAlmon.
77. James Johnson Sweeney (1900–86) was an editor of *transition*, then Curator of the Museum of Modern Art and Director of the Guggenheim Museum in New York. George Lionel Seymour Dawson-Damer, Viscount Carlow (1907–44), founded the Corvinus Press in 1936 in London. In October 1937, he published a luxurious edition of Joyce's 'Work in Progress' fragment, *Storiella as She is Syung*, which became parts of Book II, Chapter II, of *Finnegans Wake*.
78. Valery Larbaud (1881–1957) championed Joyce's works from 1920. Still located at 171, boulevard du Montparnasse, the Closerie des Lilas has been a legendary meeting place of artists, writers and intellectuals since it opened in 1847.

79. Les Trianons, located at the junction of the boulevard du Montparnasse and the rue de Rennes, was Joyce's favourite restaurant in the 1920s.
80. Chez Francis is still located at 7, place de l'Alma.
81. Alexander Troubnikoff was a Russian art historian and dealer based in Paris. Lucie is most likely referring to a trip Joyce took to Lausanne at the start of February 1938 (see pp. 47–8).
82. These are all traditional regional French sweets.
83. Joyce died on 13 January 1941 following surgery for a perforated duodenal ulcer.
84. Fernet-Branca is a well-known brand of Italian bitters that was sometimes marketed for its medicinal properties.
85. Nora Barnacle Joyce (1884–1951) was born in Galway and is buried beside her husband in Fluntern Cemetery, Zurich.
86. Paul recounts similar stories about Joyce's love of rivers in his 'Souvenir de Joyce' in Chapter 4.
87. The Munich Agreement was signed on 30 September 1938. See Joyce's letter to Paul in which he announces Lucie's arrival in Dieppe (NLI; 21 September 1938). Lucia Joyce was then under the care of Dr François Achille Delmas in the *maison de santé* at Ivry-sur-Seine.
88. Beaugency is located on the Loire in north-central France and Joyce was there at the start of August 1936.
89. This is Book I, Chapter 8 of *Finnegans Wake*.
90. James Stephens (1882–1950) was a fellow Irish poet, short-story writer and novelist who became a close friend of Joyce, who toyed with the idea of having Stephens complete 'Work in Progress' for him.
91. See Chapter 1 for more information about Lucie's years as fashion editor at the *New York Herald Tribune*.
92. Lucie returned to Paris on 16 August and Paul on 4 September 1940.
93. Sylvia Beach recounts similar stories of Fargue's notorious habit of arriving late in her *Shakespeare and Company* (New York: Harcourt, Brace & Company, 1959), pp. 149–51. The storied Brasserie Lipp opened on boulevard Saint-Germain in 1880. Anne Chérie Charles (1898–1990) was a French painter and designer. She and Fargue married in 1935. The rutabaga (or swede) is a root vegetable, a hybrid between the cabbage and the turnip. Pintades are in fact guinea fowls.
94. Joyce made two recordings of the last part of Book I, Chapter 8 (*FW* 213–16), the second of which was made by C. K. Ogden at the Orthological Institute, London.

PART II

1. The so-called 'Phoney War' was the period of limited military activity at the start of World War I from 3 September 1939 to 10 May 1940. German forces defeated the Allies on 25 June, thereby conquering France and the Low Countries. Under the circumstances, it is unlikely that the Joyce circle marked Bloomsday that year for the first time since 1924.
2. The story of Jesus's triumphant entry into Jerusalem is recounted in Matthew 21.
3. The Joyces had first arrived in Saint-Gérand-le-Puy at the start of February and left on 14 December 1940 for Zurich.
4. Joyce, Nora, Giorgio and Lucia were all eligible for Irish citizenship, and Irish passports would have made it quicker and easier for all of them to travel to Switzerland. At the start of 1941, Joyce was primarily concerned with securing Lucia's transit to Switzerland and, according to Seán Murphy, Joyce 'never suggested applying for an Irish passport for

himself and . . . his son also holds a British passport although at one time, when it looked as if he might be refused a French exit visa for that reason (being of military age), he did enquire about the procedure for getting an Irish one. He did not, however, pursue the matter, presumably because he was able to get an exit visa on his British passport.' Seán Murphy to Francis T. Cremins, 13 January 1941. *Documents on Irish Foreign Policy* <https://www.difp.ie/volume-6/1941/letter-sean-murphy-to-cremins/3394/#section-documentpage> (accessed 3 February 2022).

5. While the official ban on *Ulysses* had not been lifted in Britain, John Lane published the Bodley Head edition of the book in October 1936.
6. The demarcation line dividing France was established by the Armistice of 22 June 1940. Moulins is the capital of the Allier department in which Saint-Gérand-le-Puy is located. In her biographical notes, Lucie also describes this period as 'marking time' (Noel, 'Biographical Notes', p. 4).
7. Marshal Philippe Pétain (1856–1951) was appointed President of the Ministerial Council by President Lebrun, and the Cabinet resolved to sign armistice agreements with Germany and Italy. The entire government eventually moved to Vichy in central France. It voted to transform the discredited Third Republic into the French State, an authoritarian regime that collaborated with the Axis powers.
8. Author's note: I imagine that a Joyce autograph today brings a sum many times the worth of the check written out in green ink which the Vichy banker refused to cash.
9. The Jolases' daughters are Betsy (born 1926), an acclaimed Franco-American composer, and Marie-Christine (1929–99), an anthropologist and accomplished translator.
10. See Chapter 1 for more information on Paul's work at the Archives de Philosophie du Droit et de Sociologie Juridique.
11. Author's note: See Appendix D.
12. That is, the National Library of Ireland (NLI) in Dublin.
13. Count Gerald Edward O'Kelly de Gallagh et Tycooly (1890–1968) was the Irish Special Counsellor of the Paris and Brussels Legations at the time.
14. Catherine Fahy has compiled an extremely useful catalogue of the collection *The James Joyce–Paul Léon Papers in the National Library of Ireland* (Dublin: National Library of Ireland, 1992).
15. This is presumably the Swiss Broadcasting Corporation.
16. Author's note: See Appendix E.
17. The Joyces moved to 34, rue des Vignes in April 1939 and lived there until the end of August. It was their final apartment in Paris.
18. See Chapter 1 for more about Alec Ponizowsky.
19. According to 'How much is a dollar from the past worth today?', MeasuringWorth, 2022, $700 today would be worth about $13,000; see www.measuringworth.com/dollarvaluetoday/ (accessed 3 February 2021).
20. This luxurious edition of *Pomes Penyeach* was published in 1932 in Paris by the Obelisk Press and in London by Desmond Harmsworth.
21. The Joyce family's books, manuscripts, correspondence, and some personal belongings that Paul rescued from their apartment in Paris are now in the Poetry Collection of the University Libraries, University at Buffalo, The State University of New York.
22. Author's note: See Appendix D.
23. The lists survive in the 'Papers of Paul and Lucie Léon' collection in the NLI (MSS 36,932/1–3).

24. The family's Library with their blue-covered wrappers is in the Joyce Collection at Buffalo. Lucie described this work in detail in her correspondence with John Slocum (see Chapter 3, p. 83, and Noel to Slocum; 25 March 1949).
25. See Paul's moving letters of this period in Chapter 5.
26. See Chapter 1 for more information about Lucie's wartime experiences.
27. In English: 'What was your husband actually doing.'
28. Alexander 'Sasha' Wilenkin (1882–1917), a lawyer, was Lucie's maternal uncle.
29. He was Gregory Wilenkin (1864–1930).

PART III

1. See Chapter 4 for Paul's only known critical writing on Joyce's 'Work in Progress'.
2. Author's note: Note by OH [Olga Howe]. Letter typed except signature. Spelling, etc. reproduced exactly.
3. See Chapter 1 for further details of Paul's work preparing the typescript of *Haveth Childers Everywhere* for the printers.
4. In Zurich on 15 May 1930, Prof. Vogt operated on Joyce's left eye a week before this letter.
5. The secondary cataract in Joyce's right eye was a common complication after cataract surgery which also causes blindness.
6. James Joyce, *Haveth Childers Everywhere* (Paris: Henry Babou and Jack Kahane; New York: The Fountain Press, 1930), p. 52 and see *Finnegans Wake* 547.07–8. Paul quotes the same line in his essay on that section of 'Work in Progress' (see Chapter 4, p. 108).
7. William Leonard Courtney (1850–1928) edited the *Fortnightly Review* until his death. Joyce's review 'Ibsen's New Drama' appeared in its pages on 1 April 1900.
8. The original correspondence does not seem to have survived.
9. Unfortunately, none of Paul letters to Lucie from 1929 to 1938 are known to have survived.
10. The tenor was John O'Sullivan.
11. The Faber & Faber edition of *Anna Livia Plurabelle* was in fact only published in June 1930.
12. Joyce and Soupault were coming to the Léon apartment to work on the French translation of *Anna Livia Plurabelle*, translated by Samuel Beckett, Alfred Perron, Ivan Goll, Eugene Jolas, Paul L. Léon, Adrienne Monnier and Philippe Soupault, with James Joyce. It appeared in the May 1931 issue of *La Nouvelle Revue Française*.
13. Jules Émile Frédéric Massenet's (1842–1912) opera *Werther* was loosely based on Goethe's *The Sorrows of Young Werther*. It was first performed in Paris at Théâtre Lyrique on 16 January 1893.
14. For over a decade, Beach and the circle around Shakespeare and Company regularly celebrated St Patrick's Day in Joyce's honour.
15. The Joyces were living at 42, rue Galilée at the time.
16. It is possible that this letter is misdated since the Joyces were actually in Geneva in July and August 1933. According to Harriet Shaw Weaver's 16 August 1933 letter to Paul Léon now in the NLI, she was leaving London for a holiday in Wales with her family until the end of August.
17. The Joyces stayed in Fontainebleau twice in September 1935.

18. Joyce's 'tragic' early September letter to Paul is not known to survive, but something of its tone and content can be gleaned from Joyce's 13 September 1934 letter to Paul from the Hôtel de la Paix, Geneva: 'Mrs Léon tells me you are back tonight. This cheque is better than writing Lloyd's. I want more money as I have to go [change?] Lucia on Monday. Yesterday she behaved like a complete idiot and greatly upset my wife. I kept quite calm. Asking for poison all the time. It is a dreadful position.'
19. Sir Charles Theodore Hagberg Wright (1862–1940) attended the Royal Belfast Academical Institution and then Trinity College Dublin. From 1890 to 1893 he was appointed to the NLI until 1893, when he was elected Secretary and Librarian of the London Library. He married Constance Metcalfe Tyrrell Lewis (1864–1949) in 1919.
20. The Joyces were in Copenhagen from 22 August to 6 September 1936.
21. Joyce's 25 August 1937 telegram does not survive, but in his 27 August 1937 letter to Paul (now in the NLI) he reported: 'I am getting better so don't worry. Have to eat one beefsteak after another according to Moralkoff. No vegetables. No beer or wine or cigar but have been too jaded to take to either.'
22. The Joyces were in Switzerland from 12 August to the start of September 1937.
23. The Joyces were in Switzerland for most of August 1938.
24. The Joyces left for Lausanne on 20 August and remained there until 12 September 1938.
25. See Chapter 5 for a complete transcription and new translation of Paul's letters to Lucie from Drancy and Compiègne.
26. This is letter number [29] in Chapter 5.
27. Paul was working on a major monograph on Rousseau when he was arrested (see Chapter 1 for more information).
28. This is letter number [30] in Chapter 5.
29. This line is in the final paragraph of Book I, Chapter 8, of *Finnegans Wake*, where it reads: 'Dark hawks hear us. Night! Night! My ho head halls. I feel as heavy as yonder stone' (215.36–216.01).
30. This is letter number [32] in Chapter 5.

APPENDICES

1. In a letter to T. S. Eliot on 12 July 1936 (a copy of which is in the NLI), Paul confirmed that Lucie would be delivering the revised typescripts of Books I and III of 'Work in Progress' to Faber & Faber. His concluding remarks turned out to be too optimistic: 'Mr Joyce is working steadfastly on Part II and I hope that I am not over sanguine saying that should the same continue for some time the book could be printed and out within a year.' *Finnegans Wake* was ultimately published simultaneously in London and New York on 4 May 1939.
2. See Lucie's description of their time in Saint-Gérand-le-Puy in Chapter 1.
3. John Stanislaus Joyce was born on 4 July 1849 and passed away on 29 December 1931.
4. In an earlier draft of her memoir, Lucie wrote an interesting introductory paragraph for this anecdote that she subsequently decided not to include: 'Every year to mark the anniversary of his father's birthday, Joyce was in the habit of seeking out a poor man in Paris and presenting him with one hundred francs, quite a sum in those days. He was most exacting about the conditions. The man had to be old[,] decrepit, a beggar, and have a beard. During the twelve years that Joyce's friendship with my husband lasted, they would often do this errand together. If Joyce could not go along, then Mrs. Jolas or my husband would attend to it for him. I personally have done so a couple of times too. Once, Mrs.

Jolas tells me, she was taking care of the matter for Joyce. With difficulty she found a poor old man who seemed to fill the bill. She went up to him and explained that "in memory of an old gentleman, his son marks his birthday by this generous gesture and that he does this every year." The poor man stared at Mrs. Jolas and in an incredulous voice said "sans blagues" [no kidding], Mr. Joyce was highly amused by this sally when she told it to him later' (typescript draft in the Léon family collection).

5. Paul's letter to Jean Paulhan is the second part of Chapter 4.
6. See Chapter 1 for Lucie's account of these events.
7. Pierre Seghers (1906–87) was a French poet and editor who was active in the French Resistance in World War II.
8. Louis-Érasme Le Fur (1870–1943) was Professor of Philosophy of International Law and founded the *Archives de Philosophie du Droit et de Sociologie Juridique* in 1931. He was indeed a collaborator during the Nazi occupation of France.
9. Georges Bataille (1897–1962) was an influential French philosopher, librarian and writer, who founded and edited *Critique* from 1942 to 1962.
10. Joseph Campbell and Henry Morton Robinson, *A Skeleton Key to 'Finnegans Wake'* (London: Faber & Faber, 1947).
11. The author's unbound copy of *Finnegans Wake* that Joyce and Paul corrected in Saint-Gerand-le-Puy is in the Buffalo Joyce Collection (MS VI.I.45.a [VI.H.4.a]), from which a typescript of the errata (MS VI.I.45.b [VI.H.4.b]) was prepared and dispatched to the publishers in London and New York. The corrections were first incorporated in the 1958 Viking Press edition of the book.
12. See Paul's 30 September 1941 letter to Lucie in Chapter 5 in which he writes: 'Ever since I've been here it's the memory of the Russian Orthodox Church that alone has allowed me to gain strength sometimes, and patience.'
13. Guillaume Budé (1467–1540) was a French scholar and humanist.
14. Paul spells the name as 'Ulmo' in his letters to Lucie. See Chapter 5 for further particulars about this visit to the camp and Paul's life in the camp more generally.
15. See letter no. [23; undated, 15 or 16 November 1941] in Chapter 5.
16. Author's note: Alexandre Troubnikoff.
17. Following the announcement by the Soviet Union's new government in 1921, which effectively revoked the citizenship of some 800,000 Russians living abroad, Nansen passports (named after Fridtjof Nansen, who was then High Commissioner for Refugees at the League of Nations) were originally issued to stateless persons and refugees as internationally recognized identity papers and to facilitate travel. Lucie kept her Nansen passport until she became an American citizen on 9 May 1959. See her discussion with John Slocum of the problems she encountered travelling from France to Spain as late as 1950 in Chapter 3.
18. Paul Emile Schazmann (1871–1946) was a librarian at the Swiss National Library in Berne.
19. The original manuscript has not been located and so could not be reproduced here.
20. Paul's letter in French and in its English translation can be found in Chapter 4.
21. Probably the artist Hazel Guggenheim (1903–95) who was a lover of Alec Ponizowsky before she married Milton S. Waldman in 1923.
22. Leon Fleischman was a vice president and Paris agent for Boni and Liveright and moved in the literary circles of New York and Paris. He married Helen Kastor in 1916; they had a son, David Fleischman, in 1919, and then divorced in 1929. Helen subsequently married Giorgio Joyce in 1930.

23. Joyce's *Tales Told of Shem of Shaun* was published by Harry and Caresse Crosby's Black Sun Press in Paris in August 1929.
24. Author's note: St Sylvester's in the French text.
25. The Joyces lived at 2, square de Robiac from June 1925 to 10 April 1931.
26. See Chapter 1 for more information about Paul's collaboration with Joyce on the preparation of the text of *Haveth Childers Everywhere*.
27. After her Memoir had appeared, Lucie wrote to John Slocum on 8 May 1950 that what she had transcribed as 'Llevan' was in fact 'Sullivan': 'histoire Sullivan makes sense, doesn't it?', and also that the word published as 'Pantheon' was in fact 'Parution' ('release' in English); see Chapter 3, p. 93.
28. In 1932, Paul Léon was one of several of Joyce's friends who were instrumental in encouraging Sylvia Beach to relinquish her rights as sole publisher of *Ulysses*.

CHAPTER THREE

The Story of the Publication of *The Story of a Friendship*

LUCA CRISPI

The story of the publication of *James Joyce and Paul L. Léon: The Story of a Friendship* is about another friendship as well, that of Lucie Noel and John J. Slocum. Fortunately, much of the correspondence between these two foundational Joyceans survives in their archives in the National Library of Ireland in Dublin and the Beinecke Library, Yale University.

On 18 October 1947 Slocum introduced himself to Lucie, mentioning their mutual acquaintances: Maria Jolas and Richard Kain. The latter had told Slocum how helpful Lucie had been while he was preparing his book, *The Fabulous Voyager*.[1] He also mentioned another mutual acquaintance, 'indirectly, your sister-in-law, Mrs. Hirshman,[2] who writes that you are planning to come to this country'. Slocum informed Lucie of his ongoing work on the Joyce bibliography and asked if she might have in her files 'material that would throw light on Joyce's foreign publication in Europe, or in writings about him. Naturally, I have located all the better-known fragments of FINNEGANS WAKE, etc., but I am sure there are many things that elude me, and this is the reason for writing you.'[3] He ended the letter by telling her:

> Your husband did Joyce and, incidentally, the cause of modern belles-lettres, a magnificent service in relieving him of the business details connected with his writings. Mrs. Jolas writes me that he was very helpful in rescuing Joyce's personal effects at the time they were auctioned off in Paris. I think that was truly magnificent of him, in view of the danger that he was in at that time.[4]

Paul's dedication to Joyce, his family and his works created a corresponding bond that was the basis of Lucie and Slocum's decades-long friendship. Although there must have been a reply from Lucie to Slocum's first letter, as well as further back-and-forth correspondence between them, none of it seems to have survived. Over a year passed after his first known letter, but then during her much-anticipated trip to America, she spent a productive though intense weekend with the Slocums in their home in Tuxedo Park, about an hour's drive from New York City. This was the beginning of her friendly collaboration with one of the most important early Joyce collectors and scholars. As President of the New York James Joyce Society, Slocum arranged for Lucie to give a talk to the group at Frances Stellof's iconic Gotham Book Mart. Just a week before her talk Lucie wrote to thank John and Eileen Slocum for their gracious hospitality, but then confided to him that there was 'something I <u>must</u> tell you' that 'Everyone in Paris, London & New York knows. And it never occurred to me you might have ignored this fact':

> Is it possible that you never had heard my husband Paul Léon was a Jew – & that was the reason for his arrest & subsequent assassination by the Germans?
>
> My husband never concealed his origin. It was a case of "noblesse oblige". When the Germans decreed all Jews were to declare themselves. He underwent the humiliation of wearing a yellow star . . . so did I out of solidarity,[5] until his arrest (when I found I could do more in the red ✞ without the star).
>
> His brother who lived in Venice & was a Catholic (for 40 yrs) married a real Catholic also perished in the same way.[6] Their little girl aged 7 was saved by the nuns who hid her in a potato sack for [illegible word], from the Germans. Nadia who is a Catholic & 17 today, & lovely, told me the story herself & adds "that happened because I am mixte". — That story is but one of six million, as you know — but as far as Paul & those who died with him are concerned I can say that all died the death of Christian martyrs — I was there nearly to the end & know their Calvary step by step — You must believe this.
>
> — When Eileen asked me why Paul had been arrested I thought you had not told her because it is such a terrible story. I was afraid to start talking about it at table. And I remember telling you & Dick Cain [*sic*] at luncheon that day – in Paris —
>
> — But later that evening when you put almost the same question to me — I was quite stunned — We were so deep in Joyce & so exhausted — & I had to think it over — And I had been so certain that you knew all the time.
>
> Few of Paul's friends ever "thought" of him as a Jew . . . The New Testament, the Gospels, the teaching of our Lord Christ were what he lived by, read & practiced. The only book he asked for in the horror camp were the Gospels. My priest, Father Cyprien Kern succeeded in getting the Book through to him.[7] Paul considered that changing one's religion was the betrayal of one's inner life for exterior benefits – his inner life was intensely Christian in every way. Therefore he never denied he was a Jew. There is a great deal of intermarriage in his family. I think if he had chosen not to declare himself he could have gotten away with it. He chose martyrdom — I know he would have wanted me to tell you this.
>
> — I hope you will understand & also believe I am writing you this in all sincerity — & with a heart full of sorrow.[8]

It is not known what Slocum's reaction was when he read Lucie's frank and heartfelt account. In fact, the complete version of the story of Paul's enduring faith has never been revealed in full before. Reading Lucie's description of Paul's commitment to Christian thought in their letters and in her memoir alters how we understand his heritage, his life – and tragic end.

The day after her talk (which then became the basis of her memoir of the friendship of Paul Léon and James Joyce republished here), she wrote to thank Slocum for his assistance in having her typescript prepared. She then revealed: 'There was so much, and at first I felt I could never undertake the task. Without your great help I know I never could have succeeded in presenting it.' After all he had done to arrange and prepare for her talk, Slocum was not able to attend the event in person. So Lucie reported on the audience's 'touching concentration[,] attention and interest', which she was sure he would have appreciated, and told him: 'Miss Steloff could not have been nicer nor more amiable. She told me it was the best evening they had had, and even if my part seemed shallow or insignificant it will go down in Joyce history as having started those of the audience who know Joyce off on their own reminiscences . . . all were inspired and fascinating.' Then, she continued,

> Before starting on the 2nd part, I told them all, that even if the incidents described might appear trivial they formed an entire pattern of our daily life over those twelve years. There was a good deal of emotion chez tous, Miss Steloff could hardly speak, she was chocking with tears.
>
> At the end three people asked me to let them publish it, Miss S. for one, and I think we will have to decide on her. Because it took place chez elle, and . . . because I like what she did with the "comeallyou".

The other publication offers came from Edward Titus,[9] who exaggeratedly told her 'he would like to do it "at any price." Perhaps he will not be as rash again now he has calmed down.' Lucie also mentioned that she had told 'everyone except Steloff that I had not thought about it yet but would do so (give it some thought) and whatever money was raised [by the publication] should pay dr's bills for Lucia'. She also recounted the amusing anecdote of the clerk at the telegraph office who tried to correct her report to Maria Jolas:

> The Western Union employee said: ["]<u>Joyce evenings</u>? You mean <u>JOYOUS</u> I suppose" . . . .
>
> Why did no-one ever think of that?

Lucie let Slocum know that she had posted him a set of corrections to her talk, asked him to have them incorporated in a new typescript, and ended by writing: 'If it does get published I will have to polish it off anyway.'[10]

On her return to Paris, Lucie reported that she had been 'submerged with work – fashion work – and not a moment to call my own. I covered London and also Paris openings. I could think of nothing but fashion, and there was not a second in which I could steal off and concentrate on the Joyce essay.' Nonetheless she had been able to work on her project, 'greatly enlarging upon it, checking, verifying and extending'. She described how the essay began to take on the shape it now has in the published memoir:

> I have gone over all my husband's letters to me, in the years he knew Joyce. From these letters I have extracted paragraphs referring to current events in his and Joyce's life. I have compiled something which I have called "an appendix." To this I have added several letters he wrote after his arrest, when he was in the German concentration camp.[11] They mention Joyce.
>
> A niece of my husband's has kindly lent me a letter he wrote her which is of greatest interest, and has never been published, nor made public.[12]
>
> All this material has enlarged the book something like forty pages of closely typed copy, plus another ten pages obtained by the appendix, foreword and acknowledgements. In all, now we get fifty pages which if brought out in a size about like Leon Edel's book,[13] may be seventy five at least.
>
> Will you let me know if Miss Steloff is still willing to print it or rather have it published. If not I will have to make other arrangements as it <u>must</u> appear. Off the record, if the JJoyce Society cannot afford to do it entirely, I would be willing to share half of the expense personally.
>
> Mrs. Jolas and I were trying to figure out the cost the other evening, and it looks to us as if it would be under a $300 job or about that. I think Miss Steloff underestimates the expense.
>
> I know you are a very busy man, a very bad correspondent, but will you do me a favor John. Please make the best arrangements you can with Miss Steloff, and let me

> hear what she decides. She is busy too, so if you could dictate the answer so that I know one way or another how I stand I would be truly grateful.
>
> I understand Padraic Colum is slated for the new President [of the James Joyce Society]. Personally I cannot think of anyone nicer nor more devoted to Joyce's memory . . .
>
> I have had the luck to have discussed my essay with a friend, an American, and he actually spent hours going over it with me. I am now engaged in retyping it. Believe it or not, this is the fifth time, and this time I am doing it personally . . .
>
> As soon as it is finished I will send it to you. And then you will tell me what you think. I hope to have it finished by the end of the week. If only we could get it out by St. Patrick's day, wouldn't that be fun.
>
> I suppose you know that Mrs. Joyce and Giorgio finally came to Paris. Why don't you answer Mrs Jolas's letter about the exhibition. Did you ever hear from your Unesco friend? Is it true that the person whose works are on exhibit must be a citizen of a member nation? I would appreciate knowing this. But after all he did carry a British passport. Mrs. Jolas is busy arranging details but would I know appreciate hearing from you. So please find time.[14]

Lucie's story of her work rewriting the memoir several times sounds like Joyce's own often lament-filled letters to Harriet Shaw Weaver and to others throughout his career; and, in fact, many different versions of her memoir have survived.[15] This letter also contains the first mention of the preparations for the La Hune Gallery's exhibition of the Joyce family collections in Paris, a subject they will return to again in their correspondence. For once Slocum was relatively quick to reply. Excusing himself for his long silence, he thanked her for her 'charming Christmas presents' and asked if she liked the photographs of Joyce that he had recently sent her. He then reported:

> The Joyce Society would very much like to publish your essay as their first publication and assume full financial responsibility. If you will send me the corrected manuscript I will get after it right away.
>
> I am writing Mrs Jolas a long and apologetic letter, and will you please show her the enclosed from the . . . present head of Unesco . . . I think we shall have to pursue another angle.
>
> We miss you over here and I hope you will be coming back soon. Meanwhile, if all goes well, Eileen and I will be back in Paris about the 20th of May for a month or two . . .
>
> We enjoyed your article on America very much and Eileen joins me in sending our love.[16]

Busy as he was with his work at the United States Information Agency, Slocum's other great passion was as one of the foremost Joyce collectors and amateur scholars of his era. Therefore, it is unsurprising that he eagerly took on the charge of seeing Lucie's memoir of her husband and James Joyce's friendship into print on behalf of the James Joyce Society, though he did not follow through on his promise to get the Society to 'assume full financial responsibility'. Over the next several years, Lucie and the Slocum family continued to deepen their friendship, and they often relied on her expertise and connections in the fashion world when they visited Paris.

Towards the end of March 1949, Lucie replied, thanking him for his letter and for sending several copies of Joyce photographs that he had acquired. She told him that she would 'give two to Mrs Joyce. She has hardly any photos of her husband left at all', but was concerned about the fact that he had approached UNESCO on his own initiative, unsuccessfully as it turned out, which came as a 'bombshell' to Maria Jolas, who 'does nothing without consulting the family and of course it looks as if it had [been] done behind their backs'. He had also not given Jolas something for the book she was editing.[17] Setting aside these other issues, she then reported on her ongoing work on the memoir and the preparation of the Joyce collection for the Paris exhibition and eventual sale:

> My MS I trust will leave this coming week. I am addressing it to you . . .
>
> The Joyce books have been sorted and catalogued in our apartment. They are all bound in light blue paper, numbered and have corresponding cards. My two old ladies have not yet tackled the newspaper clippings, but I understand are to do this later on. I found a whole suitcase of these, rather gnawed at by the rats. But at any rate they are in order now, and we know all we have. And there is plenty of everything.
>
> This job which took the old librarian ladies six weeks is something that had to be done at all costs. For Joyce and also for Paul who went to such great lengths and risks to save the stuff.
>
> We hope the Joyces will be here again soon.[18]

What remained of Joyce's Paris library (still 'all bound in light blue paper') as well as his newspaper clippings collection that Lucie and her assistants sorted are all now in the Poetry Collection, University at Buffalo. They are there with the rest of the family's collection of inscribed copies of Joyce's works to them, as well as the largest collection of his manuscripts and letters in the world, all of which Paul Léon 'went to such great lengths and risks to save' from Joyce's final apartment in Paris.[19] Lucie followed up two weeks later with some good news:

> Well believe it or not I have finished my revising. And the revising of the revising, multiplied by five. How in Heaven's name Joyce could complete Finnegan [*sic*] in seventeen years is beyond me. Here I have been struggling with fifty eight pages – and only now feel I can send it through . . .
>
> But – if you think it is too long and therefore will be too costly, please delete nothing but charge it to me. I have tried to take out parts or incidents, but it spoils the flow and sequence. So I have put it all back; only for the sake of chronology – so difficult in a case like this (or you have to keep jumping from one year to another). I have been advised to place some of the incidents in the appendix.
>
> (See for example the story of Paul and Paulhan.[20])
>
> Will you please fill in the passage you know about and Colum referred to, please. Or at least tell the reader where he can find it if it is too long to publish (I mean the one about the Pope).
>
> If you have no objection your footnote could top my story about "getting the Gospels into the camp", and Paul's "religious feeling." I have given the whole story just as it happened. But if you think it is unsuitable, being too personal and too long, just cut it.
>
> I am also enclosing the copy of an article that appeared last week in the Journal de Geneve about my husband (see appendix[)].[21] Maybe you could have it translated. It is [an] excellent one and says just what it should.
>
> Also enclosed are copies of Fargue's and Jamaty's letters.[22] If you think they are of interest. Fargue is I know.

> I believe that is all. It is now 3 a.m. and I have been proofreading since four this afternoon. But "das ist alles" – I think. Do not fail to let me know what you decide.[23]

Slocum sent a 'hasty note to say that your completed manuscript had arrived safely and was with Leon Edel, Chairman of the Publications Committee of the Joyce Society', while the remainder of the committee consisted of 'Professor Tyndall [*sic*] of Columbia, a printer whose name escapes me and myself'. He quickly sketched their plan and did his best to exculpate himself with Maria Jolas:

> We hope to run your essay as one of the proceedings of the Joyce Society. We have not yet decided how to finance it. Possibly the financing will be done by Miss Steloff but if we should need additional help from you I will let you know.
>
> I am sorry I am in the "doghouse" with Madame Jolas. On one score, it is your fault as I seem to remember dictating the letter to UNESCO to you and it was our plan to send it off without advising anyone else on the theory that they could disclaim responsibility for our action if we got a refusal. Please straighten this matter out with her as I wouldn't offend her for the world.
>
> My reason for not communicating with her or sending her the promised material was a dreadful inertia or procrastination on my part. I had gathered in January some notes concerning the present state of Joyce criticism in America but never satisfied myself that they were well enough prepared for inclusion in her YEARBOOK. Please tell her that her approval of the program of the Joyce Society and the activities of the people interested in Joyce in America is extremely important. If there is any way I can remedy this situation, please let me know.[24]

Slocum's friendship with Lucie remained steadfast, though his relations with Maria Jolas remained complicated by his efforts to acquire the Joyce family's archive for his own magnificent collection. Slocum and his family were in Paris during the summer and he must have smoothed over these issues with Jolas himself. As soon as he returned to New York, he wrote thanking Lucie for her hospitality and assistance while they were there, as well as for some gifts she had sent for his wife, but then he returned to the more urgent matter of getting her memoir into print. He had contacted Steloff as soon as he had arrived and was anxiously waiting for the printer's estimate on the project. Then he gave her some news of his own: he had written to Bernard Gheerbrant, proprietor of the La Hune Gallery

> and made him a tentative offer of the whole Joyce library, which I am sure will be interpreted by Maria Jolas as a further indication of Slocum nefariousness. He probably won't take it, and when the sale comes off and the total returns are less than my offer, I will have a happy time saying "I told you so". As it is, I rather hope that he won't take it, as I haven't the slightest idea where I am going to come by the cash.[25]

Slocum himself was not sure what the Joyce family's collection offered for sale actually contained, but as it turned out he underestimated by half its value at auction. A month later, Lucie wrote to thank him for his efforts to get her book published and offered to subsidize the project. She hoped it would be out by Christmas 1949, but it would take considerably longer for the work to appear. Then she went on to keep him abreast of what was happening:

> Mrs. Joyce is in Paris, having arrived a week ago and I haven't even had a minute to see her. But she is coming to lunch tomorrow. Over the phone she sounds alright and

> not as depressed as last time. Her plans on the other hand seem indefinite. She hopes Giorgio will come to the opening of the show. The date has moved as you know, probably. Maria is hard at work and Mrs. Joyce seems overjoyed (that is not meant to be a pun or anything) at what has been done. Maria, I know, was most grateful at your efforts and work with her qui l'ont avancé beaucoup. I had a laugh at the part of your letter to Gheerbrandt [*sic*] . . .[26] I had Maria to lunch last week and we discussed the situation at some length . . .
>
> Well we will see what we will see. I guess that's the only way of looking at it. Because even if interest is running high it doesn't mean that financially it is a scoop.[27]

Slocum sent a long letter in reply in which he reported his current reading, 'otherwise I have just been typing and typing Joycewise' on his groundbreaking bibliography. He asked for more precise news about the exhibition as he wanted to be in Paris in November for it. He also gave her an update on the memoir, criticized Steloff for not being more effective in her support of the project, and made a case for his offer on the Joyce collection:

> I rather thought Maria would refuse my offer, and possibly she was justified if Jake Schwartz and one or two of the other dealers are there to run up prices, but I still think that the clear $5000 would benefit Mrs Joyce more that whatever money she makes after the deduction of commissions, taxes and shipping costs and everything else.[28]

Lucie replied, thanking him for his news, confiding:

> I hate to give you all this trouble about my essay, book or what have you, but from the first I was a little bit afraid that when Miss Steloff would actually find herself au pied du mur, so to speak, we should come up against just that.
>
> I hope you have found a printer who will not be too ruinous and that you will let me know what you have decided. Remember if it is to [be] a paper cover I would like it to be either blue (greek [*sic*] flag blue, Liffey, tie etc) or green, for Erin.
>
> As to further editing: John, my dear, please forgive me – but it has already been done over five times at least – and every time bits come out and spoil the sequence, and this time I just want to leave it as it is. Things I have mentioned there may seem trivial and unimportant to you, but they are, were, part of the picture just the same and I would like it left just as it is. There is one exception, however. If you think the scene I have described about Father Cyprien bringing the Gospels into the camp de trop, say so and we can cut it out. Though I do feel that it was so important to him all his life and he so truly believed, that it would be a pity. There is a curious side to that, Joyce, an Irish Catholic, brought up by Jesuits and educated as it were au sein de l'Eglise Apostolique, later breaks away from the church dogmas . . .[29] One of his best friends: Paul Léon, a Jew, who studied and knows Christian religion most thoroughly, who believes in Jesus Christ and is a frequent churchgoer (Russian Orthodox church). St. Thomas Aquinas, St. Augustine, the church of the Moyen age and the Reformation were all familiar subjects and sources. Every day he read the Gospels and that is the only thing he pines for and asks for during his martyrdom . . .[30] But of course do as you like . . .
>
> They are all working hard on the show. I have contributed all they wanted, and in general there are masses of books and material on hand.
>
> The show, as you know, begins on the 28th and will last for two weeks. The latest news is that Mrs. Joyce has decided she cannot stand the strain and is not staying in Paris for the show. Not even for the opening. We are distressed about it. But her mind

> is made up and she feels it will be too much for her. Her arthritis is pretty bad now. She can get around only with difficulty. I am seeing her tomorrow to say goodbye – for she is off to Zurich on Sunday.
>
> I will keep you au courant of how the show proceeds as of course if you aren't here you will be just crazy for news.

Besides news of mutual friends, other happenings in Paris, the weather, world events, she added in the margin: 'Mr. [Giorgio] Joyce has been very helpful.'[31] Slocum then replied: 'We are getting along a little further with the manuscript,' and that he had turned to 'Maurice Kaplan who, though not a printer, is a book or pamphlet designer and will do the whole job'. He then told her:

> The arrangement is this: Miss Steloff will be the publisher and it will a Gotham Book Mart imprint. She will not put up any money to finance the printing but will write a letter at the time any contract is signed with the printer, that she will buy 500 copies, and this should cover a great part of the cost. I have told her that she must sign all printer's contracts and must negotiate with you concerning your contribution, but I will probably end up by writing the letters although I will not accept the responsibility. My reason being that only with her having responsibility, along with you, will the book be properly plugged. My recommendation to you would be to make the issue only 750 copies, although I have asked the printer for an estimate on both 750 and 1000 copies.

He also made the following recommendations: that the title should be reversed, putting 'the name "Joyce" in front with the idea of selling it', and combining the foreword and acknowledgements into one note. He also apologized for having misplaced one of the four photos that she had sent along with the typescript,[32] and then made other suggestions about the illustrations to reduce the printing costs. Slocum continued:

> Concerning the fragment in French by Paul Leon,[33] I wonder if it is a good idea to run a translation of it, or even a transcription, in view of the number of words that we were unable to make out. I would recommend that it be run without a translation, and merely your introductory paragraph as a caption, leaving the problem to the reader. But the decision is yours.
>
> Concerning the quotation from FINNEGANS WAKE about the Pope, I would rather not have the responsibility of choosing the exact passage. As I said to you, I think it refers to the little cloud over the Vatican in SHEM AND SHAUN, but one can never be too sure about such things and for every ten students who say one thing, ten others say something else.

The issue of the legibility of Paul Léon's handwriting in the fragment would resurface after the volume was published. Slocum also asked Lucie to find out the date of the La Hune auction, writing:

> Mme. J [Jolas] was probably disappointed by the small amount of material I sent for the show, but it did not seem advisable to me to send irreplaceable material right at the time when I am endeavouring to finish my collations and the manuscript to the printer. Also, the show itself will have such a wealth of material that a few odds and ends would be lost in the shuffle . . .
>
> May I again express my deep apologies for having mislaid the snapshot and say that I hope it was not unique and that you have the negative of it. It may still turn up, but

> I have been over the mountains and mountains of papers and I am afraid it got lost in the restaurant when we were going over the manuscript there.[34]

Lucie replied a few days later, filling Slocum in on all the news about the La Hune exhibition:

> It opened today, and Maria Jolas and the Gheerbandts [*sic*] have done a magnificent job. I wanted to send you the catalogue and poor Gheerbr. almost had a fit to think I could have suspected him of not having sent you one.
>
> The place could have been twice as large and they still would have had stuff over. They arranged showcases so that everything is encl. but carefully divided into periods (Zurich, Paris, etc.) and most tastefully arranged. There will be photographs which you will no doubt see.
>
> Everybody of interest was there, the place was jammed, I arrived at four and stayed an hour and then came back again about a quarter to seven. There were still people and more coming in. Though then I really could take a look. Many told me they would come back again tranquillement to take a second look and <u>see</u> something.
>
> The Monde (our most respectable paper, the old Temps) came out with an article this evening.[35] The poor man did not seem to know much about Joyce but knew the French angle, and discovered two serious points.
>
> One was the fact that a French man was arrested and deported to Buchenwald. He had a copy of the French translation of Ulysses with him and kept it in all the transfers he made from camp to camp. I can add to this by recalling that in Nov or Dec 41, my husband sent a French professor who had been in the camp of Drancy so that I could tell him about Joyce and buy him a copy of Ulysses. I got one at the time for eleven hundred francs – almost double the original price.
>
> The second angle this French writer discovered (Jean Marc Theolleyr) is that he thought it quite curious that James Joyce works created un scandale and a sensation wherever they were published should have died in the most Puritan country of all Switzerland. Otherwise there was not very much to his story . . .
>
> The Joyce exhibit is certainly the literary sensation of the season, I think and of course it is really due to the fact that for the first time Joyce's work has been presented to the French public in its entirety. And not just his work but the man as well. You would love the <u>Joyce Tree</u>. It is quite terrific. The French Monde writer said: "At last he is taking his place among the classics." There is much more than that. I think people will see it and realize what he stood for.
>
> Between you and me, they omitted Freud – and Maria is disturbed about it. Because undoubtedly he did have an influence and played a part in the "roots" – and I would not be surprised if I were told that Freud read Joyce too.
>
> Maria will probably write you herself. She was very pleased to get your material, which unfortunately due to the fact that you mailed it late they could not get it into the catalogue. But she did not write you because she was waiting to get it and was completely taken up with arranging the exhibition.
>
> Miss Beach was there and deplored Weaver's absence, and Mrs. Joyce's, too. Philippe Soupault was there too and a wireless outfit. Several of us were asked to speak: Maria, Stuart Gilbert, Philippe Soupault, Miss Beach, myself – what other I do not know. But it will be on the air on the Friday at 22 hrs 30 on Chaine Parisienne. Too late for you to get it, I am afraid.

> At the Abbaye de Royaumont, musical and literary center outside Paris they are having a Joyce weekend. We have been asked to go and speak there. It should be quite interesting.
>
> It will be quite interesting to watch the progress of the exhibition. I suspect that it will arouse renewed interest. I do not yet know for sure what they are doing and how they will auction the things or when. But I hope to find out this week and will write you at once.

On the La Hune exhibition, see Figures 3.1 and 3.2 at the end of this chapter. Then Lucie turned to the topic of her memoir, thanking him for all that he had done, including finding the printer and convincing Steloff to take 500 copies, though the arrangement did not turn out as smoothly as Slocum had planned. Lucie thought that a print run of 1,000 copies 'would be better', but was hesitant in case the book did not sell as well they expected. She agreed to his suggestion about inverting the title, writing that 'James Joyce and Paul Léon, the story of a friendship is much better'. She continued:

> My brother's last name is Ponizovsky. His full name is Alexander M. Ponizovsky. He was educated after finishing high school in Moscow at St. John's College, Cambridge. The Germans deported him for Secret Service work – he was denounced. We never heard exactly what happened. His death is officially listed as March 7 1944 – six months before the South was liberated and three months before the Normandy landings. He never believed for a minute Germany could win – never lost faith in the allies.[36]

A few weeks later Slocum sent Lucie Kaplan's estimate for the design and printing – $1,160 for 750 copies –[37] which Slocum considered 'high' but 'not unreasonable, considering the number of pages and the plates involved', and he reassured her that the price would not be much more if she preferred to have 1,000 copies. He continued:

> I have received a number of Joyce notices from you and I am extremely grateful for them. It sounds to me as if the exhibition has been very successful, and deservedly so, in view of the time and effort involved. Please congratulate Maria Jolas for me and tell her she really came through.
>
> To return to your book, I would recommend that you ask Miss Steloff to buy from you at cost on publication 500 copies, which she would then undertake to sell for about $2.50 apiece. The other copies you could either have shipped to France or store part of them with me and ship the rest. This would mean you would be out of pocket for about one-half the cost at the time of publication.
>
> I wish Miss Steloff would underwrite some of this, but she has been complaining about her indebtedness and lack of cash for the past three months. I would like to be able to do it myself, but I find that I have to underwrite another pamphlet for the Joyce Society, which was a precommitment.[38]

Lucie replied immediately, thanking Slocum again for all of his help and seeking further advice from him under various headings. She told him that they didn't need to get a second printer's estimate and agreed with him 'that as long as I am spending a certain amount of money it would be wiser to ask him to print 1000 copies instead of 750'. She thought that 'it would be grand if Miss Steloff would undertake to act as publisher and I would be duly grateful to her. Don't you think they could be sold as high as $3.00 per copy. Two fifty seems rather low to me. Maria's is seeling [*sic*] for more (but then there are several contributors, and also she seems to think that the number of pages in mine would not warrant a higher price).' She also told him that she understands that Steloff 'would and could not share in the financing, and perhaps it is better this way', in fact she can 'scrape up the necessary', and then asked whether the printer had to be paid in advance.

She also asked that the printer send two dummy copies of the book and spelled out her instructions for the book design in detail, insisting that 'the paper cover be either Bright green or the Liffey blue if possible'. Lucie confirmed that she liked the idea of facsimiles of Joyce's and Paul's signatures on the cover, an example of which Slocum could get from one of Paul's letters to Joyce's London agent, James Pinker Jr., that he already had in his collection. She told him that if the printing could be done by the middle of January, then friends of hers who would be flying back to Paris from the New York fashion show could bring copies back in batches of a dozen at a time. Her advice was that they should 'get going now as quickly as possible, while interest is still stirred up, due to the exhibition'. She also warned Slocum of the possibility that the exhibition would be transferred to London, thereby postponing the auction, and so his plans to travel to Paris in January. She ended her letter by thanking him for his kind offer to visit them in Arizona, but told him that if she was 'going to do the job on the book I will have to be a very good girl and not move from mon coin at all for months to come'.[39]

Slocum replied two weeks later with another 'hasty note' to say that he had passed on all of her instructions to the printer, but then complained that he was 'vastly disappointed by the turn the Joyce sale is taking because it seems to me that Gheerbrandt [*sic*] is doing everything to obscure the items that are for sale and to make it difficult for those who are sincerely interested in Joyce to feel that we are being offered the whole collection, or even the collection I saw last Summer. I may decide to withdraw my bid from Gheerbrandt [*sic*] and let someone else take the rap for purchasing it and giving it to some American library.'[40] Meanwhile, Frances Steloff wrote to tell Lucie that the Gotham Book Mart was

> not only willing but eager to act as distributor for your book and you may be sure we will handle it in the same economical way we would if it were our own publication . . .
>
> We believe that the bulk of them will melt away within a short time of publication, especially if we can have them at this time while Joyce activity is at its height. We are fortunate in having Mr. Kaplan as he has excellent taste and does fine work . . .
>
> P.S. 40% is the usual trade discount and is quite acceptable to us.[41]

It seems that Steloff only thought of the Gotham Book Mart as the distributor and retailer of the book, and not as the equal partner in the venture that Slocum had hoped she would be. So, at the start of 1950, Lucie confirmed that she had sent the first instalment of the entire printing costs. She summed up the situation by saying that 'everything seems to be fine and all set. Now we must hold our thumbs and hope the whole thing wont [*sic*] be a flop. I honestly dont [*sic*] think it should be if I were studying Joyce or interested in the man I would certainly be interested in reading it.' Then, after asking for news about his wife and children, she told him:

> Alexis was down on leave for five days. That is all he could get as he had to be back in time to attend a tripartite conference at Bonn. His job is an extraordinary one. Part of his work is to sit into these Godesburg and Bonn conferences where they argue and talk and finally have to begin all over again. The rest of the time it is administrative. Nights he attends Maryland University, a branch of which has opened in Heidelberg. He has done well so far, came out with three A.s in Government, Politics and Speech.

> I found him awfully tired but happy to be home and get a taste of Paris. He calls me his social secretary and I had planned all he should do to get the most enjoyment out of his trip. Of course did not do half, but did get a taste of theaters, movies and saw all the interesting people I could think of.
>
> Life in Germany even with the US Forces is an entirely different world. Though we are no longer at war, it is pretty grim and dreary at times. They do get into a rut as far as intellectual exchange is concerned.

Lucie continued by giving Slocum news of her pets and then told him: 'The Joyce exhibit is apparently not going to London. Mrs Joyce and Giorgio were here for a short time. We paid our respects to Mrs. Joyce as she was winding up her Paris séjour. Maria tells me it may go to London later.' At the end of the letter, she told him that her nephew had reported that a story about the exhibition had also appeared in an Italian newspaper.[42]

That same day she wrote a scathing letter to the Editor of the London *Evening Standard*, vigorously defending her husband's legacy, just as she and Alexis would continue to do for the rest of their lives. It merits being quoted in full:[43]

> Sir,
>
> For the sake of bibliographical, historical and literary accuracy, as well as for the sake of the memory of both James Joyce and his friend (my husband) Paul Léon, I feel obliged to correct a story which appeared in a recent issue of your paper in the column Books and Persons.
>
> I am surprised that Mr Thorogood did not refer to the exhibition catalogue where the facts are recounted with complete accuracy. He certainly has got all his facts twisted and he is surprisingly inaccurate. One might almost imagine there is malicious distortion. Here are the corrections.
>
> a) Joyce did not "flee from Paris to Switzerland"[.] He was living in the free zone of France before France fell. When all his friends left (including ourselves and the Jolas'es) he found himself alone. It was late December that he succeeded in completing negotiations to enter Switzerland. There he had friends and could keep in contact with his publishers in England the United States.
>
> b) Joyce was the holder of British passport. Legally his landlord had no right to touch his belongings. Private property of British subjects at that time was protected by the Swiss government. My husband, a close devoted friend of Joyce did the best he could. Prior to the auction he retrieved and stored most of Joyce's books, papers, portraits, photographs, and bought back what he could at the auction held by the proprietor. The great majority of Joyce's library and belongings on display at La Hune recently (except the ones brought by Mrs. Joyce) are the result of my husband's devotion and démarches.
>
> c) The sealed parcel of letters (actually an oversize envelope) to which your correspondent refers as "too frank for contemporary publication" were my husband's property. They formed the bulk of his correspondence with Joyce over the twelve years of their friendship. This private correspondence deals uniquely with family and financial affairs, his daughter's sickness and other private matters the burdens of which he generally shared with my husband for the past twelve years.
>
> On our return to Paris in September 1940, my husband not knowing what fate awaited us, did not want these letters to fall into German hands. After Joyce's death in '41 he placed them in a large envelope inscribing thereupon that "no-one but the

immediate family or Joyce's legal advisors should have access to them in the event of his death. They were not to be made public for fifty years".

He took them for safety to the Irish minister in Paris Count O'Kelly requesting him to place them in the Dublin library. We knew of no safer place at the time. Your correspondent's epithet "too frank" is hardly suitable.

d) For further details I can refer you to firstly the archives of the B.B.C. where recordings have been made by some of Joyce's friends, myself included. To those who might be interested I can further refer you to my own book: The Story of a Friendship: Joyce and Léon published in New York and distributed in March by the Gotham Book Mart 41 West 47th Street, New York City.

Finally I take exception to the tone used by your correspondent in mentioning my husband. It has shocked <u>everyone</u> to whom I have shown [it]. In the United States this approach is known as discrimination. Mrs. Eleanor Roosevelt and thousands of civilized people are fighting just that approach which smacks too much of Nazi poisonous mentality to fit in with the world we are trying to build.

I am surprised that a paper with the high reputation the Evening Standard has in the past can tolerate anything as sickening.

To be sure my husband was a Jew. I resent your correspondent labelling his as <u>Joyce's Jewish helper</u>.

He was also a scholar, a man of the greatest erudition and culture. He was a devoted friend to Joyce, and this friendship included legal advice, and literary and practical help. Joyce had other friends who were not Jews and who also helped him in the past and during the time of his friendship with my husband. I have not noted they have ever been referred to as Protestant, Catholic, Anglican, Methodist or Presbyterian.

My husband was <u>not</u> discovered and shot because he had rescued Joyce's books and belongings. He died the death of a martyr because he was a Jew, solely, and because there are still people in the world today, like your correspondent, who label people according to the colour of their skin or their religion. Here in Paris we consider this a scandal.[44]

In reply, Slocum apologized for taking almost a month to answer her letter, but he had been away. On his return he had found a set of proofs of her memoir which he was going to check because he wanted 'this pamphlet to be a most outstanding piece of work'. He continued:

I was most distressed to read the <u>Evening Standard's</u> story and thought your reply dignified and splendid in the extreme. I think that gossipy journalists of that caliber should certainly be made to meet the people they libel, or their friends and relations, and see the grief that they can cause. I was also shocked by the frank anti-semitism [*sic*] of the article because I thought that we were the only nation suffering from it and that the British prided themselves on being far less tainted than we are here.

I think your reply, if the newspaper has the courage to run it, should more than undo the harm that the original article caused.

I am having the damnedest time over the Joyce business. As you know I was anxious to buy the library, but unfortunately it has gotten too expensive for me . . .

I must say, however, that I am glad to be back at work on the Joyce bibliography and a dozen or so other projects that I seem to get mixed up with.[45]

Unsurprisingly, the *Evening Standard* did not publish Lucie's letter, but she continued to set the record straight with Joyce scholars, whose works she read avidly if not always admiringly. In reply she told Slocum that she was on her way to Spain, but the 'rigamarole connected with an entry visa due to the fact that I am still the holder of a Nansen passport is beyond belief.[46] Iron Curtain is the nearest equivalent. So much so that my friend with whom I was to leave could not wait and went on without me – by car too – which made the proposed trip all the more tempting.' It is amazing to think that Lucie had lived and worked in Paris for over thirty years all the while retaining solely her Nansen passport. As it happened, she never assumed French citizenship. Instead, Lucie became an American citizen on 9 May 1959. She continued to keep Slocum abreast of the Joyce matters with which she and others were involved:

> I am sending you a photograph I had made of the Joyce portrait by Jacques-Emile Blanche. It was exhibited a little while ago at the Marcel Rochas collection dedicated to 'Moustache'. Isn't that something. I thought you might like this for your collection.
>
> The other night Maris Jolas called me over to hear the Third Programme (BBC) in which we all took part. Recordings from people in England, Ireland and France were pieced together, very well, I thought. But the éléments were completely déchainés and we had great trouble in hearing any of the first part. However the second part which came on later was clearer. But the noise was so awful that Maria quite seriously wondered as to who might be jamming the broadcast. I had a bit of trouble convincing her that no-one was jamming but that once again le destin had taken matters in hand.
>
> The [La Hune] show is definitely NOT going to London. For some reason Giorgio is against it and I am told we may all come and collect our belongings. So that is that. It is all very difficult. I quite see your point as to the purchasing of the Joyce books and papers. If I were you I would make a definite offer for what you want in writing and see what happens . . . I don't believe from what I know that anything definite has come up. But as I say the whole thing as usual is full of pitfalls.
>
> While you were away Mr. Kaplan sent me the proofs of my pamphlet. I read them carefully, went over all meticulously. And returned them. So you are probably busy with a million and one things, don't you bother. I think it will do as it is. Hope it appears soon. All OK with Steloff.[47]

After a long delay, at the start of April 1950, Slocum reported that he had carefully checked the proofs, which was fortunate because he found many minor errors that he instructed the printer to correct. In fact, there were so many that he had run up a large printer's bill, half of which he paid himself, because he had caught them so late. He also encouraged Lucie's plan to try and sell copies of her book in Paris, as she could not rely on the Gotham Book Mart to distribute them very effectively, especially abroad. He ended the letter by letting her know that 'Kaplan tells me that he should have your pamphlet ready shortly, and I am certainly looking forward to it'.[48] A month later, after the book had appeared, she replied to thank him and Kaplan for their work, telling him:

> I am very pleased with the book and so far I have had only compliments. Everyone, who has seen it including Maria think highly of the way it has been brought out, printed and its general appearance. I found French people particularly "admirative" as to the paper, printing, etc.
>
> I know a great deal of this is due to you, for I realize the time and trouble you have given up to it. I thank you again most sincerely.

> Personally I have the following to say – not recriminations, but just as you will see things to be noted if it ever goes into another edition as people seem to think it might do.
>
> a) The blue of the cover is too deep. It is not the shade I meant at all. (see necktie, see jacket of Ulysses, see Greek flag)
>
> b) some passages have been cut. By whom and why – non so. But if another edition comes out – back they should go. I know which ones they are. Maybe it is a question of number of pages.
>
> c) Mr. Kaplan says he found two errors. His are not important. But I have found three others. Two are entirely my fault.
>
> See the fragment reproduction of Paul's notes. I had a good look at it again and have discovered to my horror and annoyance that the words Llevan and Pantheon might have been deciphered by me in the first place, correctly. They are SULLIVAN (histoire Sullivan makes sense, doesn't it?) and Parution Haveth Childers etc.
>
> The third error is a footnote 'see Appendix C'. Well that belongs to page 38 and not page 35 and alludes to the Lefur letter and not Paul's letter to Pétain.

She urgently wanted to know at what price the book was being sold in New York and told him that a friend had encouraged her to expand on her recollection, but she confided to him:

> The only thing I can do is add various other details that have come to my memory since. But there is no time for that.
>
> Meanwhile I am contemplating translating it into French. Hope to get Marie Louise Soupault to do it. She did Kay Boyle's Year Before Last, several years back and did it well.[49] If she will consent, as she knew Joyce and was an integral part of our group though divorced from Philippe Soupault, she will "feel" the mood, which I think is important . . .
>
> I saw Geerbrandt [*sic*] yesterday. He is thrilled about going to London. The exhibition starts 12 June in Dover St. at the Gallery of Contemporary Art, he says. He confided further that he has never done a better exhibition than the Joyce one, and would love to do it over again except he can't show the same displays twice. I reminded him of his exhaustion at the time. Il en avait par dessus la tête, if you recall. Now it all seems like a fairy tale to him.

Unfortunately, the memoir was not translated into French: it may have had a more direct impact in Joyce's adopted country if it had been. Lucie was also eager to know what he thought of the volume and told him she was sending him a recent issue of the *Mercure de France* that contained 'a whole section on Joyce'.[50] Slocum replied immediately, thanking her for her kindness in sending the magazine. He informed her that the Gotham Book Mart was selling her book for only two dollars and that he had paid the bill for the printer's corrections in full, which he felt responsible for. He told her that review copies were being sent out and he would keep her informed of the critical reaction and addressed her veiled criticism about the book's production:

> I am distressed to hear of your dissatisfaction with points in the book. I claim responsibility for the cover being the wrong blue. I could not match the ULYSSES blue from the stocks that Kaplan made available to me, and I saw so many that I must have gone color blind. Forgive me. As to the cuts in the manuscript, I will check it with the original when it is returned to me and see what they are. I hope they were not

> serious and would be happy if you could tell me. I am sorry to hear about the errors in the text . . .
>
> I feel the book is a good-looking piece of printing and I am only sorry that for the cost we could not have had stiff covers. I have the greatest confidence in Kaplan and am going to have him do my bibliography when it is ready . . .
>
> This is a hasty letter . . . but I just wanted to say in closing that I have been reading a stack of Paul Léon's letters to Pinker and I think he was the most true and loyal friend that a man like Joyce could ever have had. I cannot tell you with what admiration that correspondence fills me. Some day I want you to read it over, and you will see what I mean.
>
> Meanwhile, thanks again for everything and I hope, on second thought you will feel a little bit better about the book, as I feel personally responsible for anything you did not find to your liking.[51]

Several thousand of Paul Léon's letters to Joyce's agent, publishers, translators, solicitor, as well as to Joyce himself, his patron, friends and admirers survive, all of which attest to Paul's dedication to Joyce personally and to the best interests of his family and works. Lucie replied immediately to reassure Slocum about her real feelings about the book and his pivotal role in getting it into print:

> PLEASE do not imagine I am displeased with the book. On the contrary, everyone seems to think it good and very well brought out. I am most appreciative of all the trouble you took to help me as I have written you countless times.
>
> The cut may not have been the printers [*sic*] fault. Or it may have been if it ruined his page count. It pertains to the part where I describe Joyce's gifts and there is a paragraph dealing with Joyce giving Paul canes which he always left in taxis and Paul asking for his last one which he had not lost when he was in the Drancy camp.[52] Also that Joyce liked hickory one.
>
> If ever there is a second edition, and if it ever comes out in French I am going to add another page or two – things I have remembered. Strange how suddenly one [*sic*] memory registers – a chance word or thought and you suddenly remember a string of events or an incident.
>
> Personally I did not think the cover would be as stiff as it is. It does not matter one way or another though you seem to feel a bound volume would have been better.
>
> Some time ago, upon receipt of Mr Kaplan's bill, I instructed the financial dept of [the] paper to send him the outstanding amount. I trust they have done so and that he has received the sum. But I do not see why you would pay for the corrections.
>
> The coquilles I have found – two of which are both your and my faults are the following: will you correct them in your copy.
>
> Fragment in Paul's hand. When we read it we could not make out the word Llevan, it is <u>Sullivan</u> (tout simplement). Then line below <u>Panthéon</u> is <u>Parution</u> and makes sense alluding to the publishing of HCE.
>
> On page 36, there should be an asterisk at intellectuels' See Appendix E.
>
> On page 35. Please delete footnote "see appendix" which has not business there.
>
> Page 38 refers to <u>Appendix C</u>. (after Paulhan incident.)
>
> There are some accents missing in French words – the Schatzmann letter for example. I have also made a mistake about Fouquet maitre d'hotel's name – it's not Celestin—but [53]

Then she returned to the theme that was the foundation of their friendship:

> I was very touched about what you say regarding the Pinker correspondences. I have an inkling – more than that even – of what you mean. Paul's devotion and the trouble he took for Joyce's affairs is and did always amaze me. For anyone as flegmatic [*sic*] as he was it was deeply curious. Joyce as a person must have aroused in Paul not only a deep friendship, but pity because of his entire helplessness to cope with that side of his life and business. To anyone engaged on a task as important as Joyce was, it would not have been humanely possible to interrupt his creative process and do the rest besides. I must say that Paul who was absolutely no good at all as far as his own affairs were concerned and who always had the deepest mépris for money defended Joyce's interests most incredibly. You will recall what Huebsch had to say about this at the Steloff bookshop the night I read my paper. "Had it not been for Léon, Joyce would have been far more lenient with his publishers.["]
>
> Well I believe this is all for the moment. Thanks again, a thousand times for everything.[54]

The following month, Lucie replied to Slocum's letter of 13 June 1950 to thank him for returning the remaining photographs and she gave him the fragment of Paul's manuscript for his collection. She promised to send him a copy of a transcript of a recent BBC broadcast on Joyce as well as a catalogue of London exhibition. She also told him:

> Maria has been to see the Joyces quite recently, Mrs. J. is quite sick. The cortisane [*sic*] cure she underwent helped at first so miraculously that she thought her arthritis has quite disappeared. But, as is frequently the case, with these new drugs – the suite – and results were terrible. She is crippled almost completely. It takes her five minutes to get out of a chair and at the moment I imagine Giorgio has been obliged to take her to the hospital. Their finances at the moment are in a bad way as London has not sent any money, transfers from country to country are still complicated . . .
>
> Have you any idea how my book is going? Here everyone admired the edition very much indeed, paper, printing, appearance, etc. Adrienne Monnier said to me "Quelle jolie plaquette". Miss Beach to whom I felt more or less obliged to present a copy seemed quite delighted, but will undoubtedly feel less so when she sees the mention in the Fragment of Histoire Beach Monnier. Tant pis. As Maria said too "after all that all history now."[55]

In July Slocum told her that he had been to the Gotham Book Mart and that they 'had sold 388 copies of her book, meaning that there were still 612 copies left, 'which is not at all bad and many more will be sold when the New Yorker does the piece they promised [Steloff]. May I reiterate my congratulations to you on the text and my regrets for any vagaries in the format.' He asked her to find out 'off the record what American University bought the Joyce Library':

> I rather think it was Harvard, but I don't know for certain and I would like to know as soon as possible as Yale wants to exhibit my collection and I don't want to see the situation of rival exhibits.
>
> It is a great disappointment to me that I couldn't have purchased the Joyce library . . .
>
> I am glad, however, to hear that it has gone to a library rather than a private individual and I only hope that whatever library it is makes it available equally to all students.[56]

Lucie's reply does not appear to have survived, but in his next letter Slocum thanks her for sending him a 'curious review' about her memoir from the *Times*, commenting:

> Ain't it peculiar the way the British nation dislikes Joyce?
>
> Reading between the lines the review practically said: "This would be a wonderful book if it had not been about Joyce". I don't understand it, but once the English get a hate on somebody or something they never get over it.
>
> How about taking time off from your multitudinous duties and dropping me a line in answer to my last couple of letters, as I miss hearing from you.[57]

After all the letters in which Lucie complained of not receiving a reply from Slocum, because he was so busy, now the shoe was on the other foot. She wrote him a long letter in reply and recounted a recent visit from Harriet Shaw Weaver to Paris and a get-together she arranged for the Joyce circle:

> I asked them all over for tea. The party lasted until 8 p.m. There were Sylvia Beach who is tout miel – as we say here (was afraid she'd never speak to me again because of the quotation "histoire Beach-Monnier"). Miss Harriet Weaver, the Jolases, Moune Gilbert (Stuart G. was not back in Paris yet, neither was Sam Beckett), Fanny Ventadour . . . and a young couple, Mr. and Mrs. Thomas Hess, editor of the Art news. I opened their first copy and there was a portrait of the artist by Jacques-Emile Blanche, a twin to the one I had photographed at the Rochas exhibit of Moustache (standing on my desk) . . . That was funny. The Gheerbrandts [*sic*] were also present.[58]
>
> Nothing in particular happened at the party except that it was nice to see everyone again.
>
> Yes I know about the sale and am happy it is all over. I understand Giorgio was in town to collect some money. I did not see him. I feel we all have done our duty, more than that, and now as far as I am concerned there is nothing more I can do. If they are careful they should have enough to live on for at least ten years.
>
> It was really a piece of luck. Without Maria Jolas and all the buildup and excitement, nothing would ever have been achieved. Even Janet Flanner did a great deal with her N. Yorker stories. It all helped. Have you seen the releases the University at Buffalo University has sent out. They might be interesting for your collection . . .
>
> My boy is due on leave tonight. I am waiting for him, he gets in at 3 a.m. He has done awfully well at his studies, got 8 A's out of 9. The 9th (American history) is a B. The University of Maryland have given him some kind of high award, brightest students in the US zone or some thing to that effect, judging by the little he told me on the phone and a letter received from his colonel's wife.
>
> He can get transferred to Baltimore or Harvard. Latter would be preferable.[59]

In reply, Slocum told Lucie:

> I have been up to Buffalo and seen the collection. Abbott, the Librarian, is a most agreeable person and I think it is in good hands, although from the point of view of American scholarship I would have preferred to see it in an Eastern library. The amount of use it will get in Buffalo will be proportionately less than it would get in Boston or New York, based on relative populations and accessibility. I think it is splendid that Maria was able to sell the library for $10,000 which, from the point of view of an open market, is considerably more than it is worth, and am glad to hear that it means security to the Joyce family. I was under the impression they already had a certain

> amount of security based on continuing royalties from the sale of Joyce's books, but I suppose the problem is getting money out of England . . .
>
> I hope your son decides to come to Harvard. He sounds like a brilliant student, and Harvard these days needs brilliant students. Do let us know if he should come over, as we would love to put him up for a while and help him get acclimatized here.[60]

Given the price that Joyce material achieves at auction today, it may sound incredible that Slocum, someone who certainly knew what he was talking about, would assert that $10,000 was 'considerably more than it is worth', but that was indeed the state of the market in Joyceana seventy years ago.[61] It is not known if Lucie replied, but Slocum was keen to keep her appraised of the Joyce events in New York:

> You might also tell her [Maria Jolas] that we had Sam Roth at the last meeting of the Joyce Society and that there were the most extraordinary fireworks you ever saw, as Roth tried to blame the whole thing on Ezra Pound and Ezra Pound's biographer, a serious young man named Edwards who was in the audience.[62] Roth did not deny that he pirated Joyce but said that Joyce had benefitted [*sic*] more from this piracy than he had, which is doubtless true, as Roth both went bankrupt and to jail, and the piracy got tremendous publicity for the book. It was a great affair with angry recriminations, resignations from the Joyce Society, and Lord knows what else. I haven't enjoyed myself so much in a month of Sundays. Next time, however, we have a very serious meeting with Abe Klein of Montreal as the principal speaker . . .
>
> Joyce plans proceed apace. Yale plans, as I think I wrote you, to exhibit my library – plus a few additions, opening the 12th of January and lasting for a few weeks. The bibliography is still almost finished, delayed by the fact that I have bogged down in the preparation of a chronology of Joyce's life and my colleague, Herbert Cahoon of the Public Library, is on his fifth revision of the collation of the individual volumes.[63]

With her memoir finally in print, Lucie's work at the *New York Herald Tribune* in Paris kept her very busy. Meanwhile, Slocum was spending more time in Arizona, though he continued to travel to Europe, making a point of seeing Lucie whenever he was in Paris. Nonetheless, their correspondence began to trail off. In one of her last letters to him, she wrote:

> I do know something I had to find out from Bob Kastor [Helen Joyce's brother], who wanted to tell Stevie Joyce, about Mrs. Joyce. She has been, as I told you, seriously ill, and from a letter from Maria I gather it was even more serious that I first thought. Maria, whom I have not seen, did tell me in a letter that there is a slight chance of Mrs. Joyce pulling through – but that if she does recover, she will be an invalid for life.[64]

Slocum wrote in his last reply that he was going on business to Frankfurt, but unfortunately there would not be an opportunity to come and see her in Paris. He recounted that he was in 'the middle of the most furious bickering with Yale over my Joyce library', which they wanted to break up 'and spread it all over their enormous library and I will not consent to this in any way, shape or form'. He ended the letter in this way:

> Sorry to have the bad news about Mrs. Joyce, because she is certainly such a nice person and certainly doesn't deserve the hard luck she has been having. I wish she could be persuaded to go back to Ireland, because I am sure that in many ways her heart is there. I blame the wretched bigotry of that country for not bringing Joyce's body home.[65]

Exposition en Hommage
A
JAMES
JOYCE

SA VIE : portraits de famille, objets personnels, photographies.

SON ŒUVRE : manuscrits, éditions rares, traductions, éditions piratées, illustrations originales de Matisse.

SON RAYONNEMENT : œuvres dédicacées de contemporains, livres et revues critiques.

Sa dernière bibliothèque.

15 OCTOBRE - 10 DECEMBRE 1949
Librairie-Galerie La Hune
170, BOULEVARD SAINT-GERMAIN, PARIS-6e

FIGURE 3.1: La Hune *Exposition en Hommage à James Joyce*, Paris (1949) – Courtesy of the Poetry Collection of the University Libraries, University at Buffalo, The State University of New York.

FIGURE 3.2: La Hune Gallery exhibition 'Family Tree' panel – Courtesy of the Poetry Collection of the University Libraries, University at Buffalo, The State University of New York.

Less than a month after Slocum's final surviving letter to Lucie, Nora Barnacle Joyce died on 10 April 1951. She is buried beside her husband in Fluntern Cemetery in Zurich, Switzerland. A decade later, Harriet Shaw Weaver, Joyce's publisher, patron and literary executrix, died on 14 October 1961, having left her extensive collection of Joyce manuscripts and letters to the British Library and the National Library of Ireland. Almost exactly a year later Sylvia Beach, founder of Shakespeare and Company and the first publisher of *Ulysses* and *Pomes Penyeach*, died on 5 October 1962. Her vast Shakespeare and Company collection is in the Firestone Library, Princeton University, while her equally impressive collection of Joyce material complements the Joyce family's collection in the Poetry Collection, University at Buffalo.

Born in Moscow on 21 November 1899, Lucie Ponisowsky Léon (Noel) passed away on 3 May 1972 in Paris after a long and successful career as a fashion journalist. She continued to be concerned with James Joyce's family and works throughout her life. Maria McDonald Jolas, translator and peace activist, died on 4 March 1987. A decade later, John Jermain Slocum, Sr., retired Foreign Service officer and prominent early collector, whose 1953 Joyce bibliography is still the standard reference in the field, died on 12 August 1997 at the age of 83, and so another circle of Joycean friends came to a close.

NOTES

1. Richard M. Kain, *Fabulous Voyager: James Joyce's Ulysses* (Chicago: The University of Chicago Press, 1947).
2. Henriette (Genia) Léon was married to Wladimir Hirschmann.
3. This work became John J. Slocum and Herbert Cahoon, *A Bibliography of James Joyce, 1882–1941* (New Haven: Yale University Press, 1953).
4. 18 October 1947; John J. Slocum to Lucie Noel. The top copy of this letter is housed in the National Library of Ireland (NLI MS 36,937/11), along with the rest of Slocum's correspondence with Lucie and some bottom copies of her letters to him. Hereafter cited by date; correspondents and NLI. There is also a bottom copy of this letter at the Beinecke Library, Yale University, James Joyce Collection, GEN MSS 112, Box 27, Folder 538, which contains Lucie's letters to Slocum and many bottom copies of his correspondence to her. Hereafter cited by date; correspondents and Beinecke. All of Slocum's correspondence is in typescript, and unless otherwise specified Noel's correspondence is also in typescript.
5. Although non-practising, Lucie (Ponizowsky) Léon was also Jewish.
6. This was Alexander (Choura) Léon (1894–1944).
7. Lucie recounts the story in her memoir (see Chapter 2, Appendix G).
8. 10 November 1948; Noel to Slocum; Beinecke; holograph.
9. Owner of the At the Sign of the Black Manikin bookshop and founder of the Black Manikin Press, Edward W. Titus (1870–1952) was a well-known American expatriate, collector, publisher and book dealer in Paris in the 1920s and 30s. He and his wife, Helena Rubenstein, were friends and supporters of Sylvia Beach and her Shakespeare and Company.
10. 19 November 1948; Noel to Slocum; c/o Marre Kahler; 427 Park Avenue, New York City; Beinecke.

11. Paul's letters to Lucie before 1940 are not known to survive. See Chapter 5 for the letters Paul wrote to Lucie from Drancy and Compiègne.
12. See Chapter 2, pp. 56–7.
13. Leon Edel, *James Joyce: The Last Journey* (New York: Gotham Book Mart, 1947), which is forty-four pages long, whereas Lucie's book ended up being sixty-three pages.
14. 28 February 1949; Noel to Slocum; Beinecke and copy in duplicate at NLI.
15. Several versions of her talk and of her memoir survive, including one copy of the memoir marked '3rd copy' of the latter in the Slocum Collection, a copy of the talk in the NLI (MS 36,932/18) and a pre-final version of the memoir in the NLI (MS 36,932/22). Further copies of both the talk and the memoir are currently still in the Léon family collection.
16. 11 March 1949; Slocum to Noel; Beinecke. There is a clipping of Lucie's article in Slocum's files.
17. Maria Jolas, editor, *A James Joyce Yearbook* (Paris: Transition Press, 1949).
18. 25 March 1949; Noel to Slocum; only her copy at NLI survives.
19. After the La Hune auction was completed, Slocum was disappointed that he had not at least acquired Joyce's newspaper clipping collection. Harriet Shaw Weaver generously gave him her equally extensive collection, which is also now part of the Slocum collection at the Beinecke Library.
20. See Chapter 2, Appendix C, as well as Paul's 'Souvenir de Joyce' in Chapter 4.
21. This is Appendix H in memoir.
22. This is Appendix E in memoir.
23. 15 April 1949; Noel to Slocum; Beinecke and copy at NLI.
24. n.d. [late April 1949]; Slocum to Noel; NLI.
25. 31 August 1949; Slocum to Noel; NLI and copy at Beinecke.
26. These are Lucie's ellipses.
27. 26 September 1949; Noel to Slocum; Beinecke and copy at NLI.
28. 6 October 1949; Slocum to Noel; NLI and copy at Beinecke.
29. These are Lucie's ellipses.
30. These are also Lucie's ellipses.
31. 14 October 1949; Noel to Slocum; Beinecke and copy at NLI.
32. There are only three photos in the memoir and it is not known what the fourth photo may have been.
33. Appendix I.
34. 20 October 1949; Slocum to Noel; NLI and copy at Beinecke.
35. Jean-Marc Théolleyre, 'James Joyce à Saint-Germain-des-Prés', *Le Monde*, 26 October 1949.
36. 25 October 1949; Noel to Slocum; Beinecke and copy at NLI. See Chapter 1 for more information about Lucie's family.
37. 15 November 1949; Maurice Kaplan to Slocum; NLI.
38. 30 November 1949; Slocum to Noel; NLI and copy at Beinecke.
39. 5 December 1949; Noel to Slocum; Beinecke and copy at NLI.
40. 14 December 1949; Slocum to Noel: Beinecke.
41. 27 December 1949; Frances Steloff to Noel; NLI and scribal typescript copy at Beinecke.

42. 6 January 1950; Noel to Slocum; Beinecke.
43. Here is the text of Horace Thorogood's article Lucie prepared for John Slocum, which is in his collection in the Beinecke Library:

BOOKS AND PERSONS

I learn that the James Joyce exhibition, big Paris success in the autumn is [being] brought to London by the Institute of Contemporary Art, will open early February in the National Book League's gallery.

It is time for it, John Lane is publishing, January 12, the first cheap edition on this country of Ulysses (18 s).

When, during the war, Joyce fled from Paris to Switzerland, leaving unpaid rent, his landlord auctioned his effects except those snatched beforehand by friends.

Pictures went for the price of their frames. Many items thus dispersed have been recovered.

Joyce's Jewish helper Leon, deported by the Germans, even risked underground "return" to rescue certain unsold remainders from the flat – was discovered and shot.

One sealed parcel of letters, too frank for contemporary publication, rests with the Dublin National Library, not to be opened till fifty years hence. But Patricia Hutchins JAMES JOYCE OF DUBLIN will throw light on the subject.

44. 6 January 1950; typescript copy in Beinecke.
45. 5 February 1950; Slocum to Noel; NLI and copy at Beinecke.
46. Nansen passports were originally issued by the League of Nations to stateless persons and refugees as internationally recognized identity papers and to facilitate travel.
47. 17 February 1950; Noel to Slocum; Beinecke.
48. 7 April 1950; Slocum to Noel; Beinecke.
49. This appeared as *Avant-hier* (Paris: Calmann-Lévy, 1937).
50. 8 May 1950; Noel to Slocum; Beinecke. This was the 1 May 1950 issue of the *Mercure de France* that contained reminiscences by Sylvia Beach, Stuart Gilbert, Maria Jolas, as well as translations of a selection of Joyce's poems by Auguste Morel and Annie Hervieu.
51. 18 May 1950: Slocum to Noel; Beinecke; copy in NLI.
52. Lucie had the following paragraphs in an earlier draft of the memoir: 'As I have said, Joyce never forgot a friend's birthday. I can see him arriving carrying a gift which he and Mrs. Joyce had taken the time and trouble to select. They had given the matter a great deal of thought. They shopped at Mappin and Webb's, and at Dunhill's in the rue de la Paix. My husband had an assortment of presents – a clock, a Dunhill ashtray, a silver cigarette lighter, a Jensen cigarette box, also a number of canes he invariably left in taxis . . . I have some bibelots, an antique box, a Louis Phillipe lamp and a number of other gifts.

    'There was a shagreen handled cane my husband always carried, this one somehow survived from being left in a taxi. It was later one of the things he had wanted most when he was in the German concentration camp and which I got to him before he was taken off on his last journey to an "unknown destination."' Lucie provided the following note: '"Unknown Destination" is the official name the Germans used when deporting millions of innocent people for mass murder and extermination' (typescript in Léon family collection).
53. Lucie left the change blank.
54. 24 May 1950; Noel to Slocum; copy only in NLI.

55. 30 June 1950; Noel to Slocum; Beinecke; copy at NLI.
56. 9 July 1950; Slocum to Noel; NLI; copy at Beinecke.
57. 23 September 1950; Slocum to Noel; NLI; copy at Beinecke.
58. The ellipses in this paragraph are Lucie's.
59. 22 October 1950; Noel to Slocum; Beinecke.
60. 4 November 1950; Slocum to Noel; copy only at Beinecke.
61. According to the website MeasuringWorth.com, '$10000 in 1950 has a relative price worth of $108,068.52 today using the Consumer Price Index' (accessed on 3 February 2022). For comparison's sake, Sotheby's sale of the much smaller remainder of the Stanislaus Joyce Estate in July 2007 sold for £721,620, including a record-breaking £240,800 for just one 1909 letter from Joyce to Nora Barnacle. The NLI acquired the 'Joyce 2002 Papers' from Sotheby's for €12.2 million.
62. See John Hamilton Edwards, *A Critical Biography of Ezra Pound: 1885–1922* (PhD dissertation: University of California, Berkeley, 1952).
63. 12 December 1950; Slocum to Noel; NLI; copy at Beinecke.
64. 14 February 1951; Noel to Slocum; Beinecke.
65. 16 March 1951; Slocum to Noel; copy only at Beinecke.

CHAPTER FOUR

On James Joyce

PAUL L. LÉON

ON JOYCE'S *HAVETH CHILDERS EVERYWHERE*

A five-page fair copy holograph manuscript sketch is all that survives of Paul's critical reflections on James Joyce's 'Work in Progress'. It is unfortunate that he did not revise and complete this essay or return to the topic again, given his decade-long engagement with the book that he helped to usher into the world as *Finnegans Wake*.

Although undated, it is most likely Paul's initial reaction to *Haveth Childers Everywhere*, which was published in June 1930 by Henry Babou and Jack Kahane in Paris and by the Fountain Press in New York. Made to Joyce's precise instructions, it was a lavishly produced large-format book, of which 685 copies in four states were published.[1] The essay is of historical and critical importance because it reveals Paul's earliest attempts to express his ideas on 'Work in Progress' as he was actively working with Joyce. It is also one of the first critical studies to specifically link Joyce's latest work with that of both Picasso and Proust.

Joseph Prescott edited the text in 1958, while the manuscript was still in Lucie's possession.[2] We have chosen to reproduce an edited version of Paul's essay based on that original manuscript, which is now in the National Library of Ireland.[3] The elliptical nature of the sentences and the numerous revisions throughout indicate that Paul left it as an incomplete draft, or that it was merely a series of ideas that he planned to elaborate and complete at a later stage. Therefore, we have taken the liberty of providing the complete quotations and citations that he certainly would have included himself. We have also silently emended his relatively few misspellings and clarified some of his paratactical constructions.

On 3 June 1930, Paul wrote to his brother Alexander (who was known as Choura):

> Currently, I find myself very busy with literature. — I have been working with Joyce. This name probably means nothing to you, but he is great, the greatest writer in the world in our time. And first of all he writes in a way no-one can understand . . . You might call it a kind of pidgin-English, which no doubt is perfect in its way. It is also perfectly amusing to translate into incomprehensible formulas the simplest ideas and to believe that they are works of art.

Lucie, who planned on publishing this letter in French and English after 1945, added an editorial note at the bottom of the sheet: 'This was in 1930. As time passed I must add that my husband had completely changed his mind about Joyce's work. He did not doubt for one moment his entire "creation" WAS a chef-d'oeuvre.'[4]

* * * * * *

This then is the latest work — a fragment of Joyce's book — the Picasso of modern literature. The association of these two names seems to me symbolical of a spiritual relation that is more than paradoxical or skin-deep. I remember some of Picasso's work, at least one of them, the Lady with the fan,[5] being defined <u>as a corpse of beauty</u> and in fact such pictures are at first sight disintegrations and dissociations of what [in] life 'natural' had been a woman with a fan. Dissociated and disintegrated there were left only triangles, squares, semi-circles, [and] circles each carrying its own personality — its own colour. But are dissociations & disintegrations anything else but the typical phenomena of death? The death of the 'Lady with a Fan' was however as necessary for her reincarnation in colours as death is necessary for nature to create its unity, for unless the seed dies . . .

Another parallel seems obvious — when Picasso disintegrated his model, he wanted to free himself from the conventional rule — called perspective — which had alone allowed the painter to add a third dimension to the two of his canvas. This solution of the problem of depth in pictures was cramping him — or should I say cramkrieging or perplauging him[6] — Haveth Childers or Anna Livia were confronted with a parallel problem that was cramping the writer — time! place![7] — logical perspective and unity obsessing not only the writer but the reader — Liberty! And you will find the names of 600 rivers and of some 50 cities interwoven in Mr Joyce's text — so that you will be bound to obtain flashes and visions of the world. Freedom from logical perspective that makes a hero to be born on the first page and marry, divorce or die on the last, a cramkrieged and perplauged life — as if life was not continuing after the hero — any hero died! Take an aeroplane, rise high enough and you might see a river from its sources to the moment where it dies in the sea. I purposely say where because the notion of time is thus translated into a notion of space — for if you let your motor stop you will hear the flowing of the river — the zooming drops transformed into waves — ceaselessly, endlessly . . . Just walk in a city and you will hear the zooming of the city, its inner life changing as years go on, imagine yourself in the heart of this rhythm and you will feel at once the owner of this city — you will live by its growth, we all do, we model our life according to the city we live in — in fact it is ourselves who make a city what it is — we give it decoration, its lighting, its shops its food, the numberless efforts of many generations they are all but one continuous action that lives again in us — ceaselessly, endlessly — . . . to die in the sea as rivers do, to pass into earth again . . . for cities die and are born. You surely know the city of Les Baux in the Provence — in the Middle Ages a city of magnificent distances, goodwalledabout[8] with Talus and counterscaps and pale palisades — then thousands of people sought shelter under its goodcountsinturns, today its population is 80 spitfired perplauged and cramkrieged citizens . . .

> ἔσσεται ἦμαρ ὅτ' ἄν ποτ' ὀλώλῃ Ἴλιος ἱρὴ
> καὶ Πρίαμος καὶ λαὸς ἐυμμελίω Πριάμοιο,[9]

<u>Haveth Childers</u> is about a city — the city of Dublin — it is an epic description of Dublin — it is a poetical work. It seems to be written in prose for the usual attributi of verse cannot be found. But let us take the most general division of prose & poetry and we shall then be sure of not committing an error.

A piece of prose always serves a purpose, it exists in order to convey a certain thought. It will then have served its purpose when the thought will have been assimilated by the reader to such an extent that he will be able to render it in his own words. The piece of prose will have then ceased to exist — the thought alone will then continue to live in its logical nudity.

A piece of poetry is different — if it conveys a thought — it conveys it in very precise form and it will exist only as the form into which the writer will have shaped it. [It] will continue living — and no reader will ever be able to recreate it unless he recreates the same words.

Try and render in your own words a sentence like this:

> I wound around my swanchen's neckplace a school of schells of moyles marine to swing their saysangs in her silents: and, upping her as king's count, her aldritch cry olos unheading, what though exceeding bitter, I pierced her beak with order of the Danabrog (Cunnig's great! Soll leve! Soll leve![10]

and yet it is quite understandable. The city sent out little resorts[11] near the sea that were founded round the river encircling it like a wonderful necklace,[12] and in the evening amorous pairs go out of town to sing or make some music in the silences of the city. Does not a river resemble a Swan, but you know Swans (in Latin they are called Olos)[13] are considered regal birds in England and are marked with the King's initials near their beak — and it is a Danish custom, and Swans sing only once in their life before they die — just like a river before it dives into the sea . . .

But the complete thought of the author will exist only in the form he shaped it for logic in a poetical work demands a garment — sometimes a beautiful garment. I think this is a beautiful one: Why?

As every work of art — a poetical creation — is emotional, and its artistical worth, if such a formula were possible, could be expressed in an 'intellectualised emotion' — or an emotion sifted through with the brain. What really counts is the overwhelming force which urges a writer to decipher within his soul that world which is the only reality: the world of truth, of beauty of eternity.

> Car l'instinct dicte le devoir et l'intelligence fournit les prétextes pour l'éluder. Seulement les excuses ne figurent point dans l'art, les intentions n'y sont pas comptées, à tout moment l'artiste doit écouter son instinct, ce qui fait que l'art est ce qu'il y a de plus réel, la plus austère école de la vie, et le vrai Jugement dernier . . . cet écrivain, qui, d'ailleurs, pour chaque caractère, aurait à en faire apparaître les faces les plus opposées, pour faire sentir son volume comme celui d'un solide devrait préparer son livre minutieusement, avec de perpétuels regroupements de forces, comme pour une offensive, le supporter comme une fatigue, l'accepter comme une règle, le construire comme une église, le suivre comme un régime, le vaincre comme un obstacle, le conquérir comme une amitié, le suralimenter comme un enfant, le créer comme un monde, sans laisser de côté ces mystères qui n'ont probablement leur explication que dans d'autres mondes et dont le pressentiment est ce qui nous émeut le plus dans la vie et dans l'art.[14]

It is not a romantic author — it is not Rousseau — it is Proust I am quoting and though probably Mr Joyce would strongly object to me I think it is in this instinctive regrouping, constant victory over obstacles, perpetual architectural construction, conquests of friendship, and above all in that musical connexion with what is probably a different world that the real life of book lies[15] — and makes it sound like a prayer: to Whom?

But I have probably overlooked the principal — Haveth Childers — is about Dublin — it is an epic about any city — which feeds millions of people and is proud of it, and [it] is vain. Hence next to the prayer and often pitched in a higher key you will find a good healthy laugh — 'Amtsadam, sir, to you',[16] and on on . . . till 'Joahanahanahana!'[17]

'Joahanahanahana!' — that laugh which kills every proud, self-satisfied and vain feeling which spells quietude, motion-lessness hence means death:

for I waged love on her: and spoiled her undines
And she wept: O my lors!
— Till we meet!
— Ere we part!
— Tollollall!
— This time a hundred years![18]

It is good to remind people that when their head is touching Heaven as a rule their feet are in the mud! It happens so often.[19]

So should one be 'firm with her. And did take the reached of my delights';[20] one is responsible to it, unless one wishes to fall entirely into death.

These seem to me to be the elements of the dissociation and disintegration of the life we come into contact with every day, but this death was necessary in order to create new life — life of and in art which is as eternal as the life of nature. I have started this by speaking of a corpse of beauty — does not the end of it spell a new life — from the disintegrated & dissociated remnants of former beauty there has been constructed a new — eternally youthful cathedral where in a comic mysterious way one hears the rhythm of nature itself — unless the seed[21] dies . . .

'SOUVENIRS DE JOYCE'
BY PAUL LEON

The text presented here is based on what appears to be Paul's original letter to Jean Paulhan (revised by him in black ink and pencil) that survives in an eight-page typescript copy in the National Library of Ireland.[1] A few minor typographical errors have been silently emended.

* * * * * *

Cher Monsieur,

Huit mois se sont déjà écoulés depuis la dernière fois que j'ai vu Mr. Joyce, et bientôt quatre que les journaux nous ont apporté la nouvelle de sa mort. Votre petit mot cause autant plus de peine et de regrets que je n'ai jamais consigné par écrit aucun fait, aucune conversation échangés avec lui pendant les quelque douze années au cours desquelles nous nous sommes vus au moins une ou deux fois par jour, sauf pendant les vacances et les voyages que nous prenions et faisions chacun de notre côté. Le temps fait déjà du sien ; les souvenirs s'estompent et s'effacent . . . Je crois cependant qu'il est mon devoir de vous répondre, mais cette réponse sera forcément plus générale que je ne le voudrais, surtout parce que je n'ai plus accès á la correspondance que nous avons échangée, soit pendant nos séparations, soit même parfois d'une rue à l'autre, entre deux entrevues. Elle sera peut-être aussi moins impersonnelle qu'elle ne devrait être, et vous me le pardonnerez, je l'espère, car c'est là le grand écueil de tous les souvenirs écrits après coup, même par des mémorialistes professionnels, dont je ne suis pas.

L'impression la plus générale que je garde et garderai de l'homme est son exquise douceur liée à une infinie compréhension. Il ne s'agit pas ici d'une qualité du cœur que je voudrais mettre en relief et qui toucherait à des côtés trop personnels et intimes pour en écrire aujourd'hui, mais d'un trait plus général faisant en quelque sorte partie des forces élémentaires de sa nature. Aussi, douceur et compréhension ne signifiaient pas chez luis faiblesse ou même indifférence, mais elles s'alliaient à une force intérieure, une activité spirituelle contenue que je n'ai rencontrées que chez lui. Le destin a voulu que cette force et cette activité, il eut à les employer tous les jours. Il viendra un temps où l'on pourra écrire sa vie – et l'on jugera alors combien le destin s'acharna contre lui, combien il eut besoin de tout son courage pour combattre, pour dominer les évènements . . . Aujourd'hui il suffira de l'indiquer pour mettre sur la piste le futur biographe.

Dès maintenant, toutefois, celui qui est curieux de l'âme humaine n'aurait qu'à se pencher avec quelque attention sur <son œuvre> celle-ci pour <les> la découvrir car, et c'est là, je crois, la clé de son œuvre, il n'existait pour lui aucune séparation entre la vie vécue et l'œuvre littéraire. Son œuvre est une perpétuelle confession et par là, il s'apparente aux plus grands romantiques. Je sais bien que nous nous trahissons dans nos écrits, même les plus objectifs, mais je sais aussi qu'en voulant se décrire et se peindre on se travestit sans jamais pouvoir se décrire et se peindre fidèlement, pleinement, entièrement. Les influences du milieu, de l'époque, de la vie quotidienne, de nos rencontres fortuites comme de nos liaisons nous cachent à nous-mêmes. Or, Joyce veut atteindre à la sincérité absolue, à de qu'il y a de plus humain en nous. Abolir le papier blanc que l'on couvre de caractères, abolir la convention de l'expression de soi-même, abolir jusqu'au corps même qui s'interpose entre le 'moi' le plus profond, le 'moi au delà de l'âme' de Pascal et le monde extérieur, abolir la main qui écrit, l'oreille qui entend, l'œil qui voit . . . En ce dernier point le destin impitoyable lui a fait faire plus de la moitié du chemin . . . Mais alors, est-on réduit au silence ? L'œuvre de Joyce est une preuve éclatante du contraire ; mais elle est là pour prouver aussi le courage, la persévérance, la force intérieure, l'énergie spirituelle nécessaires et à peine suffisants pour vaincre tous les obstacles, pour surmonter toutes les douleurs, pour atteindre la perfection. A la juger à sa juste valeur, comme la jugera postérité, son œuvre effraiera par la peine qu'elle à dû coûter ; la vie d'un homme apparaîtra comme conçue sur une échelle trop petite en comparaison avec l'immensité du labeur.

La liaison intime et indissoluble entre la vie et l'œuvre comporte un autre aspect qu'il est, peut-être, plus important encore de consigner ici, car il échappera forcément à la postérité : c'est l'influence de l'œuvre sur la vie. Perpétuelle confession signifiait pour Joyce création perpétuelle : il créait l'ambiance, le climat qui l'entouraient, et il les créait à chaque instant. On a suffisamment parlé de dévots, de chapelle, de tour d'ivoire dans laquelle il aurait vécu retiré et inaccessible à personne. Rien ne peut être plus faux. Je ne connais personne qui eut autant que lui la haine de pontifier, d'enseigner, de poser. Sauf de rares exceptions ; ses disciples sont ceux qu'il ne connut pas et qui ne le connaîtront jamais, car il s'agit d'un phénomène qui relève de l'histoire de la littérature. Ce à quoi je fais allusion, ce sont ses connaissances et ses amis. Faire une connaissance nouvelle, se créer une nouvelle liaison, était pour lui toujours un problème difficile à résoudre, une œuvre à créer. Aussi je crains que bien peu de gens ont su et ont senti combien derrière son silence il se cachait de pensées mûries, de précautions infinies, de tendre bienveillance, de véritable respect de l'humanité. En l'approchant on était enveloppé comme dans un fin réseau tissé de demi-pensées, de demi-sentiments, dans une ambiance si douce qu'il était difficile d'y résister, et d'autant plus douce qu'il n'y entrait aucune contrainte. Mais pour y pénétrer il faillait faire un effort personnel, il y avait danger véritable de s'y laisser aller sans réfléchir, car elle ne donnait qu'une amitié à toute épreuve, un attachement combien désintéressé, un délice spirituel. Elle ne donnait pas ce que le grand nombre y cherchait : les uns la découverte de la vérité, les autres des relations mondaines. Cette attente déçue explique peut-être le fait, noté par son récent biographe, que bien des amitiés se sont durant sa vie muées en haines implacables et sans espoir. Mais c'est sûrement elle qui explique la réputation d'inapprochable qui fut la sienne.

Que cette création perpétuelle, cet effort spirituel constant comportassent des risques pour lui-même aussi bien que pour son entourage nul n'en disconviendra, et c'est une raison des mille précautions qu'il prenait, de son conformisme extérieur aussi complet que possible, de son exquise politesse, car il était conscient combien cette création cachait de force quasi-titanesque qui pouvait dominer toutes les conventions et bouleverser , les traditions les plus enracinées, les 'vérités' les plus établies. Bien des écrivains illustres ont dominé toute leur œuvre, d'autre ont été dominés par lui ; je crois que Joyce restera l'exemple le plus parfait de l'effort le plus constant et le plus réussi de rendre la vie adéquate à l'œuvre. Aussi malgré le tourment et la douleur, le doute et la passion, la cruauté et les déchirements que le destin ne lui a pas épargnés et que lui n'a pas épargnés à son œuvre, je garde et je garderai toujours le souvenir d'une sérénité faite de douceur et de compréhension qui constituait le climat de son âme rappelant la sérénité de la nature dont il ne cessait d'être l'observateur émerveillé.

Un souvenir me revient à la mémoire. Je partais en vacance fin septembre 1930 et Joyce tint à m'accompagner à pied un bout du chemin vers la Gare de Lyon. Je suis un bien pauvre marcheur, tous le contraire de Joyce, aussi aimais-je modérément nos flâneries, mais, je crois qu'il se sentait plus sûr pour traverser les rues lorsque je m'appuyait sur son bras. Nous devions faire bien piètre figure tous les deux dans les rues de Paris – aussi Philippe Soupault nous avait – il baptisés : l'aveugle et le paralytique. Nous cheminions tranquillement le long du Boulevard Raspail lorsque surgit soudain devant nous une jeune fille qui l'arrêta pour lui dire avec quelque gaucherie mais bien gentiment un compliment sur son œuvre. Joyce leva ses pauvres yeux vers le ciel encore ensoleillé, puis les ramena sur les arbres clôturés du boulevard et dit : « Mais admirez plutôt la nature, Mademoiselle, le ciel et même ces pauvres arbres. » Si cette jeune fille lit, par hasard, ces lignes elle se reconnaîtra peut-être, mais je voudrais qu'elle sût combien de vérité se cachait derrière ses paroles qui paraissent banales, non pas de modestie d'emprunt, mais de réelle admiration pour l'univers créé, pour ses couleurs qu'il ne distinguait qu'avec peine et que cette peine même lui faisait apprécier avec plus de plénitude, pour ces formes conventionnellement belles ou laides mais toujours en mouvement, pour ces sons que dernièrement encore, couché sur l'herbe dans l'Allier nous écoutions ensemble pour êtres humains qui le peuplent et l'animent de leurs pensées, de leurs passions, bonnes ou mauvaises, belles ou laides, harmonieuses ou discordantes.

Cette admiration devenait chez lui véritable nostalgie lorsqu'il s'agissait de l'eau. Le bord de la mer exerçait sur lui une attraction insurmontable. Mais où qu'il fût en vacances, son premier soin était de chercher un fleuve, une rivière ou, à défaut un rû. Sa première promenade était pour eux ; combien d'heures avons-nous passé à observer le calme écoulement de la Seine du parapet de l'Alma ou du Pont Royal.

Le mystère de l'attraction de l'eau sur Joyce . . . mais il est là, décrit en toutes lettres, dans son bouleversant, étonnant, pantagruélique et romantique « Finnegans Wake » et surtout dans dernières page faites de phrases courtes, saccadées, remuantes, ondoyantes, courantes, se précipitant et chevauchant les [unes] sur les autres. N'est-ce point là le retour du fleuve, de la Liffey qui se jette en s'évanouissant dans les bras de son père l'Océan, pour se muer sous les rayons chauds du soleil en nuage remontant vers les sources où elle redeviendra goutte d'eau pour retomber et grossir le fleuve qui revient à la mer.

Parmi les mille et une critiques que j'ai parcourues, je n'ai pas remarqué ce qui pourtant saute aux yeux. L'étonnant post-scriptum qui termine l'ouvrage finit sur une phrase inachevée, un article « le » (the). Le substantif auquel il se rattache forme le premier mot du volume, et c'est « cours d'eau » (riverrun). Il ne m'appartient pas de déchiffrer tous les sens de ce qu'on est enclin parfois de considérer comme un cryptogramme ; c'est et ce sera la tâche des générations futures de critiques et historiens de la littérature, je voudrais simplement apporter le témoignage de celui qui a assisté à l'écclosion de l'œuvre. Ce post-scriptum était mûri et porté dans le prodigieux cerveau qui l'enfanta il y a peut-être des années. Son premier jet constituait une ou deux pages et demie et écrit en une après-midi de décembre 1938. Ce fut comme une délivrance. Joyce me l'apporta vers huit heures et demie à notre rendez-vous habituel chez la bonne Madame Lapeyre à son bistro du coin de la rue Grenelle et de la rue Bourgogne. Il partit ensuite pour rejoindre à diner Madame Joyce au Fouquets où je le rejoignis une heure et demie plus tard. Se [*sic*] belle-fille nous l'y lut une première fois – et on pouvait observer le plaisir que Joyce prouvait à écouter les mots écrits revivre dans la plaisante lecture, prendre consistance et couleur. Ce fut une des rares occasions où je le sentis satisfait ou même fier de lui-même, lorsque'au milieu d'une orchestration de vaisselle remuée, entrechoquée et tintante ses mots à lui créaient une harmonie au sein de la discordance des autres sons. Après . . . après ce fut fiévreux de toutes les heures, de toutes le minutes du jour comme de la nuit. Je crains bien que Joyce ne dormît que bien peu durant un mois ou six semaines. Nous étions pressés par l'imprimeur qui m'avait promis d'envoyer un exemplaire pour l'anniversaire de Joyce, le 2 février. Il fallut même abandonner la lecture des troisièmes épreuves. Le Post-Scriptum prenait de l'ampleur et de la consistance. De deux pages manuscrites il finit par devenir une douzaines de pages imprimées. Et les péripéties . . . Tous les amis de Joyce se mirent à taper. Madame Jolas tapait à Neuilly, Mr. Gilbert tapait rue Jean du Bellay, je dictais rue Casimir-Périer. Tout se centralisait vers sept heures rue Edmond Valentin au siège du cerveau directeur. Un jour j'allais chercher le pensum de Mr. Gilbert j'arrive rue Edmond Valentin et parvenu au quatrième je m'aperçois soudain que j'avais oublié l'enveloppe dans le taxi. Course chez moi, téléphone à Londres, demande de nouvelles épreuves car les additions se faisaient déjà sur les placards. Mais cela signifiait trois jours, de retard, trois jours perdus car nous étions un vendredi soir et je n'avais trouvé à Londres qu'une secrétaire de service. Heureusement j'avais eu affaire avec un chauffeur de probité éprouvée. Deux heures plus tard l'enveloppe nous était restituée dans son intégrité. Ce furent cependant deux heures bien dures pour Joyce mais je n'entendis durant ces deux heures ni une plaine, ni un reproche. Les épreuves une fois envoyées ce ne fut pas la fin. Il n'y avait plus le temps de les envoyer par la poste, aussi le téléphone marchait-il avec l'éditeur à Londres et l'imprimeur à Glasgow. Téléphone et télégraphe marchaient à plein rendement. Je crains bien d'avoir empoisonné pendant un mois la vie du directeur littéraire de MM. Faber & Faber, Mr. Richard de La Mare. Mais le livre parut enfin le 2 février, bien que pour des raisons commerciales il ne fut mis en vente que le 4 mai. Finnegans Wake n'appartient plus à Joyce, il a sa vie propre . . .

Mais l'homme n'est plus . . . Il me coûte de vous l'écrire et je voudrais ne pas y croire. Les événements nous avaient séparés et l'absence qui se prolonge me rend d'autant plus difficile d'admettre que je ne le reverrai plus . . . La porte est plus grande car ce cerveau infatigable enfantait quelque chose de nouveau . . . un réveil de Finnegan : Wait until Finnegan awakes, me disait-il.

Mais je ne puis finir cette lettre sans que ma pensée n'aille à ceux qui lui étaient plus cher, à Madame Joyce, à son fils et à sa fille. Il m'est pénible que dans les circonstances actuelles c'est la seule manière dont je puisse me rappeler à leur souvenir . . .

Veuillez agrée, cher Monsieur, l'expression de mes sentiments les meilleurs,

X.X.X.

'IN MEMORY OF JOYCE' BY PAUL L. LÉON (TRANSLATED BY LUCIE NOEL AND MARIA JOLAS)

While Paul wrote the essay on *Haveth Childers Everywhere* at the start of their friendship, the reflections on Joyce that he recorded for posterity in the letter he wrote to Jean Paulhan in May 1941 represent a dozen years of virtually daily contact. For over a decade, Paul selflessly helped Joyce and his family cope with the many personal issues that they had to confront, as well as managing the writer's complex legal and financial affairs, all the while working with him to ready 'Work in Progress' to become *Finnegans Wake*. Given all of his own intellectual interests and scholarly work, it is unsurprising that Paul had no intention of being Joyce's Boswell. Nonetheless, in the letter he confesses a certain 'sadness and regret that I should never have set down any of the conversations I had with him'.

Once she and Alexis had escaped from Paris to relative safety in Monaco, Lucie recounts the great joy she felt when she saw that Paul's letter had finally been published in *Poésie*, a French Resistance journal edited by Pierre Seghers. She writes:

> Paul was so shattered that for days he could not bring himself to speak of Joyce. Jean Paulhan, then publisher of the *Nouvelle Revue Française*, approached him for an article, which would appear in the Free Zone, but he refused to write anything. We all tried in vain for two weeks to persuade him to write *something*, and then suddenly he told me he had decided to write just a letter to Paulhan, in which he would "speak of Joyce." But he would just sign it with three asterisks, for he felt that the Germans might hear about it and pry into our lives. He wrote the letter and took it to Paulhan. The next day we heard that Paulhan had been arrested by the Germans along with other French intellectuals.[1]

In this, the only story of their friendship he ever wrote, Paul himself recounts the many long days and nights of work that were required to bring forth *Finnegans Wake*, but it is also a much more personal portrayal of Joyce's illusive character. As Lucie puts it, Paul 'fully appreciated Joyce's achievement as a writer, defending it tooth and nail when the occasion arose, but he was more interested in Joyce as a person'.[2] Therefore, as best he could under the circumstances, Paul tried to reveal certain aspects of his friend's disposition for the reader's benefit as well as for those who would come to admire the steadfast way in which Joyce faced the many difficulties that beset his final decade. Therefore, it is unfortunate that his biographers and most critics have neglected the insights of someone who knew Joyce so well for so long.

It is quite possible that Paul spent more time with Joyce than anyone outside of his immediate family at any period of his life, and he paints quite a different portrait of the man than the one we have become familiar with in Richard Ellmann's biography, for example. Paul recalls that his 'lasting impression' of Joyce was of his 'exquisite gentleness, together with his infinite power of comprehension'. While the latter attribute is a characteristic that most of Joyce's readers are likely to discern, only an intimate friend would have experienced the former, and only an astute judge of human nature would be able to describe it so eloquently. Tellingly, Paul attests to the fact that these two traits 'were allied to an inner strength, a directed spiritual activity, such as I have never seen in anyone else'. More than anyone else during that difficult final decade, Paul would know 'how much ripe reflection and infinite precaution, warm kindliness and genuine respect for humanity was hidden by [Joyce's] silence'. He goes on to describe how, '[a]s one grew to know him, one became, as it were enveloped by a fine network of half expressed thoughts and feelings that created an atmosphere of such suavity that it was difficult to resist, all the more so because it contained no element of constraint'.

According to Paul, Joyce 'was conscious that his creative effort was generated by an almost titanic force' and that 'his continuous creation, this unremitting effort of the mind, entailed hazards for him as well as for those near him'. Besides being Joyce's most dedicated collaborator on his final work, Paul was certainly privy to more of the personal aspects of Joyce's life than any friend he had ever had. This was why Paul was able to write with the conviction of first-hand experience that Joyce 'had the necessary courage, perseverance, inner strength and energy of mind — any one of which might have easily been insufficient — to overcome all obstacles, all suffering, and to attain perfection'. Through all the adversity, Paul writes that he will 'always retain a memory of his serenity', which he sees reflected both in how Joyce approached the difficulties in his life and also in the undercurrents of *Finnegans Wake*. Throughout the letter Paul links the life and the work. As he saw it, the work was a 'long self-confession', but he qualifies the claim by revealing: 'Continuous self-confession, for Joyce meant continuous creation; it was he who created the atmosphere and general conditions that surrounded him, and he never stopped creating them.' Knowing the difficulties Joyce faced in his life and work, Paul presciently concludes: 'When his work comes to be judged according to its true value, as posterity will judge it, it will appear overwhelming, if only because of the crushing labour that it obviously represents, and one man's life will seem to have been conceived on too small a scale in comparison with the effort involved.'

The text of Paul's letter to Paulhan is based on the revised manuscripts and typescripts that Lucie and Maria Jolas prepared for its first appearance in English translation.[3]

* * * * * *

Dear Monsieur Paulhan,

Eight months have now gone by since I saw Mr. Joyce for the last time, and it will soon be four months since the papers announced his death.[4] Your little note can only add to my sadness and regret that I should never have set down any of the conversations I had with him during this last twelve years, when we met at least once or twice a day, except if one or the other of us was on holiday, or travelling. Time has already taken its toll; memories become blurred and fade . . . I consider, however, that I owe you a reply. But my reply will necessarily be of a more general nature than I should have wished it, especially since it is no longer possible for me to refer to the letters that passed between us during our various separations or occasionally even, in the interval of two meetings, from one street to another.[5] It will also, perhaps, seem more personal than it should which I hope you will forgive, for therein lies the great danger of all memoirs written after the event.

The most general and lasting impression I shall always retain of Joyce the man is his exquisite gentleness, together with his infinite power of comprehension. By this I do not mean a quality of heart, which I should like to bring out one day, but which touches too personal, too intimate a side of his nature to be discussed now. I am referring to a more general characteristic, one that partakes, as it were, of the elementary forces of his make-up. For gentleness and comprehension, in his case, did not spring from weakness or indifference, but were allied to an inner strength, a directed spiritual activity, such as I have never seen in anyone else. Fate decreed that he should be obliged to put his strength and activity to daily use. The time will come when the story of his life may be written, and it will be possible then to estimate to what extent he was pursued by misfortune, how much courage he needed to combat and dominate events . . . Today I simply mention this fact, for the guidance of future biographers.

Meanwhile, however, the student of the human soul should read attentively Joyce's writings in which it is mirrored, for Joyce made no distinction between actual life and literary creation. His work is one long self-confession, and in this respect he is akin to the greatest of the romantics. I well realize that any writing, even the most objective, is self-revealing. But I also realize that in the desire to describe and portray ourselves, we only misrepresent ourselves, and the description or portrayal are never quite faithful or complete. The influences of time and environment, daily life, chance acquaintances, as well as more durable ties, tend to conceal us from ourselves. Joyce, however, seeks to attain absolute sincerity, to all that is most human within us; he seeks to do away with writing that merely aims at covering the page, to do away with conventional self-expression, to do away with the very body which intervenes between the most secret 'I', Pascal's 'I beyond the soul', and the exterior world. He also seeks to do away with the writing hand, the listening ear, the seeing eye . . . and on this last point a pitiless fate met him more than half way . . . But should one then be silent? Joyce's work offers brilliant proof of the contrary, but it serves also as proof that he had the necessary courage, perseverance, inner strength and energy of mind — any one of which might have easily been insufficient — to overcome all obstacles, all suffering, and to attain perfection. When his work comes to be judged according to its true value, as posterity will judge it, it will appear overwhelming, if only because of the crushing labour that it obviously represents, and one man's life will seem to have been conceived on too small a scale in comparison with the effort involved.

There exists yet another aspect of the intimate and indissoluble tie between Joyce's life and work, which is perhaps even more important to mention here, since it will necessarily be something of a closed book to posterity, and that is the influence of his work on his life. Continuous self-confession, for Joyce meant continuous creation; it was he who created the atmosphere and general conditions that surrounded him, and he never stopped creating them. There has been much talk of disciples, of a coterie, of an ivory tower in which he was supposed to have lived in an inaccessible retirement. Nothing could be more inexact. I know no one who was more averse to preaching, teaching, and every kind of pose than he was. With rare exceptions, too, his followers were persons who did not know him and did not get to know him — here we come to a phenomenon which belongs to literary history, one which concerns his friends and what, for the sake of precision, we may call his acquaintances. Meeting new people, or creating new ties was always for him a difficult problem to be solved, something to be created. For this reason I fear that very few sensed how much ripe reflection and infinite precaution, warm kindliness and genuine respect for humanity was hidden by his silence. As one grew to know him, one became, as it were enveloped by a fine network of half-expressed thoughts and feelings that created an atmosphere of such suavity that it was difficult to resist, all the more so because it contained no element of constraint. But in order to partake in this atmosphere, a personal effort was necessary, and it was a mistake to enter it without due reflection. For its only reward was that of unfailing friendship, disinterested attachment, the delights of the mind. It did not offer what the majority of people were looking for: neither, as in some cases, the direct road to truth, nor, as in others, social relations. These disappointed hopes may perhaps account for the fact, which was noted by his most recent biographer, that in the course of his lifetime, many friendships gave way to undying hatred.[6] Without any doubt, too, they explain the fact that he had a reputation for being unapproachable.

There is no disputing his continuous creation, this unremitting effort of the mind, entailed hazards for him as well as for those near him. This explains in part his tendency to take infinite precautions, his close outward observance of convention, and his exquisite politeness; for he was conscious that this creative effort was generated by an almost titanic force, one that was capable of dominating all conventions and revolutionizing the most deep-rooted traditions, the most accepted 'truths'. Many celebrated writers have retained mastery over their work; others have been mastered by it. I believe that Joyce provides the most perfect example of unremitting and supremely successful effort on the part of an artist to give equal value to his life and to his work. Indeed, despite the anxiety and suffering, the doubt and passion, the cruelty and heartbreak which fate did not spare him and which he in turn did not hesitate to manifest in his work, I shall always retain a memory of his serenity, a serenity that was all gentleness and comprehension like that of nature itself, whose enchanted observer he was, and with whose serenity his whole spirit was imbued.

*

I recall a day in late September 1930. I was leaving for a holiday and Joyce had insisted on walking with me part of the way towards the Gare de Lyon. I am a very poor walker, just the opposite of Joyce, and our strolls aroused in me only moderate enthusiasm. I believe, however, that he felt safer crossing the streets when I held his arm. But the two of us must have made a sorry pair in the streets of Paris and, in fact, Philippe Soupault had baptized us 'the halt and the blind'.[7] That day, as we walked quietly along the Boulevard Raspail, Joyce was suddenly stopped by a young girl who, somewhat awkwardly but charmingly, complimented him on his work. Joyce lifted his unfortunate eyes towards the still-sunny sky, then brought them back to the boxed trees growing along the Boulevard: 'You would do better,' he said to the girl, 'to admire the sky or even these poor trees.' Should that young girl chance to read these lines, perhaps she will recognize herself, but I should like [her] to know how great a truth lay behind this apparently banal suggestion. This was not false modesty, but a genuine admiration for the natural universe; for its colours which he could hardly distinguish, but which he appreciated all the more fully in consequence; for the constant mobility of its forms, whether pleasing or unshapely; for its sounds, to which only recently we listened together, stretched out on the grass in the Allier;[8] for the human beings who people and quicken it with their thoughts, their passions, whether good or evil, noble or base, harmonious or discordant.

Joyce's feeling for all bodies of water amounted almost to nostalgia, and he was drawn to the seashore by an irresistible attraction. Wherever he went on holiday, he immediately looked for a river, a stream or even a brook, and his first walks led him along its banks.

How many hours we passed together, watching the calm flow of the Seine from the Pont de l'Alma or the Pont Royal!

The mystery of this attraction towards water has been revealed to us by Joyce himself in his revolutionary, astonishing, Pantagruelian, romantic *Finnegans Wake*, especially in the last dozen or so pages, which are composed of short, choppy, restless, rippling, flowing sentences that follow each other in rapid, turbulent succession. Here we have the homecoming of the river Liffey, as it rushes swooning into the arms of its father the Ocean, there to be transformed by the heat of the sun's rays into cloud, which in turn, floats back upstream and dissolves into raindrops that swell the river as it flows down to the sea.

Among the innumerable critical reviews that I have gone through, I recall no mention of a point which, it seems to me, should strike us immediately: and that is, the fact the amazing postscript which concludes the work ends on an unfinished sentence, with the article 'the'; and the noun that follows this article is the first word of the book, that is to say, 'riverrun'.[9] It is not for me to spell out all the meanings of what people are inclined to consider as a cryptogram; this task belongs to future generations of critics and literary historians.[10] All I should like to do here is introduce the testimony of one who witnessed the growth of this work. This postscript had probably been carried in its completed form for many years in the prodigious brain that engendered it.

The first version, which was only about two and a half pages long, was written in one afternoon, in December 1938.[11] It was a veritable deliverance. Joyce brought it with him when we met that evening for our usual half-past-eight rendez-vous in Mme Lapeyre's pleasant *bistrot*, on the corner of the Rue de Grenelle and the Rue de Bourgogne. He then left to join Mrs. Joyce for dinner at Fouquet's, where he was accustomed to go regularly, and where I met him a little later. While at dinner his daughter-in-law read the fragment for us for the first time,[12] and Joyce's pleasure at hearing his written words come to life and take on consistency and colour through this agreeable rendering was very evident. This occasion, when to an orchestral accompaniment of clattering dishes and clinking glasses, his own words created harmony in the surrounding discordance, was one of the rare times when I sensed he was proud of himself.

Then began a period of feverish labour, which filled every hour and every minute both day and night. I am afraid Joyce got little sleep during that month or six weeks. We were being pressed by the printer, who had promised to send a copy for Joyce's birthday on February 2nd, and we had even to give up reading a third proof.[13] Meanwhile the postscript was growing in length and consistency, so that from two pages of manuscript it developed into a dozen printed pages.[14]

And then the countless misadventures . . . All Joyce's friends were pressed into helping with the typing. Mrs. Jolas was typing in Neuilly, Mr. Gilbert was typing in his Rue-du-Bellay apartment, and I dictating in our flat in the Rue Casimir-Périer. Around seven in the evening, the different fragments were assembled at the headquarters of the masterbrain in the Rue Edmond-Valentin. One day having gone to fetch Mr. Gilbert's *pensum*, I returned to the Rue Edmond-Valentin and had reached the fourth floor when I suddenly realized that I had left the envelope in the taxi. I rushed home and called London to ask for another set of proofs, because we were already making additions on the galleys. But this would mean a delay of three days, three days lost, since it had happened on Friday evening and the only person I had been able to reach in London was a lone secretary. Fortunately, my taxi-driver proved to be exceptionally honest, and two hours later the envelope was returned to us unopened. Those two hours were difficult ones for Joyce, but he neither complained, nor reproached me during that time.

When the proof was finally posted, it was not yet the end. Additions and corrections poured in, and there was no longer time to send them by post, with the result that there were telephone calls to the publisher in London, even to the printer in Glasgow. Both the telephone and the telegraph wires, in fact, were kept humming, and I fear for a month I must made life intolerable for Messrs Faber & Faber's literary director, Mr. Richard De la Mare. Finally the book appeared on February 2nd, and only commercial reasons kept it from being put on sale before May 4th. *Finnegans Wake* was now out of Joyce's hands and launched on a life of its own . . .

But the man himself is gone . . . It is hard for me to write this, and I wish I could not believe it. Events had separated us, and as this separation lengthens it becomes all the more difficult to believe that I shall never see him again . . . But the loss is greater than that, because his indefatigable brain was about to give birth to something new . . . to a new confession . . . a new creation . . . to the awakening of *Finnegan*: 'Wait until Finnegan wakes,' he used to tell me.

Very sincerely yours,
L ——

NOTES

On Joyce's *Haveth Childers Everywhere*

1. Copy number XLIII of the seventy-five unsigned writer's copies of *Haveth Childers Everywhere* on pure linen handmade Vidalon Royal paper is now in the Paul and Lucie Léon/James Joyce Collection in McFarlin Library University at Tulsa.
2. Joseph Prescott, 'Two Manuscripts by Paul L. Léon Concerning James Joyce', *Modern Fiction Studies*, Vol. 2, No. ii (Spring 1958): 71–6.
3. Paul Léon's manuscript is NLI MS 36,932/4.
4. A typescript copy of Paul's letter to Alexander Léon letter is among the family's correspondence in NLI MS 36,907/3.
5. Léon is presumably referring to Picasso's painting that is known in English as 'Woman with a Fan' (1907), which is now in the State Hermitage Museum in St Petersburg, rather than the better-known 'Lady with a Fan' (1905), now in the National Gallery of Art, Washington, DC.
6. See 'perplagued and cramkrieged' (*HCE*, pp. 28–9; and *FW* 539.11–12).
7. This is a reference to 'Time, place!' (*HCE*, p. 51; *FW* 546.23).
8. Léon has interspersed several words and phrases taken directly from *HCE* in the essay. On the final typescript of *HCE*, Joyce instructed the same amanuensis (most likely Paul Léon) to change 'good & walled' to 'goodwalldabout', to add 'and pale of palisaded', and change 'kingsabout' to 'kingsinnturns' (BL MS 47484b, f. 438; *JJA* 59:179). On the other hand, 'spitefired, perplagued and cramkrieged' remained unchanged from its appearance in *transition* 15 (p. 234) to *Finnegans Wake*.
9. 'The day will come when sacred Ilios will be laid low, and Priam, and the people of Priam of the good ashen spear' (Homer, *The Iliad*, Book IV.164–5 (see also Book VI.448–9), translated by A. T. Murray, revised by William F. Wyatt, Loeb Classical Library (Cambridge, MA: Harvard University Press, 1924).
10. This is how the text appears in *HCE*, p. 57 and *FW*, pp. 548.32–549.01. Although Léon's recollection of the exact wording of text was imprecise when he was writing this

manuscript, he was very familiar with Joyce's work. In fact, he copied the significant addition to this text on the page proofs of *HCE* (signalled by the paired caret marks).

11. Léon replaced 'watering places' with 'resorts' in his text here.
12. Léon replaced 'collar' with 'necklace' here.
13. They are rendered as 'olos' in *HCE* and as 'oloss' *FW*, but in Latin swan is 'olor'.
14. Marcel Proust, *Le Temps retrouvé II* (Paris: N.R.F., 1927), pp. 26 and 210–11. 'For instinct dictates the duty to be done and intelligence supplies the excuses for evading it. But in art excuses count for nothing; good intentions are of no avail; the artist must at every instant heed his instinct; so that art is the most real of all things, the sternest school in life and truly the Last Judgment . . . for this writer, who, moreover, would have to shew the most contradictory sides of each of his characters in order to give his volume the effect of a solid, would need to prepare it with minute care, constantly regrouping his forces as if for an attack, endure it like an exhausting task, accept it like a rule of conduct, build it like a church, follow it like a regimen, overcome it like an obstacle, win it like a friendship, feed it intensively like a child, create it like a world, without overlooking those mysteries whose explanation is probably to be found only in other worlds and the presentiment of which is the quality in life and art which moves us most deeply', *The Past Recaptured*, translated by Frederick A. Blossom (New York : Albert & Charles Boni, 1932), pp. 1001 and 1112.
15. Paul crossed through what he had previously written here making it basically illegible.
16. *HCE*, p. 7; *FW* 532.06.
17. *HCE*, p. [73]; *FW* 554.10.
18. *HCE*, p. 52 and see *FW* 547.07–13
19. See Paul's 23 May 1930 letter to his niece, Olga Howe: 'so I am taking the stand when I read | "But I waged love on her and spoiled her undines" | that it is good to remind people that while their heads touch heaven their feet are often in the mud. It happens so often' (Chapter 2, p. 57).
20. *HCE*, p. 53 and *FW* 547.13–14.
21. Paul replaced 'person' with 'seed' here.

'Souvenirs de Joyce'

1. This is NLI MS 36,939/1. Paul's letter was published as 'Le souvenir de Joyce' in *Poésie*, Vol. 42, No. v (November–December 1942): 35–40.

'In Memory of Joyce'

1. Chapter 2, Appendix C.
2. Chapter 2, p. 36.
3. This text was published as Paul Léon, 'In Memory of Joyce', in *A James Joyce Yearbook*, edited by Maria Jolas (Paris: Transition Press, 1949), pp. 116–25.
4. Paul last saw Joyce when they said farewell to one another in Saint-Gerand-le-Puy in September 1940 and Joyce died on 13 February 1941.
5. Paul no longer had access to his correspondence with Joyce because he had recently deposited the entire folder with Count O'Kelly, Head of the Irish Legation in Paris.
6. Herbert Gorman's *James Joyce: A Definitive Biography* (London: John Lane The Bodley Head, 1941) was published in January 1941.

7. In French: 'l'aveugle et le paralytique'.
8. Joyce was in Saint-Gerand-le-Puy, Perigny and Vichy, all in the Allier department of Auvergne-Rhône-Alpes in central France, from 24 December 1939 to 14 December 1940. Paul joined him there on 17 June 1939 and returned to Paris on 4 September.
9. Paul may have been thinking of B. Ifor Evans's review of *Finnegans Wake* in the *Manchester Guardian* on 12 May 1939. Paul and Lucie's collection of newspaper clipping of reviews of Joyce's works are now at the NLI (MSS 36,932/34/1–2, MS 36,933/1–6 and 36,933/8/1–2).
10. For an insightful study of the book's 'ending', see Dirk Van Hulle, 'The Lost Word: Book IV', in *How Joyce Wrote 'Finnegans Wake': A Chapter-by-Chapter Genetic Guide*, edited by Luca Crispi and Sam Slote (Madison: University of Wisconsin Press, 2007), pp. 436–61.
11. The first draft of the final section of Book IV of *Finnegans Wake* is indeed three pages long (BL MS 47488, ff. 120r, 119v, and 126r; *JJA* 63: 208–10).
12. Joyce's daughter-in-law was Helen Kastor Joyce.
13. The final page proofs of *Finnegans Wake*, which have been corrected and revised in both Paul's and Joyce's hands, are in the Paul and Lucie Léon/James Joyce Collection in the McFarlin Library, University of Tulsa.
14. As published, the finale of Book IV is *Finnegans Wake* 619–28.

CHAPTER FIVE

Paul Léon's 'Letters from Hell'

TRANSCRIBED, TRANSLATED AND EDITED BY MARY GALLAGHER

Paul Léon was interned in Drancy, France's main Nazi transit camp on 21 August 1941 and was transferred to a different camp, Royallieu in Compiègne, on 12 December 1941. His first letter to Lucie from Drancy was written on 22 August 1941 and his last, from Compiègne, was dated 26 March 1942, the eve of his deportation to Auschwitz-Birkenau. Paul was a passenger on the very first convoy that left France for the perfected Nazi death camps of Central and Eastern Europe. In all he had sent Lucie at least forty-nine letters during his detention: thirty-four were sent from Drancy, all of them written in French, and fifteen from Compiègne. Of the letters from Compiègne, ten were in French, four in Russian and one partly in Russian and partly in French. Of course, the vast majority of these letters were written in extremely unfavourable material and psychological conditions. In that context, the existence of this collection so carefully preserved by Paul's family – his wife Lucie, son Alexis and daughter-in-law Anna Maria – constitutes a miracle of survival.

In Drancy internees had two ways of getting letters out of the camp. First, there was the official correspondence channel that allowed them to send and receive two (censored) missives per month; and then there was the hidden channel. Most of Paul's letters from Drancy and probably all of the letters from Compiègne were sent via the unofficial channel. The less intimate tone of the official letters usually makes these clearly recognizable as such. Internees had their unauthorized letters smuggled out, sometimes with the assistance of the Red Cross or perhaps through bribery. Not to write official letters could attract suspicion, however, so Paul sent letters through both channels to Lucie. Although all of the letters published here in both the French original and in the English translation were from husband to wife, the surviving correspondence does include a (clearly official) letter written to one Simone Perréon very early on, in which Paul asks her to pass on information to Lucie, and it also includes letters to Paul from Lucie – with postscripts from his son Alexis, and from his sister, Catherine. The English translations of these latter letters are included in an appendix to the present chapter.

Many of Paul's letters mention his own letter-writing and/or the cards that he has received from Lucie, Simone Perréon (who identifies herself as his secretary in a note to him at the bottom of one of Lucie's missives) and Catherine. Several of his letters, particularly the earlier ones, mention the difficulty of writing in the dreadful circumstances that prevailed in the camp. To a gentleman-scholar accustomed to writing in a bourgeois Parisian apartment, surrounded by his prized library of at least four thousand volumes, perhaps on the polished wood table at which he worked for hours on so many Thursday afternoons with James Joyce,[1] the environment of the makeshift, grossly overcrowded camp must have been unbearable. In his first letters from Drancy, Paul tells Lucie about the lack of paper and the embargo on writing, except for the two authorized missives per month. They also mention the lack of light, the overwhelming ambient din, the absence of privacy and, of course, the hunger and health worries, the nervous exhaustion, anxiety and anguish that were all obstacles to the calm concentration required to write letters.

The circumstances of Paul's detention in Drancy and Compiègne had an immense impact on the materiality of his letters to Lucie, a materiality that is difficult to render in words. In his very first letter he asks Lucie to send him paper: he had forgotten, he writes, to pack both writing paper and handkerchiefs. This must mean that for his first letters he had to borrow paper – though not pens or pencils – from other internees. Yet, at the beginning there appears to be no shortage of writing paper; after all the writing style is fluid, the paragraphs are nicely spaced, and the full page is not filled. As time goes on, the format and size of the page can vary considerably from letter to letter; some letters were clearly written on lined writing-paper, some on plain and some on graph paper with rectangular boxes, while others were written on squared paper. There are also telegram-type letters called 'pneumatiques'. These were normally written on smaller, light-blue 'airmail-type' pages where the envelope is part of the letter.[2] Although it was not possible to distinguish from the scans on which I was working between page colours or sizes (A4 or A5, for example), or to judge the quality of the paper, it is nonetheless clear that, when Paul is writing from Compiègne, some of his notes are written on what looks like dark wrapping paper. Even when the paper seems to be of reasonable quality, the words can still be difficult to decipher, partly because, when Paul was apparently writing with a pencil, the tip seems to have been quite blunt. At other times, he appears to be using pen and ink, but then there is often much blotting and sometimes the ink has bled through to the other side of the sheet.

The fact that paper becomes scarce in the camp no doubt explains why the writing is sometimes extremely cramped, with every millimetre of space being used. Postscripts are frequent and are often added quite conventionally beneath the signature; in that case they seem to correspond to afterthoughts rather than to a concern to use up the all the available paper. However, sometimes there is no room in the bottom margin for these afterthoughts, and so they are written in the top margin or vertically along the right- or left-hand margins.

All of Paul's letters were affectionately signed and they were almost always dated. Many, if not most of the letters themselves bear Lucie's name and address and telephone number, sometimes in his own hand, but sometimes (as occasional misspellings of the street name seem to demonstrate) in that of the person who posted the letter for him. Along with the letters, the family also preserved the envelopes in which the letters were posted, though the frequently less than legible postmarks were usually of little help in dating the letters.

A very basic editorial challenge was the decision about what constituted a separate letter. Some were written over just one page, though most span two pages, often recto and verso. However, as time went on and as conditions became more difficult in the camp, and no doubt with the additional uncertainty associated with the logistics of getting letters out of the camp in secret, Paul started several of the letters on one day but finished them on another. Thus several letters bear more than one date and signature. Typically, what happened was that a date was added when Paul picked up his interrupted letter where he had left off, but sometimes there is no indication of when the letter had been started. In general, though, regardless of the presence of a date (or of more than one date) and regardless of the number of signatures or sign-offs, the general continuity and separateness of a given sequence of pages indicates whether or not it should be regarded as a single letter. This means, of course, that a small number of letters resemble entries in an epistolary journal more than a correspondence proper.

As all the foregoing indicates, Paul Léon's letters from the Hells of Drancy and Compiègne constitute an extraordinary historical document. Of course, they were not written as such; indeed, despite the sequences that read more like diary entries, it is the phatic or relational function of the writing that is stressed. This correspondence was, literally, a lifeline for the writer, and its form – including the way dates were noted (or not), the urgency with which Lucie is so often invoked and the frequency of postscripts – is part of the particular eloquence of the letters. For this reason, it was very important to ensure that the transcription reflects as far as possible the layout of the letters as written. No less than in the case of poetry, the form is part of the message and so the way the letter looks on the page is meaningful. To be clear: at the start of his detention Paul's letters were beautifully composed. And indeed, the rhythm of his perfectly indented paragraphs is no less significant than the wordplay with which he occasionally amused himself in the first missives. As time went on, however, the layout became much more variable and the rhythm manifestly less measured and serene. As the writer's understanding of his situation developed and as his emotions intensified, the number of postscripts grew and the classically composed symmetry of the nicely aerated and balanced early letters deteriorated. What took its place was much more densely and intensely structured writing, sometimes introspective, sometimes limited to practical details such as lists for food parcels, 'to do' lists, etc. While the present translation from manuscript (that is from paper and pen/pencil) to print necessarily distorts the impact of the embodied script that has carried Paul Léon's voice across the past eighty years, every effort has been made to ensure that the transcription reflects his scriptural pulse as closely as possible.

Missing words or ellipses are supplied in the transcription in square brackets but they are not marked in the English translation. Many other minor infelicities and slips – grammatical or orthographic – are corrected without being marked at all (such slips are in fact quite rare). Completely illegible words are noted as such both in the transcription and the translation, whereas my best guesses at illegible words are noted in the transcription within square brackets with a question mark. When Paul underlines words, it is always for emphasis and, while these underlinings are reproduced as such in the transcription, the emphasis is rendered by italics in the English translation. English words and the titles of published works including newspapers are italicized in the transcription and in the English translation. While normal postscripts are positioned exactly as they are in the manuscript letters – without paragraph indentation and below the signature, vertical postscripts in the margins of the letters are identified both in the transcription and in the translation by one asterisk (for left-margin postscripts) and two asterisks (for right-margin ones). Three asterisks indicate postscripts written in the top margin. The French transcription observes, of course, the conventions of French punctuation: for example, a space both before and after colons, semicolons, exclamation marks and question marks, a lower-case initial letter for the names of months, etc.

In relation to both the materiality and the content of Paul Léon's 'Letters from Hell', it must be said that, in comparison with other letter or series of letters smuggled out of Drancy or Compiègne, his constitutes a singularly rich and varied archive in all possible respects. There are three particularly noteworthy groups of letters, each with its very own distinctive rhythm: first of all, the letters he wrote in Drancy at the beginning of November 1941; then those written at the end of November; and finally the letters sent from Compiègne in March 1942. Throughout his first two months of captivity in Drancy Paul is resolutely focused on release or liberation and on his family's domestic concerns. At the beginning of November, however, he seems to have experienced a very acute crisis. On 5 and 6 November he sent a number of very terse, extremely anguished notes to Lucie. This flurry corresponded to a turning point in his understanding of his chances of release from the camp. At the end of that month there was an extremely dense and sustained series of letters in which his reflective introspection reached a sustained high point of analytical concentration. These letters are all written in the same very neat, unusually legible hand. The third set of letters coincides with the fourth month of Paul's incarceration in Compiègne in what was called the 'Jewish camp'. This was located beside the so-called 'Russian camp'.

Conditions in Compiègne were even worse than they had been in Drancy. It took some time before the Russian solidarity network started to work in Paul's favour, opening precious communication channels and thus allowing him to assist his fellow-internees in the Jewish camp. This partly explains why he wrote the March 1942 letters mostly in Russian. All in all, though, there was a far more ominous sense of desperation, doom and dread in Compiègne than in Drancy. Paul did not describe the physical conditions in any detail, but he did mention the extreme hardship, the cold, the disintegrating clothing and footwear and, particularly, the starvation and the need to lock food away or otherwise protect it from theft. However, in his final letter of 26 March he mentioned the older men, including Pierre and Roger Masse, who had been initially transferred with him from Drancy but who had been sent back to Drancy from Compiègne. Those internees who, like Paul, were not moved back to Drancy knew that their fate was going to be, if anything, even worse than that of these unfortunates.

Naturally, the principal labour involved in preparing the Drancy letters for publication was the meticulous deciphering required to produce a stable version of the text. This necessitated a long, emotionally demanding effort of research, imagination and reconstruction, along with a technical expertise that was sometimes beyond my range. Some of the research registers of course in the annotation, but the vast proportion of the toil went into deciphering the handwriting. I took comfort from the fact that Lucie, who produced the first transcription/translation of certain excerpts of Paul's camp letters, openly admitted that she had encountered similar transcription difficulties with her husband's writing. As she acknowledged in correspondence with the editor of her memoir of Paul and Joyce's friendship, the main problem that she, too, had faced was correctly recognizing some of the names mentioned by Paul.[3] If Lucie, who knew Paul's life so well and his world so intimately, had difficulty deciphering some of the patronyms mentioned in his letters, what hope could there be for a complete stranger to his life and times?

The low-resolution black-and-white scans of the originals on which I worked were sometimes very blotchy and dark. If they were often extremely difficult to decipher, this was mainly, however, because of the idiosyncrasies or inconsistencies of Paul's handwriting in the camp, or – far more often – because of the lack of any, or of sufficient contextualization. Sometimes no amount of research or magnification could unlock the secret sequence of letters. As far as the deciphering of words other than proper nouns was concerned, much assistance was provided by family, friends and colleagues. May Chehab, Bertrand Faust, Sylvie Lacrampe, Roger Little and Claude Thiébaut were all particularly helpful and I thank them warmly. I must also single out the invaluable assistance provided by Judith Devlin and Lana Ilyin in relation to the Russian dimension of Paul's writing.

[1]

22 août '41

Ma très chère Lucie,

Me voici logé & nourri aux frais de sa gracieuse Excellence—j'ai été pris avec les avocats du barreau de Paris—c'est à tort car je ne suis ni Français ni membre du Barreau. Toutefois, cela nous vaut une chambrée spéciale et des égards particuliers—et comme il faut être mangé—il vaut mieux être mangé à cette sauce-là qu'à une autre où je n'aurai pas ces avantages.

Nous couchons sur des lits en planches. Je regrette de n'être pas plus gros—car mes os s'en ressentent mais on nous promet du grand luxe—des paillasses.

Surtout ne tente rien en particulier. Garde ta dignité—c'est le plus important. On parle de triage, vérification etc. En tout cas ici à Drancy nous sommes déjà environ 8.000 et il en arrive tout le temps. J'en conclus que nous ne resterons pas ici pour longtemps. Les âges vont jusqu'à 61 ans. Je ne vois donc pas de raison valable qui puisse me libérer tout à fait—alors il vaut mieux être dans cette chambrée que dans une autre.

En tout cas mets-toi bien dans la tête que tu n'y es pour rien. C'est une mesure générale qui s'éclaircira elle-même. Il faudra par la suite envoyer de la boustifaille—mais ce sera par la suite—tu pourras toujours mentionner camp de Drancy 'groupe des avocats'. Quand et si on libère sans risque d'être repris—alors je suis d'accord pour être libéré, mais si ce n'est que pour être arrêté à nouveau, ce serait de la peine perdue.

Voilà à peu près tout—j'aurai besoin de papier—simple et à lettre—que naturellement j'ai oublié—aussi des mouchoirs. Mais tout ça lorsque la correspondance et les colis seront autorisés.

Je risque cette lettre sans savoir si elle te parviendra. Mais souviens-toi qu'il vaut mieux être ici qu'à Pithiviers.

Je t'embrasse très fort—aussi Alexis et comme je m'apitoie sur mon propre sort, j'embrasse tout le monde autour de toi, à commencer par Mlle Simone—qu'elle le veuille ou non—et finissant par la concierge—dans les mêmes conditions.

Embrasse Catherine et tranquillise-la, dis-lui qu'elle ne s'inquiète pas outre mesure.

Toujours ton
Paul

[2]

23 août 1941

Ma très chère Lucie,

Voici la deuxième nuit de passée. J'ai bien dormi sauf mes cuisses mais on s'y fait.

Il court beaucoup de 'on dit' différents—la seule chose officiellement annoncée c'est que nous sommes au camp des représailles. Le traitement malgré cette annonce ne s'est ni amélioré ni empiré.

Comme je t'ai dit, je trouve naturellement qu'il fait beaucoup mieux chez nous qu'ici mais être libérés un jour pour être repris demain cela n'en vaut pas la peine. Néanmoins renseigne-toi et Ostafreff doit te tenir au courant.

22 août 41

Ma très chère Lucie,

Me voici logé et nourri aux frais de sa gracieuse Excellence – j'ai été pris avec les <u>avocats du barreau de Paris</u>. c'est à tort car je ne suis ni français ni membre du Barreau – Toutefois cela nous vaut une chambrée spéciale et des égards particuliers – et comme il faut être mangé – il vaut mieux être mangé à cette sauce là qu'à une autre où je n'aurai pas ces avantages.

Nous couchons sur des lits en planches je regrette de n'être pas plus gros – car mes os s'en ressentent mais on nous promet du grand luxe – des paillasses.

Surtout ne tente rien de particulier – garde ta dignité c'est le plus important. On parle de tri âge vérification etc. En tout cas ici à Drancy nous sommes déjà environ 8.000 – et il en arrive tout le temps – j'en conclus que nous ne resterons pas ici pour longtemps – les âges vont jusqu'à 61 ans. Je ne vois donc pas de raison valable qui puisse me libérer tout-à-fait – alors il vaut mieux être dans cette chambrée que dans une autre.

En tout cas mets toi bien dans la tête que tu n'y es pour rien – C'est une mesure générale qui s'éclaircira elle-même. Il faudra par la suite envoyer de la boustifaille – mais ce sera pour la suite – tu peux toujours mentionner Camp de Drancy "groupe des avocats" – Quand et si on libère sans [illegible]

FIGURE 5.1: Paul to Lucie, 22 August 1941 (recto) © The Léon Estate.

d'être repris – alors je suis d'accord pour être libéré mais
si ce n'est que pour être arrêté à nouveau ce serait de la
peine perdue.

Voilà à peu près tout – j'aurais besoin de
papier – simple et à lettre – que naturellement
j'ai oublié – aussi des mouchoirs. Mais tout ça
lorsque la correspondance et les colis seront autorisés

Je risque cette lettre sans savoir si elle te
parviendra. Mais souviens toi qu'il vaut mieux
être ici qu'à Pithiviers –

Je t'embrasse très fort – aussi Alexis
et comme je m'apitoie sur mon propre sort j'embrasse
tout le monde autour de toi à commencer par
Mlle Lemoine – qu'elle le veuille ou non et
finissant par la concierge – dans les mêmes conditions

Embrasse Catherine et tranquillise la
dis lui qu'elle ne s'inquiète pas outre mesure –

Toujours ton
Paul

FIGURE 5.2: Paul to Lucie, 22 August 1941 (verso) © The Léon Estate.

Mlle Simone a dû te remettre les 5.000 fr. qui étaient à la maison. Faites attention à la dépense. Struve doit te rapporter de l'argent et vendre encore. Popoff doit te donner pour la fin août 2.000 fr. Tu peux les lui réclamer en mon nom quand tu voudras. D'autre part, Pierre doit rentrer de vacances le 26.

Maintenant il faut payer toutes les factures qui viendront pour nous et en haut. Tu connais les appointements à payer chez nous. Pour Jeanne, il lui faut 400 francs d'appoint et toutes mes cigarettes, auxquelles tu ajouteras 100 fr. pour les consommations et 100 fr. en plus. Cela en tout doit faire quelque chose comme 750 fr. Donne aussi 100 fr. à la concierge. Je crois que c'est tout.

Je vous embrasse tous et attends avec patience une libération qui peut-être viendra plus tôt que nous ne pensons,

Toujours à toi,
Paul

As-tu vu Catherine, comment va-t-elle ? Il faut qu'elle tienne tranquillement

Toute correspondance est encore interdite [mots illisibles] 10 jours. Les colis [mots illisibles].

* L[ettre] à envoyer à cette adresse : Mme Léon, 27 rue Casimir-Périer, Paris 7ème
** 27/VIII Pas moyen jusqu'ici d'envoyer cette lettre. J'ai comme tout le monde assez faim, sinon très. Il y a 3.000 colis à la poste mais il est défendu de nous les remettre. J'espère toutefois qu'il y en aura un pour moi.

J'embrasse tout [le monde?],
Paul[4]

[3]

Madame Léon,
27 rue Casimir Périer,
Paris 7e

5 septembre 1941

Ma très chère Lucie,

Je crois que j'ai un moment de lucidité et je veux en profiter pour t'écrire car jusqu'à présent je n'ai écrit que des lettres et notes idiotes. Je ne vais pas mal—au contraire le moral est bon et le régime d'amaigrissement ne m'affecte pas outre mesure sauf les chevilles—mais comme je marche peu je ne m'en plains pas trop.

Pour les visites, c'est Weber qui pourrait t'aider. Il connaît François de la Préfecture de Police qui pourrait négocier ceci. Je serais très content de te voir. Je ne compte pas recevoir ton colis avant une semaine car on les trie et on les fouille si longtemps qu'on n'en délivre qu'une cinquantaine par jour. Or nous sommes 4.250. Si tu ne l'as pas encore envoyé—ou à ta visite—je voudrais une boîte de pastilles Valda, une tube d'inorhynyl, une tube d'Eska, une boîte d'aspirine ou Aspro. Il y a beaucoup de rhumes autour de moi.

Comment va Catherine—et Alec est il rentré à Paris ? J'ai l'impression que nous sommes ici pour assez longtemps, peut-être jusqu'à la fin de la guerre et je me demande ce que je trouverai à la maison à la rentrée. Je ne crois pas que quelqu'un s'inquiète de nous, et on nous laissera comme nous sommes sans bouger, à moins qu'on ne nous ait pris pour la durée de l'exposition anti-juive, mais je n'ai pas encore vu de cars avec touristes qui viennent nous voir.

Comment va Alexis ? Je te conseille beaucoup de prudence et de patience. Toute la responsabilité pour la famille tombe sur toi maintenant. Tu dois gouverner tes nerfs et te tenir en main. Je ne t'en aimerai que plus si possible. La meilleure solution pour toi et Alexis serait peut-être d'aller en zone libre et c'est sûr qu'Alexis doit y aller dès l'année prochaine si je ne suis pas encore libéré jusque là. C'est à lui qu'il faut penser en premier lieu. Comme je te l'ai dit, j'ai grande confiance dans le bon sens de Mlle Simone. Prends conseil chez elle lorsqu'il le faudra. I make it a point que toutes les factures pour notre appartement et celui d'Alec soient payées par toi. Et tous les contrats signés et passés à leurs noms.

Je crois que c'est tout ce que j'ai à te dire sauf que je t'aime toujours beaucoup et [crie chagrin?] de ne pas te voir.

Je t'embrasse très, très fort,
Toujours ton Paul

Téléphoner Littré 00-52 à Mme Weill.
Mr Ulmo remercie pour les 3 colis et on va bien.

[4][5]

Nous avons eu aujourd'hui la visite du bâtonnier qui nous a annoncé comme une bonne nouvelle que les visites sont supprimées. J'ai donné ton téléphone pour que [l']on te prévienne. Il n'en reste pas moins que j'en suis chagriné et dois te demander et sans plus attendre le colis vestimentaire autorisé. Pour plus de sûreté, voici une liste, mais chaque fois que je le fais, j'oublie quelque chose—je m'en remets donc à toi.

1) Pantoufles de nuit 2) lames de rasoir 3) chaussettes 4) essuie-mains (2 ou 3) 5) papier (gd format) sous la fenêtre quadrillé 6) mouchoirs 7) le volume de Rousseau qui est sur ma table de nuit 8) le volume de Balzac 9) mon béret basque 10) le costume beige-brune.

Voici d'autre part une liste de ce qu'il faut faire transférer au mois de Melle Simone : le téléphone, l'électricité et le gaz. Il faut qu'elle fasse une déclaration pour la TSF en son nom. L'assurance.

La même chose qu'en haut pour Alec et les Ostafreff.

Tu dois tout payer—dans les deux cas. Tu peux toujours prendre de l'argent chez Pierre mais ne dépense pas trop. Mlle Simone sait mieux que toi la valeur de l'argent—demande-lui conseil. Si tu peux, glisse-moi dans les poches de mon costume 2 ou 3 billets de 100 francs. Cigarettes et nourriture toujours interdites mais la vérification est sommaire dit-on—essaie un peu sans trop insister—ni dépenser.

Voici ma situation

Je fais partie de la chambrée des avocats qui ont un statut d'otages. Ne t'effraie pas—cela ne veut rien dire. On prend des listes d'âge et d'anciens combattants. J'écris au verso mes états de services—car ici on ne parle que de service dans l'armée française.

Bien que nous soyons administrés par la gendarmerie et la police judiciaire française, c'est d'eux que dépend tout élargissement et jusqu'à présent on n'a élargi que ceux qui leur étaient utiles. Il faut donc attendre. Sois tranquille—reste le plus de temps possible chez toi car chaque fois que je peux je te fais téléphoner. Struve si nécessaire peut vendre tous les bouquins Mme de Staël mais il ne faut pas toucher à Rousseau ni aux doctrines politiques.

Mme Paul Léon
27 rue Casimir Périer
Paris 7^{e}

Voici mes états de service

Léon, Paul, né le 25 avril 1893 à St Petersburg, Russie
Réfugié russe
Marié et fils français
Professeur de droit
Guerre 1914–1918—Armée Impériale Russe
Volontaire au 33e en ligne de combat
du 15 juillet 1915 au 1er mai 1917
(proposé à la Médaille St Georges 1è^{re} classe)
Ecole d'officiers de l'Empéreur Paul I 1er mai–1er septembre 1917
promu Sous-Lieutenant 1er septembre 1917
2e régiment de mitrailleurs
1er septembre 1917–1er février 1918
détaché à l'école d'officiers—instruction de tirailleurs mitrailleurs
Retour à la vie civile

Guerre 1939–1940
Conseil de révision pour les réfugiés russes
9 avril 1940 reconnu apte mais non appelé

[5]

9 septembre 1941

Ma très chère Lucie,

Voici la lettre que j'avais écrite le 5 mais qui n'a pu partir. J'espère que tu as reçu celle du 7—on ne sait jamais lorsqu'on les envoie si elles parviennent. Tu connais maintenant mes désidérata—béret basque, pastilles Valda, inorhynyl, Eska, lames de rasoir. Papier quadrillé grand format—tu en trouveras sous la fenêtre enveloppé dans du papier brun.

On nous promet de jour en jour l'autorisation des colis de victuailles. Lorsque ce sera possible je le laisse à ton imagination mais jusque là nous avons faim. C'est d'ailleurs la seule raison qui me fait croire que notre détention a un caractère plus ou moins provisoire—au cas contraire je ne trouve pas de sens aux rigueurs exagérées.

Dis bien à Catherine qu'il ne faut plus qu'elle s'inquiète. On s'en sortira, j'en ai la conviction.

Quant à la sortie d'ici, que veux-tu que je t'en dise ? Tu en sais peut-être plus long que moi. Je crois qu'il faut jouer sur l'ancien combattant que je suis mais ici on n'a pris que les listes de ceux qui ont combattu dans l'armée française. On verra si les armées alliées peuvent être bénéficiaires de ces mesures par la suite.

Aucune lettre ne nous parvient encore. C'est encore une rigueur plutôt inexplicable. A la tête de notre repaire se trouve le lieutenant [Daneker], grand-maître de la juiverie—mais agissant par l'intermédiaire des autorités françaises—Commissaire Voineau et la gendarmerie. Mais je crois que Weber peut mieux te renseigner que quiconque.

Embrasse tout le monde à la ronde.
Je t'embrasse bien, bien fort comme je t'aime.
Toujours ton
Paul

Ceci doit être la 5ième lettre que je t'écris. Si tu m'envoies un paquet de papier hygiénique (j'en ai déjà deux et c'est trop car je suis constipé) glisse-y deux ou trois billets de 100 fr. et colle les côtés. J'en ai cherché en vain, dans le 1er colis. La jaquette sport était attachée à la valise par une corde sans être enveloppée. Est-ce ainsi qu'elle a été envoyée ?

[6]

10 septembre 1941

Mme Paul Léon
27 rue Casimir Périer
7^{e}

Ma très chère Lucie,

Le vent est au pessimisme complet aujourd'hui. Après une visite avec photographie qui était en réalité une humiliation, on vient d'annoncer que notre chambrée sera disloquée, c'est-à-dire que nous serons couchés dans différentes chambres et par terre avec les autres ce qui ne promet guère. Je voudrais beaucoup savoir ce que tu as pu obtenir de promesses fausses ou vraies par Engelmann—tout dépend d'un lieutenant Dannecker, mais on doit connaître ceci dehors mieux que nous. Je veux espérer que tu as au moins de l'espoir car cela va être dur. Les vieux au delà de 60 ans et les jeunes de moins de 18 qui devaient partir ne sont pas partis et j'ai l'impression que nous sommes ici pour longtemps sinon pour jusqu'à la fin de la guerre. Tâche de savoir. Nous n'avons encore aucune nouvelle du dehors. Il en sera autorisé 2 par mois—écris-moi donc à mots couverts.

En plus j'ai oublié de te dire que j'ai acheté et payé chez Petrossian une bouteille de cognac Monnet qu'il devait livrer et qu'il n'a pas livrée—tu peux aller la prendre.

Je t'embrasse bien, bien fort
Toujours ton
Paul

[7]

11 septembre 1941

Mme Léon
27 rue Casimir Perrier
Paris

Ma très chère Lucie,

Merci beaucoup pour ta carte et le sac de couchage. Tout cela m'est précieux—mais cela tardait et je me sens plus faible des nerfs. Or avec tous les bobards qui courent il faut tenir coûte que coûte.

Il faut aussi penser à l'avenir. Si je suis libéré il faut partir et si je reste ici il faut aussi que toi et Alexis partiez. Alexis peut passer au lycée de Nice ou Grenoble. Je connais un peu un professeur à la faculté des Lettres de Grenoble. A Nice je ne connais personne.

Le dernier bobard qui circule est que nous sommes en quarantaine mais que les Français anciens combattants seraient relâchés avant terme. En ce sens il serait peut-être important d'établir comme tu l'as fait mes états de service militaire.

On nous déplace aujourd'hui—je crois que je vais coucher par terre mais grâce au sac cela ira ; surtout ne m'envoie plus rien jusqu'à l'hiver, autrement si je sors d'ici je ne saurais comment rapporter le tout.

En tout cas comme je n'ai plus d'argent si tu ne peux m'en envoyer comme je t'ai écrit, verse à la Police 100 fr. à mon crédit au camp de Drancy—au moment de [la] sortie je pourrai les toucher.

Ma nouvelle chambre est Escalier 16 chambre 13/14.

Je t'ai écrit 7 lettres au moins. Les as-tu reçues toutes ? Comment va Alec ? As-tu de ses nouvelles ?

J'embrasse Catherine et aussi Mlle Perréon que je remercie pour ses quelques mots. Toi je te serre dans mes bras bien, bien fort.

Toujours ton Paul
qui t'aime bien

12 Septembre 1941

Merci ma très chère Lucie, j'ai très bien dormi dans le sac—ma dernière nuit sur des planches. Demain j'espère que ce ne sera pas pire sur le plancher.

Mon numéro matricule est le 5203—comme chez les bagnards.

Tu as dû lire l'article du *Paris Soir* et du *Petit Parisien*. Quelle honte et quel mensonge.

[8]
[Sans date][6]

Lucie Léon
27 rue Casimir Périer, Paris 7e
Inv. 70.04
Block IV escl 16 chambre no.13
NUMÉRO MATRICULE 5203

Vu la suppression des visites pour lesquelles il faut demander une permission spéciale à la Préfecture de Police, je prie d'envoyer d'urgence le colis vestimentaire dont le détail sera donné par Mme Netter en y ajoutant un coussin tête.

P. L.

[9]

16 septembre 1941

Ma très très chère Lucie,

Cette lettre te sera à nouveau remise par un ami de mon ami Mr Guterman, qui, comme son nom l'indique est un homme très bon. Il prend soin de mes 250 gr de pain afin que je ne les mange pas tout à la fois et il m'a prêté 100 fr. Il pourra m'en prêter encore donc ne t'inquiète plus au sujet de l'argent.

Aujourd'hui on a eu un choc. Le cadre allemand du camp est parti. En réalité il en reste encore, mais ils paraissent se désintéresser du camp. Les gendarmes français sont devenus et plus sévères et plus corrompus. Quoi qu'il en soit, si tu as de l'espoir fondé, et pas seulement en l'air, dis-le moi de façon détournée dans la carte réponse que je t'enverrai jeudi. Ou peut-être par cette occasion. Le régime ici est tellement sévère que je ne peux pas croire qu'il continue longtemps. Mais on dit que Pithiviers où on était beaucoup plus libre est devenu aussi sévère qu'ici. C'est l'absence de colis de nourriture qui rend la vie aussi dure car on s'affaiblit.

Il faut tout faire pour préparer Alexis au départ en zone libre. Qu'il vende les livres, tous, de l'année dernière. Qu'il s'achète un programme de la classe de Math-Philo et qu'il commence à acheter les bouquins nécessaires. En province il est plus difficile de trouver ce qu'il faut.

Comment va tout le monde ? As-tu des nouvelles d'Alec ?—je m'inquiète à son sujet.

Et Catherine, je l'embrasse bien, bien fort.

Je suis très énervé par tous les bobards qui courent et mes nerfs commencent à flancher.

Je t'embrasse—bien, bien fort—Alexis aussi et tous autour de vous y compris Mme Perréon et Mlle Simone.

Ton Paul qui t'aime toujours.

Plus tard le 16 Sept

Ma tête travaille si mal que j'ai oublié de te dire que ton paquet de médicaments est très bien arrivé avec tout ce que tu avais mis dedans. Je regrette que tu n'aies pas enveloppé un des médicaments dans quelques mots écrits par toi pour me dire tes espoirs, car je me sens bien bas aujourd'hui ; je ne sais pourquoi. Mais j'espère, j'espère en toi.

Je t'aime et j'espère te voir bientôt.

Ton Paul qui est toujours à toi.

Mme Paul Léon
27 rue Casimir Périer
Inv 70.04 Paris 7e

[10]

18 septembre 1941

Ma très très chère Lucie,

Merci mille fois pour ton dernier colis et ta lettre avec les certificats. Mais ici on n'accepte que ceux qui ont servi dans l'armée française : peut-être te sera-t-il plus utile de l'autre côté. Attention seulement : dans le certificat de Tatisteff il y a 2 fautes : 1. Il est dit que je suis né en 1897—alors que la date est 1893. 2. Il est dit que j'ai terminé mon service le 1er mai 1917 alors que je l'ai terminé en février 1918. Si tu peux obtenir une visite, on a commencé à libérer les réformés. Le camp est entièrement sous le contrôle des Français. La corruption prévaut. J'espère que tu pourras obtenir ma libération car malgré le [carnosine?] dont j'ai immédiatement avalé une ampoule, je me sens fatigué et les nerfs usés. Le bruit de la chambrée est épouvantable.

Je t'embrasse ainsi que tous

Ton Paul

On dit que les jeunes et les vieux partiront samedi.

[11]

19 septembre 1941
Drancy
Block IV esc. 16 chambre n°13
Numéro Matricule 5203

Ma très très chère Lucie,

Voici enfin la 2e fois que je peux t'écrire. J'espère que notre détention ne se prolongera plus outre mesure. Donne-moi des nouvelles d'Alec, Catherine et de tout le monde. J'attends impatiemment de tes nouvelles. J'embrasse tout le monde autour de toi mais surtout toi-même et Alexis.

Je te remercie pour ta lettre recommandée avec mes papiers militaires. Mais il y a 2 fautes dans le certificat de la rue Guénégaud. 1) je suis né en 1893 et non en 1897 comme il est dit dans le certificat 2) mon service a pris fin en mars 1918 et non le 1er mai 1917.

Voilà tout. J'attends et j'espère te voir bientôt. On commence ici à libérer les réformés et dit-on les jeunes et les vieux ; notre tour viendra.

Toujours ton Paul
qui t'aime.

[12]

30 sept. 1941

Ma très très chère Lucie,

Je suis peiné de ne pas avoir encore reçu une réponse de toi à ma carte. Peut-être a-t-elle été censurée ?

Veux-tu s'il te plaît faire corriger le certificat de l'Office des Réfugiés Russes : date de naissance et service militaire car il me font naître en 1897 alors qu'il faut 1893 et mon service à la guerre se termine en février 1918 et non en mai 1917 (École militaire 2e rég. des mitrailleurs).

Ensuite je voudrais que Kaminsky aille voir le Père Serge Boulgakov lui demander une prière pour moi. Depuis que je suis ici c'est le souvenir de l'Église russe qui seul me permet parfois de gagner du courage et de la patience comme le conseille Mlle Simone.

Je voudrais aussi qu'Alexis achète pour moi chez Budé les pages choisies de l'Evangile ou tu peux demander mon exemplaire qui est chez l'ami de Nicolas Anatolievich auquel je l'avais prêté (j'ai oublié son nom, c'est chez lui que j'ai passé la nuit à Helsingfors).

Je suis inquiet au sujet d'Alexis, son travail, son avenir. As-tu fait quelque chose pour lui ? Tu pourrais aller avec lui, nos amis prendraient soin de moi pendant l'absence.

J'espère te revoir bientôt, bientôt, mais je ne sais. Kaminsky peut dire au père Serge que si je sors d'ici je le verrai. Je voudrais aussi qu'Alexis le voie.

Moi je t'aime toujours et je t'embrasse ainsi que tous autour de toi,
Ton Paul

[13]

8 octobre 1941

Ma très très chère Lucie,

1) Merci beaucoup pour ta carte et pour l'espoir qu'elle veut me donner mais je suis si fatigué et mon âme est [trop?] écorchée presqu'à vif pour partager ton espérance. Que veux-tu que je pense de Roger s'il n'a pu jusqu'à présent obtenir une autorisation de visite pour toi. As-tu quelque chose de notre ami Engelmann—ceci me paraîtrait plus sérieux. As-tu pensé à Vals—tu pourrais t'adresser à lui, soit directement chez Laval, ave des Champs Elysées, soit par un Monsieur [Chavert?] que connaît bien Pierre. Mais sois prudente avec lui. Il y a aussi l'ami d'Alec, près de la rue de Ponthieu, Andréas, je crois, qui pourrait te donner des renseignements—par la Police-Gendarmerie—sur moi et mon sort—mais je te prie donne-moi des nouvelles.

2) Je ne veux pas trop influencer Alexis s'il se sent plus [porté vers?] le père Maillard, qu'il le fasse après avoir vu le p. Serge.

3) J'espère que tu paies absolument tout à la maison et que tu ne laisses rien à Mlle Simone. J'y insiste encore et encore. Aussi toutes les factures convenues en haut ainsi que je l'aime. Par contre suis les conseils de Mlle Simone pour l'économie du ménage et en général—je t'en prie.

4) Enfin je t'embrasse de tout cœur. Excuse moi. J'embrasse Catherine dont les quelques mots m'ont touché plus que les tiens. J'espère qu'il n'y a plus de malentendu entre nous—s'il y en avait eu à un moment—parce que cela signifierait une séparation pour toujours car je suis si faible que je ne le supporterais pas. Pardon si je t'offense mais torturé par la faim et moralement par une monstruosité de toutes les minutes je n'ai plus la force de penser et pourtant je t'aime, je t'aime beaucoup et je ne mens pas devant Dieu.

En commençant cette lettre, comme toutes par ailleurs, j'oublie ce que j'ai à dire. J'aurai une lettre officielle à t'écrire demain ou après-demain—tu répondras, n'est-ce pas ?

Je prie Dieu . . .. Remercie ceux qui prient pour moi et ceux qui [l']ont demandé—Que Sa volonté soit faite

Je te serre dans mes bras,
Ton Paul qui t'aime toujours.

Je t'embrasse tout le monde.

Mme Léon
27 rue Casimir Périer
Paris 7e
Inv 70-04

[14]

9 octobre 1941

Ma très très chère Lucie,

Excuse-moi, ma chérie, de mes plaintes, mes tristesses, mes grossièretés—ma seule excuse est que je suis diminué moralement, physiquement, de toutes les manières. J'en suis même à me demander si cette diminution n'est pas définitive.

Une commission—as-tu vu Mme Bauh, 10 rue Claude Lorrain, Paris et lui as-tu remis ce que je te demandais ? Veux-tu lui verser la somme de 500 francs —

J'espère très peu mais je prie—pour ceux qui le font pour moi, pour toi, pour Alexis. Que Dieu vous épargne—que Sa volonté soit faite.

Je t'embrasse et te serre dans mes bras.

Toujours ton

Paul

A tous les amis [mon] souvenir, j'espère pas définitif !

Pour le certificat du Comité il faut en prendre un nouveau car il ne s'agit pas seulement de la date mais du reste des services. Enfin ici on n'accepte pas les déclarations des anciens combattants sauf ceux de l'armée française—aussi on n'accepte pas les révisions ; tu pourras donc les garder et les présenter de ta part.

Je pense beaucoup à l'organisation de la vie d'Alexis. J'espère qu'il s'est mis à travailler tout de suite, qu'il a des petits cours de mathématiques et que pour la philo il suit les conseils de M. [Schuster?] jusqu'à ce que je puisse venir, si jamais ce jour arrive.

Quant à moi, je t'embrasse ainsi que tout le monde, tous ceux à qui je pense et tous ceux qui pensent à moi.

Toujours ton

Paul

[15]

22 octobre 1941

Ma Lucie chérie, ceci est d'abord une missive de commission. Je commence par ceci, car mon orgueil et ma volonté sont encore loin d'avoir disparu.

Voici la liste : 1) Veux-tu aller chez Pierre et prendre chez lui 10.000. Tu peux dire qu'Alec m'a offert 10.000 pour moi depuis juillet et que je n'ai rien pris. Or si tu n'as pas tant toujours est-il que pour juillet je pense pouvoir disposer de ça.

2) Prends avec toi Struve ou vas-y toute seule chez Margraff, 37 rue St André des arts et verse-lui 2.000 en disant qu'il garde tout ce qu'il a acheté chez moi de la collection Benj. C.. Dis-lui que je lui garantis le prix marqué chez lui et au moins le double de ce qu'il m'a payé ainsi que quelques brochures 1815 mais ceci a moins d'importance. Le plus important—ce que je pleure—c'est la collection Constant.

3) Demande à Struve d'aller chez Rivière et de racheter Moret, Chauviré, Weill pour 1.950 francs s'il le peut.

4) Paie à Mme Bauh contre reçu 3.500—en tout (tu dois lui avoir déjà payé 500 fr., alors ajoute 3.000) 10, rue Claude Lorrain

Je crois que c'est tout—la prochaine fois je t'écrirai encore—ne pense pas que je sois devenu tout à fait fou, bien que j'en sois assez près. Mais il faut prendre ses dispositions.

Maintenant grâce à toi et au Père Cyprien je viens de passer 5 jours tolérables—où une douceur inattendue s'empare de mon cœur. Oh ! ils auront encore beaucoup à faire avec moi pour détruire mes faussetés et réveiller ma foi—mais je le veux tellement que Dieu me touchera de sa grâce. Je crois que l'épreuve que je subis où le physique avec ses crampes touche le moral et sa faiblesse vaut parce qu'il fait éviter à la famille et aux proches et aux amis des expériences plus dures. Il vaut mieux que je souffre que de perdre quelqu'un d'aussi cher que Maria était pour Choura. Aussi je prie Dieu pour tous—dis-le à Catherine. Peut-être Serge sera plus heureux par mon épreuve qui parfois me fait toucher du doigt la folie. Dis-le à Mme Perréon et à Mlle Simone que je me suis mis à les aimer très fort depuis que je suis ici parce que je sais qu'elles t'entourent de leurs soins et de leur douceur. Dis-le même aux Duttenhofer, que j'ai eu tort de ridiculiser si souvent. Dis-le à Troubnikov, à Nicolas Anatolievich, à Stein et beaucoup à Kaminsky que j'aime tous de tout mon cœur.

Quant à toi, mon amour, tu sais que je t'aime, aussi je ne le répète pas. Mais j'espère que vous avez été ensemble avec Catherine avant-hier. Tu vois aujourd'hui combien les choses, les paroles sont petites. Invite Dauphin et sa femme à déjeuner soit au Rest[aurant]. Et prépare un déjeuner avec eux et moi chez Madeleine. Mais c'est si loin, 6 semaines, et moi je te serre dans mes bras, Toujours, Paul

[16]
5/11/41
Mme Léon, 27 r. Casimir Périer
Inv 70-04

Ma chère Lucie,

Ce reçu te sera apporté par Jacob Eskis.

Veux-tu prendre de Pierre l'argent nécessaire et le lui remettre à moins que tu n'aies déjà payé à Mme Joudrie, la sœur de M. Eskis, 1.000, auquel cas tu paieras 2.500 au lieu de 3.500.

Prends mon reçu,
Paul Léon, 5.xi.41

5.xi.41

Pour me sauver je veux croire en Dieu mais je suis si près du désespoir
Je t'aime
Je t'embrasse

* 5/xi.41

J'ai dépensé hier 1.000 fr. Je suis fou. Cache un peu d'argent dans le colis—en tout tu dois payer 5.500 à Mme Bauh et 3.500 à M. Eskis.

Paul, je t'embrasse

Madame Léon
27 rue Casimir Périer
Paris 7e
Inv 70-04

Chaque jour, chaque heure ajoute à ma souffrance. Je me sens disparaître dans le néant. J'espère en toi.

[17]
6 novembre

Encore une nuit d'angoisse mon amour—pardonne-moi, je n'ai plus d'espoir qu'en toi. N'envoie <u>pas</u> le colis d'hiver. Si je le reçois, cela voudra dire que je n'ai plus à avoir d'espoir. Mais envoie encore un colis de vivres. Demande un bon chez M. Guterman que tu as dû voir. Il se confirme que l'opposition contre moi n'est pas personnelle mais question de nous tous. M. Netter est prévenu.

Vois M. Wahl et fais-lui connaître Sam Beckett.

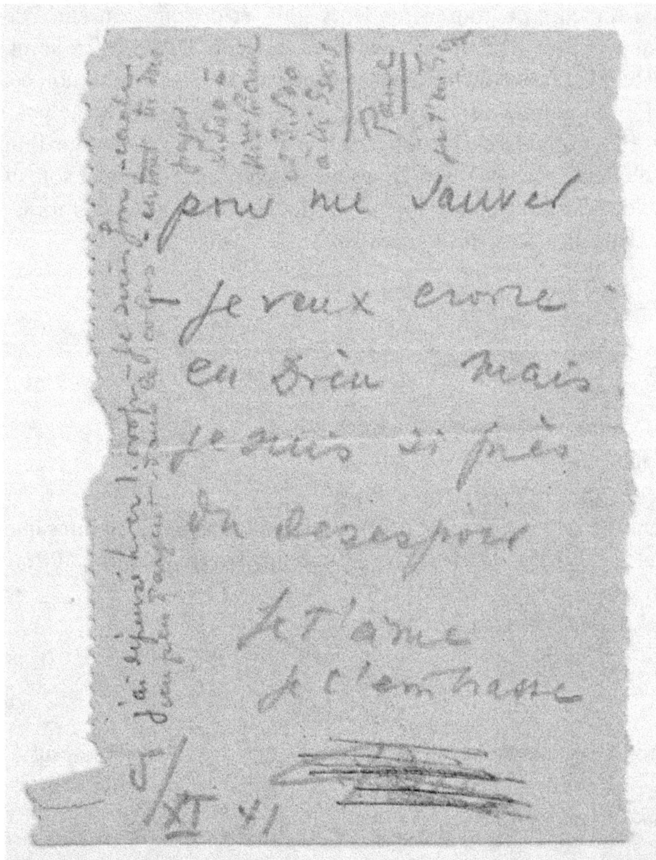
pour me sauver
je veux croire
en Dieu mais
je suis si près
du désespoir
Je t'aime
Je t'embrasse
5/XI 41

FIGURE 5.3: Paul to Lucie, 5 November 1941 (recto) © The Léon Estate.

Je t'embrasse
Je t'aime. J'ai faim
Je n'ai [pas] encore reçu aucun colis de vivres.

6/XI/41
Je vous remets ce mot et passerai pour donner des nouvelles de M. Léon [mot illisible] car rien encore ce matin.
Jean Wahl

[18]
7 novembre 1941

Lucie, ma chérie,

J'ai reçu un petit emploi aux bureaux, aussi suis-je plus tranquille. Mais je me sens très engourdi. Il m'est même difficile de penser. J'espère toujours et contre tout te revoir et t'embrasser bientôt. On m'annonce un colis, j'ajouterai quelques mots ce soir pour te dire

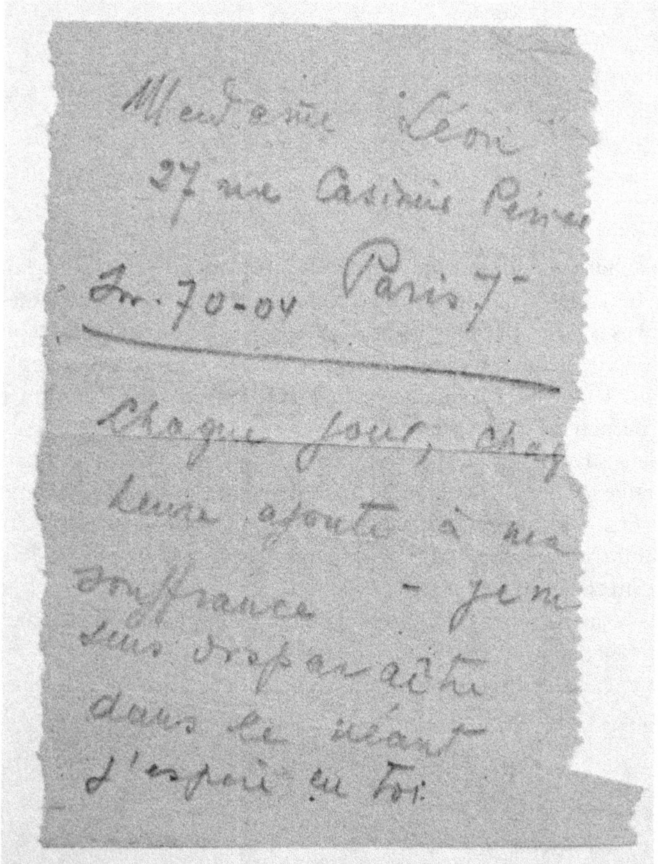
Madame Léon
27 rue Casimir Périer
Inv. 70-04 Paris 7e

Chaque jour, chaque
heure ajoute à ma
souffrance – je me
sens disparaître
dans le néant
d'espoir et Foi.

FIGURE 5.4: Paul to Lucie, 5 November 1941 (verso) © The Léon Estate.

si j'ai encore très faim. M. Guterman a dû te raconter comment nous vivons mais je t'aime toujours. A tout à l'heure.

J'ai <u>tout</u> reçu mon amour—j'ai fait des heureux. Je suis heureux et je pleure chaque 5 minutes—je te serre dans mes bras—j'ai mangé beaucoup moi-même—Je serai malade, mais tant pis.

Voici pour Wahl :

'Que de Dieux loqueteux
Que de Jésus sordides
Jésus multipliés
Jésus sans mission
Qui foulent faiblement la lente cour aride
Et qu'unit entre eux un seul espoir douteux
On chercherait en vain dans leur visage /sur leur face torride
Un dur amour de soi rôde autour de leurs yeux
Et leur regard sans foi se perd dans le vide.'

Je t'aime, je t'aime, je t'aime,
Oh ! l'obscurité dès 7 heures.
Paul toujours
*** Le colis de nourriture pour lundi ou mardi n'est-ce pas ?

[19]
8 novembre

J'ai dans ma chambrée un interné Mr Berels, âme candide et sincère—il vient d'avoir une fille qu'il ne connaît pas. Peux-tu téléphoner et aller voir sa femme—242 rue St Martin—Archives 31-76. Tu pourras dire à Mme Berels que son colis est très bien mais que dans le suivant elle devrait mettre plus de pain car tu pourrais lui expliquer le poids approximatif qu'il faut ne pas dépasser. Tu peux la faire venir chez toi et lui dire de s'adresser à la permanence de la Place J. Jaurès.

Quant au tien—il était parfait. Pour moi aussi il faut du pain—et le chocolat, chocolat, chocolat qui était exquis et qui a fait mille heureux—il n'y en a plus—M Berels maintenant a tout pris en main et me rationne. Même les deux petits paquets d'épices me sont parvenus par miracle sans se défaire et se perdre. Mais généralement il vaut mieux les mieux ficeler, autrement ils se perdent.

Je n'ai plus de lacets jaunes, ni autres d'ailleurs. Une paire s'il te plaît. Du sucre en morceaux, fromage, beurre, bacon . . .

Merci pour ta carte. Si je sors nous irons dîner tout seuls comme deux fiancés.
Je t'aime, je t'embrasse,
Paul

Pour mon colis d'hiver,
attends pour l'envoyer !

Tu pourrais écrire 2 mots à la femme de mon chef de chambre, rue des Immeubles industriels XIe. M. Guterman te dira s'il le faut.

[20]
Mme Léon 27 r. Casimir Périer, Paris 7e
Inv. 70.04
11.11.1941

Ma très chère, on annonce pour samedi une nouvelle visite médicale de tous ceux contre lesquels on a élevé une opposition. Cette visite sera passée par le Dr Tisné[t] de la préfecture et un docteur français du Palais Bourbon. Après ton colis, il est évident que mon œdème des yeux disparaît remplacé par des coliques hépatiques. Mais mes chevilles enflent. Je ne sais ce que cela peut vouloir signifier du point de vue médical mais peut-être en diras-tu un mot à M. Guterman. J'ai reçu le certificat de Debray, merci. J'espère que tu as pu voir Mme Berels et que tu donneras de bonnes nouvelles de la petite.

Quelque philosophie que je tâche de me faire j'ai des heures et des nuits d'angoisses c'est le supplice des ténèbres et de la torpeur.

As-tu vu Wahl ? je m'en souviens avec plaisir.

Je perds bien du courage—mais je tiens—j'ai voulu être de corvée pour aller chercher les colis au corps de garde mais sans succès.

8 novembre

J'ai dans ma chambrée un interné M. Berels, âme candide et sincère – il vient d'avoir une fille qu'il ne connaît pas – Peux-tu téléphoner ou aller voir sa femme et la petite – 242 rue St Martin – Archives 31-76. Tu pourras dire à Mme Berels que son colis est très bien mais que dans le suivant elle devrait mettre plus de pain – car tu pourras lui expliquer le poids approximatif qu'il faut ne pas dépasser. Tu peux la faire venir chez toi et lui dire de s'adresser à la permanence de la place J. Jaurès –

Quant au tien il était parfait – pour moi aussi il faut du pain – et le chocolat, chocolat, chocolat qui était exquis et qui a fait mille heureux. Il n'y en a plus – M. Berels maintenant a tout pris en main et me rationne. Même les 2 petits paquets d'épices ne sont parvenus par miracle sans se défaire et se perdre – mais généralement il vaut mieux les mieux ficeler – autrement ils se perdent.

Je n'ai plus de lacets jaunes – ni autres d'ailleurs – 1 paire s'il te plaît. – Du sucre en morceaux, fromage, beurre, bacon –

Merci pour ta carte – si je sors nous nous dînerons tous les deux tous seuls comme deux fiancés

Je t'aime, je t'embrasse

Paul

Pour mon colis Thirle attends pour l'envoyer!

Tu pourrais écrire 2 mots à la femme de mon chef de chambre – 12 rue des Immeubles Industriels – XI
M. Sutermann te dira s'il le faut –

FIGURE 5.5: Paul to Lucie, 8 November 1941© The Léon Estate.

Ulmo est dans ma chambrée et parle de l'admiration que t'a [ont] voué [Pithiviers?] et lui-même.

Mais j'ai hâte de te voir, de t'embrasser.

J'apprends que tu as envoyé un 2e colis. Est-ce à mon nom ?

Je t'embrasse comme je t'aime —

Pas de colis d'hiver avant de perdre l'espoir —

[21]

12/XI J'ai travaillé jusqu'à 2 heures—pour les listes des départs d'aujourdhui—après, les angoisses de la nuit reprennent—si je pouvais sortir aussi !

Ma chérie—j'en suis encore à espérer en toi, à prier pour toi et moi—Alexis et tout le monde, que je voudrais vous voir. J'apprends que samedi il s'agit d'un docteur allemand. Parles-en à Guterman : il peut être d'un bon conseil. Mais je ne veux rien te dire. Le mot te sera envoyé ou apporté par un disciple de Wahl—sa femme d'ailleurs est charmante. Vois-le demain mais je prie que ce mot te parvienne aujourd'hui pour qu'il n'y ait pas de temps de perdu.

Je t'aime, je veux te voir, j'espère te voir.
Toujours ton Paul

Ma folie fait encore des rêves de voyages culinaires avec toi.

*'Ma barbe pousse toute blanche'

[22]

M. Léon 27 r. Casimir Périer, Paris 7e

12/11—Mon amour, merci pour le colis. Je fais une colique hépatique sans douleur d'ailleurs mais ma faim s'arrête et je redeviens humain. J'ai même envie d'une cigarette de temps à autre.

J'ai tant de choses à te dire. Je suis assez blessé par de petites choses qui ne veulent pas guérir. Les doigts, les pieds, etc. Je crains que ce ne soit le manque de matières dans le sang—maintenant tout va guérir.

Je viens de déjeuner—un peu avec Ulmo un peu avec mon garde Berels. Et de ton colis—tu vois si les coliques vont reprendre mais c'est ou plutôt c'était exquis. Maintenant évidemment pour notre bien-être l'administration vient d'ordonner de boucher toutes les cheminées afin qu'on ne puisse faire ni thé ni bouillon, c'est te dire combien on s'occupe de notre confort.

Aussi mon amour je te répète ce que je te dis dans le petit mot que t'enverra Mme Berels. La commission des médecins avec participation des Allemands doit avoir lieu samedi. Il faudrait que le médecin allemand soit prévenu et consente à me laisser passer, au cas échéant réclame de me voir pour me libérer.

Pour le prochain colis un peu ou beaucoup de confiture et si tu réussis des cigarettes ou du tabac et quelques billets de 100 fr—je n'ai plus un sou—mais bien cachés. J'ai trouvé dans les sabots le chocolat. As-tu vu Mme Berels et la petite fille ? 242 rue St Martin-Archives 31-76.

Le père est celui qui prend soin de moi. Son âme est candide et pure. Il voudrait sortir et voir aussi sa femme et sa fille—j'en parlerai au docteur—a Mlle Monod qui est exquise.

Mais aujourd'hui il y a une nouvelle liste de partants, 200 environ—du travail pour toute l'après-midi—nouvelles angoisses pour ceux qui restent. Pour moi.

Et quand te reverrai-je ?

Que dit Guterman ? Il m'avait promis samedi dernier—or—nous voici de 8 jours en retard ! A-t-il oublié ?

[23]
[sans date][7]

Je sais ma chérie que je t'ai à nouveau fait très mal. Pardonne-moi si tu peux. Mais quelque philosophie qu'on se fasse il y a des moments d'angoisse et de douleur. D'ailleurs le jardin de Gethsemanie est tellement plus proche de moi que le Sermon de la Montagne. Tellement plus proche que par avance j'abdique ma vie spirituelle entre les mains du pr Serge ou du pr Cyprien, ma vie sentimentale entre les tiennes et ma vie matérielle entre celles de Mlle Simone à laquelle tu peux dire qu'elle court de grands risques car depuis que je suis ici je n'ai jamais pensé à vous tous sans elle—et comme toujours sans Catherine. Mais voilà, il y a encore la vie intellectuelle que je voudrais garder pour moi et que je ne puis abdiquer sans me perdre entièrement et les 14–15 heures de ténèbres la font sentir si menacée. Cette nuit j'ai eu tout à coup le sentiment que tu n'as pas été chez Margraff—J'en ai eu la sueur froide. As-tu vu Mme Bauh et Eskis ? Tu peux juger de ma bêtise, mais en même temps maintenant que, grâce à toi et à Berels, la vie animale ne prime plus, je suis redevenu comme un enfant et les visions de caramels, de bonbons, de chocolats me poursuivent de jour comme de nuit. Même les cigarettes ne jouent encore pas ce rôle. Confitures, beurres, mes jambes vont mieux sauf que les plus légères éraflures s'enveniment et font [de] petites plaies mais ça passera. Des demandes : bougies, allumettes et alcool calorifique pour chauffer le café—tout ceci [est] interdit mais peut peut-être passer dans le colis d'hiver. Tu vois, j'en parle. C'est que je me soumets à contrecœur en souffrant mais ça passera.

Téléphone et vois Mme Pierre Masse que son mari a prévenue, aussi Mme Jean Jarnaci, mon chef et dis-lui l'admiration que nous trois lui portons. Je sais aussi combien toi tu dois être admirée et je t'aime et je t'admire toujours, toujours ton

Paul—
16/11/41

Des gamelles en aluminium à 2 compartiments ronds, eau de cologne, des feutres. . . Mon amour, ton 8e colis surpasse tout. Tous y compris M. Ulmo demandent les adresses des confiseurs et des laiteries ? Nous avons fait un festin.—Merci. Merci. As-tu vu Mme Berels—il est si gentil pour moi qu'elle me pèse sur le cœur. Comment va la petite et comment la nourrit-elle ?

Je t'aime, je t'embrasse,
*Un peu d'huile pour une veilleuse—As-tu vu Wahl ?
Paul

Reçu toutes les épices nicotinisées.

Je viens de voir M. Bauh qui me demande <u>où en est le règlement de Mme Bauh</u>
et <u>Eskis, et Margraff</u>—j'ai trouvé 3 billets.

Je tâche de remettre cette lettre au rayon de soleil qui nous éclaire de sa croix.

[24]

Mercredi 19-11-41

Ma chérie—enfin j'ai vu Mlle Noel—à mesure que le gendarme se fâchait j'avais plus de courage. Je suis devenu si faible d'imagination que je ne pouvais plus me l'imaginer—m'a-t-elle trouvé très vieux ? Merci pour ta carte. J'espère que tes vœux s'accomplissent mais rien d'individuel n'a été noté, le seul souvenir qu'il peut avoir sont des jambes enflées et le fait que j'étais le seul à pouvoir parler allemand. Il me tarde de te serrer dans mes bras et depuis cet après-midi mes angoisses reprennent—quand, quand te reverrai-je ?

A en juger par ta carte tu as réglé Mme Bauh et M. Eskis, Margraff et peut-être Rivière. Aujourd'hui M. Bauh me dit qu'il n'y a que 3.500 à régler or je lui dois en tout 6.000. Tu pourras s'il te plaît donner à sa femme soit 2.500 en complément soit 500 si tu lui as déjà payé 5.500 comme je te le demandais.

Demandes—j'ai terriblement faim aujourd'hui et rien à manger comme colis. Aussi voici des suggestions : un colis de 2 kg environ de pain, 1 kg de pommes de terre cuites en robe de chambre et condiments, sel, moutarde, thé, le 2e matières grasses, bacon, beurre, lard,—tout est bon. A partir de demain nous faisons notre popote avec M. Ulmo—et conserves ou pâtés et viande, poisson, figues, dates, fruits. As-tu reçu les bons donnés pour Mme Berels et toi à notre rayon de soleil ? Invite-le chez nous.

J'ai dans la tête 4 travaux à faire et un 5e—la révision du texte français de *l'Ulysse* de Joyce.

Moutarde, bouillon Kub ou viandox, olives, papier hygiénique, lacets—le manteau chaud pourrait aller dans le colis de vivres de M. Ulmo—Un colis alimentaire vient de lui être signalé, j'espère qu'il y aura un pour moi demain matin. Du sucre, du citron, des caramels—en quantité, du chocolat.

Comment te plaît J. W. ? Voici pour la fin :

Cependant ces blasphèmes, ces cris, ces racles
Qui fusent des rives de toute éternité
Feront reculer devant les tabernacles
La pensée barbare et toute sa cruauté

Il me tarde. Je veux te voir.—Nous irons dîner à deux tout près de chez nous, chez Marius—j'ai trop mal aux jambes.

Embrasse Mlle Noel comme je t'embrasse

Toujours ton
Paul, avec
angoisses et amour

As-tu vu Paulhan ?—parle-lui d'un *Ulysse* pour la Pléiade, ainsi par Beckett, moi et J. Wahl.

J'espère à bientôt. Je t'aime.

Je laisse le colis à ton initiative comme tout. Ils étaient si bons que je ne pourrais mieux faire.

Je n'ai jamais rien écrit au sujet de Maroussia et Larissa. J'y pense souvent et je les embrasse, Maroussia pourrait être ma marraine—qu'en pense-t-elle ?

Du savon à laver le linge—et fruits, fruits, des matzès, des galettes, biscuits, etc. etc. et du chocolat en grandes tablettes si possible. Encore mille baisers

*Rien n'est encore arrivé pour moi—je mange à crédit et j'ai faim et je t'embrasse encore une fois.

[25]

[Sans date][8]

Note pour Mlle Noel

Aff[aire] Paul : Les nouvelles reçues ont encore plus exagéré l'angoisse car elles dressent comme un mur entre les deux camps. On ne se comprend plus et chaque minute paraît pour lui un siècle de torture tandis qu'il paraît suffire de 2 semaines d'absence pour qu'un homme comme Guterman oublie tout ce qu'il a souffert lui-même—quant aux raisons de l'opposition il est assez difficile de les deviner si les explications sur les malentendus ont été véritablement fournies et d'ailleurs certains avocats sont partis sans opposition. Peut-être faut-il songer à ce qui s'est passé l'année derrière—les 3 descentes [suites de?] délation pour expliquer l'opposition. Mais je ne veux pas que tu t'en fasses des cheveux gris, même s'il en est ainsi. . . peut-être peux-tu en parler à quelqu'un. Ma barbe grandit toute blanche c'est te dire ce que je suis.

Aff[aire] faim : La faim est devenue une idée lancinante et psychologique avec dysenteries ou faiblesse des muscles, inquiétant, ennuyeux, mais rien à faire. Un colis dure un jour et demi, deux jours. Aujourd'hui avons l'invitation de André Cohen que nous devrons rendre dès que colis viendra. Il faudra pouvoir recevoir deux colis par semaine mais comment te procurer le bon supplémentaire. Ici impossible peut-être pourras-tu. Tu dois avoir pour cette semaine un bon supplémentaire remis par le rayon de soleil. Il y a aussi des difficultés de se procurer les denrées. Remercie tout le monde, embrasse-les. Je répète je n'ai jamais rien écrit au sujet de Maroussia et Larissa, mais je pense à elles et Maroussia pourrait peut-être être ma marraine.

Aff[aire] Berels : Je te remercie beaucoup pour ce que tu as fait et lui aussi. Il faudrait que sa femme ou toi obtienne d'un docteur complaisant un certificat de mauvaise santé, foie, cœur, jambes, n'importe quoi afin d'être porté sur la liste des malades et afin d'être convoqué à la visite du Dr Tisné lorsqu'il viendra ici. Pourrais-tu te charger de cette négociation ? Mme Kuperberg a négocié cette chose avec succès et son mari est annoncé pour la prochaine visite.

Tous les miens : Je pense toujours au pain. Il faudrait aussi de la viande et du pâté pour inviter A. Cohen et des confitures, du miel etc. etc. Je crois que c'est ce qu'il y a de plus simple et j'attends, j'attends comme un fou. Comme ici on peut se procurer depuis les colis certaines denrées il faudrait de l'argent—peut être pourras-tu confier des billets de 100 ou de 1.000 à notre rayon de soleil. Si tu peux fais-le vite très vite ; une partie—ce que j'en donnerai ici te sera rendue là-bas—tout ce que je prêterai ici, si je le fais. Aussi envoie tout ce que tu peux, du chocolat dans le colis—peut-être quelques épices, miel, merci. Je sais que je suis égoïste, que je te tourmente mais je suis à moitié fou. Et quand je m'abandonne, je pleure, je voudrais tellement en avoir fini pour le 4 décembre !

Je t'aime mon amour, pardonne-moi.

24 novembre 1941

Pommes de terre cuites dans mon colis ! si possible chocolat. J'ai bien reçu le manteau d'hiver. Il est un peu étroit et court mais très chaud et il fait encore chaud. J'ai donné le gris à un pauvre ici—je veux te voir mon amour. Je suis triste [et] angoissé jusqu'à la nuit. Invite notre rayon de soleil chez nous afin qu'elle connaisse Alexis. Comment est-il ? A-t-il grandi ?!

Quant au pain que tu peux m'envoyer, surtout ne te prive pas. Mme Moreau peut te vendre un grand pain par semaine sans ticket et les galettes. J'insiste pour que tu ne te prives pas. N'emploie pas les bons que je remets pour moi—ils sont pour Berels et il s'ensuivrait des explications—remets-les simplement à Mme Berels s.t.p.

Excuse encore une fois cette lettre. Je voudrais tellement écrire des paroles de tendresse et d'amour, mais je suis en pleine torpeur et engourdissement, ce qui ne m'empêche pas de t'aimer d'ailleurs.

Je suis heureux que J. W. te plaît. Je pense que Beckett est moins bien. Tu pourrais faire un pont entre Dauphin et J. W. J'ai déchiré ta note et j'ai beaucoup oublié. Vas voir Paulhan avec J.W. à la NRF et dis-lui que Beckett, J.W. et moi réviserons *Ulysse* pour la Pléiade quand il voudra, je t'aime toujours, Paul

On m'annonce ton colis, merci—aussi Ulmo—sommes en joie—pardon—demain invitons A. Cohen et Gaston Weill, moi aussi je t'aime, je veux te voir vite, vite, au plus tard le 4 décembre.

Si la consultation Berels-docteur Tisné devait coûter quelque chose il paiera avec bonheur donc ne te gêne pas. Demande à Guterman si nécessaire.

Aujourd'hui à déjeuner nous avons eu la poire en compote, exquis, divin comme toi mon amour le/les colis sont superbes—Il y en a pour 4 jours—Or il faudrait qu'il y en ait pour ce temps mais s'il y en a pour 2 c'est toujours ça de gagné sur le temps, sur la mort qui nous gagne de sa main froide, qui nous étreint et qui m'empêche de t'embrasser.

Il est honteux, mais il n'y a que le colis qui nous fait sortir d'un état de torpeur et d'engourdissement qui tue la mémoire, interrompt la pensée, le travail, l'émotion, oh que j'envie ceux qui sont sortis !!!

Au sujet des oppositions on dit que le Dr Tisné a insisté sur le fait qu'il voulait libérer les avocats parce que véritablement malades d'où la visite des docteurs allemands il y a 10 jours mais nous n'avons rien entendu depuis. As-tu des nouvelles—ma tête travaille très mal comme tu vois et j'écris par morceaux.

Pardonne-moi, mon amour, si tu peux—argent, cigarettes par le rayon de soleil—cette note est d'un égoïsme éhonté—je le sais mais j'ai mal de toi.

[26]

26 novembre. Les jours se succèdent, se ressemblent dans leur tristesse, dans leur torpeur, dans leurs ténèbres et rien ne vient. Quand donc cela finira-t-il—Grâce aux colis je fais des rêves à demi endormi, des rêves de travail. Ces colis d'Ulmo et les miens sont éblouissants. Le déjeuner aujourd'hui s'annonce comme si nous allions au Ritz. Je t'aime mon amour mais ma plaisanterie elle-même devient lourde et ennuyeuse. Je t'embrasse.

Nous sortons du festin éblouissant avec A. C. et Gaston Weill. Nous avons été avec vous en pensée et quant à moi vous nous avez manqué, oh combien j'aurais préféré du pain sec près de toi et Dieu sait si je me rends compte de ce que je dis. Fais-moi rentrer si tu peux—toujours ton Paul.

'Lucullus a dîné chez Lucullus' grâce à toi.

Je joins [bon de?] colis. Peut-être pourras-tu l'employer encore cette semaine—pain, pommes de terre. Je pourrai désormais me passer de beurre, c'est trop cher pour toi, biscottes et biscuits et galettes.

Je crains beaucoup l'absence de Bosqui pour Alexis. Dis-lui que j'insiste pour qu'il prenne des cours chez lui. Aussi invite le rayon de soleil chez nous avec Wahl et Alexis. Je t'aime toujours, je suis malheureux—[une phrase en russe]—Voilà à peu près ce qu'on ressent.

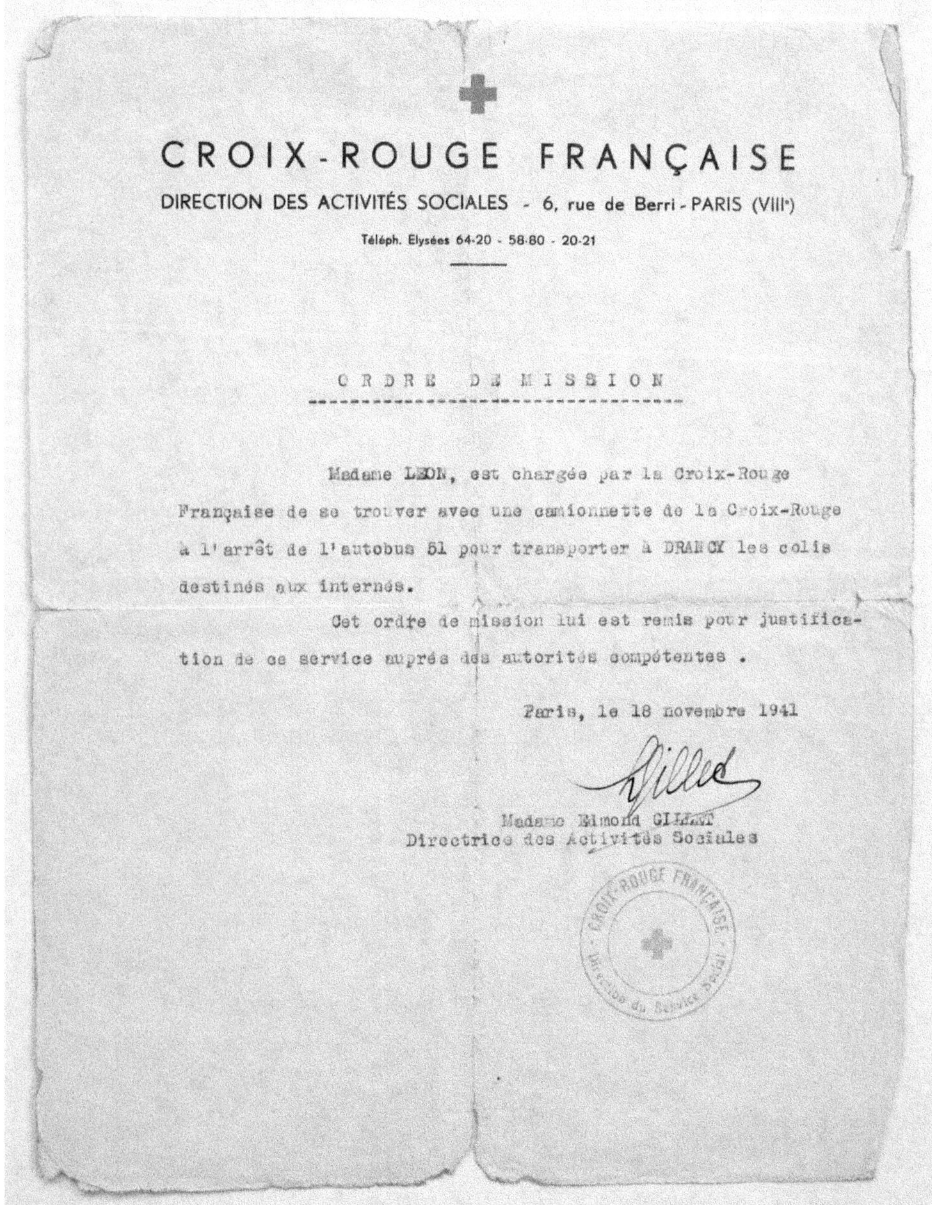

CROIX-ROUGE FRANÇAISE

DIRECTION DES ACTIVITÉS SOCIALES - 6, rue de Berri - PARIS (VIIIe)

Téléph. Elysées 64-20 - 58-80 - 20-21

ORDRE DE MISSION

Madame LEON, est chargée par la Croix-Rouge Française de se trouver avec une camionnette de la Croix-Rouge à l'arrêt de l'autobus 51 pour transporter à DRANCY les colis destinés aux internés.

Cet ordre de mission lui est remis pour justification de ce service auprés des autorités compétentes .

Paris, le 18 novembre 1941

Madame Edmond GILLET
Directrice des Activités Sociales

CROIX-ROUGE FRANÇAISE
Direction du Service Social

FIGURE 5.6: Croix Rouge travel authorization for Lucie, 18 November 1941 © The Léon Estate.

Si tu as un bon supplémentaire j'attendrai un colis vendredi ou samedi. Colis simple, compote au poire et confiture et miel, chocolat, caramel.

Merci pour le pardessus ; à toi, à Catherine, à tous—je vous aime tous, je vous embrasse—je veux vous voir.

Mercredi 19-11-41

Ma chérie - enfin j'ai vu Melle Nael - à mesure que le gendarme se fâchait j'avais plus de courage - je suis devenu si faible d'imagination que je ne pouvais plus me l'imaginer - m'a-t-elle trouvé très vieux? Merci pour ta carte - j'espère que tes vœux s'accompliront - mais rien d'individuel n'a été noté le seul souvenir qu'il peut avoir sont des jambes enflées, et le fait que j'étais le seul à pouvoir parler allemand - Il me tarde de te serrer dans mes bras - et depuis cette après-midi - mes angoisses reprennent - quand, quand te reverrai-je?

A en juger par ta carte tu as réglé Mme Bank et M. Estribs, Marxgraff et peut-être Rivière - Aujourd'hui Mr Bank me dit qu'il n'y a que 3.500 à régler or je lui dois en tout 6.000 - Tu pourras s'il te plaît donner à sa femme soit 2.500 en complément soit 500 fr si tu lui as déjà payé 5.500 comme je te le demandais -

Demandes - j'ai terriblement faim aujourd'hui rien à manger comme colis - Aussi voici des suggestions: Un colis de 2 kgs environ de pain 1 kg. de pommes de terre cuites, en robe de chambre et condiments sel, moutarde thé - le 2-me matières grasses - bacon, lard beurre, 1 tout cotton. A partir de demain nous faisons notre popote avec Mr Ullmo - et conserves ou pâtés. De viande, de poisson, fromage dattes fruits. As tu reçu les bons donnés pour Mme Busch à toi à notre rayon de soleil - Invite le chez nous -

J'ai dans la tête 4 travaux à faire - et surtout la révision du texte français de l'Ulysse de Joyce -

Moutarde, bouillon Kub ou viandox, olives - papier hygiénique lacets - Le manteau chaud pourrait aller dans le colis d'hiver de Leon Ullmo - Un colis alimentaire vaut de lui être signalé - j'espère qu'il faudra

FIGURE 5.7: Paul to Lucie, 19 November 1941 (recto) © The Léon Estate.

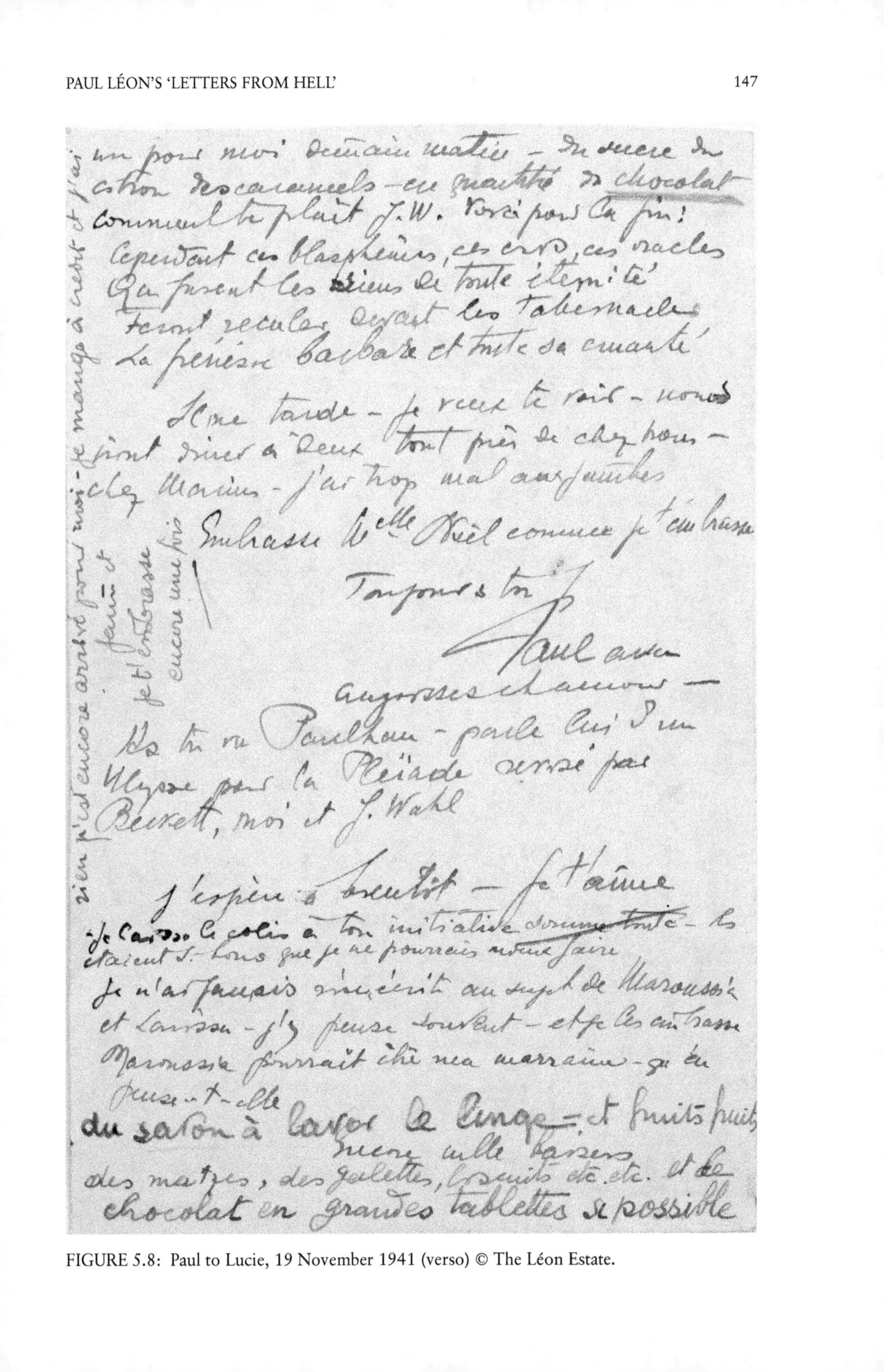

FIGURE 5.8: Paul to Lucie, 19 November 1941 (verso) © The Léon Estate.

FIGURE 5.9: Paul to Lucie, 24 November 1941 (recto) © The Léon Estate.

FIGURE 5.10: Paul to Lucie, 24 November 1941 (verso) © The Léon Estate.

FIGURE 5.11: Drancy envelope : 28 [November?] 1941 © The Léon Estate.

[27]

26 novembre. Il est triste de se voir sans pouvoir se parler. J'avais tellement envie de pleurer en te regardant qu'après que le gendarme m'a[va]it apostrophé, j'ai couru parler à notre rayon de soleil et lui ai remis une lettre que je sais mauvaise. J'ai donc manqué ta visite au camp que les services m'ont ensuite racontée. Je ne sais même pas si j'aurais pu me retenir de pleurer si je t'avais vue de plus près. C'est en somme l'incertitude qui me tourmente. Maintenant que la faim est plus psychologique on peut la dominer—mais quitter cette prison, ces étrangers, ces inconnus—quelle espérance—quand ?! En as-tu une idée ? L'ombre d'une idée ? Je sais que tu dors bien—je dors aussi—mais la journée et la soirée sont une torture et les idées sur les choses qu'on aurait pu faire, qu'on fera, viennent comme des mouches entamer et distraire le sommeil. Le désir de mon cœur va vers toi et tout ce qui a été ma vie, aussi faut-il faire un effort continuel pour maintenir son équilibre. Les colis pour moi et Ulmo ont été éblouissants et nous avons déjeuné comme toi tu n'as pas déjeuné depuis 3 ans : œufs mimosa, poulet rôti, pâté de foie et salade, camembert, tarte aux pommes, fruits, café à la crème, biscuits aux raisins de corynthe et amandes. Ulmo était dans son élément. André Cohen (auquel j'ai en plus du déjeuner donné 1 boîte d'Eleska, la ½ du beurre et 2 oeufs) etait était ravi comme d'ailleurs son ami Gaston Weill qui est un peu gauche mais sympathique. As-tu jamais remis du tabac à Mme Bauh ? Tu sais pour combien je lui suis redevable mais c'est surtout pour du pain. Ce n'est pas recommendable, surtout de la part de quelqu'un qui se dit avocat mais comme sans lui je n'aurais rien eu, il faut sourire et payer. As-tu maintenant payé tous les

6.000 francs ; or tu peux m'envoyer 1.000 ou 2.000 par le rayon de soleil, tout sera plus facile ici. Mais tout ceci n'est rien. Comment sortir d'ici, voilà la question. Le rayon de soleil t'aime et t'admire de façon qu'il est fâché contre moi parce que je te fais souffrir. Quant à Guterman j'ai été frappé par ce qu'il t'a dit. Je ne m'attendais pas à cela, surtout après tout ce qu'il a enduré ici. Si tu peux me faire parvenir des cigarettes par le rayon—je crois aussi par colis c'est trop risqué—c'est un miracle que tout soit arrivé jusqu'à moi. J'oublie aussi de te demander si tu as payé 3.500 à M. Eskis ou à sa sœur. Je tâche de te faire parvenir un bon de colis par M. Berels. Remets-le simplement à sa femme—elle doit savoir comment le constituer. Mais toi tu ne me dis rien sur toi-même. Tu as bonne mine mais tu as l'air si triste ! Je pense, j'espère que je pourrai te distraire, te rendre heureuse. Oui—j'en suis sûr—j'y travaillerai. [Pour] la première fois de ma vie je sais ce que je veux faire. Je t'aime, je t'aime, je t'aime.

Toujours ton, Paul

'La vengeance féroce d'une fausse divinité'.

Ceci est une nouvelle version de la dernière ligne de Wahl

Les journées traînent et cependant elles se ressemblent tellement qu'on ne les distingue guère et le soir on est tellement lourd que l'on dort comme un sac de plomb. Ah—mon amie—je ne connaissais guère la vie jusqu'à présent, je veux dire certains aspects de la vie, de ma vie, de mon caractère. Je crois que vraiment je te suis attachée par ma faiblesse surtout mais aussi par une certaine force qui n'admet pas certaines choses et je crois ne les admettra jamais. Tu es pour moi comme une mère—et je t'aime beaucoup comme telle—mais tu es aussi autre chose. Alors tu ne dois pas me trahir, nous serons encore heureux ensemble, n'est-ce pas ? As-tu des difficultés financières ? J'espère que non, qu'Alec t'a donné des pouvoirs étendus et que tu en profites. Je t'ai pris beaucoup et si tu veux—écris à Alec que c'est moi qui demande. Aussi tu connais mes préjugés. C'est nous qui devons payer toutes les factures de la vie chez nous. Aussi pour les Perréon de manière à ce qu'elles n'aient aucun frais, sauf ce qu'elles veulent. N'est-ce pas mon amour ? Maintenant ou du moins aujourd'hui que je me sens mieux je voudrais tellement te voir, te parler, pouvoir même t'écrire en russe, le français dont j'ai rempli ces pages me paraît artificiel et ne rend pas mon sentiment. Je t'aime tout de même. J'ai profité comme tu vois ce matin d'une accalmie dans mon cerveau—autrement mes lettres ont dû te sembler être écrites par un fou tellement il y avait de désordre en elles. Excuse-moi, aime-moi comme je t'aime toujours. Malgré ma folie, ma torpeur, mon engourdissement—cela passera—je crois, j'espère—Paul toujours.

Voici donc une suggestion pour un colis ou deux ou trois

1) pain noir juif (Mme Berels te dira où l'avoir)
biscottes galettes, matzés etc. ce que tu voudras
2) Khalva (autant que possible, même source d'information)
Confitures, miel
3) Chocolat—en grandes tablettes ou boîte chez Marquis
beaucoup
4) Fruits—nouilles, riz cuit (on l'ajoute à la soupe)
Pommes de terre cuites
5) Conserves : pâté, thon etc. dans la mesure du possible
Sauce tomate, viande, légumes etc.
6) Bonbons acidulés ou autres, quantité et bon marché vaut mieux que qualité et prix.

Je vais peut-être avoir à changer de chambrée et en conséquence à me séparer de M. Ulmo. Je m'organiserai alors avec des jeunes gens qui me paraissent très gentils et qui travaillent dans mon service. Il y aura, dit-on, de la lumière. La constitution des colis vaut la même n'importe comment.

Comme matières grasses, ce qui est meilleur marché : margarine, huile. Avec le beurre on mange tout son pain. On a confisqué le réchaud d'alcool méthyl ; on confisque les bougies—alors inutile de les envoyer sauf par le rayon de soleil s'il veut, mais dans la nouvelle chambrée on nous promet de la lumière.

J'attends les épices et [les] billets et peut-être avant mardi par le rayon de soleil. Une grande tablette de chocolat en quarts serait la très bien venue, je n'ai où cacher autre chose car mes valises ne ferment pas à clé. Autrement une boîte sans ticket chez Marquis. Si tu viens encore dans le camp demande à être conduite chez Mlle Monod—elle me fera chercher.

As-tu parlé à Mme Masse qui sera heureuse de te voir. Elle est prévenue par Monsieur Masse. Une idée me vient : peut-être dans les démarches serait-il utile d'insister sur le fait que je suis secrétaire de l'Institut international de Philosophie du Droit qui a des membres partout (ce n'est pas les Archives dont j'ai donné ma démission mais l'Institut où je suis toujours). Ceci n'est pas marqué dans la 'Bürgschaft' en allemand dont tu m'as envoyé [la] copie.

[28]

27 novembre 1941

Je me sens beaucoup mieux et plus fort mon amour ce matin. Est-ce le fait de t'avoir vue, de penser à toi, rêver de toi ? Je ne sais, mais mes jambes mêmes font moins mal—Dieu te garde ! J'ai encore moins d'espoir ce matin, malgré que dans moi-même je veuille espérer te revoir en liberté vite, très vite, mais j'ai moins de douleur et il me semble que si je pouvais travailler cela deviendrait tolérable. Inutile de dire que tout travail est défendu et qu'il faut se cacher pour écrire et voler le papier qu'on ne nous donne pas. J'ai une idée pour les colis, tu vois que je continue à être goinfre et égoïste. Tu pourrais envoyer du Khalva qui se veut du pain dans une boîte en fer blanc—donne-le à goûter à Alexis. Quelqu'un m'en a donné ici et je l'aime après n'en avoir guère mangé depuis 25 ou 30 ans. Mme Berels te dira où on peut l'avoir à bon marché. Je te fais parvenir le bon de M. Berels : dis à sa femme de l'employer à nouveau encore cette semaine. Pendant que j'avais faim je n'ai jamais eu le désir de fumer. Maintenant cela commence à me prendre et je fume une par jour et encore pas tous les jours car elles coûtent encore 20 francs pièce (au lieu de 12 fr. pièce il y a un mois).

Pour le khalva, Petrossian doit savoir où on le trouve mais il est trop cher et Mme Berels te donnera une meilleure adresse, c'est-à-dire meilleur marché. As-tu été chez Margraff pour sauver ma collection Constant ? C'est ce qui me tient à cœur, très à cœur.

Pour le bon Berels et que Mme doit employer avant le 30 novembre il faut aussi qu'elle remplisse l'adresse de l'expéditeur c'est-à-dire une note à elle—remets-le lui et dis-le lui.

Eh bien mon amour je compte sur toi, je m'accroche à toi, je t'aime. Toujours ton Paul
27 novembre 1941

[29]

28 novembre 1941

Ma chérie je ne sais aujourd'hui si c'est le fait d'avoir entendu ta voix, lu ta carte, espéré aucun nouveau colis, mais je crois que je pense mieux, toutefois l'exaspération continue, mais je la maîtrise. C'est en ce sens que je me rends compte comment expliquer ce que j'ai ressenti, ce à quoi j'ai presqu'abouti. Durant ces derniers 100 jours j'étais effectivement presque fou et je n'en suis pas encore sorti, la torpeur, l'oubli, l'impossibilité d'écrire une lettre, les souffrances et les tourments que j'ai ressentis et que je t'ai fait souffrir. Pardonne-moi. Mais maintenant je sais ce que c'est que de sombrer ou presque dans la folie. Je suis encore diminué. J'espère que si nous sommes rendus à la vie normale, je pourrai remonter la pente mais je sais que je risque de demeurer diminué pour la vie.

29 novembre

Très chère, je n'ai pu continuer hier. Le colis est venu depuis, aussi je t'ai vue. Pourquoi as-tu hésité avant-hier lorsque je t'ai demandé si tu croyais que nous sortirions d'ici—je ne te le reproche pas—mais avec les nerfs dans l'état où nous les avons, chaque petite chose compte et cette nuit je n'ai fait que penser à ceci. Le colis est trop beau, trop cher et on le mange trop vite. Je prévois que dimanche à partir de midi nous n'aurons plus rien jusqu'à mardi—je ne me plains pas—au contraire—mais c'est pour te montrer l'état de bêtise où nous sommes. Encore qu'en travaillant j'ai quelques 5 heures où je puis ne pas penser à l'estomac. On m'a pris toutes les cigarettes—et le papier blanc que tu avais mis dans le colis. Y avait-il quelque-chose d'écrit dessus ? A ce qu'il paraît, nous n'avons pas le droit d'avoir du papier à écrire. Te rends-tu compte de la bêtise des règles? J'ai su où se trouvait J.W. Je crois que vous ou tout au moins Alexis devrait le rejoindre. Nous en déciderons ensemble lorsque nous nous verrons. En tout cas il y a eu ici pendant 60 jours des Français de son âge. L'incertitude de notre sort est ce qui me ronge et rend fou à nouveau et à nouveau. Dorénavant je saurais ce que cela veut dire de perdre la raison.

Il fait froid aujourd'hui, [un] froid d'hiver, mais les chambrées sont encore chauffées et d'autre part le pardessus de Catherine est très chaud. Je suis tellement faible, même qu'il m'écrase, mais ça va. C'est toutefois l'idée que nous sommes ici pour l'hiver qui me poursuit. Comme je voudrais être près de toi, faire un travail. Il se peut que ce soit aussi une illusion, mais j'ai dans la tête les 5 tâches à faire : révision d'*Ulysse* avec Beckett, Souvenirs sur Joyce, édition Constant, édition Rousseau, livre à finir sur Rousseau, sauf tout ce qu'on peut faire en plus. Dis à Mlle Simone qu'elle aura à me prendre en main pour que j'accomplisse tout ce que je te promets ici. L'intelligence s'affaiblit et cède, l'engourdissement gagne ; le matin on se réveille encore capable de penser, deux heures plus tard tout s'envole, on a perdu toute capacité de réfléchir. C'est dur mon amour, c'est dur. Le soir c'est en sens envers ; on se couche la tête lourde et sans pensée ; puis petit à petit on se réveille, les puces aidant, l'incertitude du temps qu'on doit passer ici vous remonte comme un relent de galère et on est prêt à pleurer. C'est douloureux mon amour, c'est surtout triste. J'insiste pour qu'Alexis prenne au moins 1 fois par semaine une leçon chez Bosqui.

Déjà l'année dernière il a perdu 1 trimestre et il ne faut pas que cela se renouvelle. Je t'en prie fais le nécessaire, il s'agit de tout son avenir. Je t'embrasse pour l'instant. Je ne sais si notre rayon de soleil va venir aujourd'hui. Il se peut que je ne la verrai que mardi. En tout cas je t'aime et t'aimerai jusqu'à mardi et plus tard. Une date pour le retour je t'en prie. Te verrai-je le 4 ?!! Le premier assaut fait à ton colis aurait été visible. Ulmo était heureux parce qu'il avait faim. Il a fallu [se cacher d'un troisième convive qu'il n'aime pas?]. On a dévoré le pâté de foie, le chocolat (la tablette je l'ai cachée avant pour la manger tout seul) dont j'avais distribué la moitié [aux associés?] de Masse, Bloch et les grands chefs (dont Masse est le seul vraiment sympathique et grand esprit) vois donc Mme Masse—les biscottes (dont je devais la moitié à 1 camarade). Et sur ce arrive A. Cohen avec lequel nous partageons son pot de confiture avec les biscottes et finissons le chocolat. Ce sont des jeux d'enfants mais c'est encore la partie sympathique où il y a des sentiments ridicules et enfantins. Mais combien souvent il y a la haine, l'envie, la jalousie et c'est tellement humiliant. L'idée que je t'aime, que je t'aime toujours est mon seul aide et m'annoblit un peu l'esprit, l'âme.

Je ne sais que te demander pour le colis d'hiver ; peut-être une ou deux paires de caleçons car le lavage ici est [terrible?] il n'y a pas de savon, de l'eau de cologne contre les puces.—Mais je t'en prie si tu as de l'espoir ne l'envoie pas encore ; je t'en supplie et je t'aime toujours.

Des suggestions pour colis bon marché, lard, bacon si possible, savon pour lessives de linge.

Pour le 4 je te souhaite tout le bonheur que tu mérites, que tu peux avoir, si nous ne nous revoyons pas, songe à Alexis : fais-en un homme, apprends-lui à faire ce que tu veux et aime-le.

Aime-moi aussi comme je t'aime,
Toujours ton Paul

[30]

29 novembre : Chérie, il est curieux ce sentiment qui me pousse à vouloir t'écrire, à formuler une ou deux phrases et immédiatement à perdre le fil des idées, à penser à la nuit qui va venir, à la faim qui s'enchaînera, à l'idée du colis—en un mot à tout ce qui tourne autour de ma petite personne physique, physiologique et nerveux et cependant je crois que mon 'moi' véritable est près de toi, plus près qu'il n'a peut-être jamais été, c'est une exagération mais enfin je veux y croire. C'est d'ailleurs un des traits de la vie ici, que l'incapacité de faire quoi que ce soit de suivi, d'intelligent, de sensé, je suis ici depuis 3 semaines 1 mois, nous faisons le 6e fichier, nous allons commencer le 7e, à quoi est-ce nécessaire, peut-être me répondras-tu avec meilleur sens que moi-même. Lundi doit venir une nouvelle commission allemande qui peut-être mettra fin à la suspension des départs qui dure voilà déjà 2 semaines et demie. Et comme je voudrais être chez moi, chez nous avant ou au plus tard pour jeudi, pour te dire que je t'aime, je crois que je respirerais plus facilement si je pouvais le faire. Ma tête tombe, pas de sommeil, mais de torpeur. My, how his head falls, ça c'est de l'Anna Livia, et elle résonne comme dans un vaste vide résonne une chute

au revoir pour l'instant—je t'aime—

[31]

2 décembre 1941

Chérie, le nouveau colis a été divin—et tiendra 2 jours au moins. Il n'y a que le pauvre Ulmo qui est encore dans l'état où j'étais la semaine dernière par rapport au pain et qui le dévore. Je ne dis pas que je m'en prive mais j'en mange surtout avec, tandis que lui en prend pour commencer, avec le dîner et comme dessert, sans compter le reste du temps. Aussi le pain et [les] matzès [ont] filé. Quant au reste, tout est tellement bon et somme toute après 5 semaines nous sommes rassasiés. Sauf le désir de se reconstituer, la faim demeure surtout psychologique, c'est-à-dire devient une gloutonnerie. On m'annonce le colis vestimentaire, je ne l'ai pas encore vu, et si je le reçois avant le départ de cette lettre, j'ajouterai quelques mots de tristesse. Mais je veux te dire que je me sens mieux, ne souffre pas pour moi, je le fais moi-même suffisamment, je veux que jeudi soit pour toi un jour de fête, et que tu sentes que je suis avec toi, de tout mon cœur et de toute mon âme, faute de présence réelle, je reviendrai vers toi comme l'enfant prodigue, et je m'oublierai dans tes bras avec plus de bonheur que jamais, tu vois je ne perds pas l'espoir de vous revoir et je te laisse le soin d'Alexis et de son avenir en toute tranquillité. Mais va-t-il chez son professeur Bosqui ? Explique-lui s'il te plaît qu'il faut qu'il y aille encore cette semaine—jeudi, jeudi—je voudrais être avec toi, avec tous nos amis. La seule idée me fait venir une légère sueur d'angoisse, mais je me domine—et je t'aime, je t'aime, je t'aime. Il me semble même que j'ai raffermi, tellement j'ai du plaisir à redire ce mot, tellement il me pénètre. C'est ton ambiance que je cherche avec toute celle de nos amis. Si tu veux invite Maxime pour jeudi. Il me semble que je serai heureux si tu peux l'être. Au revoir mon amour, je laisse cette page pour demain. Les papiers concernant l'Institut de Philosophie du Droit se trouvent dans mon cartonnier, troisième ou quatrième carton du haut ; mon nom y est dans l'en-tête avec tout le bureau—Je t'embrasse pour ce soir.

3 décembre Note—pour colis alimentaire—trop beau—on peut supprimer le beurre, trop cher. Pain d'une boulangerie juive (pain noir), chocolat en tablette (le beefsteak était admirable mais aussi trop cher), confiture si facile (tout d'ailleurs exquis). On nous promet colis pour laver le linge, veux-tu m'acheter encore une chemise avec col attaché car ce colis prendra 2 semaines et moi je te renverrai 2 chemises et 2 caleçons—je voudrais que tu m'envoies 1 chemise et 1 caleçon pour que je puisse attendre 2 semaines si nécessaire. Aussi 2 paires de chaussettes en très grosse laine si possible pour mettre dans les sabots. Tu vois mon amour que j'ai presque perdu tout espoir de te revoir bientôt : je suis triste—aujourd'hui le Destin est impitoyable—je t'aime tout de même et pour toujours. Gaston Weill, l'ami d'André Cohen, a été évacué à l'hôpital. Vois-tu sa fille qui est amie avec la fille d'André Cohen. Tu as ma carte de textiles avec bons, les chaussettes se déchirent toutes en glissant dans les sabots. Je viens de recevoir le colis où il n'y avait rien pour moi sauf l'eau de cologne. Merci—doublement merci—pour l'espoir que tu me laisses, que tu me donnes—j'ai tout remis à André Cohen qui s'en charge pour G. Weill qui comme je l'ai dit est depuis hier à l'hôpital évacué. Ce qu'il me faut ce ne sont pas des chaussettes mais des kroumirs à mettre dans les sabots.

Encore une fois, je t'embrasse, je te souhaite tout le bonheur dont tu es digne et je t'embrasse de tout mon cœur et de toute mon âme

Toujours ton
Paul

Bien qu'Ulmo déteste l'oignon, je m'en suis délecté dans la soupe, de même si tu peux une gousse d'ail, du bouillon kub ou viandox.

[32]

[Lettre avec des dates illisibles, toutes avant le 10 décembre]

[Des mots illisibles] suggestions pour colis
1) Pain juif, demande à <u>Mme Berels</u> adresse boulangeries
2) Un peu de matzès, pâtes dans la mesure du possible, pommes de terre
3) Oignons, ail etc
4) Bouillon kub
5) Confitures et miel

6) Caramels
7) Chocolat, en tablettes surtout, un peu de bonbons croquants
8) Conserves : Pâté, poisson, viande
9) Bacon, lard, très peu de beurre, seulement pour les pâtes et les pommes de terre
10) Fruits

Dans le colis d'hiver, si tu en envoies un, tu peux mettre tout le pain que tu veux, et les conserves les plus denses et peut-être ce que je t'avais demandé en épices et chocolat.

Voilà la journée de passée et rien de nouveau. Je suis chargé d'un travail à la tête d'une équipe de 10 que fait la Préfecture de Police pour vous. As-tu dû le faire et Alexis y est-il allé ?

Sauras-tu jamais combien on peut être affamé de nouvelles de liberté, du désir de sortir—à demain et j'espère qu'il y aura des nouvelles.

[Date illisible] décembre

Afin que je n'oublie pas le 13 est la Sainte Lucie. Veux-tu demander à Beckett d'envoyer quelque-chose à Lucia Joyce, et lui donner pour ça 200 ou 250 frs. C'est en souvenir de son père. Tâche aussi de me faire parvenir un peu d'argent. Tu peux m'envoyer un mandat de 50 frs. Nous avons souvent besoin de pain.

[Date illisible] décembre

Ma chérie le colis d'hier est remarquable. Il y en a pour 7 repas. C'est superbe, mais trop cher. Comme 2 autres de nos popotes en ont reçu aussi le leur, nous tenons jusqu'à mardi ou mercredi. Le chocolat est superbe. Je l'ai avalé tout seul, sauf 8 ou 9 bonbons que j'ai dû remettre à des personnalités. Exquis, exquis, exquis. Le papier hygiénique est venu à point en 5 parties. J'attends encore 2 ou 3 petits paquets pour ne pas risquer tout à la fois. Par contre les cigarettes ont été prises. La gamelle—superbe, le tout admirable mais peut-être trop cher. La liste ci-dessus est peut-être plus réaliste.

Ta note par André Cohen m'inquiète pour beaucoup de raisons. Je me demande s'il s'agit des associés immédiats de ma chambre ou des dirigeants seulement. Je ne vois plus le rayon de soleil qui évite de se montrer à moi, mais j'espère le voir mardi. Je lui donnerai ou j'essaierai de lui donner un bon. Tu pourras y changer la date.

Je t'embrasse mille fois.

Je me sens mille fois mieux. Mes jambes sont pratiquement désenflées.

Ce n'est que sous les yeux qu'il y a des poches terribles. Pour le docteur que tu es allée voir il ne m'a pas convoqué et j'étais sur les listes sans intervention particulière. J'ai d'ailleurs quelques absences de vue. Encore une fois je t'embrasse ainsi que tout le monde autour de toi, tous ceux que tu aimes, tous ceux qui t'estiment.

Les kroumirs sont allés à Ulmo : le gilet chaud, est-il pour moi ?

En t'adressant à Mme Berels pour le pain juif, demande-lui comment on prépare le gebackene [Pretzel?] à mettre dans la soupe et à envoyer cuit et où on les achète. Tu pourrais peut-être aussi envoyer un sachet de poudre de caséïne à mettre dans le potage. Tout ceci et ce genre de spécialité juive et autre (œuf cuit—vermicelles—qui nous ont donné un plat exquis) sont, je pense, meilleur marché que les délices que tu envoies qui sont admirablement appréciées mais qui me paraissent très chères. En tout cas, merci mille fois.

La note que m'a remise A. Cohen sans m'inquiéter m'a paru exacte et là-dessus nous en parlerons, je voudrais seulement savoir si les personnes visées par toi sont des associés directs ou des chefs.

Je me sens beaucoup mieux. Je t'aime toujours. Je travaille au recensement—Alexis l'a-t-il fait ?—et le temps passe plus vite. Pour ton recensement qu'as-tu fait en tenant compte de ton père ?

Je t'embrasse très, très fort et tous ceux que je t'aime, que tu aimes et qui t'entourent,

Toujours ton Paul

Dans le colis de linge 1 pyjama, 1 chemise, 2 caleçons, chaussettes très grosses et bon marché—je te renverrai aussi mes [chaussures?] [mots illisibles]

*La dernière date pour l'envoi du colis d'hiver est le 10 décembre 1941.

[33]

4 décembre—Chérie, je sais par le rayon de soleil que tu as à nouveau été frappée par ma lettre et que tu as été chez le docteur. Comment te dire qu'en réalité cela ne va pas bien mais que tu n'y peux rien et que je suis sorti de la liste des malades. Hier Ulmo lui-même était très abattu—anniversaire de la mort de sa femme. Mais lui extériorise ceci en paroles, chez moi cela me mord l'intérieur, le cœur, l'âme. Je ne peux me retenir de te le dire et si je le dis d'une façon aussi décousue, c'est parce qu'effectivement je suis diminué et continue à me demander si cette diminution ne restera pas pour toujours. Engourdi, endormi à moitié, butant contre des pierres, des perrons, voyant mal, voilà ce que je suis devenu, là-dessus moralement humilié, [dégradé?], écorché. Tout cela sont des faits. Le simple fait de sauter dans mes lettres d'un sujet à l'autre—du souvenir du colis, pour passer à la religion, te montre suffisamment l'état de demie-folie où je me trouve. Un mois s'est passé depuis que j'aurais dû sortir et je sais aussi peu que toi des raisons de l'opposition. Mais tout ceci dit, je ne veux pas que cela détruise ta vie, surtout un jour comme aujourd'hui pour toi. Songe à toi, à Alexis auquel tu es indispensable, il n'y a rien à faire pour moi, individuellement : il faut attendre le sort de tout le monde. Il faut se faire à cette idée que l'on est pris comme dans une meule qui nous écrase ce n'est guère agréable je regimbe mais cela n'aide guère. Je crois et je veux croire que nous nous relèverons mais c'est tout. Toi tu dois être prudente, ne pas risquer inutilement ni ta vie ni les amitiés de l'avenir. Tu dois en premier lieu te sauver toi-même et Alexis, ma vie à moi est ou sera bientôt fini. Alors laisse-moi. Le colis d'Ulmo dont une grande partie m'était destinée était très bon. Nous avons bien mangé ce soir, nous verrons demain. Peut-être le mien viendra-t-il aussi. Nous pourrions alors tenir jusqu'à mardi. Je t'ai envoyé par le rayon de soleil le bon pour cette semaine. Peut-être pourras-tu enfin l'entrer pour la semaine prochaine.

Mais pour la composition des colis, simplifie même si Ulmo, comme aujourd'hui, est déçu.

Moins de matzès. Je t'avais demandé du pain juif et Mme Berels devait te donner l'adresse de la boulangerie où on pouvait l'avoir peut-être sans tickets. Ce n'est pas des matzès mais du pain. Tu peux supprimer le beurre, trop cher, du lard le remplace d'ailleurs avantageusement. Ulmo d'ailleurs ne mange ni beurre ni fromage. Le bacon d'ailleurs aussi. Mais la difficulté est, je le répète, que toutes les bonnes choses se mangent avec du pain, d'où le résultat que le pain manque. Tu peux envoyer riz cuit et pâtes ou macaronis. En voilà bien long sur les colis—Dieu veuille que je n'en aie plus besoin mais quand, quand, quand ? Il suffit de se le demander pour que la nervosité, les angoisses, les douleurs reprennent, pardonne-moi.

Toujours ton Paul

[34]

[Lettre sans date, terminée le 22 janvier]

Chérie, ton pain est arrivé quand nous étions 10 rassemblés affamés. Rien n'aurait pu être mieux ni donner un plus grand bonheur. Je t'aime comme toujours mais je suis abruti par le froid et la gloutonnerie. Je n'ai [pas] encore reçu que des aliments. Je dors tout habillé. Mr C. est charmant mais très sévère—aussi n'ai-je pas d'argent. Peux-tu m'envoyer 2.000 francs ? Merci d'avance. Roger Masse dont le fils est marié à la fille de Crémieux a reçu son colis. Par contre Pierre n'en a plus depuis 15 jours. Avec Ulmo nous faisons popote le soir, mais il vaut mieux séparer les colis—il y a des fuites. Mais il est charmant et m'aide énormément. Il voudrait avoir des nouvelles de chez lui et qu'on dépose 2.000 francs chez Mme Hakoune, 8 rue de Montyon pour lui être remis à son mari—ici aussi des colis pour lui personnellement. On nous autorisera les colis après le 1er février. Il y aura un moment difficile à cause de la limitation de tout le camp. Mes pieds sont en marmelade. Je te prie des chaussons ou coussins, des sabots, ma couverture, mon sac de couchage. Je t'aime, je t'embrasse très fort. A tout le monde merci—baisers—22 I 42. Encore un peu de force !! chaussettes de laine. Alfred a très très faim. J'ai été vu par le docteur allemand mais il est muet. Personne ne peut rien faire ici mais si quelqu'un de l'extérieur pouvait me sortir d'ici !?!? Quel bonheur—même pour une résidence forcée !

[35]

6.II.42 Trésor chérie—à la lettre d'hier j'ajoute—je viens de recevoir petit colis—auquel il manquait les gants et le ½ l. de pain (enveloppé dans l'enveloppe des gants) mais je crois qu'il m'a été volé devant le nez—et qu'il est parvenu jusqu'à nous. Il faut pour colis sucre p. la popote. D'après ta lettre il me manque encore 2 colis—aussi les deux pour Ulmo ne sont pas parvenus. J'ai bien reçu 500, ce qui m'a permis de payer les dettes les plus criantes. Je te prie donc de suivre ma demande de la lettre d'hier pour que je puisse donner à Alfred. Celui-ci demande à dire à Simone qu'il remercie pour les nouvelles qui sont les seules qui lui parviennent. Il a aussi reçu le début du colis de l'associé de [Necker?]—le reste doit suivre mais rien, encore, de Sagliès. Nos cartes officielles devaient partir il y a 8 jours—mais punition ou non elles ne sont pas encore parvenues—donc prudence—et d'autre part M. Claude Polack qui va bien n'a reçu que boîte vitamines par Albert. Il voudrait avoir par toi nouvelles et indications exactes sur l'envoi des colis avec dates (Passy 44-13) Si tu peux ai[e] les réponses pour ta visite mardi. Pour l'argent d'Ulmo et le mien c'est Hakoune 6-82—Montyon qu'il faut dire. Le khalva était tellement bon qu'il n'en reste rien. Les deux Masse ont été ravis. Répète si tu peux. Alfred demande essence pour briquet, encre, stylo, brosse à habit, serviette, cologne. . .. La valise avec nos choses peut avoir 10 kgs. Ceci vaut pour Alfred et Polack, etc. Je te remercie et il est inutile de te le dire pour tout ce que tu fais pour moi. Embrasse Catia, Simone, Mme Perréon, dis à Alexis que je l'aime et espère en lui. Jean prie de prévenir Gilberte, la belle-sœur de Maurice, de constituer le 1er colis alimentaire et de casser le poids et [il] la prie d'insister auprès de Thierry pour qu'il se présente devant l'école de Lyon—Gilberte verra utilement Chauveau, le patron de [Corcelen?], l'ancien camarade de Jean dans la guerre 1914, puis fruits séchés, pruneaux, bananes séchées, conserves, cela vaut pour toi aussi.

Réponse à une de tes questions oubliée. J'ai avec moi la petite valise en carton que tu as envoyée à Drancy. Il me faudrait quelque chose qui ferme—boîte en bois avec cadenas. [Le reste serait dommage?].

Mille et mille baisers,
Ton Paul[9]

[36][10]

6.II.42

Chérie, la situation s'aggrave. Mme Raymond de la rue Navarin a l'occasion d'envoyer un nouveau colis vestimentaire avec des aliments. Mme Masse se mettra en rapport avec toi pour mon supplément mais je n'ai encore rien reçu sauf par Gilberte et Alfred. Si tu peux ajoute à mon colis vestimentaire tout ce que tu peux, pain, chocolats etc etc J'ai surtout besoin de chaussettes. . . apporte le tout le plus vite possible. M. Raymond veut des gants chauds. Mme Pierre et sa nièce apporteront à moi ce qui est écrit dans sa lettre spécifiquement.

Je t'embrasse je t'aime, Paul

[37]

[Lettre non datée, vraisembablement écrite vers le 12 février 1942]

Chérie, il fait froid + [j'ai] faim. Rien ne nous parvient. Voici à titre d'indication : Les choses chaudes, personne ne sait où elles sont, peux-tu m'acheter un pantalon foncé et assez chaud, ski ou souple, c'est tout ce qu'il faut, le reste ne vaut rien après dix jours. Je suis abruti et je m'abandonne à toutes les initiatives. Puissions-nous nous revoir un jour. Le désespoir saisit tout le monde. Ulmo est très bas et très las. Pour colis, pense à une popote à 4, moins de variétés, plus de quantité. Pâtes pour potages, farines solubles—pâtés de lapin—un poulet serait le rêve, desserts : khalva, confitures, miel, sucre—saccharine. Nous gardons chacun pour soi pain (et nous avons besoin de ça, je te prie de me croire), chocolats, bonbons, biscuits. Je n'ai pas encore reçu le mot de mardi. J'attends demain mardi. Je n'ai donc pas de sous car le livre ne peut rien faire parvenir. Avec ça tout est très, très cher, même la cantine, pas les harengs. Pour la popote, conserves. Je n'ai pas reçu les chaussettes ni les gants. Les miennes sont en loques. Smoliak demande qu'on avertisse la Croix Rouge—2 rue de Navarin, Trudaine 52-73, prévenir sa bonne Marie. Lucien Lévy, Wagram 24-45, demande des nouvelles de sa femme, de même M. [nom illisible], 15, rue Trousseau—par petit bleu que Mme vienne te voir. Pour la popote, Eleska, Banania, Blédine, si possible Nescafé, farines solubles, caséine, macaronis, gâteau aux macaronis ou nouilles. Un paquet devrait faire 2 jours 2 repas. Vois Mme Masse, sois gentille,—comment est sa santé, lui s'inquiète. Pour moi aussi, biscuits, chocolats, pain, pain, pain, J'ai faim. Pommes de terre cuites œufs durs.

Je t'aime, je suis abruti, j'ai froid, je m'endors,

PL

[38]

Compiègne, 19 février 1942

Ma chérie

Tu peux m'envoyer et sans limitation de poids une valise de linge, chaussures, vêtements et objets de toilette.

J'ai besoin surtout de : couverture, sac de couchage, chaussettes, chemise col-tenant, caleçon chaud, sabots, kroumirs, chaussons si possible, eau de cologne, pâte dentifrice, 2 musettes, 1 pantalon chaud foncé, paire lacets, rasoir, lames.

Actuellement la correspondance et les colis alimentaires ne sont pas encore autorisés.

Je t'embrasse comme je t'aime

Toujours ton

Paul

[39]

Compiègne, le 19 février 1942
Ma chère Lucie
Veux-tu payer à Monsieur Sichel 1.000 fr (mille francs) que je lui dois dès qu'il sortira.
Paul Léon

Mme Léon
27 r. Casimir Périer
Paris 7e

[40][11]

21.II.42

Au lieu de boîte à cadenas il vaut mieux une valise à clef mais si tu en as déjà envoyé une la boîte restera ici. Le beau-frère de Gilberte demande de communiquer d'urgence qu'Humbert a fait retourner les colis mais qu'à partir du 1er mars il faudrait s'adresser à son ami Emile Marcotte No 971. AC demande aussi des nouvelles [à] Mme Nicolle, Ave Carnot 18-92.

Catherine [mots illisibles] mais je suis abruti, affamé, gelé.[12]

[41]

23.II.42
Ma chère Lucie,
Veux-tu payer à M. Marcus les 200 francs que je lui dois à sa demande.
Paul Léon
Reçu de M. Léon 200 francs.

[42]

[Lettre entièrement en russe, non datée.]

[43]

11 mars 1942

[Lettre majoritairement en russe, mais comportant les trois phrases suivantes en français.]

Albert a reçu la lettre et en est content. Il n'est sûr de rien pour la libération. Pour le colis d'hiver il en est fâché car tout est inutile et encombrant sauf [les] chaussettes et les mouchoirs [mots illisibles].

[44]

11 mars 1942

[Lettre en russe.]

[45]

[Lettre en russe, non datée.]

[46]

15 mars 1942

[Lettre en russe.]

Absender:

Vor- und Zuname: Paul Léon

Gefangenennummer 3030

Lager-Bezeichnung: Compiègne (Oise)

Deutschland (Allemagne) Frontstalag 122

Gebührenfrei!

An Madame Paul Léon

Empfangsort: Paris (7me)

Straße: 27 rue Casimir Périer

Land: France

Landesteil (Provinz usw.)

Kriegsgefangenenpost

FIGURE 5.12: Paul to Lucie, 19 February1942 (recto) © The Léon Estate.

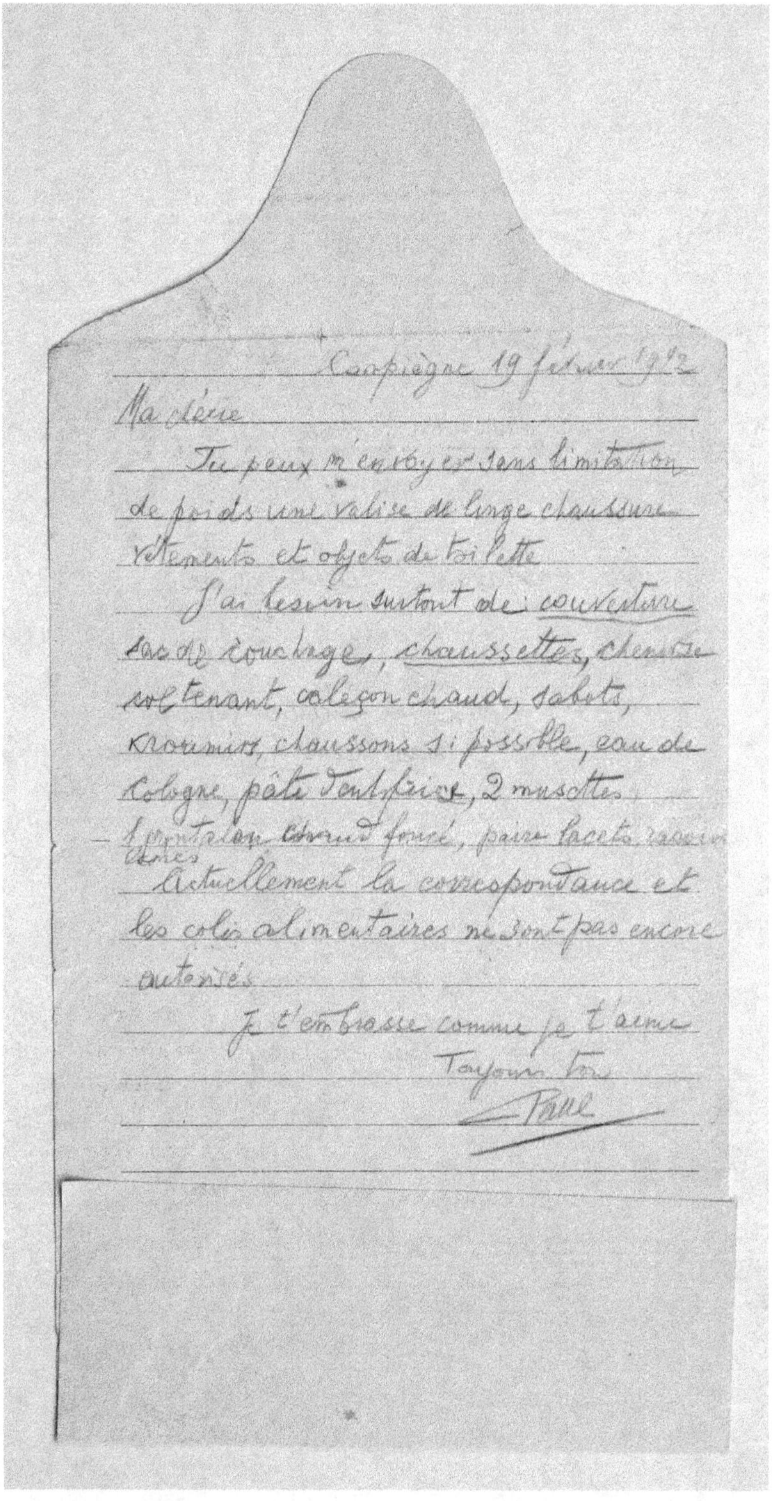

Compiègne 19 février 1942

Ma chérie

Tu peux m'envoyer sans limitation
de poids une valise de linge chaussure
vêtements et objets de toilette

J'ai besoin surtout de: couverture
sac de couchage, chaussettes, chemise
col tenant, caleçon chaud, sabots,
kroumirs, chaussons si possible, eau de
Cologne, pâte dentifrice, 2 musettes,
1 pantalon chaud foncé, paire lacets rasoir
lames

Actuellement la correspondance et
les colis alimentaires ne sont pas encore
autorisés

Je t'embrasse comme je t'aime

Toujours toi

Paul

FIGURE 5.13: Paul to Lucie, 19 February1942 (verso) © The Léon Estate.

[47]
22.III.42

Chérie, voici un rapport qui devrait toucher PM le plus tôt possible.

Ma vie est changée du tout au tout grâce à Mme Raymond et grâce aux 2 colis que le Sauveur m'envoie la popote est aujourd'hui très riche.

Le mauvais sort s'est attaché au 1er des 2 derniers colis. On le livra[it] par petites tranches chez Masse qui, ne sachant pas à qui il était en distribua[it] une partie. D'ailleurs une autre a été volée—je n'ai eu ni beurre ni sucre, ni [confitures?] ni sardines ni chocolat ni pain. J'espère mieux de celui-ci dont nous avons déjà goûté les pommes de terre et les harengs exquis—hier le dîner à 6 était mieux que chez soi.

Je ne vis que de l'espoir de te voir. J'ai passé la visite (2e) allemande.

J'ai hâte de t'embrasser les mains les pieds. Tous mes baisers autour de toi.

Toujours, Paul

Notre sort est inconnu

[48]
jeudi 26 mars, 1942

Chérie—nous sommes comptés et demain on part, je ne sais ni où ni comment. On parle de Troyes—c'est ce que semble dire l'Allemagne, mais on ne sait rien. Quoi qu'il en soit notre sort ne peut être que pire que celui des plus vieux, c'est-à-dire pire que Drancy—alors ?!?!

Je veux que tu te souviennes de toute ma tendresse pour toi et Alexis—dis-le aussi à Catherine et à Simone. Dis-le à tous les amis qui se sont révélés être de vrais amis. Je les aime tous et toutes. Je prie Dieu tous les soirs pour Toi et Alexis et elles et eux tous. J'espère vous revoir mais mon espoir n'est pas très fort. [Schoenfeld?] et les deux [nom illisible] sont avec notre lot, de même [nom illisible], dis-le à Paul [Bernstein?] et les Smoliak dont tu trouveras les adresses dans ma valise et de même des choses à M. Smoliak, 2 rue Navarin.

Mais le plus important pour moi est de te dire que je t'aime comme il y a 20 ans et si je ne te revois pas—ce sera toi que j'aimerai toujours.

Que Dieu te garde, toi et Alexis
Je t'embrasse comme je t'aime
Toujours ton
Paul

Mme Paul Léon
27 rue Casimir-Périer
Paris 7ème
Inv. 70-04

Salut et amitiés spéciaux à Kaminsky, Troubnikoff, Nouvel, etc etc. Comme nous sommes loin de tout ça. Je prie Dieu pour Catherine, Simone, sa mère etc etc et tous les amis qui nous ont aidés ici—!?

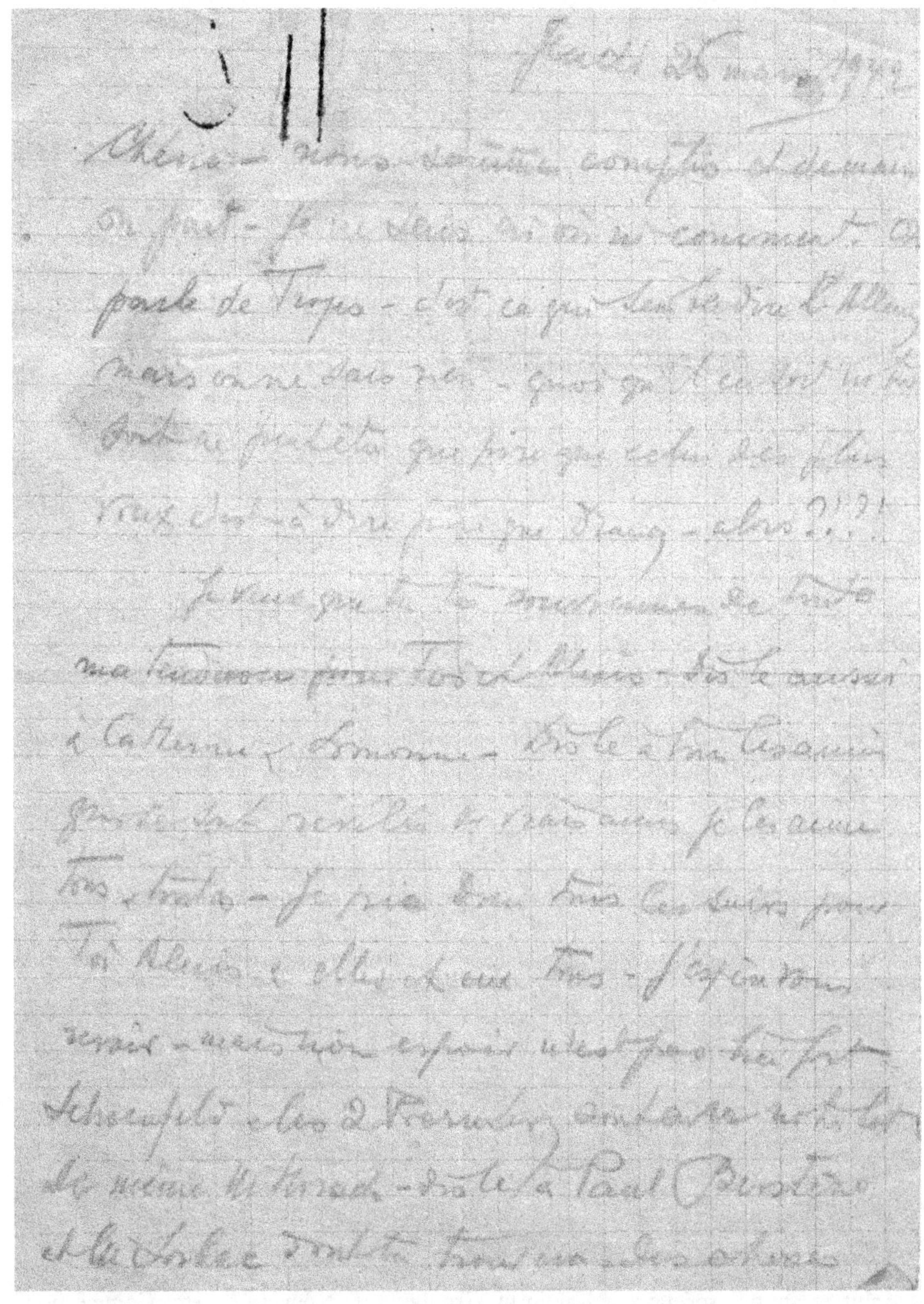

FIGURE 5.14: Paul to Lucie, 26 March 1942 (recto) © The Léon Estate.

FIGURE 5.15: Paul to Lucie, 26 March 1942 (verso) © The Léon Estate.

Léon Paul 15.12.49

M. 1246.

PRÉFECTURE DE LA SEINE

Mairie du 7e Arrondissement

EXTRAIT des Minutes des Actes de Décès

231 / 1501

Coût de cette expédition : 1 NF (Décret du 6 octobre 1958.)

Les droits de timbre ont été supprimés par la loi du 6 janvier 1943 ; le présent extrait est seulement soumis aux droits d'expédition.

C N° 0906941

CC

MINISTÈRE des ANCIENS COMBATTANTS et VICTIMES de --- GUERRE.-/ Le cinq avril mil neuf cent ~~quatre-vingt-treize~~ quarante-deux, est décédé à Auschwitz (Pologne) Paul LEON, né à Petrograd (Russie) le vingt- -- cinq avril mil huit cent quatre-vingt-treize, domicilié en dernier lieu à Paris, rue Casimir Périer 27 fils de Léopold LEON et de Ida RATTNER, époux de --- Elisabeth PONISOWSKY. Le présent acte a été dressé, par Nous, Officier de l'Etat Civil au Ministère des Anciens Combattants et victimes de Guerre, à Paris - le cinq décembre mil neuf cent quarante-neuf.- Transcrit le quinze décembre mil neuf cent quarante-neuf, par Nous, adjoint au Maire du septième arrondissement de Paris.-/

P.E.C.

Paris, le vingt-trois janvier mil neuf cent soixante

Approuvé la rature de trois mots nuls.-/

Le Maire-Adjoint Officier de l'État-Civil

RÉPUBLIQUE FRANÇAISE ... PARIS

Le Maire-Adjoint Officier de l'État-Civil

3174 Co 8. - Imp. mun. - 400.000 ex. - 10-59. - Cde 15958.

FIGURE 5.16: French Death Certificate: 5 April 1942 (1949) © The Léon Estate.

ENGLISH TRANSLATION

Paul Léon was, himself, an interpreter and translator par excellence. His first published volume was the French translation of the letters exchanged in Russian between Tsar Nicholas II – the last Tsar of Russia – and his mother Maria Federovna.[1] In addition to the translation, he also wrote the introduction and annotations for this correspondence, published by Simon Kra in Paris in 1928. Having produced several articles and books on the ideas and writings of Benjamin Constant and Jean-Jacques Rousseau, his last full-length volume, published in 1939, was also a translation: namely the French version of Nikolai Timacheff's *Introduction to the Sociology of Law*.[2]

When he first met James Joyce in 1928, Paul Léon was not yet the established scholar and writer that he would become, but he was already an accomplished translator. He began, almost immediately, to work with Joyce on the French translation of an extract from the 'Anna Livia Plurabelle' chapter of *Finnegans Wake* (I.8).[3] The Drancy letters refer several times to his dreams of revising the French translation of Joyce's *Ulysses* with Beckett and with the philosopher-poet Jean Wahl. These dreams of translating Joyce seem to have been just as vivid and just as vital for him during his internment as his dreams of completing major book-length studies on Benjamin Constant and Jean-Jacques Rousseau. One of the most moving aspects of Paul's camp letters is the fact that, at the very end, just before his voice was snuffed out by the barbarian usurpers of Europe, he had reclaimed his first language. Indeed, his last letters from Compiègne fulfil the observation made to Lucie in an earlier letter from Drancy about his longing for the spontaneity and the emotional authenticity of communicating with her in Russian.

The translation into English of Paul's camp letters was quite uncomplicated on the whole. The minor challenges encountered included the choice of the correct English spelling of Russian names that had already been transliterated/translated into French. The twentieth-century transliteration of Russian names into French was notoriously inconsistent and even the spelling of Lucie's family name shows this. The spelling that she herself used (Ponisowski) is different from the spelling (Ponisovski) on her French tombstone, for example, and from the spelling found in most family documents (Ponisowsky). Another minor challenge concerned the translation of Paul's (rare) use of French slang, for example, the word 'boustifaille' used in the first letter and 'popote', which crops up regularly over the entire correspondence. Both terms refer to food. The word 'boustifaille' would translate as 'grub' if that slang weren't so anachronistic. As for 'popote', it means shared food or shared meals, but similarly there is no specific word in contemporary English that would communicate the idea of 'pooled' food other than 'potluck' dining, which would also be an anachronistic translation and unfaithful to the popular register of 'popote'.

Other translation details perhaps worth noting are the conventions adopted for the translation of titles. 'Pr' (the abbreviation of 'Père') has been translated as 'Fr' (short for 'Father'). 'Mme' for 'Madame' has not been translated into English as 'Mrs' but has rather been retained as Mme. However, the abbreviations 'M' or 'M^{r}' for 'Monsieur' have not been translated into the English 'Mr', but rather the abbreviated form has been spelled out in the translation as 'Monsieur', and where the full title is given as 'Monsieur' in the original it is retained in the translation. The reasons for this choice of non-translation are well illustrated by the standard English non-translation of the title in Flaubert's masterpiece

Madame Bovary. As that point shows and as any reader who can read both languages will readily agree, reading Paul's letters in the original is a completely different experience to reading them in translation. This is precisely the tenor of Edward Weekes's comment to Paul's sister Henriette Hirschmann about the publication of one of Paul's letters about Joyce. Concerning the question as to whether the letter should be published in translation (only) or not, Weekes wisely noted that it 'will be most effective when read in the original French and without the change of a word'.[4] This approach to translation also explains, of course, the decision to include in this volume not just the annotated English translation of Paul Léon's letters from Hell, but also the original French text.

[1]
22 August 1941

My dearest Lucie,

Here I am, enjoying bed & board courtesy of his gracious Excellency—I've been detained along with the lawyers of the Bar council of Paris—mistakenly of course, for I'm neither a Frenchman nor a member of the Bar council.[5] Nonetheless, this means that we're housed in a room apart with special perks. And since we're all for the chop in any case, better to be gobbled up along with the lawyers than in circumstances where I wouldn't enjoy these privileges.[6]

We are sleeping on bare wooden planks and I regret not being plumper, for my bones are suffering. But we've been promised that there's great luxury ahead—straw mattresses!

Under no circumstances should you take any particular action. The top priority is to retain your dignity. There is talk here of triage, checks, etc. but in any case here in Drancy we already number approximately 8,000 and more people are arriving all the time.[7] This all leads me to conclude that we won't be remaining here for long. As some are as old as 61, I can't see any reason why I should be released definitively—in that sense I'm better off being housed with the lawyers than in any other quarters.

In any event, you must get it into your head that you are not to blame in any way for this. It is, rather, a general measure and everything will become clear in due course. Some food rations will have to be sent in soon—but all in its own good time—you can specify 'Lawyers Group', Drancy camp— If and when they start releasing people—without any risk of rearrest—then I'll be happy to be freed. But if it's just going to be a question of getting arrested all over again, it would only be a waste of energy.

That's about it for the moment. I'm going to need paper, both plain paper and notepaper for letters—naturally I forgot all about bringing some with me—and also some handkerchiefs. But all that must wait until letters and parcels are allowed.

I'm taking a chance on sending this off without knowing if it will reach you. But don't forget that I'm better off here than in Pithiviers.[8]

I send all my love to you—to Alexis too and, since I'm feeling sorry for myself, I also send my love to everybody around you, including Mlle Simone, whether she wants it or not and even the *concierge*, in the same spirit.[9]

Give Catherine my love too and reassure her.[10] Tell her not to worry too much,

Ever yours,

Paul

[2]
23 August 1941

My dearest Lucie
Well, I've got through the second night. I slept well apart from my upper legs, but one gets used to the discomfort.

Lots of different rumours are circulating. The only thing that has been officially announced is that our detention is a reprisal measure.[11] Despite this announcement, our treatment has neither improved nor disimproved.

As I already told you, naturally I feel I would be much better off at home than here, but being released one day only to be picked up the next is not worth the trouble. All the same, do try to find out what's going on—Ostafreff should keep you informed.[12]

Mademoiselle Simone must have given you the 5,000 francs that were in the house. Be careful, both of you, with expenditure. Struve is supposed to bring you some money and has more items to sell.[13] Popoff is to bring you 2,000 at the end of August.[14] You can ask him for this sum in my name whenever you wish. Also, Pierre is due back from holidays on the 26th.[15]

From now on you'll have to pay all the bills that come for us and also for upstairs. You know the various amounts due from us. Jeanne is to get 400 francs in cash,[16] along with the price of all my cigarettes and 100 francs for drinks, plus 100 francs extra. That should come to something like 750 francs. Also, give 100 francs to the *concierge*. I think that's everything.

I send my love to you all and patiently await a release that will perhaps come sooner than we think.

Ever yours,
Paul

Have you seen Catherine and how is she doing? She's got to stick it out with serenity.

All correspondence is still forbidden and [illegible words] ten days. The parcels [illegible words].

*L[etter] to be sent to this address: Madame Léon, 27 rue Casimir-Périer Paris 7e.

** 27/VIII No possibility so far of sending this letter off. I am quite hungry, in fact very, as indeed are we all. There are 3,000 parcels in the camp office but there's an embargo on distributing them to us. Still, I hope there's one there for me.

Give my love to everybody,
Paul

[3]
5 September 1941

My dearest Lucie,
I think I'm enjoying a moment of lucidity and I want to make the most of it by writing to you, for up until now the only letters and notes I've written were idiotic. I'm not doing badly; on the contrary my morale is good and the slimming diet isn't having an excessively adverse effect on me, other than on my ankles. But given that I'm not walking a lot, I can't complain too much.

Regarding visits, Weber is the person who might be in a position to help you.[17] He knows Monsieur François of the police *Préfecture*,[18] who might be able to negotiate all this. I would be very happy to see you. I don't expect to receive your parcel for at least a week, for they are spending so long sorting and searching them that only about fifty are actually delivered each day, and there are 4,250 of us here.[19] If you haven't already sent all this, or if you aren't going to bring it with you when you're coming here on a visit, I would like a box of Valda lozenges, a tube of inorhinyl, a tube of Eska and a box of aspirin or Aspro.[20] There are a lot of head colds around here.

How is Catherine and has Alec come back to Paris yet?[21] I have the impression that we are going to be here for quite a long time, perhaps right up to the end of the war and I wonder what I will find at home when I get out. I don't think that anybody is particularly bothered about our fate and I think that we'll just be left as we are, without a stir, unless we're to be interned for the duration of the anti-Jewish exhibition,[22] but then I've yet to see coachloads of tourists come to gawk at us.

How is Alexis? I advise you to adopt an attitude of great prudence and patience. Full responsibility for the family rests on your shoulders now. You must manage your nerves and keep a grip on yourself. I will only love you all the more for this, if that were possible. The best solution for yourself and for Alexis would perhaps be to leave for the Free Zone.[23] Certainly, Alexis absolutely *must* go there as of next year anyway if I've not been freed before then. He's the one we have to put first. As I already told you, I have every confidence in the good sense of Mademoiselle Simone. Ask for her advice as often as you need to. *I make a point of* ensuring that all the bills for our apartment and for Alec's apartment as well are paid by you.[24] And all the contracts should be signed and transferred into their names.

I think that's all I have to say other than that I love you so much still and am so sorrowful not to see you.

I send you my love and big hugs,

Forever yours,

Paul

Phone Littré 0-52 to speak to Madame Weill.

Monsieur Ulmo says thanks for the three parcels and that we're well.[25]

[4]

[undated; around 7 September 1941]

Today we received a visit from the 'President of the Bar Council' who announced as though it was good news that all further visits are cancelled. I gave your telephone number so that they could alert you. I'm still upset, nonetheless, and I must ask you without further ado to send in the authorized clothes parcel. Just to be sure, here is a list, even though every time I make one I forget something. So I'm counting on you to remember.

1) Bed slippers 2) Razor blades 3) *Socks* 4) Hand towels (two or three) 5) Big sheets of paper (which you'll find by the window) 6) Handkerchiefs 7) the Rousseau volume that's on my bedside table 8) the Balzac volume 9) my Basque beret 10) the beige-brown suit.

Here is another list of what you need to get transferred to Mademoiselle Simone's account: the phone, the electricity and the gas; she'll need to make a declaration to the TSF in her name and there's the insurance. You'll need to do the same thing for upstairs—for Alec and the Ostafreffs. You must *pay for everything*—in both cases.[26]

You can always get some more money from Pierre but don't spend too much. Mademoiselle Simone knows the value of money better than you do so ask for her advice. If you can, slip two or three banknotes (100 francs) into the pockets of my suit. Cigarettes and food are still forbidden but people are saying that the searches are cursory, so try to include a little without going too far and without spending too much.

This is my situation:

I'm housed in the same quarters as all the lawyers, who are being held as hostages. Don't let this frighten you because it means very little. We are drawing up lists of people's ages and veteran status. I'm writing on the back of this letter the details of my own military service, because here we're only concerned with service in the French army.[27]

As we're administered here by the *gendarmerie* and the French judicial police,[28] they are the ones who decide whether the net will be widened or not and up until now they've only widened the criteria to include those people who can be useful to them. So we'll have to wait. Stay calm and stay at home as much as possible, because any time I can I'll make sure that you are called on the phone. Struve can, if necessary, sell all the Madame de Staël books but don't go near the Rousseau collection or the books on political thought.[29]

Mme Paul Léon
27 Rue Casimir Périer
Paris 7e

Here are the details of my military service:

Léon, Paul, born 25th April 1893 in St Petersburg, Russia
Russian refugee
Married with a French son
Law professor

1914–1918 War—Russian Imperial Army
Volunteer with the 33rd regiment
Mobilized to the front from 15 July 1915 to 1st May 1917
(nominated for decoration with the Medal of St George, 1st class)
Emperor Paul I Military Academy 1st May–1st September 1917
Promoted to Second Lieutenant 1st September 1917
2nd artillery regiment 1st September 1917–1st February 1918
Seconded to the Military Academy as artillery and machine-gun instructor
Demobilized

1939–1940 War
Review Council for Russian Refugees
9 April 1940 deemed fit for active service but not called up

[5]
9 September 1941

My very dear Lucie,

Here is the letter that I wrote on the 5th but which couldn't be sent. I hope that you received the one I wrote on the 7th.[30] When we're sending off a letter from here we never know whether or not it will be delivered. You know all my desiderata now—a beret, Valda lozenges, inorhinyl, Eska, razor blades. And large sheets of squared paper—you'll find some wrapped in brown paper beneath the window.

From one day to the next we're being promised parcels of food. Once they've been authorized I'll leave the contents up to you, but until that day dawns, we will be going hungry. This is indeed the only reason I have for believing that our detention is more or less provisional—otherwise, I can't see the point of this exaggerated harshness.

Do tell Catherine that she doesn't need to worry any more. We'll get through all this, I'm convinced of it.

As for getting out of here, what can I say? You know more about this, perhaps, than I do. I think that we have to play the war veteran card, given that I am indeed a war veteran. But here in the camp only the names of those who have fought in the French army have been registered. We'll see if veterans of the allied armies can also benefit from these same measures in due course.

We're not receiving any post yet. This is another harshness that seems quite inexplicable. At the head of our secret lair is Lieutenant Dannecker.[31] He's the grand master of the Jewish question but acts through the intermediary of the French authorities—through Commissioner Voineau and through the gendarmerie.[32] But I think that Weber is better placed than anyone else to inform you about this.

Do give my love to everyone.

I send you big hugs and I love you,

As ever,
Your Paul

This must be the fifth letter that I've written to you.[33] If you are sending me a roll of toilet paper (I already have two, which is too many because I'm constipated), do slip two or three 100 franc notes into them and then stick the edges together. I looked in vain in the first parcel for some cash. The sports jacket was attached to the suitcase with a piece of twine and was not wrapped at all. Is this how it was sent?[34]

[6]
10 September 1941
Mme Paul Léon
27 rue Casimir-Périer
7[e]

My dearest Lucie,

Today the mood has turned to complete pessimism. After an inspection along with a photography session that turned out to be a pure exercise in humiliation, we've just been told that our cell is to be disbanded.[35] That's to say that henceforth we will be dispersed across different rooms, sleeping on the floor with all the others, so it's not exactly a promising prospect. I would very much like to know what kind of false or true promises you've received through Engelmann. Everything depends on a certain Lieutenant Dannecker, but all this must be much clearer on the outside than here inside. I would like to believe that you at least have some hope because this is all going to be very difficult. The older men, the ones over 60, and the young, those under 18, who were supposed to leave are still here and I have the feeling that we are going to be here for a long time, if not right up to the end of the war. Try to find out. We've still had no news from the outside. We will be allowed two letters each month—so write to me in code.

Another thing that I forgot to tell you is that I bought and paid for a bottle of Monnet brandy from Petrossian's.[36] They were supposed to deliver it but it never arrived—you can go and collect it.

I send you all my love and hugs,

Yours as ever,

Paul

[7]
11 September 1941

Mme Léon
27 rue Casimir Perrier
Paris

My dearest Lucie.

Thank you so much for your card and for the sleeping bag. Both mean so much to me, but I had been waiting for them for so long and now I feel so much weaker regarding the state of my nerves. Yet with all the rumours that are circulating at the moment it's so important, come what may, to remain strong.

It's also vital to think of the future. If I'm released, we'll have to leave Paris. And even if I stay here in Drancy, you and Alexis will have to leave. Alexis can move to a *lycée* in Nice or Grenoble. I'm slightly acquainted with an arts professor at the University of Grenoble. In Nice I know nobody.

The latest rumour doing the rounds is that we're being quarantined, but that the French war veterans could be released ahead of time. In that respect it might be important to continue the work that you've been doing to establish my military service records.

We're being moved today—I think I'm going to be sleeping on the floor, but thanks to the sleeping bag I'll be alright. Under no circumstances should you send me any more things until winter—otherwise, if I get out of here I won't be able to take everything home with me.[37]

In any event, as I have no money left, and if you can't send me some in the way I suggested, then give the Drancy Camp Police 100 francs in my name. In that way when I can go outside the building I'll be able collect the money.

My new room is Staircase 16, Room 13/14.[38]

I have written at least seven letters to you.[39] Did you receive them all? How is Alec? Have you had news of him?

I send my love to Catherine too and also to Mademoiselle Perréon. I'm grateful to her for her few words. As for you, I'd like to wrap my arms tightly around you,

As ever your Paul
who loves you

12 September 1941

Thank you, dear Lucie. I slept very well in the sleeping bag—my last night sleeping on the floor. I hope it won't be worse tomorrow on the floor.

My registration number here is 5203—as though I were a convict.

You must have read the article in *Paris Soir* and in *Le Petit Parisien*.[40] What a disgrace and what lies!

[8]
[No date; after 11/12 September 1941]
Lucie Léon
27 rue Casimir-Périer, Paris 7[e]
Inv. 70.04
Block IV Stairway 16, Room 13
Registration Number 5203

Given the suspension of those visits requiring special permission from the Police *Préfecture*, I request the urgent dispatch of the clothes parcel as itemized by Madame Netter to which a pillow should be added.[41]

P.L.

[9]

16 September 1941

My very, very dear Lucie,

This letter also will be brought to you by a friend of my friend Monsieur Guterman who, as his name suggests, is a very good person.[42] He takes care of my 250 grams of bread so that I don't eat it all in one go and he has loaned me 100 francs. He will be able to lend me more, so stop worrying about money.

Today we got a shock. The German camp administration has left. In actual fact there are still some Germans in charge but they seem to have lost interest in the camp. The French police have become both more harsh and more corrupt.[43] Nonetheless, if you have any hope, but hope that is *well founded* and not based on wishful thinking, please let me know indirectly or secretly in the reply coupon that I'll send you on Thursday. The regime here is so punative that I cannot believe that this will go on for much longer. Yet some people are saying that in Pithiviers, where the regime gave internees much more freedom, things have become just as harsh as here. It's the absence of food parcels that makes life so hard, because it makes us weak.

No effort should be spared to prepare Alexis for leaving for the Free Zone.[44] He must sell last year's schoolbooks, all of them. And he needs to get the prospectus for the Maths/Philosophy course and start purchasing the prescribed books. It's harder to find what one needs down the country.

How is everybody? Do you have any news of Alec–I'M worried about him.

And give Catherine a big, big hug from me.

I'm very stressed about all the rumours that are circulating and my nerves are starting to give way.

All my—very biggest—hugs to you—and to Alexis and all those who are at your side, including Madame Perréon and Mademoiselle Simone.

Your own Paul who loves you forever.

Later on September 16th

My head is working so badly that I forgot to tell you that your package of medicines arrived safely with all that you had put into it. It's a pity that you didn't wrap one of the medicines in a few words in your own hand, telling me of your hopes, for I feel very low today. I don't know why. But I am hopeful, full of hope in you.

I love you and hope to see you soon

Your Paul

who is yours forever.

Madame Paul Léon

27 Rue Casimir-Périer

Inv 70.04 Paris 7e

[10]

18 September 1941

My very, very dear Lucie,

Thanks so much for your latest parcel and for the letter with the certificates. However, here they will only accept men who served in the French army, so perhaps this will be more useful to you outside? Be careful, however, because in Tatisteff's certificate there are two errors:[45] 1) my birth date is given as 1897, whereas the year should be 1893. 2) I'm said to have completed my military service on May 1st 1917, whereas I finished it in February 1918. Do organize, if you can, a medical examination for me. They have begun to liberate those declared unfit for military service. The camp is entirely under the control of the French—and there is corruption everywhere. I hope that you will be able to have me freed because in spite of the phial of [carnosine] that I took immediately,[46] I feel tired out and my nerves are frayed.

The noise in the room is horrific. I send you and all the others my love,

Your Paul

They are saying that the young and the old will be leaving on Saturday.

[11]

19 September 1941

Drancy

Block 1V Stairway 16 Room 13

No. 5203

My very, very dear Lucie,

This is the 2nd time that I'm finally able to write to you.[47] I hope that our detention will not be prolonged for much longer. Do send me news of Alec, Catherine and everybody. I am waiting impatiently to hear from you. I send my love to all those around you, but especially to you and Alexis.

Thank you for your registered letter with my military papers enclosed. But there are two errors in the certificate from the rue Guénégaud.[48] 1) I was born in 1893 and not, as the certificate says, in 1897. 2) My military service ended in March 1918 and not on May 1st 1917.

That's all for now. I'm just waiting and hoping to see you soon. They are starting now to release those declared unfit for military service and also, it's being said, the young and the old. Our turn will come.

Forever your own Paul

who loves you.

[12]
30 September 1941

My very dearest Lucie,

I am pained not to have received a response to my card from you yet. Perhaps it was censored?

Would you mind, please, having the certificate from the Bureau of Russian Refugees corrected? That is, my date of birth and also the dates of my military service which ended in February 1918 and not in May 1917 (in the military academy with the 2nd artillery regiment).

I would like, furthermore, if Kaminsky could pay a visit to Father Serge Boulgakov to ask him to pray for me.[49] Ever since I've been here it's the memory of the Russian Orthodox Church that alone has allowed me to gain strength sometimes, and patience too as Mademoiselle Simone advises.

I would also like if Alexis could buy for me from Budé the selected Gospel extracts.[50] Or else you could ask for my copy back from that friend of Nicolas Anatolievich to whom I lent it (I've forgotten his name now but he's the person I stayed with that night in Helsinki).[51]

I'm worried about Alexis, about his work, and about his future. Have you done anything for him? You could always leave [Paris] with him because our friends here would take care of me in your absence.

I hope to see you soon, but I don't know that I will. Kaminsky can tell Father Serge that if I ever get out of here, I will go to see him. I would like if Alexis would see him too.[52]

As for me, I still love you and send my love to you and to all who are close to you.

Your own Paul

[13]
8 October 1941

My very dearest Lucie,

1) Thank you very much for your card and for trying to give me some hope. But I am so tired and my spirit is so battered, to a pulp almost, that I cannot share your hope. What would you have me think of Roger, given that he hasn't been able by now to obtain permission for a visit for you? Have you heard anything from our friend, Engelmann? This would seem to me to be a more delicate matter. Have you thought of approaching Vals? You could get in touch with him either directly at Laval's on the avenue des Champs Elysées or via a certain Monsieur Charvet whom Pierre knows well. But be careful about him. There is also that friend of Alec's from beside the rue de Ponthieu. His name is Andreas I think and he might be able to give you some information.

2) I don't want to influence Alexis too much—if he feels more [drawn towards] Father Maillard then let him do it after having seen Fr Serge.[53]

3) I hope that you are settling *absolutely all* the domestic bills and that you are not leaving any of them for Mademoiselle Simone to pay. I must stress this over and over again. You must also look after all the expenses for upstairs as agreed. And again do follow Mademoiselle Simone's advice as far as budgeting and everything else is concerned.

4) Finally I send you all the love in my heart. I'm sorry but I also send my love to Catherine whose words touched me more deeply than yours. I hope that there is no

further misunderstanding between us, if there ever was one at a certain point, because that would bring about an eternal separation. I am so weak right now that I wouldn't be able to bear it. I am sorry if I am offending you but in my current state, tormented by hunger and by a monstrousness that never ceases, I no longer have the strength to think and yet *I love you, I love you* and, as God is my witness, I am telling the truth.

As soon as I began this letter, like all my letters indeed, I forgot what I wanted to say. I have to write you an official letter tomorrow or the day after tomorrow. You will reply, won't you?

I am praying to God! Will you thank those who are praying for me and also those who have asked for prayers for me? May [His] will be done.

I take you in my arms,

your Paul who loves you forever.

I send my love to everybody.

Mme Léon
27 rue Casimir Périer
Paris 7e
Inv 70-04

[14]
9 October 1941

My dearest, dearest Lucie,

Please forgive me, my love, for my complaints, my sadness, my lack of refinement—my only excuse is that I am diminished morally, physically, and in every other way too. I have got to the point where I even wonder if this diminished state is not a definitive one.

A request—have you been to see Madame Bauh,[54] 10 rue Claude Lorrain, Paris and have you given her what I asked you to? Can you pay her 500 francs? I have very little hope but I am praying—for those who are praying for me, for you and for Alexis. May God spare you—may His will be done.

I send you my love and hold you tightly in my arms,

Forever yours,

Paul

My fond thoughts go out to all our friends—I just hope these are not my final thoughts.

As for the certificate for the committee, another one will have to be requested because it's not just the erroneous dates, but the rest of my service record. Here they won't accept any war veteran certificates except those of the French army and they won't accept the military service review. You can therefore hang on to this certificate for yourself.

I'm thinking a lot about how best to organize Alexis's life. I hope that he has begun to study right from the start, that he is taking some classes in maths, and that as far as philosophy is concerned he is following the advice of Monsieur [Schuster?]. At least until I can come home, if ever that day dawns.

For my own part, I send my love to you and also to everybody who is in my thoughts and all those who are thinking of me.

Forever yours,

Paul

[15]
22 October 1941

My beloved Lucie, this missive is first and foremost a to-do list for you. I will start with that, because my pride and my willpower are far from having deserted me.

Here is my list: 1) Will you go to Pierre's and get 10,000 from him? You can say that Alec gave me a sum of 10,000 for myself in July but that I didn't actually take any of it. However, if you don't receive that much, it's still the amount that I thought I would have for July.

2) Go to Margraff's,[55] 37 rue St André des Arts, either by yourself or taking Struve along with you, and give them 2,000 francs. Tell them to put aside for me all the books that they bought from me belonging to the Benj. C. collection. Tell them I will stand over the price that they have fixed and give them at least double what they paid me, along with a few 1815 brochures, as these are of no great importance. The most significant books—the ones that I mourn—are the Constant collection.

3) Ask Struve to go to Rivière's and to buy back Moret, Chauviré, Beaudoin, Weill, for 1,950 francs if he can.[56]

4) Pay Madame Bauh 3,500 francs *in all* and get a receipt (you must have given her 500 already, so just add 3,000 now). She's at 10, rue Claude Lorrain.

I think that's all till the next time I write—don't think that I've completely lost my mind, even though I'm not too far removed from madness. But it's important to put some order on one's plans.

Now that, thanks to you and to Fr Cyprien,[57] I have just spent 5 tolerable days, my heart is filled with an unexpected gentleness. Oh, they will still have their job cut out for them to get rid of my falseness and to reawaken my faith but I want so very much for God to touch me with his grace. I think that my present trials, which are causing such suffering to my physical being and affecting in turn my moral being and its weaknesses, are of some value because they mean that family, friends and relations can be spared the worst. It is better that I suffer than that I lose someone as dear to me as Maria was to Choura.[58] That is why I am praying to God for everybody. Do tell Catherine. Perhaps what I'm going through now, these trials that are driving me to the very edge of madness, will mean that Serge will know greater happiness. Tell Madame Perréon and Mademoiselle Simone that I have begun to love them intensely since I've come here because I know that they are supporting you with their care and their gentleness. Tell this to the Duttenhofers also, whom I wronged by making fun of them on so many occasions. Tell Troubnikov, Nicolai Anatolievich,[59] Stein and of course Kaminsky too: tell them that I love them all from the bottom of my heart.

As for you, my love, you know that I love you and so I won't say it again. But I hope that you were with Catherine the day before yesterday. You can see that words and objects are things of nothing. Do invite Dauphin and his wife to lunch at our place or out to a restaurant.[60] And start to plan a lunch for them along with myself at Madeleine's.[61] But six weeks' time seems so far away and I am holding you in my arms, as ever, Paul

[16][62]
5 November 1941
Mme Léon, 27, r. Casimir-Périer
Inv 70-04

My dear Lucie,

This receipt will be brought to you by Jacob Eskis.[63]

Will you please get the necessary cash from Pierre and give it to him, unless you have already paid 1,000 to Mme Joudrie, Monsieur Eskis's sister, in which case you will pay him 2,500 instead of 3,500.

Do get a receipt for this.

Paul Léon, 5.xi.1941

[5 November 1941]

In order to be saved I want to believe in God but I'm so close to despair.

I love you.

I embrace you.

5.xi.41

Yesterday I spent 1,000 francs. I'm mad. Hide some money in the parcel—you must pay 5,500 in total to Madame Bauh and 3,500 to Monsieur Eskis.

Paul, with love.

Madame Léon,
27 rue Casimir-Périer
Paris 7e
Inv 70-04

Every day, every hour adds to my suffering. I feel myself disappearing into the void. I place my hope in you.

[17]
6 November [1941]

Another night of anguish, my love. Forgive me—I have lost all hope except for my hope in you. *Don't* send the winter parcel. If I receive it, that will mean that I must abandon all hope. But do send another food parcel. Ask for a coupon from Monsieur Guterman whom you were to see. It has now been confirmed that the reason that my release is being opposed is not personal but rather concerns all of us. Monsieur Netter has been told this.

See Monsieur Wahl and introduce him to Sam Beckett.

I send you hugs,

I love you.

I'm hungry

I have yet to receive a single food parcel.

6/XI/41

I'm sending you this note and will call to give news of Monsieur Léon [illegible word] for there is still nothing this morning

Jean Wahl[64]

[18]
7 November 1941

Lucie, my darling,

I've got a little job in one of the camp offices, so I'm easier in my mind. But I still feel very heavy and numb. I even find it difficult to think. I am still hoping against hope that I will see you and hold you soon. I've been told that there's a parcel for me, so I'll add a few words to this letter this evening to say if I'm still very hungry. Monsieur Guterman must have told you how we live here but I love you as ever. I'll be back soon.

I've received *everything*, my love, and I've been able to make my companions very happy. I'm overjoyed and am bursting into tears every five minutes. I want to take you in my arms. I have eaten such a lot. I'll be sick, but never mind.

Here is the Wahl piece:

'What ragged Gods,
What decrepit Jesuses
Multiple Jesuses
Jesuses without a mission
Who feebly tread the bleak courtyard
United by one doubting hope
That you would be hard put
To find on their parched countenances.
A harsh self-regard hovers around their eyes
And their hopeless gaze fades into the void.'[65]

I love you, I love you, I love you.
Oh that darkness that falls already at 7 p.m.
As ever, Paul.

***The food parcel will come on Monday or Tuesday, isn't that so?

[19]
8 November [1941]

There is an internee in my room whose name is Monsieur Berels.[66] He's an ingenuous and sincere soul and he has just had a baby daughter whom he has never seen. Can you phone and visit his wife—at 242 rue St Martin, Archives 31-76.[67] You can tell Madame Berels that her parcels are very good but that she should put more bread into the next one. You could tell her roughly the weight limit. You can ask her to come to the apartment and tell her to go to the office on the Place J. Jaurès.[68]

As for your own parcel, it was perfect. But I too need bread. And regarding the chocolate, the chocolate, the chocolate, that was so delicious and that made thousands so happy, there is none left. Monsieur Berels has taken matters in hand and is rationing my food. Even the two little packets of spices reached me safely by some miracle without becoming undone or going astray.[69] But in general it's best to parcel them more tightly or else they will be lost.

I have no more yellow shoelaces, no laces at all in fact. Could you send me a pair, please. And sugar lumps, cheese, butter, bacon. . .

Thank you for your card. If I get out [of here] we will go out to dine by ourselves like two lovebirds.

I send you my love and hugs,

Paul

You must hold off sending me my winter clothes parcel!

Could you write a few lines to the wife of my room leader, Rue des immeubles industriels, XIe. Monsieur Guterman will tell you more if necessary.

[20]

Mme Léon, 27 r. Casimir Périer, Paris 7e

Inv. 70.04

11 November 1941

My dearest, a fresh medical examination has been announced for next Saturday for all those whose release has been opposed. This examination will be conducted by Dr Tisné from the Police *Préfecture* and by a French doctor from the Palais Bourbon.[70] After I got your parcel, it seems that the swelling of my eyes was replaced by colic of the liver. But my ankles are swollen. I don't know what that means from a clinical point of view but perhaps you could mention it to Monsieur Guterman. I received the Debray certificate and thanks for that. I hope that you have been able to see Madame Berels and that you will be able to give a good report on the baby girl.

No matter how philosophical I try to be, I still go through hours and entire nights of anguish in a torment of darkness and torpor.

Have you seen Wahl?[71] I have such good memories of him.

I am losing heart but I'm still holding on. I did try to be part of the team that is sent to get the parcels from the guardroom but I wasn't chosen.

Ulmo is in the same dormitory as me and has spoken to me of the admiration that he and [Pithiviers?] have for you.[72]

But I'm so anxious to see you, to embrace you.

I have just found out that you sent a second parcel. Does it have my name on it?

I embrace you as I love you—

Please don't send a winter parcel until all hope is gone—

[21]

12 November 1941

I worked until 2 a.m. on the list of departures for today. Afterwards, the night-time anguish starts up again. If only I could get out of here too!

My darling, I'm still placing my hope in you, and I'm praying for you and for Alexis and everybody else. How I long to see you all. I have learned that on Saturday it's going to be a German doctor. Speak to Guterman about this: he might have some good advice. But I don't want to mention anything about it to you here. This message will be sent or brought by a disciple of Wahl's, whose wife is charming incidentally. See him tomorrow but I am praying that this message will reach you today so that no time will be lost.

I love you, I want to see you, I hope to see you

Forever yours,
Paul

My madness is producing dreams of culinary expeditions with you.

*'My beard is growing snow white'

[22]
12 November 1941
Monsieur Léon, 27 r. Casimir Périer, Paris 7e

Thank you, my love, for the parcel. I am suffering from an attack of colic. It's actually painless but it has put a stop to my hunger and so I am feeling human again. I even feel like smoking a cigarette from time to time.

I have so many things to tell you. I'm quite bothered by tiny ailments, sores that just won't clear up. On my fingers, on my feet, etc. I'm worried that they might be caused by the lack of trace elements in my blood. But everything is going to heal now.

I have just had lunch, shared with Ulmo and also with my guardian, Berels. And it all came from your parcel. You can imagine the rounds of colic that are going to start up again, but it is all, or at least it was all, absolutely delicious. Of course now, purely in the interests of our well-being of course, the camp administration has ordered that all the chimneys must be blocked up so that we can in future make for ourselves neither soup nor tea. All this by way of illustrating the pains being taken to see to our comfort.

On another note, my love, I want to repeat what I have already put in the message that Madame Berels is going to send to you. The medical review in which the Germans are involved is to take place on Saturday. The German doctor must be made aware of my situation and consent to let me be seen. If necessary, he must actively ask to see me so that I can be released.

For the next parcel, some (or a lot of) jam and if you can at all, some cigarettes or tobacco and a few 100 franc notes. I don't have a penny left, but if you do send money, hide it well. I found the chocolate hidden in the shoes. Did you go to see Madame Berels and their little daughter? It's 272 rue St Martin-Archives 31-76.

He's the one who is taking care of me. He's got a pure and ingenuous spirit and wants to get out of here to see his wife and daughter. I'll mention him to the doctor and also to Mademoiselle Monod, who is a beautiful person.[73]

But today there is a new list of releases, 200 approximately. That will make enough work for the whole afternoon and it will bring new pangs of anguish for the ones who are not leaving—including me.

For when am I going to see you again?

And what does Guterman have to say? He promised it would be last Saturday so there's been an eight-day delay. Has he forgotten?

[23]
[no date; probably 15 and 16 November 1941]

I know, my treasure, that I have hurt you yet again. Please forgive me if you can. The truth is that no matter how philosophical one tries to be, there are still moments of anguish and pain. Indeed the Garden of Gethsemane is far, far closer to me than the Sermon on the

Mount. So very close to me is it that I must now place my spiritual life entirely in the hands of Fathers Serge or Cyprien, my emotional life in your hands and my material life in the hands of Mademoiselle Simone. You must indeed tell the latter that she is in grave danger because since I arrived here in Drancy I have never thought of you without Mademoiselle Simone and also—as ever—Catherine coming into my head. But then, there is also my intellectual life, and that one I would like to keep for myself and I cannot indeed hand it over without completely falling apart. This is the part of my life that is most severely threatened by the 14–15 hours of darkness that must be endured each day. Last night I was all of a sudden overcome by the feeling that you hadn't gone to see Margraff and my blood ran cold. Did you see Madame Bauh and Monsieur Eskiss? You can see from this how foolish I am but at the same time, now that, thanks to your and to Berels, my basic physical needs are no longer controlling me, I have become like a child again and am haunted both day and night by visions, hallucinations of caramels, sweets and chocolates. It's not yet the same thing with cigarettes. Jam, butter. . .. My legs are in better shape now except for the smaller sores, which are getting worse and are turning into small open wounds. But that will pass.

I have some requests: for candles, for matches and for some methylated spirits for heating up coffee. All of this is forbidden but there might be a way of sending it in the winter parcel. And so, as you see, I can bring myself to mention the latter. I am submitting to it, against my own better judgement and with a heavy heart, but that will pass.

Can you phone Madame Pierre Masse and meet with her: her husband has told her that you will. And can you also contact Madame Jean Jarnaci,[74] [the wife of] my boss and tell her how much we all admire her. And I know how much you too are admired, and I love and admire you forever, forever your own

Paul—

16/11/41

Aluminium containers with two round compartments, eau de cologne and pens.

My love, your eighth parcel surpassed itself. Everybody here, including Monsieur Ulmo, is asking for the addresses of the confectioners and dairies. We had a real feast. Thank you, thank you. Have you seen Madame Berels? Her husband is so good to me that when I think of her it's always with a heavy heart. How is their little girl and how is she managing to feed her?

I love you and embrace you

Paul

All the nicotined spices arrived safely.

I have just seen Monsieur Bauh and he wants to know what is happening about the payment to Madame Bauh, Eskiss and Margraff. I found the three banknotes.

I'm going to try to give this letter to the Ray of Sunshine who is lighting us up with her cross.

***Some oil for a night-light. Have you seen Wahl?

[24]

Wednesday, 19 November 1941

My beloved, I've finally seen Mademoiselle Noel. The angrier the policeman became, the more determined I felt. My imagination has become so weak that I can't picture what I look like to others. Did she find me very old? Thank you for your card. I hope that your prayer will be granted but nothing specific was noted in relation to me. The only memory that he can have are of my swollen legs and also of my being the only person able to speak German. I cannot wait to hold you in my arms—after this afternoon my attacks of anguish have started up again. When, when, oh when am I going to see you again?

Judging from your card you have settled my debts with Madame Bauh and Monsieur Eskiss and Monsieur Margraff and also perhaps Rivière. Today Monsieur Bauh told me that there are only 3,500 francs more to be paid. But the total amount owing to him is 6,000 fr. Could you please give his wife either 2,500 or 500 if you have already paid her the 5,500 that I asked you to give her previously?

Requests—I am dreadfully hungry today and have no parcel food to eat at all. So here are some suggestions: a parcel with about 2kg of bread, 1kg of boiled potatoes in their jackets and condiments such as salt, mustard, tea, and a second parcel with butter, bacon, ham, anything like that would be good. From tomorrow on we will be 'cooking' and eating with Monsieur Ulmo and so will need preserves, or pâté, meat, fish, figs, dates, fruit. Did you receive the coupons that were given to our Ray of Sunshine for you and Madame Berels? Do invite the latter to our home.

My head is full of the four projects to be completed, plus a fifth—the revision of the French translation of Joyce's *Ulysses*.

Mustard, stock or Oxo cubes, olives, toilet paper, shoelaces. The warm coat could be put into Monsieur Ulmo's winter parcel. He has just had news of a food parcel for him, I hope that there will be one for me tomorrow morning. Sugar, lemon, caramels, lots of them, and some chocolate. . ..

How do you like the Jean Wahl piece? This is the final section:

Meanwhile these blasphemies,
these screams and death rattles
that resound from the edge of all eternity
Will drive back from the tabernacles
Barbaric minds and all their cruelty

I am so tired of waiting. I want to see you. We will go to dine just the two of us right beside us, at Marius's—my legs are so sore.

Give my love to Mademoiselle Noel as I send my love to you,[75]

Forever yours, in love and anguish,

Paul

Have you seen Paulhan?[76] Can you speak to him about the publication of *Ulysses* in the Pléiade in a translation by myself, Beckett and J. Wahl?

I hope I will see you soon. I love you.

Like everything else, I will leave the parcel list to your own imagination. Your hampers have been so wonderful that I wouldn't have been able to better them myself.

I've never mentioned Maroussia and Larissa.[77] I think of them often and send them my love. Maroussia could be my godmother—what would she say to that?

Soap for washing clothes, and fruit, salt herrings, galettes, biscuits, etc. etc. and chocolate, in big bars if possible. Again, lots of hugs and kisses.

*Nothing has come for me yet. I'm incurring debts in order to eat and I'm hungry and I send you my love once again.

[25]
[Undated; probably 23–4 November 1941]

Note for Mademoiselle Noel[78]

Regarding Paul: The news that we've received has increased anxiety levels here because it erects a division, like a wall, between the two sides.[79] We no longer understand each other and while each minute is for him [Paul] like a century of torture, it appears that a mere fortnight of distance has sufficed for somebody like Guterman to forget everything that he himself went through here. As for the rationale for blocking his [Paul's] release this is quite difficult to work out (assuming, of course, that the explanations regarding the misunderstandings and confusion in the certificate were in fact provided). Furthermore, some lawyers have been released without any challenge being made. Perhaps we should be considering what happened last year—the three raids [following] denunciations—as the most likely explanation of the opposition to my release.[80] But I don't want your hair to turn grey on account of this, if indeed this is what is going on. Perhaps you could speak to somebody about it. My beard has turned completely white: enough said about my state of mind at the moment.

Concerning hunger: Hunger has become a burning psychological idea and is causing dysentery as well as muscle weakness. It's bothersome and worrying but nothing can be done about it. A single parcel lasts a day and a half to two days. Today we have been invited to dine with André Cohen,[81] an invitation that we will have to return when our own parcels arrive. We would really need to be receiving two parcels per week but where are we to find the extra coupon? Here it's quite impossible but perhaps you might be able to do something. You should get a supplementary coupon for this week via the Ray of Sunshine. It is also extremely difficult to get hold of the staples. Thank everybody and send my love to everybody. Once again, I know that I haven't written until now about Maroussia and Larissa but I am thinking of them and Maroussia could perhaps play the role of godmother.

Concerning Berels: Thank you so much for all that you have done and he sends his thanks also. Either you or his wife should try to get a certificate from a friendly doctor, confirming that he is in poor health, that he has liver, heart, limb problems: just whatever it takes in order for his name to be on the list of the sick and for him to be seen by Dr Tisné when the latter visits the camp. Could you take charge of this? Madame Kuperberg negotiated a similar arrangement successfully and her husband has been placed on the list for Dr Tisné's next visit.

My loved ones: The thought of bread is never far from my mind. I'll need meat and pâté as well for receiving A. Cohen and jams, honey etc., etc. I always think this is going to be the easiest thing in the world and then I wait and wait, like a madman. Since the parcels started getting through, we're able to source certain foodstuffs here in the camp. So I'll need money for those. Perhaps you could give some 100 or 1,000 franc notes to our Ray of Sunshine. If you can't do this soon, then try to do it as soon as possible. A certain amount of it, whatever I spend or loan here, if I do lend any of it, will be reimbursed to you on the other side. So please send what you can, anything, chocolate, for example, in the parcel, perhaps some spices and some honey. I know that I'm being selfish, that I'm tormenting you, but I'm half crazy. And when I let myself go, I start to cry, I would so wish all this to be over by December 4th.[82]

I love you, my darling, forgive me.

24 November 1941

Some boiled potatoes for my parcel! And chocolate too, if you can. I received the winter coat safely. It is a little tight and a little too short but it is very warm, especially as it's still quite warm here. I gave away the grey one to a poor fellow here. I really want to see you, my love. I am sad and in a state of anxiety which will last until night falls. Do invite the Ray of Sunshine to our home so that she can meet Alexis. How does he look? Has he grown?

As for the bread that you might be able to send in, please don't go short yourself. Madame Moreau can give you a big loaf of bread each week without any need for a coupon. And *galettes* too. . . I must emphasize that I don't want you to go without.[83] (Don't use the coupons that I'm sending you—they are for Berels and they would give rise to questions—so just pass them on to Madame Berels, please).

Once again please forgive this letter—I would so love to write words of love and tenderness to you but I am immersed in a state of torpor and numbness, although that doesn't prevent me from loving you.

I am glad that you like J. W[ahl]—Beckett isn't quite as good I think.[84] You should mediate between Dauphin and J. W. I tore up your note and I've forgotten much of what was written on it. Go with J.W. to see Paulhan at the NRF and tell him that Beckett, J.W. and I will revise *Ulysses* for the Pléiade whenever he wishes.

I love you as ever, Paul

I've just been told about your parcel, all my thanks—Ulmo's too—we're overjoyed—I'm sorry—tomorrow we'll invite A. Cohen and Gaston Weill to share it. I love you too, I long to see you soon, soon, at the very latest on December 4th.

If Berels's medical consultation with Dr Tisné was to cost anything he would gladly pay it so don't be worried about that. Ask Guterman if necessary.

Today for lunch we had the stewed pears, delicious, divine like yourself, my love. The parcels are superb and there is enough for four days. Well, there needs to be enough for four days but even if there's enough for two, that's still something to keep time at bay, to ward off death whose chilly reach is catching up on us, encircling us and preventing me from embracing you.

It's shaming to admit it, but only parcels force us out of the state of torpor and numbness that kills memory and stops us thinking, working and feeling. Oh how I envy those who have got out of here!!

On the question of the opposition to our release, it's being reported that Dr Tisné is adamant about wanting to release the lawyers on account of them being genuinely sick. That's why we had the inspection by the German doctors ten days ago, but since then we've heard nothing. Do you have any news? My head isn't working properly at all as you can see, which is why I'm writing in fits and starts.

Forgive me, my love, if you can—money, cigarettes—via the Ray of Sunshine—this note is full of a shameless egotism—I'm well aware of it but it's the pain of missing you.

[26]
26 November [1941]

The days pass by one after another, each one as sad as the previous one, the same torpor, the same darkness and nothing changes. When will this end?—Thanks to the parcels I have dreams while half awake, dreams of working. The hampers for Ulmo and for me are dazzling. Today's lunch makes us feel we're going to the Ritz. I love you, my darling, but this joke is becoming a bit awkward and tired. I want to embrace you.

We have just left a dazzling feast with A. C. and Gaston Weill.[85] We were with you all in spirit and, speaking for myself, how sorely we missed you. How much I would have preferred to have been eating unbuttered bread had you been at my side, and God knows that I'm fully aware of what I'm saying. Bring me home if you can, as ever your Paul.

'Lucullus dined with Lucullus (thanks to you)'.[86]

I'm sending the parcel coupon with this letter. Perhaps you can use it this week again. Bread, potatoes—I can do without butter from now on, it's too expensive for you, crackers, biscuits, *galettes*.

I'm very worried about the effect of Bosqui's absence on Alexis.[87] Tell him that I'm insisting that he take private lessons from Bosqui. Also, do invite the Ray of Sunshine to the house along with Wahl and Alexis. I love you as ever and am unhappy. [Sentence in Russian.]: That's more or less how we are feeling here.

If you have an extra coupon I'll be hoping for a parcel on Friday or Saturday. Just a basic parcel: stewed pears and jam and honey, chocolate, caramel.

All my thanks for the overcoat to you, to Catherine and to everybody, I love you all, I embrace you and I long to see you.

[27]
26 November [1941]

It's sad to see one another but not to be able to speak. Looking at you I wanted so badly to burst into tears that after the policeman addressed me, I ran over to speak to our Ray of Sunshine and asked her to hand you a letter. That's why I missed your visit to the camp, which my colleagues told me about later. I don't even know if I'd have been able to hold myself back from crying if I had seen you up close. In essence it's all the uncertainty that is torturing me. Now that our hunger is more psychological than physical we're better able to handle it. But what hope is there of leaving this prison, these strangers, these unfamiliar people, and when might that happen? Have you any idea at all? The slightest shadow of an idea? I know that you are sleeping well. So am I during the daytime, but the evenings are pure torture. Thoughts of what we could have done and of what we are going to do are like flies that interfere with our sleep and distract us from it. My heart yearns for you and for all that my life has been to date, so a continuous effort is required in order to hold firm. The parcels for myself and for Ulmo have been dazzling and we have been dining at noon like you have not dined for three years. Eggs mimosa, roast chicken, liver pâté and salad, camembert, apple pie, fruit, white coffee, biscuits with raisins and almonds. Ulmo was in heaven. A. Cohen with whom I shared not just lunch but also a box of Eleska, half the butter and 2 eggs was absolutely delighted, as also was your friend Gaston Weill (who is a bit awkward but a nice man). Did you bring the tobacco to Madame Bauh? You know how much I owe her husband, mainly in terms of getting hold of bread. It's not something to be proud of, especially from someone who calls himself a lawyer, but since I'd have had nothing without him, I have to smile and pay up. Have you paid the full sum of 6,000 francs to them? You could send me 1,000 or 2,000 francs via the Ray of Sunshine. It would make things easier in here. But none of this is really important. How to get out of here, that's the real question. The Ray of Sunshine likes you and admires you to the point that she's cross with me because I'm making you suffer. As for Guterman I was very struck by what he said to you. I wasn't expecting that, especially after all that he endured here himself. Could you possibly send me some cigarettes via the Ray of Sunshine? I agree with you that it's too risky to conceal them in the parcels. It's a miracle that everything has got through to me. I think I forgot to ask you if you've paid 3,500 to Monsieur Eskis or to his sister. I'm trying to get hold of a parcel coupon for you via Monsieur Berels. Just pass it on to Madame Berels since she will know what to put in the parcel. But you are telling me nothing about yourself. You look well but you have such a sad expression. I think, I hope that I will be able to make you feel better, even to make you feel happy. Yes, I'm sure of it, I will work at it. For the first time in my life I know what I want to do. I love you, I love you, I love you.

As ever yours, Paul

'The ferocious revenge of a false god'

This is a new version of the last line of the Wahl text.

The days are dragging on and yet they are all so similar to each other that there's no difference between one day and the next. In the evening we feel so heavy that we sleep like bags of lead. Oh my beloved, I knew barely anything of life until now. I mean of certain aspects of life, aspects of my own life and of my own character. I truly believe that I'm attached to you above all by my own weakness but also by a certain inner strength that renders certain things unacceptable to me, things that will never, I believe, be acceptable to me. You are like a mother in my eyes and I love you very much as such but you are also something else for me. For this reason you must not betray me. We will be happy together again in the future, won't we? Are you having financial problems? I hope not, and I hope that Alec has given you extended powers and that you are able to use them. I really implore you to do this, and if you like, write to Alec telling him that I'm the one asking for this for you. Also, you know what I want and what I don't want. And especially that I want us to be the ones who are paying all the living expenses at home. And that includes the Perréons' bills. I don't want them to have any expenses apart from the ones that they want to take upon themselves. Won't you do as I say, my love? Now that I, at least for today, feel better I would so much love to see you, to speak to you even to be able to write to you in Russian. The French in these pages seems so artificial to me and it just doesn't allow me to express my feelings. I love you none the less for that. As you can see I have taken advantage of an episode of mental calm to write to you: otherwise my letters must have seemed to you to have been written by a madman, for there was so much disorder in them. Forgive me, and love me as I always love you. Despite my madness, my torpor, my numbness, which will pass, I believe—I hope—Paul, forever.

Here are suggestions, then, for a parcel or two or even three:

1) One loaf of Jewish brown bread (Madame Berels will tell you where to get it)

Crackers, *galettes*, matzah,[88] etc., at your own discretion

2) Khalva (as much as possible and as per the recommendation from the same source)

Jams and honey

3) Chocolate—in big bars or a box of chocolates from Marquis[89]

lots of it

4) Fruits—noodles, cooked rice (to add to soups)

Boiled potatoes

5) Tinned foods: pâté, tuna etc as far as possible

Tomato sauce, meat, vegetables etc.

6) Sweets (tangy fruit drops or others) quantity and good value trump quality and price.

I will perhaps have to change rooms and as a result part company with Monsieur Ulmo. I'll try to manage afterwards with some young men who seem very pleasant to me and who are working on my team. There will be better light, apparently. The composition of the food parcels will be the same no matter where I am.

In terms of fats, get the best value: margarine, oil. The problem with butter is that we eat all our bread with it. The methylated spirits were confiscated and also the candles so there's no point in sending those in unless you get them in via the Ray of Sunshine if she's willing. But in the new room we've been promised good lighting.

I'm expecting to receive the spices and banknotes perhaps by Tuesday via the Ray of Sunshine. A large bar of chocolate in squares would be very welcome. I have nowhere to hide anything else because my suitcases can't be locked. Failing that, a box of chocolates (which won't require coupons) from Marquis would be good. If you are coming to the camp again, ask to be brought to Mademoiselle Monod and she will send for me.

Have you spoken to Madame Masse? She who will be happy to see you and has been notified by Monsieur Masse that you'll be in touch. I've just had an idea: perhaps when you're making inquiries it might be useful to stress the fact that I am Secretary of the International Institute of Legal Philosophy which has members all over the world (this is not the *Archives*, from which I resigned but rather the Institute where I've retained my membership).[90] This fact is not noted in my official identity papers in German (you sent me a copy of these).

[28]

[27 November 1941]

I feel a lot better and much stronger this morning, my love. Is it the fact that I've seen you, thought of you, dreamed of you? I don't know, but even my legs aren't as painful. May God preserve you! I have even less hope this morning, even though deep within myself I want to be able to hope to see you again as a free man, soon, very soon. However, I am in less pain physically and it seems to me that if I could work things would become bearable. I needn't tell you that all work is forbidden here and that we have to write in secret and steal the paper that they refuse to give us. I have an idea for the food parcels. As you can see I haven't stopped being an egotist and a glutton. You could send in some Khalva which passes itself off as bread and comes in a white tin. Let Alexis taste it. Somebody here gave me some and I find I like it after not having tasted it at all really for twenty-five or thirty years. Madame Berels will tell you where it can be bought for a reasonable price. I am sending you Monsieur Berels's coupon. Tell his wife to use it again for this week. When I wasn't hungry I had no desire to smoke. But the desire for cigarettes is starting to return now and in fact I'm smoking one a day (well not quite every day because they still cost 20 francs each whereas a month ago they only cost 12 fr. each).

As for the khalva, Petrossian's should know where to source it but they are too expensive. Madame Berels will be able to recommend a better, i.e. cheaper, source. Did you get to see Margraff so as to save my Constant collection? That's what I really, really care about.

For the Berels coupon which Madame Berels has to use by November 30th, she has to fill in the sender's address on the letter, so give her the form and let her know this.

And so, my love, I am placing my trust in you, I am counting on you and I love you.
Forever your own
Paul
27 November 1941

[29]
28 November 1941

My darling, I don't know today if it's the fact of having heard your voice, read your card, or the fact of not waiting for another parcel, but I feel that my thinking is clearer. Certainly the exasperation is ongoing but I am able to control it. It's in this way that I have figured out how to express what I've been feeling and also the state in which I almost ended up. Over the past 100 days, I was to all intents and purposes on the verge of insanity and I haven't completely come out of that state yet. The torpor, the amnesia, the impossibility of writing a letter, the suffering and torment that I went through and that I induced in you, please forgive me for all that. But now I know exactly what it is to go under, or almost to drown in madness. I am still diminished. I hope that if we are ever to recover a normal life, I'll be able to climb back up the hill to sanity, but I know that there's a risk that I will remain diminished for the rest of my life.

29 November

Dearest, I wasn't able to go on yesterday. In the meantime I've received the parcel and I've seen you. Why did you hesitate the day before yesterday when I asked if you thought that we would be released from here? This is not a reproach. It's just that with our nerves in the state they are in, every little thing is significant and all I could think about through the whole of last night was that.

The parcel is too wonderful, too expensive and we are eating its contents too fast. I predict that on Sunday from noon onwards we won't have a thing left to eat until Tuesday. Not that I'm complaining. Quite the opposite in fact: it's to show you how foolish we have become here. And yet, thanks to the work I do here there are at least five hours when I can't think about my stomach. *All my cigarettes were taken, and so was the blank paper that you had placed in the parcel*. Was there something written on it? From what I can tell, we are not being allowed access to writing paper. Can you believe the stupidity of the regulations? I have found out where J.W. is. I think that you, or at the very least Alexis, should join him there.[91] We will decide all that together when we see each other. In any event there were French boys of his age here for sixty days. The uncertainty of what lies in store for us is what is eating away at me and driving me insane over and over again. At least now I can say that I know what it means to lose one's wits.

It is cold today, wintry cold, but the rooms are still being heated and also, the overcoat that Catherine sent in is very warm. I am so weak now that it's squashing me beneath its weight, but it's alright. It's just the idea that we are going to be here for the whole winter that is tormenting me. How much I long to be close to you and to be doing some real work. It is possible that this too is an illusion, but I have in my head the idea of five tasks to be accomplished—the revision of *Ulysses* with Beckett, the composition of my Recollections of Joyce, the Constant edition, the Rousseau edition, the completion of my study on Rousseau, not to mention all that could be done besides. Tell Mademoiselle Simone that she will have to take me in hand if I'm to accomplish everything that I'm promising to do.[92] Here our intelligence weakens and crumbles and numbness takes over. In the morning we awaken still capable of thinking but two hours later everything has vanished, we have lost all our ability to reflect. It's hard, my love, it's hard. When I try to put it into words, I can see that in fact it's the other way round. We go to bed with a head that is very heavy and empty of thought. Then little by little we awake, helped by the fleas, and the uncertainty regarding the amount of time we are going to have to spend here rises up within us like the stink of a galley ship, bringing us to the verge of tears. It's painful, my love, and above all, it's sad. I must stress that Alexis needs to go at least once a week to a lesson with Bosqui.

As it is, last year he lost a whole trimester of instruction and this must not happen again. I beg of you, do whatever it takes, because his whole future is at stake. I send you my love for now. I don't know if our Ray of Sunshine will come today. It is possible that I won't see her before Tuesday. In any event I love you and will love you up to Tuesday and beyond. A date for my return, I beg of you. Will I see you on the 4th?!! The first assault on your parcel was clearly [visible]. Ulmo was [unhappy] because he was starving and we had to hide [from a third guest because he doesn't like him]. We devoured the liver pâté and the chocolate too. I had hidden the bar so as to be able to eat it all by myself but had shared half of the rest with Masse's associates, Bloch[93] and the other big shots here (Masse is the only really nice man amongst them all and the only real intellect) so do please go and see Madame Masse. I owed half of the crackers to a friend. And with that, A. Cohen joined us and we shared his pot of jam with the crackers and polished off the last of the chocolate. It's just fun and games, but it's the nicest sort of child's play in an atmosphere that's silly and immature. But how often there is instead an atmosphere of hatred, envy and jealousy. And this is so humiliating. The idea that I love you, that I love you forever is my only succour, giving some nobility to my thoughts and my soul.

I don't know what to ask for in my winter parcel. Perhaps one or two boxer shorts because the laundry situation here is terrible. There's no soap. And we need eau de cologne to keep the fleas away—but I beg of you, if you have any hope left, don't send that parcel yet. I implore you and I love you forever.

Suggestions for a cheap parcel: streaky or smoked bacon, if possible some soap for washing clothes.

For the 4th, I wish you all the happiness that you richly deserve, all possible bliss, and if we don't see one another, think of *Alexis*, make a man of him, teach him to do what *you* would have him do and love him.

Love me too as I love you,

Forever yours, Paul

[30]
29 November [1941]

Darling, the feeling that impels me to write to you is strange. I want to formulate a couple of sentences before losing at once my train of thought, before being beset by thoughts of the night that is going to fall, of the hunger that will start up again, of the image of parcel food hamper. In a word, thoughts of all that concerns my own small physical—physiological and nervous—person. And yet I believe that my true 'self' is close to you, closer than it has perhaps ever been. This is an exaggeration but I really want to believe it. And that, indeed, is one of the characteristics of life here, this inability to do anything coherent, intelligent, sensible. I have been here for about three weeks or a month and we are now onto the 6th dossier and will be beginning the 7th soon. What is it all for, I wonder?—perhaps you can answer me more rationally than I can myself. On Monday, a new German inspection team is coming and it will perhaps put an end to the suspension of releases which has gone on for two and a half weeks already. And how I long to be at home with you before or at the latest by Thursday, at home so that I can tell you that I love you. I think I would breathe more easily if I could do that. My head is nodding, not with sleep but with torpor. *My, how his head falls*;[94] this is from 'Anna Livia' and it reverberates like a fall resounds in a vast void. So long for the moment—I love you—

[31]
2 December 1941

Darling, the new parcel was divine and it will last us for two days at least. The only one of us still in the state that I myself was in last week regarding the bread, the only one who is devouring all round him, is Ulmo. I can't say that I'm depriving myself but I'm mainly eating the bread with my meals whereas he is taking some before, during and after dinner too (as a dessert), not to mention in between meals as well. And so the bread and the matzah have disappeared. As for the rest of the parcel, everything is so delicious and so, all in all, after five weeks we are satiated. Beyond the need to restore our strength, hunger remains above all a psychological phenomenon, that is to say, it turns into a sort of gluttony. I've been told that the clothes parcel has arrived. I haven't seen it yet, though, and if I do receive it before this letter is sent, I'll add a few words of sadness. But I want to tell you that I do feel better in myself, and so you mustn't suffer on my behalf. I am suffering enough as it is for myself. I want Thursday to be a day of celebration for you and I want you to feel that I am with you, with all my heart and with all my soul. If I can't be there as a real presence I will return to you like the Prodigal Child and will lose myself in your arms with more bliss than ever. You can see that I'm not losing all hope of seeing you again. And it's in a spirit of complete serenity that I'm leaving to you the responsibility of caring for Alexis and for his future. But is he going to see his tutor Bosqui? Explain to him if you can that he must go back again this week. Thursday, oh Thursday, I would so much like to be able to be there with you and with all our friends. The mere idea of it causes me to break out in a cold sweat, but I can check myself. And I love you, I love you, I love you. It seems to me in fact that I've become stronger, so much pleasure do I derive from repeating these last words, so deeply do they seep into me. If you want, do invite Maxime on Thursday. I believe that I will be happy if you can be happy. Goodbye my love, I am leaving this page until tomorrow. The documents relate to the Institute of Legal Philosophy and they are in my box file, a couple of boxes—third or fourth—from the top. My name features in the heading (on the headed notepaper) along with the names of the whole committee. I send you my love for this evening.

3 December—Regarding the food parcels—too wonderful—you can omit the butter, it's too expensive. Get bread from a Jewish bakery (brown bread), bars of chocolate (the steak was marvellous but too expensive as well), jam is so easy (and also delicious indeed). We are being promised a laundry parcel now. Would you mind buying me another shirt

(with a collar) because this parcel is going to take two weeks to arrive and I will then send back two shirts and two pairs of boxer shorts. I would ask you to send me one shirt and one pair of boxer shorts so that I can wait for two weeks if necessary for the parcel to come. Also can you send two pairs of socks (in very thick wool if possible) for tucking into my clogs. As you see, my love, I've lost almost all hope of seeing you soon. I am sorrowful—destiny is merciless nowadays—but I love you still and forever. Gaston Weill, André Cohen's friend, has been moved to hospital. You do know that this is the man whose daughter is friendly with the daughter of André Cohen? You have my clothing ration card along with the coupons. My socks get torn when they slide around inside the clogs. I have just received the parcel and there is nothing for me in it except for the eau de cologne. Thanks very much, on the double indeed, for leaving me some hope. I have passed everything on to André Cohen and he will look after it for G. Weill who, as I already said, has been evacuated to hospital. What I need are not socks, really, but rather *kroumirs* to put inside my clogs.[95]

Once again, I send you my love. I wish you all the happiness that you deserve and I embrace you with my whole heart and my whole soul.

Yours forever,
Paul

Even though Ulmo detests onions, I really loved them in the soup along with, if you can, a clove of garlic and some stock cubes or Oxo cubes.

[32]
[Illegible date, before 10 December][96]

[Illegible words] suggestions for parcels
1) Jewish bread, ask Madame Berels for the addresses of the bakeries
2) Some matzah, some pasta in so far as possible; potatoes
3) Onions, garlic, etc
4) Stock cubes
5) Jams and honey
6) Caramels
7) Chocolate bars, especially, but also some chocolate sweets
8) Tins of pâté, fish, meat
9) Streaky bacon, very little butter, only for the pasta and the potatoes.
10) Fruit

In the winter parcel, if you're sending one, you can put in all the bread you like and the most filling preserves. And perhaps I've already mentioned spices and chocolate.

And so a whole other day has passed without anything new. I've been tasked with heading a project team of ten regarding a piece of work that the Police *Préfecture* is doing for you.[97] Have you been able to do that thing? And did Alexis go to that place?[98]

Have you any idea of what it's like to be so starved of news of freedom—and can you imagine how intensely we yearn to get out of here? Until tomorrow then, and I just hope that there will be some news.

[Illegible numeral] December

Before I forget all about it, the 13th is the Feast day of Saint Lucie. Would you please ask Beckett to send something to Lucia Joyce and give him about 200 or 250 fr. to do that. It's in memory of her father. Do try also to bring me some cash. You could send me a money order for 50 fr. We often need to get bread.

[Illegible numeral] December

Darling, yesterday's parcel is amazing. There's enough in it for seven meals. It's superb but too expensive. As two other pals that share their rations with me have also received parcels, we are going to be able to hold out until Tuesday or Wednesday. The chocolate is wonderful. I gobbled it up, all of it except for eight or nine chocolate sweets that I had to offer to the big guns. Delicious, delicious, delicious. The toilet paper arrived just in time in five sections. I am still waiting for two or three small parcels, better not to risk everything in one go. On the other hand the cigarettes were taken. The fare, all of it, was superb, absolutely magnificent, but perhaps overly extravagant. The list I've made out above is perhaps more realistic.

The note that you sent via André Cohen is a worry to me for many reasons. I am wondering if you're referring in it to my immediate associates or just to the leaders. I see no sign of the Ray of Sunshine who doesn't seem to want to show herself to me but I hope to see her on Tuesday. I'll give her a smile or will try to pass on a food coupon. You can always change the date on them.

I send you all my love.

I feel a thousand times better. The swelling in my legs has practically disappeared.

It's just that I have terrible rings under my eyes. As for the doctor that you went to see, he never called me and so I was on the list without any specific 'intervention' recommended. I do have some vision problems, some blind spells. I send my love to you as well as to everybody who is looking after you, to all those whom you love, all those who care about you.

The *kroumirs* have been given to Ulmo. As for the warm jacket, is that for me?

When you are asking Madame Berels about the Jewish bread, could you also ask her how to make gebackene [Pretzels] and where to buy them? They are sent pre-cooked and are for putting in soup. You could also perhaps send a packet of caseine powder to put into soup.[99] All of this food and that kind of Jewish speciality (cooked egg, or vermicelli—that make for a delicious dish) are, I suspect, better value than the delicacies that you have been sending in. These are deeply appreciated but they appear to me to be very expensive. In any event, a thousand thanks.

The note that A. Cohen gave me didn't really worry me and seemed quite accurate. We will speak about it again, but I would just like to know if the people that you are concerned about are the people I'm directly involved with or the chiefs.

I am feeling a lot better. I love you still. I'm working on the camp census (did Alexis do that thing by the way?)—and so the time is passing more quickly. What have you done census-wise in relation to yourself, bearing in mind your father?[100]

I send my most tender affection to you and to all those I love, as well as to those whom you love and who are helping and supporting you,

Forever yours, Paul.

For the clothes parcel: one pair of pyjamas, one shirt, two boxers, very thick, cheap socks. I'll send you back my [shoes] [illegible words].

*The last day for sending the winter parcel is 10 December 1941.

[33]
4 December [1941]

My darling, I have heard from the Ray of Sunshine that you were badly affected yet again by my letter and that you have been to see the doctor. How can I impress upon you the fact that, yes in truth, things are not good but you can do nothing about it and that I have been removed from the list of the sick. Yesterday, Ulmo himself was very low: it was the anniversary of his wife's death. But, whereas he externalizes his feelings in words, in my case they eat me up on the inside, burrowing into my heart and soul. I cannot prevent myself from telling you all this and if I am telling you about it in such an incoherent manner, it's because I am, in point of fact, diminished, and I cannot stop wondering if this impairment is going to remain with me forever. Paralysed, half asleep, bumping into stones, into steps, unable to see properly—this is what I have become—and on top of all that psychologically humiliated, [damaged], flayed alive in fact. These are the facts. The simple act of jumping about in my letters from one subject to the next, hopping from the arrival of a parcel to the question of religion, is enough to illustrate the state of near insanity in which I find myself. A month has passed since the moment when I should have been released, and I know as little as you do about the reasons behind the opposition to my release. But that said, I don't want this to destroy your life, on this day above all other days, given what it means for you. Think of yourself and think of Alexis and of how indispensable you are to him. There is nothing more that can be done for me as an individual. We just have to wait to see what is to become of the whole group. We need to accept this idea that we are caught beneath a millstone that is grinding us down. It is not at all pleasant, but there is no point in complaining. I believe—I need to believe—that we will arise again but that's all [I can do]. For your part you must be prudent, and not take any pointless risks for your life or for your future friendships. You must in the first instance save yourself and save Alexis. My life is over or will soon be over. So let me be. Ulmo's parcel, most of which was intended for me, was excellent. We ate very well this evening and we shall see what tomorrow brings. Perhaps my parcel will arrive too. In that case we'll be able to hold out until Tuesday. I sent you the coupon for this week via the Ray of Sunshine. Perhaps you could use it for next week.

Regarding the composition of the parcels, do try to simplify this, even if Ulmo is disappointed (as he was today).

Less matzah. I had also asked you for Jewish bread and Madame Berels was to give you the address of the bakery where it could be purchased without coupons. So no more matzah but rather more bread. You can also cut out the butter, which is too expensive. Bacon fat would be much better in its place. In fact Ulmo eats neither butter nor cheese. Nor bacon indeed. But the difficulty, to repeat myself, is that all the nice things are eaten along with bread and so, as a result, we quickly run out of it. You can also send cooked rice and pasta or macaroni. So that's a long parenthesis on the parcels. Please God soon I won't be needing them, but when, when, oh when will that be? The instant I articulate this question the nervous anxiety and suffering starts up again. Forgive me.

Forever your own
Paul

[34]
[undated letter, completed 22 January 1942]

Darling, your bread arrived when there were ten of us gathered together, starving. Nothing could have tasted better or have given more happiness. I love you the same as ever but I'm worn down by the cold and by gluttony. The only things I've received as of now is food. I am sleeping in my clothes. Monsieur C. is charming but very strict,[101] and so I have no more money. Could you send me 2,000 francs? Thanks in advance. Roger Masse whose son is married to Crémieux's daughter has received his parcel. But Pierre on the other hand has received nothing at all for the past fifteen days.[102] Ulmo and I share our rations in the evening but it's better to send separate parcels for us because things go missing. Still, he's a lovely man and is enormously helpful to me. He would like to have news from home and requests that 2,000 francs be deposited with Madame Hakoune, 8 rue de Montyon to be sent to her husband here. And he also requests parcels to be sent to him individually—they will be allowed in after February 1st. In the meantime, though, there will be a few difficult days because of the limits imposed on the whole camp. My feet are like putty.[103] I am begging you to send in slippers or *kroumirs*, clogs, a blanket, and a sleeping bag. I love you and I send you all my kisses. Hugs too to everybody else—22 I 42. Just a little more strength!! woollen socks. Alfred is very, very hungry.[104] I was examined by the German doctor but he didn't utter a word. Nobody can do anything to help me here but if somebody from outside could get me out of here!?!? What happiness that would bring, even if I were only to be released into house arrest!

[35]
6 February 1942

Dearest treasure—to yesterday's letter I want to add that—I have just received the little parcel from which the gloves were missing and the half-litre of bread (that had been wrapped up in the gloves) but I think this was stolen from under my nose—and that it had actually got as far as our quarters. We need sugar for the shared meals. According to your letter,[105] it seems that I'm still missing two parcels that were sent to me—and the two for Ulmo haven't arrived either. I received the 500 [francs], though, and that allowed me to pay the most urgent debts. Please try therefore to follow the requests I made in yesterday's letter so that I can give something to Alfred. He is asking that Simone be told that he is grateful to her for the news.[106] Her letters bring the only news that actually reaches him. He also received the first part of the parcel sent to [Necker?]'s associate; the rest will no doubt follow, though nothing has yet been received from Sagliès. Our official cards should have been sent out eight days ago but whether it's as a punishment or not they haven't yet been delivered, so we must be prudent. And on another point, Monsieur Claude Polack, who is well, has only received one box of vitamin tablets through Albert. He would like to have news via you and also some precise information on the sending of parcels with dates (Passy 44-13). If you can have answers to these queries when you come here on a visit on Tuesday, that would be good. Regarding the money for Ulmo, it's for Hakoune 6-82 rue de Montyon. And also, just to say that the khalva was so good that there is none left. The two Masses were delighted.[107] Send us the same again if you can. Alfred is asking for fuel for his lighter, ink, pen, clothes brush, towel and cologne. . .. The suitcase with our things in it can weigh up to 10 kg. The same goes for Alfred and Polack, etc. Thank you so much and I needn't tell you how grateful I am for all that you are doing for me. Give my love to Catia,[108] Simone and Madame Perréon and tell Alexis that I love him and place my hope in him. Jean is requesting that you let Gilberte, Maurice's sister-in-law, know that she should put together the 1st food parcel (keeping the weight down). Could you also ask her to approach Thierry about applying to go to college in Lyons. It might be useful for Gilberte to try to ask Chauveau about this; he's Corcelet's boss (Corcelet was Jean's old friend in the 1914 war). Also, dried fruits, prunes, dried bananas, jams. Could you do likewise?

This is an answer to one of the questions that you put to me and that I forgot all about. I have with me the small cardboard suitcase that you sent to Drancy. I need something that can be locked, a wooden box with a padlock. [Anything else would get damaged].

A thousand kisses,
Your Paul

[Several sentences in Russian.]

[36]
6 February 1942

Darling, the situation is getting worse. Madame Raymond of the rue Navarin is going to be able to send a new clothes parcel along with the food.[109] Madame Masse will be in touch with you about the additional items for me but I've received nothing as of yet except through Gilberte and Albert. If possible, please add to my clothes parcel anything that you can, bread, *chocolates* etc. etc. I especially need socks—*please bring it all as quickly as possible*. Monsieur Raymond wants warm gloves. Madame Pierre and her niece will bring me what has been noted specifically in [his] letter.[110]

I love you and I embrace you, Paul

[37]
[undated letter, probably written around 12 February 1942]

Darling, it is cold and we are hungry. Nothing is getting through to us. Here, just for your info is the list: warm clothes—nobody knows where they are—can you buy me a pair of dark trousers, a warm pair, maybe ski trousers. Or ones that are soft and loose. Only these are suitable because the others are no use at all after ten days of wear. I am worn out and am just going along with all the initiatives being taken. If only we could see one another again some day. Everybody is overcome with despair. Ulmo is very low and very weary. Regarding parcels, don't forget we need food for 4, less variety but more quantity. Noodles for soup, flour, rabbit pâté, a chicken would be magnificent, desserts: khalva, jams, honey, sugar, saccharine. Each of us is hanging on to his own bread (and we need that, you'd better believe it). Plus chocolates, biscuits. I still haven't received Tuesday's message. I'm hanging on for tomorrow, Tuesday. I have no money left because there's no point in relying on the slate any more for getting things.[111] What's more, everything is very expensive, even the canteen food, though not the herrings. For our shared meals we need tinned food. I still haven't received the socks or the gloves. The ones that I have are in rags. Smoliak is requesting that the Red Cross be alerted (2 rue de Navarin, Trudaine 52–73) and that his maid Marie be informed. Lucien Lévy, tel. Wagram 24-45 is asking for news of his wife. The same thing for Monsieur [illegible name], 15 rue Trousseau, who is sending a message to his wife by *petit bleu* asking her to come and see you. For our shared meals, Eleska, Banania, Blédine and if possible Nescafe and powdered starch, also caseine powder, and macaroons and a cake made of macaroni or noodles.[112] One parcel should last two days, two meals. Do go to visit Madame Masse and be nice to her. How is her health? Her husband is worried. As for me, I too need biscuits, chocolates and bread, bread, bread. I'm hungry. Cooked potatoes, hard-boiled eggs.

I love you. I'm worn out. I'm cold. I'm falling asleep.

[38]
Compiègne, 19 February 1942

My darling,

You can send me—without any limit as to weight—a suitcase full of underwear, clothes, shoes and toiletries.

What I especially need is a blanket, a sleeping bag, socks, a stiff-collared shirt, a warm pair of boxers, clogs, *kroumirs*, slippers if possible, eau de cologne and toothpaste, two lunchboxes or containers, one pair of warm dark trousers, a pair of shoelaces, a razor and razor blades.

No correspondence or food parcels are allowed yet.[113]

I embrace you and love you,
Always yours,
Paul

[39]
Compiègne, 19 February 1942

My dear Lucie,

Would you please pay Monsieur Siechel the 1,000 fr. that I owe him as soon as he gets out.[114]

Paul Léon

Mme Léon
27 r. Casimir Périer
Paris 7e

[40]
21 February 1942

[Several paragraphs in Russian.]

Instead of a box with a padlock it would be better to have a suitcase that can be locked but if you have already sent one in then the box can remain here. Gilberte's brother-in-law is asking that it be made known as a matter of urgency that Humbert has sent back the parcels but that, as of 1 March, people should contact his friend Emile Marcotte No. 971.[115]AC is also asking for news from Madame Nicolle, Carnot 18-92.[116]

Catherine [Illegible words] but I'm numb, starving, freezing.

[41]
23 February 1942
My dear Lucie,
Would you please pay Monsieur Marcus the 200 francs that I owe him at his request?
Paul Léon
Received from Monsieur Léon 200 francs.

[42]
[Undated letter entirely in Russian.]

[43]
11 March 1942

[Letter almost entirely in Russian, with these three sentences in French.]

Albert has received the letter and is very happy. He has no certainty regarding release. As far as the winter parcel is concerned he is upset about it because everything is useless or too cumbersome, except for the socks and the handkerchiefs [illegible words].

[44]

[Letter in Russian, dated 11 March 1942.]

[45]
[Undated letter in Russian.]

[46]
15 March 1942

[Letter in Russian.]

[47]
22 March 1942

Darling, this is a report that should reach PM as soon as possible.[117]

My life has changed completely. Thanks to Monsieur Raymond and thanks to the two parcels that the Saviour sent to me, our meals today are very rich.

Bad luck hit the first of the two most recent parcels. It was delivered in small portions to Masse. Not knowing whose it was, he shared out part of it. In fact, another part of it was stolen—so I got neither butter nor sugar nor jam nor sardines nor chocolate nor bread. I'm hoping for better things from this one. We've already enjoyed some of it—the potatoes and the delicious herrings. So yesterday's dinner, shared amongst 6 of us, was better than dinner at home.

The only thing that is keeping me alive is the hope of seeing you. I've got through the German inspection (the second one).

I am impatient to kiss your hands and your feet. I send my love to all those close to you.

As ever,
Paul

We don't know what our fate is to be.

[48]
Thursday, 26 March 1942

Darling—we've been counted and tomorrow we leave—I don't know where we are going or how. There's talk of Troyes, that's what the German[s] seem to be saying but we know nothing for certain—regardless, our fate cannot but be worse than that of the oldest men: in other words it cannot but be worse than Drancy—so go read?!?![118]

I want you to remember all my tender love for you and for Alexis. And tell Catherine and Simone too. Give my love to all our friends as well, the ones who turned out to be true friends. I love them all. I pray to God every evening for you and for Alexis, as well as for all our friends. I hope I will see you again but I don't have much hope. [Schoenfeld] and the two [illegible names] are in our group, and so is [illegible name]. Tell Paul [Bernstein] and the Smoliaks—whose addresses you should be able to locate in my suitcase along with some items belonging to Mr Smoliak, 2 rue Navarin.

But the most important thing for me is to tell you that I love you as much as I did 20 years ago and that—if I don't get to see you again—it is you that I shall love forever.

May God preserve you—you and Alexis both.

I embrace you as I love you,

Forever your own

Paul

Mme Paul Léon,
20, rue Casimir-Périer
Paris 7
Inv. 70-04

My greetings and my especially friendly regards to Kaminsky, Troubnikoff, Nouvel etc. etc. How far away all that seems to us now. I pray to God for Catherine, Simone, her mother etc. etc. and for all the friends who assisted us in this place—!?

APPENDIX

[A]
[Paul Léon to Mlle Simone Perréon]

[undated; posted in August/early September 1941]

Mademoiselle S. Perréon,
27 rue Casimir Périer
Paris 7e

Dear Miss Perréon,

Could you kindly request of Madame Lucie Léon, née Ponisowsky, to come to see me and to bring with her the documentation pertaining to the various contracts that we are to sign. Since two persons are permitted to visit at the same time you will be allowed to accompany her to help her to make sense of the material. She should come here in the afternoon two days after receiving this card. At the entrance she just needs to ask for the lawyers' parlour. She will have to bring her identity papers and a clothes parcel, but it would be best to wait until I have been able to advise Madame Ponisowsky regarding what it should contain.

M. Paul Léon, Camp d'Internés de Drancy
Block N° 1, Escalier N° 1, Chambre N° 4
Drancy

[B]
[Lucie to Paul Léon[1]]

Monday 9th

My darling, it's been disappointment after disappointment. I missed your call, just as I also missed Maître P[ierre] who called yesterday. He had documents for you, the typescript of your military service etc. I still have hope that all that this will sort itself out. Did you receive the suitcase via the Red Cross? Tomorrow there will be a sleeping bag. Plus a pillow and, if it's allowed at long last, some food too. Everybody is thinking of you. I've been to the camp six times but wasn't able to get anything in. However, things do seem to be getting a little more organized by degrees. The wives and daughters of your colleagues and myself are sharing information and news and we're trying to cheer ourselves up mutually. I'm seeing a lot of Madame André Cohen and am helping out twice a week at the rue de Berri. Alexis will be home on the 15th. He hopes that you are in good spirits and sends you all his love as do I. Everybody wants to be remembered to you. Don't be worried about us. All our friends are wonderful and will not forsake us. I'll send you the books as soon as I can. I embrace you.

*Your secretary also sends you her regards and her best wishes for strength and patience.
S. Perréon

[C]
[Lucie to Paul Léon]

29 September [1941]

My dear Paul,

It's been eight days now since I received your card and since then I've had no news of you. The others have received long letters. Are you allowed to send letters as well? I really hope so. Let me know where to find the Choura Maillard file—I need to see him about [Alexis?], because he has sent further material. I am running around all day long, seeing lots of people. Everybody is thinking of you and are hoping that the sorting will shed light on your case very quickly, because we are really anxious to get you home. Alexis and S. are returning home tomorrow. The schools will reopen soon. Don't worry about the books. Alec is well. I've had news of him recently. He would be very glad to come if he could help me. I'm following his advice in addition to the advice of hundreds of other folk. What do you need sent in? Ask the R+ [Red Cross] to tell me what's allowed. Will you be getting a label for the parcels? You are in everybody's thoughts and I do have hope.

[D]
[Lucie to Paul Léon]

Paris, 3 October [1941]

My dear Paul, your card made me feel very sad, even sadder than I already was if that's possible. You must not lose hope. I am certain, as are we all, that the worst is over and that we shall see one another again soon. Roger, Léon-Paul,[2] Georges Yamat have as much faith in this as I do and so I am hopeful that the mistake will soon be recognized. You will need to correct the discrepancy in the date yourself because the typist misread the year [of your birth]. Father Cyprien is praying for you and we are going to go to see Father S[erge]. Alexis will go to see him with Kam[insky]. He will also buy you the Gospels. I send you my love, as does Alexis. I have written to you several times and I am thinking of you and praying. So take heart. All our thoughts are of you and we are full of hope. Choura knows everything. All my tenderness.

[E]
[Catherine Berline (née Léon) to Paul, with a postscript from Lucie]
4 October 1941

My dear Paul, we have received all your sad and depressed letters. We are suffering for you as you can well imagine and we're hoping that we will see you soon again. Lucie is so unhappy. She is doing everything that a human being can do and we have full confidence in the outcome. Choura for his part is doing the needful also and his friend, whom you know, is going to join Lucie. All this to say, my darling, that you must hold firm. For Lucie who loves you, for Alexis, but also for me, for without you I am completely unable to go on. Without Lucie nothing will happen. For my part, all I can do is to suffer, to pray and to weep. I can assure you that we are certain of prevailing. So take heart, my darling. With deep and tender affection, Katia.[3]

*From the very start everything has been and is being done according to your wishes. I've been to see everybody and I have well-founded hope. Alexis is working with [Struve] and is studying very diligently, keeping you in his thoughts. He has Russian and German twice a week. He has school in the mornings every day except for Sundays and is studying then every afternoon. I am suffering with you and am doing all I can to find a solution. Take heart. I embrace you most tenderly. [Lucie]

[F]
[Madame Berels to Lucie Léon]

[Undated]

Madame,
I am forwarding to you herewith a message from both your husband and my own spouse, who are going through the same difficulties. Would you be so kind as to phone me tomorrow, Thursday, at 9.30 a.m., to make an urgent appointment to meet.
Respectfully yours,
Berels
GOB 44-79[4]

[G]
[Simone Cohen, wife of André Cohen, to Lucie Léon]

[Undated]

Wed. evening
My dear friend,

I am thinking of you and of Paul. We must remember that he wrote this ever so poignant letter in a moment of terrible demoralization. But his state of health really does allow us to hold on to the hope that he will be sent home. I know that you are remaining active and strong as you need to be so often, alas!

It's a beautiful thing to help others so much when one is oneself put to such a hard test. Thank you for this message, you are a source of salvation.

In faithful friendship. Sim. A. C. [Simone André Cohen]

Adresse d'Alf = no 11539
Bloc I Escalier 4 Chambre 13

[H]

[Lucie to Paul, with postscript by Alexis Léon.]

[undated; after 4/5 November 1941]

My beloved,

Thank you for your letter. I've done everything you asked except for seeing Madame [illegible] though I have spoken to her and ten days ago we looked after her. I will go to see her as soon as I can. I saw your friends and they are all thinking about you. I introduced Beck[ett] to JW [Jean Wahl] and Beckett had lunch with us today. Father C[yprien] is waiting for news of you and as for me, I'm awaiting the outcome of the [illegible word]. I am sorry that you have such sore eyes and ankles and an upset stomach. Everything will get sorted out once you are home. We'll have to get you to see a good doctor. I'm delighted that you [liked] the food parcel. The meat was a Bristol ham pinched from a dinner party. We're all thinking about you. Did you share it with André Cohen? Remember me to Maître Ulmo. Does he know that it was for him that I got involved to begin with? I am seeing his mother-in-law. We are awaiting your arrival with the greatest of impatience. It cannot be long now. I would like to send you the warm overcoat that Catia gave me for you. Give your grey one away to someone else when you receive it. I don't want to discourage you but rather to save you from the cold, which must be very hard to bear. Everybody sends you their loving thoughts. I embrace you. Phone me from the bistro.[5] L.

* Dear Papa, we are all thinking of you and looking forward to your arrival with great impatience. Hopefully it won't be long now [illegible words] Alexis

[I]

[undated; early November 1941]

[Lucie to Paul, with postscripts from Dauphin and from Alexis Léon.]

My dear Paul, we cannot wait for you to arrive. I have seen your friends and they are all certain that your return is imminent. God's will be done. I am doing everything I can to follow through to the end. Right now I am bringing in a food parcel with your label on it. You will get your clogs via A[ndré] Cohen. Leave him your bed quilt when you are getting out. He needs one. Phone me from the bistro and I will come and collect you. I embrace you tenderly and cannot wait.

*My dear friend, I am with your darling and courageous wife. We are speaking about you, thinking of you and acting for you as hard as we possibly can. Take heart and be patient. The end of your trials is perhaps [illegible] at hand. In faithful and devoted friendship, Dauphin.

**Dear Papa, we cannot wait for you to come, especially now. We are all thinking of you and waiting to be able to send you a food parcel. As for me I am working hard at school and am pleased with my results. Maman is going to see your friend tomorrow, your son Alexis.

[J]
[Monsieur Thévenin to Lucie Léon.[6]]

Bagnères-de-Bigorre

11 September 1945

Dear Madame Léon,
I have just received your letter and I want to reply without a second's delay.
I knew Monsieur Léon well in Compiègne and I remember well that he often came to play bridge with Monsieur [illegible name]. We were deported together to Birkenau and I also remember having seen him in this camp during the first days of our stay in that hell. I must confess to you that he was in a very bad way when I saw him for the last time around the 3rd or 4th April 1942. From that time onwards I had no news of him ever.
At present I am living in Bagnères with my wife and my daughter and I'm receiving medical treatment. For, ever since my return from the camps I have been sick. Even though I've regained all my weight, I feel in all other respects worse than at the time when I left the camp.
I cannot therefore make an arrangement to meet you in Paris since I cannot foretell exactly when and where I could get there. But it will probably be towards the end of October. However, Madame [illegible name] will be advised of all this and will be able to keep you informed.
I hope that you will forgive me for giving you such [illegible word] and such incomplete information and ask you to accept my best wishes,
Thévenin

[K]
[Monsieur Thévenin to Lucie Léon].

Bagnères-de-Bigorres

19 September 1945

Dear Madame Léon,
You are wondering if it would be possible to have more information about the death of Monsieur Léon. I am perhaps less knowledgeable on that subject than you are, for since my return I haven't been able to be in touch with the outside world. My health still leaves a lot to be desired. Perhaps other comrades, deported on the same day as us from Compiègne, could give you some information. Personally I only have one contact: it's Monsieur [Lachmann] whose address you will doubtlessly be able to obtain from the Federation of the rue Leroux.[7] If you find any other names, please be so kind as to let me have them too. As for Monsieur Lattès, I certainly did get to know him at Compiègne but my memory has faded since then. I don't remember him from Birkenau and I don't know

what became of him. He was perhaps with Monsieur Léon on the last day we saw each other but I didn't notice him there. Monsieur Léon was at that time very tired and exhausted by the various trials that we had had to endure and I saw him falling down. I was about twenty feet away from him but I wasn't able to stop because we were advancing in rows surrounded by SS guards.

Thanking you for your good wishes, I send you my best regards,

Thévenin

NOTES

1. In 1988, Alexis and Anna Maria Léon presented the table from their apartment at 27, rue Casimir-Périer to the James Joyce Centre in Dublin, 35 North Great George's Street, where it is still on display.
2. The French pneumatic (pressure-driven) postal service sent messages underground through sealed lines in the sewers of Paris. The 'cartes pneumatiques' were sometimes called 'petits bleus' because of the colour of the paper. This term is used in Letter [37].
3. Although he described himself as an 'avocat' (lawyer) in the 1926 census and as a 'Law Professor' both in his 1926 application to study for a doctorate in Paris, and again in the 1936 Paris census, Paul never formally practised law and never held a university position in France.

Transcription

4. Une seule astérisque indique un postscriptum ajouté dans la marge gauche. Deux astérisques précèdent un postscriptum placé dans la marge droite et trois un postscriptum écrit dans la marge supérieure.
5. Lettre sans date, écrite sans doute vers le 7 septembre (vu la liste d'objets demandés, les questions d'intendance domestique qui préoccupent encore l'expéditeur ainsi que la question obsédante des états de service militaire).
6. Ce message semble dater du 12/13 septembre.
7. Cette lettre fut sans doute écrite le 15 et le 16 novembre.
8. Il s'agit manifestement d'une lettre écrite entre le 23 et le 24 novembre.
9. Cette lettre comporte un message écrit en russe (sur environ six lignes).
10. Cette lettre comporte un message écrit en russe (s'étendant sur cinq lignes).
11. Cette lettre de plusieurs paragraphes ne comporte qu'un seul paragraphe en français : tous les autres sont écrits en russe.
12. Cette lettre est terminée et signée en russe.

Translation:

1. For a more comprehensive account of Paul Léon's career as a scholar and writer, see Mary Gallagher, 'Paul Léon and the Republic of Letters', *Dublin James Joyce Journal*, Nos. 11–13 (2018–20): 205–27.
2. Timašev, Nikolaj Sergeevich, *Introduction à la sociologie juridique, version française d'après le manuscrit anglais*, translated with Paul L. Léon (Paris: A. Pedone, 1939).
3. See Megan M. Quigley, 'Justice for the "Illstarred punster": Samuel Beckett and Alfred Péron's Revisions of "Anna Lyvia Pluratself"', *James Joyce Quarterly*, Vol. 41, No. 3 (Spring 2004): 469–87.

4. Edward Weekes to Henriette Hirschmann; 1 March 1946; NLI MS 36,937/1.
5. One of the most complete sources on the history of Drancy, Paul Léon's first detention centre, is Annette Wievorka and Michel Laffitte, *A l'intérieur du camp de Drancy* (Paris: Perrin, 2012). The centre was originally a social housing project (Cité de la Muette) located in the 'new' industrial and largely communist Paris suburb of Drancy, just three miles from the north-eastern edge of Paris *intra muros*. Built between 1930 and 1935 (when it ran out of money), the project was only partially completed when it was commandeered as a prison for communists between September 1939 and May 1940. It was the first prefabricated complex ever built in France and shared with one other complex the distinction of including France's first skyscrapers (five 14-storey towers). After housing *Wehrmacht* soldiers following the fall of Paris on 14 June 1940, the complex was used to hold the Germans' largely French POWs (in its horseshoe-shaped entrance complex or 'cours d'entrée', located right beside the five tower complexes). On 20 August 1941 the Nazis began their major round-up of Jewish people in Paris. They targeted 5,784 men and boys to begin with, all aged 15–50 years. However, only about 3,000 were arrested on the first day. The internees were normally arrested in their homes and were mostly taken by bus to Drancy. Among those arrested on the following day were some forty to fifty men (several much older than 50), identified as Jews with legal connections, including Paul Léon.
6. When the bus carrying the 'Lawyers Group' arrived in Drancy on 21 August 1941, the rank-and-file internees who had been held there since the previous day gave these professional advocates, ironically perceived as their saviours, a standing ovation. See Wievorka and Laffitte, *Drancy*, p. 84.
7. Drancy, as the camp became known metonymically, was close to three major railway stations. The complex was thus ideally located for its role as the main Nazi concentration, transit and deportation camp in France. Of the estimated 74,000 internees deported from France between 1942 and 1944, about 67,400 men, women and children were deported directly from Drancy, the vast majority of them French Jews. It is estimated that only about 2,000 of those interned in Drancy survived. While at its peak occupation the camp did indeed hold close to 8,000 internees, Paul's is an inflated figure for the end of August 1941 and indeed he revises it downwards in Letter [3].
8. Pithiviers, located about 80 kilometres south of Paris in the Loiret region, was a converted train station. It was the first Nazi concentration camp to be established in France and was operated as such from May 1941 to August 1944. Like Drancy, it had served as a POW prison in 1940, before serving to house Jewish detainees.
9. Simone Perréon was a trusted family friend. During Paul's detention, she and her mother Madame Perréon were living in an apartment owned by the family at 27, rue Casimir-Périer, probably in Paul and Lucie's own apartment.
10. Catherine Berline was Paul's sister and also lived in Paris.
11. It was reported at the time that the arrest of the Jewish lawyers on 21 August 1941 was a reprisal measure. It was claimed that Jewish lawyers and intellectuals were fomenting communist resistance to the Nazi occupation. See Richard H. Weisberg, *Vichy Law and the Holocaust in France* (London: Routledge, 1996), most especially ch. 3: 'The Special Treatment of Jewish Legal Professionals'. Also note the title of Nissim-Noël Calef's eyewitness account: *Drancy 1941: Camp de représailles, Drancy la faim.* [*Drancy 1941, Camp of Reprisal and Starvation*] (Paris: Éditions de l'Olivier, 1997). Calef wrote his testimony in French in Italy between 1942 and 1943. The Italian translation appeared first (*Campo di rappresaglie*, Rome: Di Carlo, 1948) before the original French version was located by Shoah memorialist Serge Klarsfeld, who deposited it in 1991 with the association of Sons and Daughters of Deported Jews from France (*Fils et Filles de Déportés Juifs de France* or FFDJF). Klarsfeld also wrote the preface to the French version, published in 1997.

12. Paul's letters confirm that the utility bills, including insurance, for a second apartment owned by the Léon-Ponisowsky family at 27, rue Casimir-Périer were put into the name of the Ostafreffs (note that the spelling of this Russian name is unstable).
13. This is a reference to an intermediary belonging to the Struve family, who was going to help Lucie to buy back some of the books from Paul's library, books that had essentially been pawned. The person in question could have been Gleb Struve, who was from St Petersburg, a scholar and Paul's contemporary. Struve had followed essentially the same trajectory as the Léons after the Russian Revolution. Emigrating first, like them, to England, where he studied in Oxford and became friendly with Nabokov, he too moved on to France in 1924. However, he left for the USA in the 1930s. Gleb Struve's less famous brother Alexei also lived in Paris and was a distinguished Russian scholar and bibliophile. Therefore, this reference could be either to him or indeed to the brothers Gleb and Alexei's political scientist father Piotr (Peter) Struve, who was still alive and working as an intellectual in Paris in 1941.
14. Like Paul, Alexander Alexandrovich Popoff had been an officer in the Russian army in World War I. Popoff emigrated to France in 1919 and opened an antique shop in Paris opposite the Elysée Palace. His business grew into a world-famous art gallery. In 1935 the famous Popoff gallery won the Paris Grand Prix for the quality of its exhibitions and art collections, which were mainly of nineteenth-century watercolours and eighteenth-century Russian porcelain. This is another reference to Paul and Lucie's efforts to sell off family treasures. Lucie wrote that from the summer of 1940 she and Paul 'lived off the sale of stamp collections, my husband's first editions, and much of our furniture' (Noel, 'Case History', p. 6).
15. Paul and Lucie both refer to this person as Maître Pierre, a notary who seems to be helping the family to manage their finances.
16. No information is available about 'Jeanne', but she was most probably the proprietor of Paul's local *café-tabac* where he would have bought his cigarettes and drinks. Only certain cafés in France are licensed to sell tobacco products.
17. Paul suggests more than once that a man named Weber may have information that could assist Lucie in securing his release from Drancy. It is possible that this is Roger Weber, the proprietor of the Café Weber mentioned by Lucie in her Memoir and apparently mentioned as 'Roger' in one of her cards to Paul (see Appendix, Letter [D]).
18. Jean François was the deputy head of the Paris *préfecture* (police department).
19. This revised figure is closer to historians' estimates of the internee population in Drancy at this time than the one Paul gives in Letter [1].
20. Valda and inorhinyl are proprietary medications for the upper respiratory conditions to which Paul, as an apparent asthmatic, was susceptible. Eska may be Eleska (hot chocolate powder): Paul was known for his love of chocolate.
21. Alec is Lucie's brother, Alexander Ponisowsky, who was deported to Auschwitz from Monaco towards the end of the war.
22. A rabidly anti-Semitic propaganda exhibition on 'Le Juif et la France' opened on 5 September 1941 at the *Maison Berlitz* in Paris and didn't close until 15 January 1942. It was financed by the German Security Bureau and the German Embassy in Paris.
23. The Free Zone was the area in the southern part of France that was not occupied by Nazi Germany, at least not until July 1942. It was not exactly 'Free', however, in that it was under the control of the quisling French government put in place by the Nazis: the 'Vichy' administration.
24. While it would seem that it was Paul and Lucie's apartment that was now (ostensibly or officially) being inhabited by the Perréons, the second family apartment ('upstairs') had

originally been inhabited, according to the 1931 census, by Henriette Hirschmann (née Léon) and her family until that family's dispersal in 1936 after the death of Paul's brother-in-law, the art dealer Wladimir Hirschmann, and the emigration of Henriette to the United States in 1940. This second apartment appears to have been owned by Lucie's brother Alec in 1941 but was also put into the Ostafreffs' name. The reason why Paul wanted all the utility bills for these apartments to be paid by the Léons was that the Perréons and the Ostafreffs were in effect protecting these family properties.

25. Mme Weill is probably the wife of Gaston Weill, a fellow internee of Paul's in Drancy, whom Paul mentions several times in his letters. He belonged to the 'Lawyers Group'. Albert Ulmo also belongs to this group and is mentioned both in Paul's and in Lucie's letters and in Lucie's memoir.
26. TSF (Télégraphie sans fil) was the French wireless (radio) company, founded in 1918.
27. Although several of the internees in the Jewish 'Lawyers Group' had multiple military decorations for service in the French army, there was still absolutely no chance of their being released on that basis. It eventually became clear to Paul that medical grounds, not military veteran status, provided the only possible hope of a reprieve. By the end of September, sanitary conditions, malnutrition and starvation in the camp were catastrophic.
28. Paul is confirming here that the French *gendarmerie* participated, at least initially, in the movement of money, mail etc. into and out of Drancy.
29. Paul's critical edition of the correspondence between Benjamin Constant and Germaine de Staël as well as his biography of Constant were both published in 1928. He was writing a major work on Jean-Jacques Rousseau throughout the 1930s.
30. There is no specific letter from Paul to Lucie dated 7 September, though the undated letter [4] may well have been written on this date. Various details, including the list of items that Paul is asking to be brought to the camp for him and the list of administrative tasks set for Lucie, would seem to suggest that this letter was written at some point prior to 12 September when Paul changed rooms in Drancy. This chronology would also seem to be confirmed by his concern with domestic administration and by the expression of a mistaken belief, founded on his office work in the camp, that his war veteran status might favour an early release.
31. Paul misspells [Daneker] the name of SS officer Theodor Dannecker (1913–45), who masterminded not just France's main concentration camp in Drancy, but the entire Jewish purge in France until August 1942. As early as 1934, he had developed a precocious taste for this line of work in his role in developing Germany's first concentration camp near Berlin. His reign of terror in France was extreme in comparison with his somewhat less successful genocidal career in Bulgaria and then Italy, before he was eventually arrested by the US army in 1945. In theory, the French police and *gendarmerie* were in charge of administering Drancy. However, the fact that Paul knew Dannecker's name testifies to the latter's notoriety as someone who gloried in the dread that he was given free rein to inspire during his visits and inspections of the camp.
32. The French commission for Jewish affairs (*Commissariat générale aux questions juives*) was a further administrative puppet for the Nazis, along with the French police department (*préfecture*) and the quasi-military police, the *gendarmerie*. No individual matching the name 'Voineau' features in the relevant historical accounts, so it is possible that Paul meant to write 'Vallat'. Xavier Vallat headed the so-called Jewish Affairs Commission at this time.
33. This letter dated 9 September would indeed be the fifth (unofficial letter) of the extant collection, including the undated, presumably 7 September, letter (numbered [4] here).
34. The parcels that had reached Paul by this point did not include food. It is important to remember that the 'lawyers' and 'doctors' benefited from better conditions that the

majority of internees. For the latter, starvation set in from the end of August with an effective famine taking hold of the camp in September, when it was reported that some internees had lost 30 kilograms. Normal camp rations were two meals of watery soup and tiny amounts of bread. Dysentery was rife and so was tuberculosis. See Wievorka and Laffitte, *Drancy*, pp. 36–7.

35. As rumours circulated about conditions in the camp, a public relations exercise was mounted with the help of the collaborationist Paris press. This focused specifically on the so-called 'luxurious' conditions in which the lawyers in particular were supposedly being held. Photographers and journalists visited the camp on 10 September and their anti-Semitic reports were published two days later. These reports included photographs of the best-known Jewish legal figures, some of whom Paul frequently refers to in his letters. They were designed to incite anti-Jewish hatred and resentment in a population suffering from food shortages and rationing.

36. The Armenian Petrossian family had founded their still world-famous delicatessen and vintner shop in Paris in 1920.

37. This request not to send in any more clothes before the winter takes on ever more urgency as the 'winter parcel' with warm clothing comes to symbolize the loss of hope of being released before winter arrives.

38. Paul's address at Drancy was Bloc 1, Escalier 1, Chambre 4 until 12 September. Conditions in these quarters reserved for the lawyers were far superior to the regular dormitory conditions of Block 4, to which Paul was moved on 11 September, along with most of the 'Lawyers Group'. Coincidentally, the internees who were moved, or who had not been selected for the more high-profile administrative roles with perks reserved for those who got to stay on in Block 1, were men like Paul or the highly distinguished Pierre Masse, and they held a far less elitist and deluded understanding of themselves and of their position than their apparently more favoured counterparts who managed to remain in the more salubrious quarters. Wievorka and Laffite's book vividly outlines the internal politics and the internal divisions within the so-called 'Lawyers Group' of Drancy as well as the enormous gulf between the conditions in which numerous distinct categories of internees were held (at least in the first months of the camp's operation). They devote separate sections of their study to the 'Nazi Obsession with Lawyers' and to the camp's initial social geography. They note, for example, that one quarter was nicknamed the 'Champs-Elysées', as it was inhabited by the aristocrat internees (assimilated professionals and intellectuals), whereas another was dubbed 'Belleville', since it was the 'fiefdom of Proletarians and Poles'.

39. If the undated letter [4] is included, this is indeed the seventh letter that Paul sent to Lucie.

40. On 12 September these two collaborationist newspapers, *Paris Soir* and *Le Petit Parisien*, ran stories on the Jewish 'Lawyer' internees at Drancy, specifically dwelling both on the extravagant luxury to which they were allegedly accustomed and to the relative luxury in which they were being detained. The photographs accompanying this infamous act of anti-Semitic incitement, which were taken on 10 September, do not include Paul Léon, but they do include three figures who feature prominently in his letters: the senator Pierre Masse and the two lawyers Albert Ulmo and Gaston Crémieux.

41. Léon Netter also belonged to the group of lawyers interned in Drancy.

42. Although his name appears several times in the letters, it has not been possible to identify who Monsieur Guterman was. He was most probably also an internee, who seems to have been released early. Paul is very disappointed that, knowing how dreadful conditions are in the camp, Guterman does not prove more helpful to Paul's case from outside.

43. Historical accounts of Drancy confirm this testimony of corruption and inhumanity on the part of some of the French guards who helped to run the black market and to impose an arbitrary reign of terror in the camp; see Wievorka and Laffitte, *Drancy*, pp. 66–77.

44. Paul knew that Alexis was in danger in Nazi-occupied Paris and urged Lucie on more than one occasion to consider getting him to leave for the Free Zone.

45. Paul's military record was certified by the French Bureau for Russian refugees, whose director was one Monsieur Tatisteff. The certificate is dated 15 September 1941.

46. Carnosine is the most likely transcription of the medication that Paul is referring to here. It is a dietary supplement regarded as effective in treating stress, but also in treating nerve damage due to diabetes. It is not clear whether Paul had diabetes, though he was most likely pre-diabetic while in Drancy.

47. This is apparently Paul's second 'officially authorized' letter to Lucie, which accounts for its rather stilted form and for the fact that it repeats information contained in the more informal letters.

48. The Bureau for Russian Refugees (*Office des réfugiés russes*) was located at 7, rue Guénégaud.

49. Serge Kaminsky is also mentioned in the Foreword to Lucie's Memoir as a person with whom Paul discussed his 'own reactions to Joyce's creative process' (Chapter 2, p. 34).

50. The Latin Quarter bookshop Guillaume Budé, named for the French Renaissance scholar and humanist, was founded in 1926, along with an associated series *Les Belles Lettres*. Both the bookshop and the publishing house specialized in history.

51. This reference to Helsinki recalls the fact that, in his reminiscences of his father, Alexis, Léon mentions his parents' encounter there on their way from Russia to Western Europe (Chapter 6, p. 219). Many other so-called 'white Russian' émigrés travelled through Finland en route to England, France, Germany, etc.

52. Father Serge Boulgakov (1871–1945) was a famous Russian Orthodox theologian based in Paris in the 1930s and 1940s.

53. No information has been found on Fr Maillard, although one of Lucie's letters to Paul in Drancy mentions a file on 'Choura Maillard' (Appendix, Letter [C]). It is not altogether clear why Paul would so want Alexis to contact these Russian Orthodox priests.

54. A moneylending and black-market economy rapidly began to operate inside Drancy. This was largely facilitated—and indeed run—by the *gendarmerie*. Mme Bauh is the wife of a Monsieur Bauh who lends Paul money inside the camp. Lucie then reimburses Mme Bauh on the outside. See Wievorka and Laffitte, *Drancy*, pp.70–7.

55. Margraffs is the name of a famous second-hand Paris bookshop founded in 1878 by Gustave Lehec. Although Alphonse Margraff, who took it over from Lehec, sold it in 1908 to Jean Clavreuil, the shop kept the name 'Margraff' for several decades. It traded from 37, rue Saint-André des Arts in the Latin Quarter. Paul's letters refer to this bookshop very frequently and he seems to have had the Margraff catalogue with him in Compiègne, since one of his letters in Russian seems to quote from it.

56. The bookseller Marcel Rivière founded a socialist bookshop and publication company in Paris in 1902, which outlived his death in 1948. His was one of the leading scholarly publishing houses in France; its list included works on political theories, sociology, economics, law, etc. The bookshop was originally located in the 6th arrondissement on the rue Jacob. The books that Paul wanted to buy back are scholarly works, including most probably Roger Chauviré's study of Jean Bodin, a sixteenth-century philosopher of sovereignty and professor of law at Toulouse. Chauviré was a long-time professor of French at University College Dublin, James Joyce's alma mater.

57. Fr Cyprien is the Orthodox priest who features so prominently in Lucie's Memoir, where he is identified as Fr Cyprien K. As Lucie recounts, he succeeded against the odds in having the Christian Gospels brought to Paul in the camp (Chapter 2, Appendix G).

58. Alexander (Choura) Léon was Paul's brother. He lived in Italy and was married to Maria (née Farina), who predeceased him. Alexander Léon was also deported to Auschwitz.

59. While no information can be found on the Duttenhofers, Lucie's 'Memoir' mentions Alexander Troubnikov, who was an art historian associated before his French exile with the Hermitage museum in Russia and thereafter with the Louvre in Paris. Nikolai Anatolievich Kouomzine was a professor of New Testament studies in the Orthodox Institute in Paris. Born in 1912, he died in 1993 and is buried in the Russian Orthodox cemetery of Sainte-Geneviève-des-Bois outside Paris, where Lucie, Alexis and other members of their family are also buried.

60. This friend, who is never referred to as Monsieur Dauphin, but rather simply as 'Dauphin', also featured in Letter [15] as one of the couple's circle of friends. Indeed, he adds a few words of support to one of Lucie's letters to Paul in Drancy (Appendix, Letter [I]). It appears from this other reference that Paul specifically wanted Dauphin to be put in contact with Jean Wahl, who had been a fellow internee of Paul's in Drancy until his release in early November. It is possible that this person was Claude Dauphin, pseudonym of Claude Legrand (1903–78), an actor, who played roles in Beckett's plays after the war, and who, like Beckett, was quite politically active during the Occupation on the side of the *Résistance*.

61. From the context it appears that this is a reference to an unnamed bistro run by a person called Madeleine.

62. On 5 and 6 November Paul sent Lucie a series of tiny, telegraphic notes that showed the unprecedented depth of his anguish and despair. The reason for this mental suffering is clear: on 4 and 5 November, about 800 very sick internees, including Jean Wahl, were released from Drancy with many being transferred directly to hospitals in Paris. Paul must have been feeling desperate not to have been amongst them.

63. Jakob Eskiss, his sister Madame Joudrie and the Bauhs are Paul Léon's main moneylenders. Monsieur Bauh worked inside the camp, and his wife and the Eskiss–Joudrie pair worked on the outside. It is possible that Monsieur Bauh was a camp *gendarme* rather than an internee.

64. It is possible that Jean Wahl posted this 'pneumatique' for Paul and signed his own postscript as well.

65. Jean Wahl (1888–1974) was a prominent Parisian intellectual, a poet and a philosophy professor and the future founder of the Paris-based Collège International de Philosophie. In 1940, he was suspended as a Sorbonne professor under Vichy law, but continued to teach his students in secret. He was arrested, interrogated by Theodor Dannecker himself, who struck him, and had him imprisoned in the Santé prison before his transfer to Drancy. He spent just 60 days in Drancy before his release was authorized on medical grounds about nine weeks after his detention. This happened when Theodor Dannecker had returned to Germany to get married in early November. Wahl had written and published poetry before his arrest and wrote about seventy poems in and about Drancy, one of which is quoted several times by Paul in his letters to Lucie. These texts were published in Marcel Raymond, *Poèmes de Jean Wahl, accompagnés de dessins d'André Masson* (Montréal: Éditions de l'Arbre, 1945).

66. Monsieur Berels and Paul seem to have taken care of each other while in the camp, and their wives were in communication in relation to food coupons, parcels, food rationing, etc. See Appendix, Letter [F].

67. This is a telephone number: 'Archives' is the name of the telephone exchange corresponding to the district near the *Archives nationales* in the 4th arrondissement— or the Marais neighbourhood—the main Jewish quarter of Paris. The Léons' telephone number is given as Inv 40-09; Inv is the abbreviation for Invalides (the Military Hospital).
68. The Place Jean Jaurès was the Red Cross's central depot for the clothes and laundry baskets travelling to and from Drancy. Lucie's work with the Red Cross, specifically organizing the food parcels, allowed her access to the camp on a number of occasions, when she and Paul were able to see each other.
69. 'Spices' was Paul's code word for cigarettes (occasionally he uses the more revealing expression 'épices nicotinisées'). The black market in cigarettes was controlled by the *gendarmerie*.
70. Dr Tisné was the so-called 'Aryan' doctor appointed at Drancy at the start of November 1941 by the *Préfecture de Police*. He was assisted in the camp by the team of Jewish doctors working there from the end of August. The camp's team of interned doctors included Benjamin Schatzmann, who wrote an eyewitness account of his experience in Drancy in diary form: *Journal d'un interné: Compiègne-Drancy-Pithiviers: 12 décembre 1941–23 septembre 1942* (Paris: Fayard 2006). The Palais Bourbon was the French parliament building. It had been effectively occupied by the Germans by this point. At the beginning of November when Dannecker had returned to Germany for his wedding, tuberculosis, dystentery, starvation and malnutrition had already caused catastrophic suffering in Drancy. Dr Tisné appears to have been able to use the opportunity of his absence to have about 800 internees released on medical grounds, including Jean Wahl. 398 were released on 4 November and 550 the next day. When Dannecker returned to France on 11 November, he promptly suspended the liberations, which according to Paul's letter of that date, were still being planned for 12 November. The evacuation of the sick is documented in the Paul Zuckermann correspondence that is held in the Shoah Memorial Museum in Paris (CDIC 986 (19)-4). Michel Laffitte edited Zuckermann's 180 letters of testimony and they were published as *Berthe chérie* by Éditions du retour in 2014.
71. In early December, the Red Cross social worker Annette Monod discovered that Dannecker had ordered Wahl's rearrest and she was able to have him alerted. Wahl escaped from Paris with his brother's help and eventually got to Mâcon in the Free Zone before escaping to Casablanca. At this time France's African colonies were effectively part of the *Zone Libre* and could thus play a vital part in the movement of resistance to the Nazis. From Casablanca Wahl travelled to Baltimore in the summer of 1942. An intellectual support network had organized a position for him in the USA, where he worked as a professor of philosophy until 1945. See his daughter's testimony on her father's wartime trajectory: Barbara Wahl, 'Autour de Jean Wahl: textes, traces, témoignages', *Revista di Storia della Filosofia*, Vol. 66, No. 3 (2011): 517–38. An open-access transcription of Jean Wahl's interviews with Pierre Boutang is available on the website Academia and it specifically includes a section on the 1941–5 period.
72. Albert Ulmo was a widower, a lawyer and a war veteran who, like Paul, was also arrested on 20 August 1941 and interned at Drancy. Both men were transferred to Compiègne on 12 December. Ulmo was sent back to Drancy, however, most probably on 19 March (because his wife had not been Jewish). He was deported from there to Auschwitz-Birkenau in the 36th convoy on 23 September 1942. As Lucie's memoir confirms, she and Paul tried to help him as best they could to endure camp conditions because they felt sorry for Ulmo, who was quite alone in life (see Chapter 2, p. 61).
73. This is a reference to Annette Monod, who became known as the 'Angel of Drancy'. It is possible that she is the person Paul refers as his *rayon de soleil* (Ray of Sunshine) in his letters. Monod had officiated as an angel of mercy at Pithiviers and Beaune-la-Rolande in the Loiret before being sent to Drancy and then Compiègne. Besides saving Wahl from

certain death (see above n. 70 and n. 71), she was instrumental in making Drancy where she worked more humane for countless internees. If she was Paul's Ray of Sunshine, it was because she alleviated his misery by bringing money and cigarettes into the camp, as well as possibly smuggling letters in and out of the camp. After Drancy was liberated in 1945, Monod was put in charge of dismantling Drancy and of overseeing the rehabilitation of the survivors.

74. No information is available concerning Monsieur Jarnaci. However, Pierre Masse was the most eminent, and at over 60 years of age, he was probably the oldest of Paul's fellow internees at Drancy. Masse was a lawyer by profession and a former parliamentary deputy, senator and Deputy Secretary of State for Military Affairs. He had been decorated both with the *Croix de Guerre* and the *Légion d'honneur*. Like Paul, he was arrested with the other lawyers on 20 August in Paris and transferred on 12 December 1941 to Compiègne. Unlike Paul, however, he was transferred back to Drancy along with other internees whose wives were or had been identified as 'Aryan' on 19 March 1941. He was deported thence to Auschwitz in the 39th convoy of 30 September 1942. See Georges Weller's testimony *De Drancy à Auschwitz* (Paris: Éditions du Centre, 1946), most recently republished as *Un juif sous Vichy* (Paris: Éditions Tiresias-Michel Reynaud, 1991).

75. Paul had been able to see Lucie when she came to Drancy as a Red Cross assistant.

76. At the time, Jean Paulhan was the director of France's most famous literary journal, the *Nouvelle Revue française,* published by the prestigious publisher Gallimard. Gallimard also published the famous leather-bound Pléiade editions, a series that includes the French translations of Joyce's works.

77. Maroussia and Larissa are most probably the names of the two seamstresses working on the ground floor of 27, rue Casimir-Périer. In her memoir Lucie refers to them as having sympathized with the Léons after Joyce's death (see Chapter 2, p. 50).

78. The use here of Lucie's pseudonym and the fact that Paul refers to himself at the start of the letter in the third person indicates a certain strain and constraint on his part. However, this abates as the letter progresses.

79. All historical accounts of the first months of camp life, particularly first-hand testimonies (see Zuckermann's and Schatzmann's accounts, for example), stress the fact that there were very deep divisions in the camp between the 'hoi polloi' of internees and the relatively privileged internees (often professionals) who were put in charge of the day-to-day running of the camp. The latter elite included the 'Lawyers Group' of course, along with the 'Doctors Group', for example. After the transfer of most of the lawyers, including Pierre Masse and Paul Léon, and eventually Edmond Bloch himself, from the relative luxury of Block 1 to the regular dormitories and basic rations of Blocks 3 and 4, and after their demotion to petty administrative labours, divisions within this group deepened and soured. However, there was also a significant division in the camp between the self-styled French-Jewish versus foreign-Jewish internees. Later, the operative distinction operated by the authorities was whether one's spouse was Jewish or not.

80. Lucie refers to the three occasions on which the Gestapo came to the Léons' home prior to Paul's arrest and to the two thorough searches of the apartment (see Chapter 2, pp. 52).

81. André Cohen had also been arrested as part of the 'Lawyers Group'. Paul mentions him several times in his letters, sometimes as a friend of Gaston Weill, as does Lucie in her letters to Paul (see Appendix, letters [H] and [I]).

82. 4 December was Lucie's birthday and the prospect of not spending the day with her starts to assume gigantic proportions in Paul's mind. The '4th', which fell on a Thursday, is mentioned multiple times in several letters.

83. *Galettes* are a kind of large pancake made with coarser flour and eaten with savoury rather than sweet fillings.

84. This is a reference to Jean Wahl's poetry about the camp, which Paul cites several times in his letters.
85. A.C. is most likely André Cohen.
86. This reference is to Lucius Lucinius Lucullus (117–56 BCE), a politician of the late Roman Republic, known for his banqueting. In his *Life of Lucullus*, the Greek historian Plutarch attributed to him a particular appreciation of the art of dining alone.
87. Monsieur Bosqui is a tutor with whom Paul wants Alexis to take private lessons.
88. Matzah is traditional Jewish unleavened bread.
89. Marquis is a well-known Parisian chocolatier and the name of a manufacturer, a brand and a boutique.
90. When the German Occupation began to result in Jewish professors like Jean Wahl being suspended, Paul wrote to Louis Le Fur to resign from his role as secretary to the Editorial Board of the journal for philosophical and sociological legal studies, the *Archives,* a journal that he regarded as compromised. The 'Archives' were associated with a corresponding Institute.
91. 'JW' is Jean Wahl. Although Paul's formulation here seems to suggest that he thinks that Wahl is already in the Free Zone, Wahl was actually still in Paris for some time after his release and this is when Annette Monod alerted him to the fact that he might be arrested again. At that point, in early December, he fled to Marseilles and thence to North Africa and the USA.
92. In a short postscript to one of Lucie's letters to Paul in Drancy, Simone Perréon refers to herself as Paul's 'secretary' (Appendix, Letter [B]).
93. Most probably Edmond Bloch, one of the 'Lawyers Group'. This war veteran was formerly head of the 'Patriotic Union of French Israelites'. He identified with the more privileged Jewish administrative cadre of the camp, lording it, according to Paul Zuckermann, over what he regarded as the 'riff-raff' of 'foreign Jews'. Edmond Bloch features beside Pierre Masse in one of the propaganda photos published in the collaborationist press on 11 September 1941, an incident Paul mentions in Letter [7].
94. Paul is quoting here from memory the famous collaborative English translation of an extract from the 'Anna Livia Plurabelle' chapter of *Finnegans Wake*. Begun at poet Philippe Soupault's suggestion in the summer of 1929 by Samuel Beckett and Alfred Péron, this translation was originally intended for publication in Adrienne Monnier's literary journal *Bifur.* It was revised, however, after September 1930, when Beckett left Paris for Dublin, first by Eugène Jolas and Yvan Goll. However, the job was only completed after fifteen further sessions with the assistance of Joyce himself and Paul Léon, sessions that took place in the Léons' apartment. The translation was eventually published, at Joyce's insistence, not in *Bifur*, but in the more culturally embedded journal, the *Nouvelle Revue française*, on 1 May 1931.
95. *Kroumirs* is a Russian word for shoe-lining slippers or very thick socks.
96. Paul dated this letter several times in December. He no doubt began it early in the month, perhaps as early as between the 2nd and the 4th, certainly before 12 December when Paul and most of his cellmates left Drancy for Compiègne.
97. Paul's camp census work is still ongoing in early December.
98. The fact that Paul is not naming the place or the thing is significant. It is most likely that these mysterious questions refer to concerns for his family's safety since Paul has been insisting that Alexis should contact either Fr Boulgakov or Fr Maillard, two Christian/ Orthodox priests, and frequently begs her to have Alexis leave Paris, possibly with her, to the Free Zone.

99. Caseine is milk protein (available in powder form).

100. Paul's second reference to Lucie's census status was either prescient or else just an ironic coincidence. In both cases, he segues from a reference to the ongoing camp project of recording the identity status of internees' family members to a reference to what Lucie and Alexis (and finally Lucie's father) are doing outside the camp about registering their Jewish identity. On 12 December 1941, about a week after Paul wrote this letter, many internees from the 'Lawyers Group', including Paul, were moved to Compiègne. This transfer coincided with massive arrests of a host of 'new' Jewish internees in Paris, often called the 'rafle des notables'. Paul's cohort was left in Compiègne until March, when they were then divided into two groups. The first group were those who were sent back to Drancy in a deplorable state on 19 March 1942, only to be deported directly thence to the death camps further east a few months later anyway. The second group consisted of those who, like Paul, were sent straight to Auschwitz on the first convoy out of France on 27 March. It would seem that the basis of this selection was quite simply whether their spouse was 'Jewish' (direct deportation from Compiègne) or 'Aryan' (return to Drancy for later deportation). Paul was not transferred back to Drancy. Meanwhile, Lucie recounts how she had to leave their apartment and live in a series of safe houses.

101. Gaston Crémieux was another internee who belonged to the 'Lawyers Group' at Drancy from the start.

102. The implication here seems to be that Crémieux is the block leader and that Roger Masse gets preferential parcel treatment because he is Crémieux's son-in-law.

103. The image in French is rather of feet like jam (marmalade). This, coupled with the plea for footwear, underlines how difficult Paul found it to walk already in January 1942. It was because of the deplorable condition of his possibly diabetic or pre-diabetic feet that he could not keep up or even stand during forced marches or line-outs, for example from the station at Auschwitz to the newly built cell blocks of Birkenau or shortly after arrival at Birkenau, which is why he was shot.

104. All the references to 'Alfred' concern another member of the 'Lawyers Group', Alfred Valensi (1878–1944), who was from Tunis. He was a politically eminent intellectual of the Mediterranean world and the author of a noted work on Zionism.

105. Lucie did, then, get letters into Compiègne, but these don't seem to have been preserved.

106. This is possibly Simone Perréon.

107. Pierre Masse had the highest profile among the entire 'Lawyers Group' at Drancy. His brother, Roger, was not a lawyer but an engineering graduate of the *École Polytechnique* and a distinguished French army colonel and World War I veteran. In 1939 Roger was remobilized and was arrested as a POW by the Germans in August 1941, but was later released. On 12 December 1941, he was rearrested, this time as a Jew. He was brought to Compiègne on the same day as his brother Pierre, who was transferred there from Drancy (along with Paul Léon and several of the Drancy 'Lawyers Group'). Unlike Paul, the Masse brothers were sent back to Drancy on 19 March. According to the Nuremburg testimony of their fellow detainee Georges Weller, Theodor Dannecker personally selected Roger Masse to be transferred back to Compiègne from Drancy on 29 April 1942. He was then sent to Auschwitz-Birkenau on the very last Jewish deportation effected directly from Compiègne on 6 July 1942.

108. Paul's sister, Catherine Berline, was called Catia or Katia (see Appendix, Letter [E]), as was his niece, Catherine Hirschmann Henriette's daughter. It is most likely that he is referring to his sister here.

109. Mme Raymond is the wife of Raymond Smoliak, who was also deported with Paul on 27 March.

110. Mme Pierre is Mme Pierre Masse, whom Paul has already referred to on several occasions.
111. On the slate or on credit.
112. Eleska is hot chocolate powder, Banania is a banana-flavoured drink and Blédine is powdered milk.
113. This quasi-preterition confirms that Paul's Compiègne correspondence with Lucie is clandestine.
114. Although Paul Léon spells the name 'Sichel', this is probably the internee Michel (or possibly Michael) Siechel who was interned in Compiègne from 12 December 1941 and then transferred to Drancy in March 1942 (Wievorka and Laffitte, *Drancy*, p. 192). In Drancy, he appears to have been able to communicate news from the BBC received in sign language from his 'Aryan' wife who stationed herself in a house just outside the camp.
115. Gilberte's brother-in-law is identified as Maurice in letter [36].
116. 'AC' is André Cohen.
117. PM is presumably Pierre Masse.
118. Paul is referring here to the older men who were retransferred to Drancy in March in a deplorable state. They included Albert Ulmo and the two Masse brothers.

APPENDIX

1. This letter was obviously sent just after Lucie had sent Paul a sleeping bag and pillow. However, in September 1941, the 9th fell on Tuesday, not Monday, so the letter was written either on Monday 8, or Tuesday 9, September.
2. No doubt Roger is Roger Weber and Léon-Paul is the poet Léon-Paul Fargue who was a regular visitor to the rue Casimir-Périer.
3. On 8 October 1941, Paul told Lucie that Catherine's words had moved him more than hers.
4. This phone number refers to the 'Gobelins' exchange, located in the 13th arrondissement (and named for the famous tapestry manufacturing enterprise).
5. There was a bistro opposite the camp and Lucie is asking Paul to phone her from there as soon as he has been released.
6. Dr Thévenin survived Birkenau having been deported from Compiègne along with Paul.
7. Fédération nationale des Déportés et Internés, Résistants et Patriotes.

CHAPTER SIX

'Living Memories of James Joyce: Fifty Years On': A Lecture at the James Joyce Society

ALEXIS LÉON

Gotham Book Mart, 41 West 47th Street, New York City
11 February 1998

This is a lightly edited transcript of Alexis Léon's talk to the James Joyce Society at the Gotham Book Mart in New York. It was chaired by Sidney Feshbach, then President of the James Joyce Society and Professor of English at City College, City University of New York.

* * * * * *

Sidney Feshbach: In November [1948] Lucie Noel spoke here, so it's the fiftieth anniversary. Lucie Noel is the mother – and I just use the name because it is given to her, it is nothing of my doing, Madame Léon. This evening her son is speaking here and he's going to tell us about their family and their relationship to Joyce and you all know this. [. . .] I'll try to leave enough time at the end for questions and discussion. I'm going to call Alex Léon, or is it Leon?

Alexis Léon: I answer to many different names. They're all okay, whatever you are more comfortable with.

Feshbach: Please, could you please welcome him.

Alexis: Thank you. It's really a privilege to be here and I wish that time would allow me to meet every one of you individually. As Sid has said, it's fifty years, nearly, since my mother addressed this Society. Fifty years is a long time – I would imagine that few of those who attended that meeting in November of 1948, are still here, but if they are, they'll have to forgive any repetition. [audience laughter] And there will be repetition, inevitably. Why there will be repetition is very simple, you are scraping – this Society, and other Joyce Societies – are scraping the bottom of the barrel. Because if you're looking for people who knew Joyce – and remembering he was born in 1882, which means that if he were alive today, he would be what, 116 years old – anyone who knew him must be getting along there too. And, in fact, when I was in Dublin for the birthday lecture on the second of February, the point was appreciated very much.

If I can mix metaphors a bit, in this barrel that you are scraping the bottom of to find the last witnesses, you're talking to now, or you're looking at somebody, who was very young, I was fifteen the last time I saw Mr Joyce, which was in September 1940. Obviously, I'm not here to speak *at all* about the literary merit and the controversies, which are still bubbling up I notice. I'm not here to make any pronouncements at all, but just to give you a little bit of the flavour of what it was to be there at the time. Obviously, being young – at least it seems so now in retrospect – well, I didn't have any, you know, fantastic relationship with the great author. In fact, there were so many [writers] who came to the house. Although we knew Mr Joyce was one of the great geniuses, nevertheless, I was interested in some of the other people just as much, whether it was Samuel Beckett, whether it was Phillippe Soupault, the French poet, whether it was Léon-Paul Fargue, another poet, and so on.

So, there I was, the only the child, the reason I am an only child was because my parents took one look after a year or two and said, 'My God what a mistake, never again.' [audience laughter] And so, as only children do, you grow up very fast. You become an adult, at least in mind very early, the rest, hopefully, follows. And so, therefore, my reminiscences are a farrago of my direct observation, as I recall fifty years later, more than fifty years later, or they're something taken from my mother's, not only the talk given to this Society fifty years ago, but also what she wrote and what she talked about, and what my father said and so on. You'll have to forgive me if some of it sounds rehashed, but I am hopeful that'll you get some idea of the flavour of what it was to grow up and to see all these things happening at the time.

Criminals tell you – or are supposed to tell you, it may be just a joke – that you should never confess. Let the other side prove the case against you; well, maybe so. Other people also say you should never apologize. Certainly, for a speaker to apologize takes away a lot. Well, I think this is an exception. I am going to apologize three times. I'm going to apologize in the first place, because inevitably I am going to do what I was told never to as a child, I'm going to use the word 'I'. You remember, some of you, perhaps things have changed since then, that you are told not use the first person. And, so, you find all kinds of ways of getting around it, you say 'me', or you use the passive voice, or you try not to use 'I', especially in correspondence, if anybody still writes letters, which I sometimes wonder. [audience laughter] So, I'm sorry about that, there'll be a bit of that.

The other thing also, which I think merits a kind of apology is talking about the past. I mean there's nothing worse than the man like in Pushkin's poem or Lermontov poems, who talks about the battle of Borodino, where Napoleon really had problems, and he's talking to his little grandchild and on and on and on he goes, and we've all known those people who as they get on all they can do as they get towards the end of their lives is talk about the past. And if you're young and looking forward, you're looking to the future and it's amazing how one's perspective changes. It's been said many times before that anybody who was born after man landed on the moon, which to the generations prior to that seemed impossible – there was this piece of green cheese there, supposedly up in the air – and landing on the moon [was] impossible. Anyone who was born after the giant step for mankind, considers that absolutely normal. In fact, young people born afterwards now talk about landing on Mars, and then I'm sure that in the future it'll go beyond the solar system. So, one's perspective certainly changes. Nevertheless, in this particular instance I'll have to talk a little bit about the past, otherwise there is nothing to talk about [audience laughter] on this particular subject, but I hope at the end to say something about the future, the future of reputations and the magnificent work that Societies such as yours are doing. [. . .]

The Dublin talk on the birthday, on the second of February, when Joyce would have been 116 years old, since he was born on the second of February 1882, was an interesting meeting. My father was eleven years younger than Joyce. He was born in April of 1893 and, therefore, maybe even today in some societies (and I'm not talking about learned societies) perhaps less so I'm talking about some civilizations where there is still that respect for older age, my father always spoke of 'Mr Joyce'. We always spoke of 'Mr Joyce'. Here I am, fifty years or sixty years later, still speaking of 'Mr Joyce'. The life of James Joyce is very well documented. I mean every year books come out and there have been phenomenal biographies; there have been studies. I like Richard Ellmann's book, although even now with the passage of time people are finding fault with it and everything; that is in the normal way of human experience. But fewer people know about the Leons, I'll use that pronunciation, if you don't mind. So, I'd like to say a few words about Paul and Lucie.

Paul was born in St Petersburg, the sixth child of a family that was quite wealthy. They had a business, which prior to World War I still had the monopoly of the export of grain to the Baltics. In those days, before the Bolshevik revolution, Russia was a great exporter of grain, especially wheat. That was to change in years afterwards, in fact you remember, I'm sure you do, that Russia, the Soviet Union in fact, became an importer of wheat especially from the United States, a major exporter of wheat, and Argentina in particular. But in those days, somewhat halcyon days I suppose, prior to World War I, that was not the case.

He was always considered to be the smartest; he was the youngest. There were four girls and two boys in that family. They were all well-educated, of course, but he seemed to be the one who seemed to have the greatest talent. So, he got a good education. He volunteered in World War I, as just an ordinary soldier. All that was to change with the famous Russian Revolution. Changed not only for him, but for thousands upon thousands of people, millions if you count the people who stayed in Russia, or had to stay in Russia.

My mother came from a family, a rather interesting family, that was based in Moscow, and they had, my grandfather especially, had five or six textile plants. Now we're talking about prior to 1913. While the Industrial Revolution started in the UK, in England, in the middle of the nineteenth century, it was taken up with great gusto in this country and by 1913 the United States was a major industrial power. It's quite surprising to realize – I think it is because everything gets compressed in people's minds – that in the early part of the century there was quite an industrial base in Russia. So, there were these two families who knew each other vaguely. I've often said I suppose that I owe my birth to the Russian Revolution, because had that not been [. . .] we all have this kind of thing you know: the part that hazard and circumstance plays in all our lives is amazing. Well, obviously, if there hadn't been the Russia Revolution they would not have left. My mother would not have fallen in love with my father. The legend in my family was that she saw him jumping over small puddles on the beach in Finland. Finland had been a Grand Duchy in the Russian empire, but was declaring its independence at the time of the Russian Revolution of 1917.

I have often wondered about that, because in 1917 my father was 24, I have great difficulty imagining him jumping over puddles on the sand beach of Helsinkport or

Helsinki, but anyway it makes a good story. Both of them, both families, who had to leave Russia and leave everything behind, like thousands of others, ended up with some cousins that they had in England. By then, I take it – I was never told much of the details – they were very much in love. The two families, as happened often in those days, were absolutely opposed. I think my mother's family thought that she would be marrying somebody *below* her status. My father's family said you are absolutely *insane*, you haven't got a job, here we are émigrés: how are you going to support her, etc.? They were both opposed.

But my uncle, an interesting man, who became a press correspondent by the name of Poliakoff for British newspapers, principally known because he was very favourable to Mussolini, which later on turned out to be not so popular at all [audience laughter], but in this case in 1921 he organized the elopement. It wasn't like going to Gretna Green, or going away some place, and letting nobody know about it. He organized the elopement. He took them to the registrar in London and they got married and in 1921 they did that and moved to Paris.

What do Russian refugees do coming into Paris, like so many of them did? Many of them went to Berlin, many of them (I was reminded a few minutes ago that) went to Sweden. Some of them of course ended up in London. But anyway, what did they do? Many of them didn't have any kind of trade, no training to work, very often they came from relatively wealthy families; they didn't know what do. So many of them became taxi drivers. It would be interesting to see any kind of research to see how long it took them to figure out which part of the town to take you to when you jumped into the taxi.

Others ended up as doormen at nightclubs. It seemed to be that those who were very tall, who had been in the Russian army, especially the guards of the Tsar, in their uniforms, in their top hats, they looked exactly like the nightclub footmen and nightclub doorman of the time; so that's what they fitted in as. My father had some legal training. He immediately put that to help some of these poor refugees, who were struggling with the French system, which was even more bureaucratic than now, which is saying quite a lot. [audience laughter] He would help them. Since they didn't have any money, he didn't feel he should ask them for any money. He was doing all this work [as] pro bono work. Of course, my mother was absolutely furious.

She had problems of her own. When she came to Paris and they were settling there, she told me in later years that she didn't know how to boil an egg. This had all been done by servants in the past, but she was a remarkable woman, some of you who have met her know. She really not only learned how to boil an egg, but became a good cook in her own right. She was really the wage earner in the family; that's what it amounted to. She was delighted to be the wage earner. She was I suppose a kind of feminist before her time. My father was, of course, very much interested in writing and studying. He published some of the books you see here on the table and you can look at some of them after. The correspondence between Tsar Nicholas and his mother, then there was a biography of Benjamin Constant, but his magnum opus was going to be something on Jean-Jacques Rousseau, the French philosopher of the eighteenth century. He managed to publish, before the war intervened, about four or five chapters in the journal of a learned society to which he belonged.

So, there they were, with a son, who had to be put through school. The French school system then was – and still is as I understand it – rather tough; a lot of homework. The son in question was slow, which he still is. It took him hours to do some of those translations from Latin to French and French to Latin. I remember very well an occasion when my parents looked at me working, and the French–Latin or rather the Latin–French dictionary was a big fat volume. It had not only the translation of each word, but it also had after each word quotations from the Latin classics. The whole idea was if you were translating something you had never seen before you would look up every word, even the word *et* which means 'and', in the hope that you would find a whole phrase translated. You may remember some of you who have studied Latin the famous phrase, *timeo Danaos et dona ferentes*, which literally means 'I fear the Greeks and bringing gifts'. But *et* in this context means even when they are bringing gifts, which is by the way a feeling you have very much even today. [audience laughter] You are a little bit afraid of people who are too nice, bringing gifts. So, anyway, they saw me there and said to each other: 'Oh my God, we have brought into the world a pedant.' [audience laughter] I didn't know what to say at the time. There I was working away and my mother was getting madder and madder because I was only going to bed, 10 years old, 11 years, at one or two in the morning, when I had the homework done. But my father wasn't too unhappy, he thought: 'Well that's good, he's learning something anyway.' That was the atmosphere of that particular family, let's say from about the mid-20s to the mid-30s in Paris.

Paris was a wonderful place to live. In between the wars it was very cheap and that was its major attraction to a lot of Americans; American authors, American painters: Hemingway just to name one of many. I think you could live very well on 1,500 francs, which I think was about fifty dollars. Now I accept the fact that fifty dollars in the 20s or 30s is a great deal more than it is nowadays, if you translate it into today's currency. Nevertheless, it was considered very cheap. All of that changed. France became one of the most expensive countries in the world by about 1936, 1937, just before the start of the war, with the introduction of social security, which nowadays accounts for about 50 per cent at least of the cost of employing somebody on top of the salary. In those lovely days, things were much cheaper. There were lots of foreigners living in Paris, as you know.

What was their work? Well, I mentioned my father pouring over his books, working on Benjamin Constant and Jean-Jacques Rousseau, surrounded by his beloved four-thousand-book library, keeping an eye once in a while on what the son was learning, but my mother had a rather interesting job. At first, because of the cheapness of life in Paris a lot of Americans would come, ladies mostly, to buy clothes; this was in the 20s and 30s. Most of them didn't speak a word of French; that hasn't changed much. And most of the French didn't speak a word of English. So, they needed somebody to help, you know to go around, to do the translating, then take care of the shipping of the clothes, and so on. These were, of course, wealthy Americans: she did that for a while. And she became very well known in the couture, haute couture: it was something she loved very much. Then, about 1936, she got a job with the *New York Herald Tribune*. My father was wondering: 'She's going to write, what name is she going to use?' My mother said: 'Well, what are we going to do, I don't want to make you unhappy.' So, they decided they would take the name Leon and turn the letters around and come up with Noel, which was an amusing thing at the time. So that's where 'Lucie Noel' came from really.

She started working as the assistant fashion editor and the correspondent of the *New York Herald Tribune* in New York, which no longer exists, as you well know. She would rush around. Even then they had two collections a year, so she would rush around. There were no planes in those days, commercially I mean. I remember her having to race with the copy to the Gare Saint-Lazare, which was the station where the train left to Le Havre or Cherbourg, where the boat left for New York. That was something that occupied her, and she was very interested in that. But she was a very energetic person, who also managed to run a kind of salon in Paris, with all kinds of people and they seemed to mix very well. There were some Russians from the Russian Revolution, I remember in particular a Colonel Scheremetieff. And everyone joked that he had a crush on my mother, which he probably did. He was the son of the last governor general of the Caucasus. What I remember about him is a recipe he gave me for Roquefort cheese. He liked to take some Roquefort cheese, pour some brandy on it, maybe a little bit of butter, mash it and it made a wonderful thing. I haven't forgotten that in all those years. That was his claim to fame, I guess. His father may have been the governor general of the Caucasus, but he invented the Roquefort mash. [audience laughter]

Having set the background, perhaps I can get back to the subject of your Society, Mr Joyce. How did they meet Mr Joyce? Well, once again, a series of coincidences, as happens to all of us in life. My mother's brother was a sort of gad about town, also looking for a job. When you have no other job, and you have some foreign languages, you think, 'I can teach, if nothing else.' And, I don't know how, he met Joyce's daughter Lucia, but they had a nice relationship going, not in the modern sense of the term, but they certainly enjoyed each other's company. Through Lucia my uncle met Mr Joyce and started giving him Russian lessons. One thing led to another and all of a sudden what happened was that my father and Mr Joyce met at one of the social get-togethers, and they must have found something in common. I have often wondered, what did they find in common that drew them together so that they spent a lot of time.

Between 1930 and 1940, a period of a little over ten years, they met nearly every day at our apartment, our flat, in Paris. They saw each other socially as well. The wives were involved from time to time. They met nearly every day. My father didn't travel a lot, but Mr Joyce liked to go to Switzerland quite a lot, especially in those early years for one of his seventeen or nineteen eye operations. What did they see in each other? I think the number one thing was they were both exiles. Joyce had left Ireland in the early part of the century, in 1904, I believe, and had gone to Trieste and then after Trieste to Zurich and then finally had settled in the 20s in Paris. And my father, naturally, was one of those Russian exiles from the Russian Revolution, so that was already a kind of bond. Secondly, I think that Joyce needed somebody disinterested. My father refused to accept any money at all, just as he had not accepted from those poor Russians, who were trying to struggle with the French bureaucracy, he didn't even accept it from Mr Joyce. I don't think Mr Joyce insisted too hard [audience laughter], because if you look at what has been said and if you know about the magnificent efforts of people like Miss Weaver, and so on, he always, all his life, he never had enough money. That was a standard thing, and, of course, he liked to live well. It is an irony of course that the great fame of Joyce came after he was dead, after his life was over, after the Second World War was over, and led, of course, by American interest in the universities, I would say without a doubt.

So, anyway, they would meet and there were few other people in the group. There was Gene Jolas, who published one of those literary magazines called *transition*, published certain parts of *Finnegans Wake*. *Ulysses* had already been written, had been published in the early 1920s. Joyce then started on about seventeen years of work to write *Finnegans Wake*. The main problem, of course, was that in *Finnegans Wake*, as you know better than I do, Joyce tried to create a new language. Although the subtext sounds a little bit like English, a lot of the words are created words. And one of the things he would do, he would create words by introducing puns in these words, breaking the bonds of English words and very often bringing in words from other languages. Scandinavian languages in particular, with which my father couldn't help at all. He knew seven languages, but certainly no Scandinavian languages. And of course, there were lots of other languages, especially German, Spanish and Italian as well [in *Finnegans Wake*].

My memory of them is that they would be sitting around this table in our combined living room and dining room in Paris and there were long periods of silence, and then maybe one or the other would say something and there would be a sort of a little flurry of activity and then you could see them thinking and then the silence would take on again. The famous words 'silence, exile and cunning' applied, of course, to Joyce, and applied in a similar measure, I think, to my father, although the cunning was not very discernible, I must say, and that can be deduced from what happens later on.

The group also included, not only Eugene Jolas, but also Maria Jolas, an American from Kentucky, who was a remarkable person. She ran a bilingual school in Neuilly in the outskirts of Paris. She was really a very, very strong personality. I think maybe she has addressed this Society [someone in audience confirms this], yes. She was quite extraordinary. There was Samuel Beckett, for a while certainly, people like Louis Gillet, Phillipe Soupault, Léon-Paul Fargue, other poets and so on. At these lunches that my mother used to manage to do in spite of work there was always a mixture [of people]. There may have been an American there, who came from one of the department stores, because then it was no longer private customers, little by little, it was the department stores who were buying originals from the French couture. Simplifying them and making thousands, or hundreds, of them, at lower prices and simplified and so they would come over on buying trips. And there was possibly Nabokov. I hope you don't mind as it sounds terribly like dropping names, which is ghastly, but it so happened that it was very often just a normal thing, I never even thought of it at the time. My mother helped Nabokov translate one of his books, I think the one called, what was it, *The Life of Sebastian Night*, I think it was. So, there were some Russians and there was obviously Mr Joyce from time to time, although he didn't like to participate too much in these dinners. He would sit quietly on the side, didn't eat much and then there were French people as well and it became quite the tradition. Then there was Colonel Scheremetieff doing his mashed Roquefort from time to time. [audience laughter] It worked well. They were able to accomplish quite a lot because, although it took seventeen years for Joyce to finish *Finnegans Wake*, his last book, nevertheless, it wasn't work all the time. There were occasions; for example, he loved to celebrate Thanksgiving, American Thanksgiving. He would write poetry when something happened. There was the famous case of the turkey, which was being delivered from some shop to, I think, the Jolas's house. The guy skidded with his tricycle on the place Saint Augustin, if you know Paris at all, there's a big church there. The turkey went skidding about twenty or thirty yards. There was a very famous poem that Joyce wrote on this turkey that was trying to fight meeting such an end as the main course on a Thanksgiving dinner. There were quite a few occasions like that.

There I was 12, 13, 14 with my eyes wide open. When at the table my father decided to tell a risqué story, which nowadays would not even be risqué, nobody would bat an eyelash at all. He thought that my ears were not suitable to hear this risqué story, which was probably not risqué at all, he would use an expression from the French theatre of the boulevard, in other words, as opposed to the Comédie-Française, the classics. He would say 'Pauline', which was normally a maid, when the bourgeois family wanted the maid to leave because they could discuss something privately, they would say '*Pauline sortie*', 'Pauline please go out, please remove yourself'. So, he would turn to me and he would say '*Pauline sortie*'. Very reluctantly I would move to the door and I would sort of try to leave it slight open so I could hear what was going on [audience laughter], but it never worked: 'Close the door,' I was told. Then I would wait: so, 'when can Pauline come back in? how long is this story going to last?' I would try gingerly and generally I was allowed back in. This tended to happen around the salad course, and I had my eyes, of course, on the dessert. In fact, I still bear the scars as you can see. [audience laughter] There's no question that it was a very united family. It was a lot of fun, in spite of the seriousness of Mr Joyce and my father's work.

All of that, like for so many people, was completely transformed by the war. The war in Europe, the Second World War, came in stages. First there was in September '38 the famous Munich [Agreement]. The Munich [Agreement] is still being argued today because some people say, okay, it enabled the allies – France and England at the time – to have one more year to get prepared because they were not prepared at all, so that they would have a little bit of production of planes; others say no, it was a betrayal because it had opened the door. Two years previously Hitler had marched into Austria, there had been the *Anschluss* and now he was able, thanks to Munich, to take over the Sudetenland, that part of Czechoslovakia where there was a majority of German speakers, and then little by little take over the rest, with protectorates over Bohemia and Moravia and a similar friendly regime in Slovakia. So, Munich came. And, of course, everybody was afraid, people did realize this thing wasn't going to end particularly well. A lot of people started making preparations. I was sent off to a little country home we had about ninety miles south of Paris, near Orléans, where, because there were many people in the same situation, a small annex of the *lycée* was opened up in a town that was, you know, a one-horse town, or maybe two horses, let's give it some credit: Beaugency. All those towns around the Loire valley have some claim to fame going back five hundred years. Jeanne d'Arc slept here. [audience laughter] Well, in this case not only Jeanne d'Arc, but her right-hand man in the fifteenth century, de Dunois, had slept there. And there was a big square tower, it was somewhat historical, but every little town around the Loire river had some connection. Of course, Rouen could claim that the British burned Jeanne d'Arc there, but these other ones she managed to liberate them from the English who were occupying most of France at the time. I'm talking about 1429 to 1430.

So that was Munich. It wasn't yet war, but it was getting close, that was '38. In the following year '39, by the end of the year, the war had started, the 1st of September. Can you imagine Mr Joyce, seventeen years of work, finally manages to get *Finnegans Wake* published in 1939? It fell, you know – nobody noticed it – like a lead balloon, I think the expression is and that was it. He was very disappointed. He was a man who didn't really take much of a political stance. He thought there wasn't much to choose [from] in general, and politics didn't interest him at all, what he lived for was his art. So here was an enormous effort which had no resonance whatsoever. So that happened on 16 June of 1939.

Then things started going badly in an accelerated fashion. While there were a few months of phoney war, as it was called, it didn't last long. By May of '40 the German army had invaded Belgium and the Netherlands and had managed as a result to enter France. The French had a pretty good memory of what the Germans were like. In the previous war, that ended in 1918, and this was 1940 so twenty-two years before they had been occupied for a long time in northern France, they had lost two million killed, more than anyone else at the time. Of course, these figures now seem so small when we see what has happened since. But, anyway, it was a major factor.

Everybody in northern France took to the road. That was the famous exodus. Ten million people on the road. Where were they going? Well, they weren't too sure where they were going, they were going south, as far away as they could from the advancing army. Actually, the French army was also on the road going in the same direction. [audience laughter] It was thought there would be some resistance on the natural barrier, which was Loire Valley. So, the big thing is, let's get to the other side of the Loire and then maybe we can live for a second round. That unfortunately was not to be. It was a real mess, but luckily Mrs Jolas had already moved her bilingual school from Neuilly to a little château owned by the parents of one of her pupils at her school, a château called La Chappelle, which was just a few miles from Vichy. At that time nobody knew that Vichy would become so not only important, but the seat of the Pétain government and therefore the object of much opprobrium in later years, nobody knew that. She had said if anything goes wrong, 'pear-shaped', I think the word is, in English, in American rather, come to the château, come to Saint-Gérand-le-Puy, the little village next to the château.

So, from all sides of the compass, here is this motley crew, the Joyce group assembled ending up in Saint-Gérand-le-Puy. My father arrived there in a cart drawn by a donkey. We'd heard that he was arriving, everybody went out to meet him. He said, 'Well, the good Lord arrived in Jerusalem on a donkey,' but everybody said, 'No, no, wait a minute, first of all, you need a bath, because we can smell that and secondly you are going to need some white robes, if you're going to say that.' So, anyway, the mood was rather optimistic, and this was the beginning of June 1940, but dark days were ahead. On the 17th of June the Pétain government decided there was no point in continuing the war and they asked for an armistice, which was granted by the Germans on 25th June. And then everybody who was there had to make the decision, what do we do? France was divided into two parts: a part that was called occupied, a part that was called non-occupied. It became occupied too later on. But what do we do?

An aunt of mine, way back in Russia, had had a salon at which many artists came, among whom was one of her beaus, Serge Koussevitzky, who by that time had become the conductor of the Boston Symphony Orchestra, and so she had managed to get in touch with him and he organized a US visa. She and her son left through Spain, Portugal, again no planes of course (civilian planes), and managed to get to the United States. Mr Joyce and his family wanted to go to Switzerland. I'm talking June, July, August. It took some negotiation. It took several months in the case of Mr Joyce. He only arrived there in December of 1940. And, of course, that didn't last long. On the 13th of January [1941] he was dead from peritonitis.

My mother was then working for the *New York Herald Tribune*. The United States was not yet at war; that only happened a year and a half later, on the 7th of December, on the day of infamy when the Japanese attacked Pearl Harbor. There was quite a lot of isolationist feeling in the States. The *New York Herald Tribune* was still being published and she had a job – she had no other job. So, she felt, she had to go back. Of course, the apartment had been left and everything was in it. My father felt, 'Well, I am not political. I want to get back to my books, my four thousand books or so', though he never used the number, but that was what he had in mind. 'I want to continue my work. I want to finish this book on Jean-Jacques Rousseau.' And of course, there was the son's education, he had to get his baccalaureate. So they went back. Of course, that was something that had consequences that weren't known at the time. And he [my father] was dead by April of '42. That is roughly a little over a year after Joyce. So here were these two friends that had both come to the end of their lives.

Joyce in '41 was 58 going on 59, on the 13th of January, the 2nd of February would have been his birthday. [Audio recording cuts out for an indeterminate amount of time.]

[. . .] Of course, everybody knows, depending on whether you're an optimist or a pessimist, that you just have a limited amount of time and you only have one time round as far as we know because nobody has written that I am having a second time around. Although some philosophies and religions do tell you that you have several times around, maybe as an animal or some other creature, but for most people in the West, it's a one-time job and it only goes in one direction. What happens to all of us? We live on, I suppose, in the minds in the memory of those who have known each one of us and when they in turn depart, then that's the end of that. Maybe the name remains on a stone somewhere, and maybe somebody of the second or third generation takes care and puts some flowers on it, but that's it.

Artists are somewhat different. I remember very well Guillaume Budé's edition of Latin classics that my father had. He would always point to this ode from Horace which says, *exegi monumentum aere perennius*, which means 'I have built a monument more lasting than bronze', and of course an artist leaves his work behind. Horace was referring to the Odes, but every artist of some kind leaves something other of himself. So, in the case of Mr Joyce he leaves his work and that work has become sort of alive again. A new life, especially after World War II. Sparked by the universities here in the US and the younger generations and now it's a worldwide phenomenon.

What then of the future? If you look at the classics of the past, they really continue, though there are some that don't last very long. I'd like to come to a conclusion by quoting – my father tried to drum it into me, but I never could remember – about five or six lines from a French historian, by the name of Edgar Quinet, who nobody reads nowadays, like so many, but nevertheless he has this marvellous sentence – I'll try to translate it with the help of Mr Ellmann – about how nature continues these flowers through generations and they grow on the ruins of men's artefacts and it says something like this. I'll give you a translation as I go along:

> *Aujourd'hui comme aux temps de Pline et Columelle*
>
> Today as in the time of Pliny and Columella

Both were ergonomists who lived in the first century AD.

> *La jacinthe se plaît dans les Gaules*
>
> The hyacinth disports in Wales.

Not Wales at all, it's in the Gauls, I think it's a typographical error, because Ellmann knew it was the Gauls.

> *La pervenche en Illyrie, la marguerite sur les ruines de Numance*
>
> The periwinkle in Illyria, the daisy on the ruins in Numantia.

Numantia was a town in Spain which the Romans had built, which is completely destroyed and there's nothing left not even ruins nowadays.

> *Et pendant qu'autour d'elles les villes ont changé de maîtres, que plusiers sont entrées dans le néant.*
>
> And while around them cities have changed masters and have changed names and while some of them ceased to exist.

The French say entered into nothingness, that's a much stronger word.

> *Que les civilisations se sont choquées et brisées, leurs paisibles générations . . .*
>
> While civilizations have collided with each other and broken up, the peaceful generations of these flowers of which he mentions three . . .
>
> *. . . ont traversé les âges et sont arrivés jusqu'à nous fraîches et riantes comme aux jours des battailles.*
>
> . . . have passed through the ages and have come up to us, fresh and laughing as on the days of the battles.

That supposedly represented pretty much Mr Joyce's view of history. He recited it to John Sullivan, as they were walking by a cemetery on the boulevard Edgar Quinet in Paris, who nobody studies, but at least there is a street in his name. I think that's about as good an epitaph as you could think of. He translated it into the language of *Finnegans Wake*. In Dublin we had an Irishman, who much better than I can ever hope to do, read this passage from *Finnegans Wake* and the lilt and the sound of it is so close to the French, but with words that are partly English and partly the special language of *Finnegans Wake*, it was a very moving occasion. So that was it. Time marches on – and no one can stop it.

[General applause.]

Sidney Feshbach: You have any questions or comments you wish to make?

First questioner: The photos that I've seen of Joyce he looks very slim, and your parents spent so much time with him. In addition to Thanksgiving dinner, did they ever mention what else he ate?

Alexis Léon: He was always slim. I guess he must have been one of those people who no matter of how much they ate, they don't seem to put on weight. These are the people I am envious of for obvious reasons. He loved his white wine, he loved especially Neuchâtel wine, a Swiss wine. In fact, at one point if you've read the biographies, the Swiss commercial attaché wanted him to come out and officially endorse this wine in order to help their sales. [audience laughter] Mr Joyce on this particular occasion did not rise to the challenge.

There was another rather amusing incident that has to do with eating and drinking. Quite often while they were sort of sitting there in silence and working there would come a knock on the front door of our apartment in Paris. This was a regular poor man, I think he was possibly Russian, but I'm not absolutely sure. He would knock on the door and ask for alms. Two francs was a substantial thing then. My father would always give him two francs, and my mother would go absolutely mad, bananas, because she knew the man was going to drink it. She would ask: 'Why are you giving two francs? He's going to drink it?' And he would say, 'If that's his pleasure let him go and drink it.' There was a bistro about 50 or 70 yards from the apartment. A typical old French bistro with a zinc counter. After they had done their work, let's say at 11.30 or 12.00, my father and Mr Joyce, arm in arm, would go to this bistro and have some Neuchâtel wine, they stocked Neuchâtel wine. My father wore a Homburg hat. And there, of course, on one occasion, there was the guy who had just gotten his two francs drinking his glass of wine. And very courtly everyone took off their hats and started saluting each other, a little bit like some graduation ceremony at some university in England. [audience laughter] It was quite extraordinary.

Mr Joyce had two restaurants that he liked every much one was on place de l'Alma, which was along the Seine river, called Francis, and another was on the Champs-Élysées, and they even have a James Joyce room now, called Fouquet's. They would end up there, nearly always. In many cases my father would grab a cab, my father would make sure either the driver knew where Mr Joyce had to be deposited or my father would go with him. One day, the story goes that they were both walking arm in arm – I guess shuffling would be a better expression – up the rue Royale that's the street that runs across the place de la Concorde to the Madeleine. Anyway, Philippe Soupault the French poet saw them and said immediately: 'There's the lame leading the blind.' [audience laughter] They liked their food I can assure you.

Second questioner: Do you remember Mrs Joyce?

Alexis: Yes, the famous Nora Barnacle. She was a marvellous person, very quiet. I don't know how they were like in the intimity, but she was very quiet. She has been quoted a couple of times as saying, 'It's very hard to be the wife of a writer.' She also would keep an eye on the clock. So that when Mr Joyce was at a party and he felt like singing, and he would sing, and then he would drink and then he would sing. He wasn't drunk. I'd never seen him drunk, contrary to some people think today. I have never heard of him being drunk. 'Well, Jim, time to go home.' And he would go. My recollection of her is that she was absolutely perfect, they were so united. She was the mother of his two children, Giorgio, with his beautiful baritone voice, and Lucia, the daughter who had an unfortunate history of mental sickness, who is no longer with us. That was a sort of tragedy that they bore with great patience. But she was a wonderful person, no question about it.

Third questioner: Two of the names you didn't drop were Wyndham Lewis and Ezra Pound. I wonder if there was any contact in your household and whether there were any aspects of anti-Semitism as a result?

Alexis: I can't answer that because I think that those contacts were prior to my father becoming so close with Joyce. I think that must have been in the 20s, in the *Ulysses* period especially.

Third questioner: It was later also.

Alexis: Later also, well I never heard them speak of either one, but that doesn't mean a thing. I would have been the last to know of such things, simply because of my age.

Fourth questioner: Is it your memory that when they were working together on *Finnegans Wake* that they were working mostly on issues of language?

Alexis: Their work was of two kinds, one was what you might call business management, or of three kinds perhaps. There was an awful lot of correspondence involved with publishers, quite often asking for advances I would say and with dealing with translations of *Ulysses* which was beginning to appear in various languages as you know, sort of business correspondence. Joyce was delighted to leave that to my father, although naturally they discussed what the answer should be and what the procedure should be. In the case of T. S. Eliot, who as you know was head of Faber & Faber, it was sort of a mixed situation in that T. S. Eliot was already an author in his own right on top of running a publishing house. Then there was of course, as you describe it quite correctly, the question or discussing of the creation of new words, so in that respect the fact that my father had these seven languages was of interest to Joyce.

Fifth questioner: What language did they speak to each other?

Alexis: English I would say, 99 per cent of the time. Although Joyce did speak French acceptably.

Sixth questioner: And your father's English?

Alexis: His was very fluent.

Seventh questioner: Did it come from his school in Russia?

Alexis: Yes, from school in Russia and also from a lot of reading of English philosophers.

Feshbach: And you said they lived in England?

Alexis: Yes, but not for very long.

Eighth questioner: And your English?

Alexis: We'll leave that to another time. It would be too long to explain.

Ninth questioner: Joyce has so many Jewish and Hebrew expressions in *Finnegans Wake* was . . .

Alexis: I don't think they came from my father! Because I don't think he knew any of them. Well, maybe he knew a few, after all its impossible to go through life without a modicum of intelligence and education, especially international education, without picking them up. Obviously, Joyce did a lot of research in that direction himself. You have to remember that my father's friendship with him is long after *Ulysses*. And *Ulysses* is this peregrination of Leopold Bloom through Dublin on the 16th of June 1904 even though the book came out in 1922. I think already Joyce knew quite a lot on his own.

Tenth questioner: Léon, would he have known Italo Svevo?

Alexis: Personally, no. Again, I have the feeling that is from an earlier period. I think Mr Joyce sort of isolated himself during those seventeen years – of which ten or so my father participated in – in order to concentrate on the tremendous job of *Finnegans Wake*, so a lot of people he did not see.

Feshbach: Just following that same line, I always assumed Paul Léon was Jewish, yet when he was in the camp he asked for the Gospels and then it's followed by your mother actually giving these prayers to the Virgin Mary: I wonder if they had converted?

Alexis: It's a bit more complex than that. Yes, he did come from a Jewish family. He listed himself as agnostic. He was not a great fan of organized religion. However, he was very sensitive to metaphysical questions and to religious questions. For about twenty or thirty years he had very definitely been influenced by the New Testament, especially the Sermon on the Mount. He considered the Sermon on the Mount as a phenomenal expression of feeling. The story I think you are referring to is that when he was arrested and went into the Drancy camp he had forgotten to take his Gospels with him. He asked my mother in a letter that was smuggled, a letter written on toilet paper, whether she could do anything about it. With the help of a Russian Orthodox priest, although nothing was allowed, she managed to get them to him. Part of that same story was that she was a very energetic woman and really extraordinary. The camp was poorly run and there was no food, hardly any food, so the inmates quickly exhibited signs of malnutrition, which meant oedema, which is what happens when your cells fill with water and, for example, your legs become very large. In fact, he had to cut open his shoes, or somebody did it for him. My mother saw this mess because they were allowed to receive one package from the families a week, but it wasn't organized. The packages were never done properly. It was an unbelievable mess.

So my mother joined the Red Cross. In her Red Cross uniform, she organized in place de la Chapelle, which is not far from Drancy, a place where Paris ends. She organized a sort of a reception area. The families came there with all kinds of food and she repackaged it, with the help of three or four other people, so that it would be accepted in the camp. She then got onto the truck, she drove into the camp four times and met my father secretly there. But eventually the head of the inmates said, 'This is getting to become quite dangerous, not just for you and your husband but for all of us.' So, she had to give it up. She was that kind of a person; you know extremely energetic and ready to fight for what she felt was right. That's as far as I would like to go on that, because I think this lady here has a question.

Eleventh questioner: Did you ever happen to hear Joyce sing at any of these social events?

Alexis: Yes, I was never invited I must say, unfortunately. I was the wrong age to be invited. I tended to hear these things second-hand. But I did hear him I think once or twice. He had a nice voice, I think a semi-trained voice, not as well trained as his son, but it was a lovely Irish voice. Of course, there is the famous story, if I may keep you a little bit longer, with John Sullivan. Joyce was a great support of Sullivan, the Irish tenor. My mother made four trips to the United States by boat and Joyce asked her – I don't know if it was the famous day where they had to pass around the duty of taking Joyce to the cinema or to the opera – and on one of these occasions Joyce wanted to see a film called 'Ecstasy', you know the story, which starred Hedy Lamarr in the altogether or whatever they say nowadays. And there were some horses in there, doing what horses of different sexes do very well I'm told. At any rate, there was Joyce in the second row, because he couldn't see very well; nineteen eye operations. Nearly half blind in one eye and he couldn't see much out of the other. So there he was next to my mother and he kept asking: 'What's happening now?' [loud audience laughter] My mother was very embarrassed, so she would try to explain using the nicest words she could find what was going on. And then he'd ask: 'And now what's happening now?' That was when the horses were at it. And finally, he said, 'I see, I see.' [audience laughter]

After one of these forays, he knew my mother was going to New York –something to do with these buyers of French fashions – and he said, 'You know they don't recognize Sullivan enough and I think that you should give an interview at the Metropolitan Opera.' So, mother went and she was received by Mr Ziegler, who I guess was a director of the Metropolitan Opera here. Mr Ziegler was absolutely wonderful. I listened to the whole story. I suppose my mother was playing the violin about how wonderful Sullivan was as an Irish tenor and at the end he said, 'Mrs Leon, Mr Sullivan is well known to us, he has sung here.' . . . So, she slunk out and felt terrible. Then in a sort of sheepish way she told Mr Joyce and he said, 'Yes, thank you, thank you.' And he wrote a little poem for in her scrapbook about 'Oh Mr Ziegler, Oh Mr Ziegler'. [audience laughter] That is the best that I can answer your question.

Twelfth questioner: Thank you.

Feshbach: There is a line in the *Wake*, there are lots of puns on lion and Leon and Mark the lion and so on. I wonder is this sentence about your father? It's a nasty sentence as it were: 'Don't tell me, Leon of the fold, that you are not a loanshark!' (*FW* 193.04–5).

Alexis: Well, I don't remember that line, but I haven't read the *Wake* as well as you have. They did have a couple of falling-outs and it is recorded that one day Mr Joyce told my mother, 'What's wrong? Why won't Leon speak to me?' They had a big falling-out just before they met again in Saint-Gérand-le-Puy in June 1940. What it was about I don't know. My father of course admired him and loved to see him work, but sometimes he felt that Joyce made errors of judgement.

I've put here on the table some interesting things, especially a couple of the books my father had written or at least in part in the case of the last one. The interesting one, of course, is the *James Joyce/Paul Léon Papers*. As soon as he heard that Mr Joyce had died on the 13th of January 1941, he realized that something had to be done because Joyce had left his apartment in Paris with the whole family and gone because of the exodus and everything collapsing and ended up in Switzerland in December 1940. There was no way of transferring money apparently from Switzerland to France. The owner of the apartment was getting very nervous about rentals and started to make noises and wanted to sell whatever property was in there. So, luckily, through my uncle they went to the auction house, the French, poor equivalent of Sotheby's and Christie's, and bought back a lot of the stuff and hid it and it was given to Mrs Joyce at the end of war.

The interesting thing about the papers were that my father managed – and he hated doing it I know – at night he went with one of our factotums that he could get hold of with a cart and he went to the apartment, told the concierge some cock and bull story that he had some property and books of his in the apartment that had been occupied by Mr Joyce and his family, went up there, gathered it all together, brought it down, and then brought it back to his apartment. This is under German occupation, with a curfew, police and military patrols, but they managed to avoid all that. Then he made these nineteen envelopes full of these papers and put on there – and that I remember personally – that it should go to the National Library of Ireland, with an embargo, a fifty-year embargo. I remember him telling me, the reason for a fifty-year embargo was to protect the reputations of people who might not appear in a very good light and I think also because he realized that the sickness of Mr Joyce's daughter Lucia in the mental institution was not something that needed to be immediately talked about too much. I mean to protect not only the reputation, but also the sensitivity of that situation. He then took all of that to the Irish Embassy, which funnily enough was still in early '41 in Paris, although the government was in Vichy and there it stayed during the war until after the war and brought to the National Library of Ireland. The fifty years expired in 1991, long after all the principals were no longer with us. So, the Irish National Library spent about a year opening them up, cataloguing and so on. Then they had a very nice inaugural, which the Taoiseach, the prime minister, and Stephen Joyce, the grandson, and myself attended in the amphitheatre, round room, of the National Library of Ireland, which I'm sure many of you are quite familiar with. That was an interesting consequence, fifty years on.

Feshbach: Any last questions?

Thirteenth questioner: Do you own any first editions of all the books?

Alexis: No, they all ended up with University of Tulsa and that's this catalogue here, the Paul and Lucie Léon Joyce collection.

Feshbach: There's an interesting story that your mother tells that she took the first editions and distributed them among friends and then at some point a German came looking for the first editions.

Alexis: Working probably for Göring, we think. Göring, among other things, loved art, he loved anything that had any value. He would send his agents around all of Europe, they would try and requisition, or pay very low prices for things. And they turned up apparently, this must have been 1942, the last part of '42. I was no longer there. They asked for first editions. They went about it in very roundabout way: 'Where is your husband?' My mother, with her usual directness, screamed at them: 'Don't you know that you arrested him and that he is in camp?' And they asked, 'What did he do?' So, she said what he did, and then finally the word Joyce came up: 'That's it, that's it. He was Joyce's secretary.' Then she went through the whole thing: no he wasn't Joyce's secretary and that he never took any money, but they said, 'Yes, yes, but he must have some first editions', and that's when she understood that's what they were after, things of value, and, of course, by then, as you say, they had been spirited away and hidden, so they didn't get anything.

Feshbach: It's so extraordinary. I find it incomprehensible, I mean, this running over to get Joyce's business papers and getting them away. Your mother knowing in advance to get rid of the first editions, and distribute them one here, one there, and then recollecting them after the war, as I understand, and that is what became the Tulsa Léon Joyce collection. It's a remarkable sense of dedication. It's a remarkable story. Anyone else?

Fourteenth questioner: It makes it much more sad that some of the material ended up with the Joyce family, which was either destroyed or hidden.

Alexis: I'm not really qualified to talk about that, but I think I know what you're talking about. [some audience laughter] I personally think that when you are in possession of something where there is a general, collective interest and you yourself don't want the thing to be published or become used, why not put an embargo on the thing – okay a fifty-year embargo, a hundred-year embargo, put some kind of embargo that will save the reputations of someone. Of course, it will make the academics very unhappy because they will have to wait and it will be the next generation, but don't destroy things, don't destroy things! If there's anything to be learned about history, is that, after all, we should keep records, in one form or another. It doesn't even have to be the original form, nowadays you don't have to keep the originals to keep records. You can microfilm it; they've been doing that for many years. Perhaps it's better because paper only has a certain life, doesn't it?

Feshbach: I would like to thank Mr Léon very much.

[Prolonged audience applause.]

FIGURE 6.1: Alexis and Anna Maria Léon, 1996 © The Léon Estate.

SELECT BIBLIOGRAPHY

JOYCE'S WORKS

Joyce, James, *Anna Livia Plurabelle* (New York: Crosby Gaige, 1928).

Joyce, James, *Anna Livia Plurabelle* (London: Faber & Faber, 1930).

Joyce, James, 'Anna Livia Plurabelle', translated by Samuel Beckett, Alfred Perron, Ivan Goll, Eugene Jolas, Paul L. Leon, Adrienne Monnier and Philippe Soupault, with the author, *La Nouvelle Revue Française*, Vol. xix, No. 212 (May 1931): 633–46.

Joyce, James, *Finnegans Wake* (London: Faber & Faber; New York: Viking Press, 1939).

Joyce, James, *Finnegans Wake: A Facsimile of Buffalo Notebooks VI.B.29–VI B.32*, compiled by Danis Rose, in the *James Joyce Archive* [Volume 59] (New York: Garland, 1978).

The Finnegans Wake Notebooks at Buffalo: VI.B.29, edited by Vincent Deane, Daniel Ferrer and Geert Lernout, with an Introduction by Geert Lernout (Turnhout: Brepols, 2001).

Joyce, James, *Haveth Childers Everywhere* (Paris: Henry Babou and Jack Kahane; New York: The Fountain Press, 1930).

Joyce, James, *Pastimes* (New York: Joyce Memorial Fund Committee, 1941).

Joyce, James, *Pomes Penyeach* (Paris: Obelisk Press; London: Desmond Harmsworth, 1932).

Joyce, James, *Selected Letters of James Joyce*, edited by Richard Ellmann (London: Faber & Faber, 1975).

Joyce, James, *Storiella as She is Syung* (London: Corvinus Press, 1937).

Joyce, James, *Tales Told of Shem and Shaun* (Paris: Black Sun Press, 1929).

Joyce, James, *Ulysses* (Paris: Shakespeare and Company, 1922).

Joyce, James, *Ulysses* (London: John Lane Bodley Head, 1936).

OTHER WORKS

Beach, Sylvia, *Shakespeare and Company* (New York: Harcourt, Brace & Company, 1959).

Boyle, Kay, *Avant-hier*, translated by Marie Louise Soupault, (Paris: Calmann-Lévy, 1937).

Budgen, Frank, *James Joyce and the Making of 'Ulysses'* (Oxford: Oxford University Press, 1972).

Calef, Nissim-Noël, *Drancy 1941: Camp de représailles, Drancy la faim. [Drancy 1941, Camp of Reprisal and Starvation]* (Paris: Éditions de l'Olivier, 1997).

Campbell, Joseph, and Henry Morton Robinson, *A Skeleton Key to 'Finnegans Wake'* (London: Faber & Faber, 1947).

Crispi, Luca, 'A First Foray into the National Library of Ireland's Joyce Manuscripts: Bloomsday 2011', *Genetic Joyce Studies*, 11 (Spring 2011).

Crispi, Luca, '*Ulysses* in the Marketplace: 1932', *Joyce Studies Annual* (2012): 29–65.

Crispi, Luca, 'Paul, Lucie, and Alexis Léon', *Dublin James Joyce Journal*, No. 10 (2017): 119–28.

Crispi, Luca, 'Paul Léon and the Publication of *The Mime of Mick, Nick and the Maggies*', *Joyce Studies Annual* (2019): 125–61.

Crispi, Luca, Stacey Herbert and Lori N. Curtis, *In Good Company: James Joyce & Publishers, Readers, Friends: An Exhibition of McFarlin Library's Special Collections in Occasion of the North American James Joyce Symposium, University of Tulsa, 2003* (Tulsa: University of Tulsa, 2003).

Documents on Irish Foreign Policy <https://www.difp.ie/volume-6/1941/letter-sean-murphy-to-cremins/3394/#section-documentpage>.

Edel, Leon, *James Joyce: The Last Journey* (New York: Gotham Book Mart, 1947).

Edwards, John Hamilton, *A Critical Biography of Ezra Pound: 1885–1922* (PhD dissertation: University of California, Berkeley, 1952).

Ellmann, Richard, *James Joyce* (Oxford: Oxford University Press, 1982).

Encyclopaedia Britannica (Cambridge: Cambridge University Press, 1911).

Fahy, Catherine (compiler), *The James Joyce–Paul Léon Papers in the National Library of Ireland* (Dublin: National Library of Ireland, 1992).

Fargue, Leon-Paul, *Haute Solitude* (Paris: Émile Paul Frères, 1941).

Fuse, Mikio et al., 'Emendations to the Transcription of *Finnegans Wake* Notebook VI.B.29', *Genetic Joyce Studies*, Issue 3 (Spring 2003).

Gallagher, Mary, 'Paul Léon and the Republic of Letters', *Dublin James Joyce Journal*, Nos. 11–13 (2018–20): 205–27.

Gillet, Louis, 'Du côté de chez Joyce', *Revue des deux mondes*, 28 (August 1925).

Gillet, Louis, 'M. James Joyce et son nouveau roman', *Revue des deux mondes*, 84 (15 August 1931).

Gorman, Herbert S., *James Joyce: His First Forty Years* (New York: B. W. Huebsch, 1924).

Gorman, Herbert S., *James Joyce* (New York and Toronto: Farrar & Rinehart, 1939).

Gorman, Herbert S., *James Joyce: A Definitive Biography* (London: John Lane The Bodley Head, 1941).

Hine, Reginald L., *The History of Hitchin*, 2 Vols. (London: George Allen & Unwin, 1927 and 1929).

Homer, *The Iliad*, translated by A. T. Murray, revised by William F. Wyatt, Loeb Classical Library (Cambridge, MA: Harvard University Press, 1924).

Irving, Washington, *A History of New York* (New York: Doubleday, Doran & Co., 1928).

Jolas, Maria (ed.), *A James Joyce Yearbook* (Paris: Transition Press, 1949).

Jolas, Maria, 'The Little Known Paul Léon', in *A James Joyce Miscellany, Second Series*, edited by Marvin Magalaner (Carbondale: Southern Illinois University Press, 1959), pp. 225–33.

Kain, Richard M., *Fabulous Voyager: James Joyce's 'Ulysses'* (Chicago: The University of Chicago Press, 1947).

Kenny, Peter (compiler), 'Collection List No. 70: Papers of Paul and Lucie Léon' (Dublin: National Library of Ireland, n.d. [2005]).

Léon, Paul L., *Benjamin Constant* (Paris: Rieder, 1930).

Léon, Paul L., 'Une doctrine relativiste et expérimentale de la souveraineté – H.-J. Laski', *Archives de Philosophie du Droit et de Sociologie Juridique*, Nos. 1–2 (1931): 231–40.

Léon, Paul L., 'Les idées sociales et politiques du guild-socialism', *Archives de Philosophie du Droit et de Sociologie Juridique*, Nos. 3–4 (1931).

Léon, Paul L., 'Doctrines sociales et politiques du moyen âge (des origines au IXe siècle)', *Archives de Philosophie du Droit et de Sociologie Juridique*, Nos. 3–4 (1932): 247–67.

Léon, Paul L., 'Le problème des sources du droit positif', *Archiv für Rechts- und Sozialphilosophie*, Vol. 28, No. 4 (1934).

Léon, Paul L., review, R. W. and A. J. Carlyle, *History of Medieval Political Theory in the West*, Politica (1936).

Léon, Paul L., 'L'évolution de l'idée de la souveraineté avant Rousseau', *Archives de Philosophie du Droit et de Socologie Juridique*, Nos. 3–4 (1937).

Léon, Paul L., 'Le souvenir de Joyce', *Poésie*, Vol. 42, No. v (November–December 1942): 35–40.

Léon, Paul L., 'In Memory of Joyce', in *A James Joyce Yearbook*, edited by Maria Jolas (Paris: Transition Press, 1949), pp. 116–25.

Lernout, Geert, 'Finishing a Book Without Title: The Final Years of "Work in Progress"', *Joyce Studies Annual* (2013): 3–32 (30).

Nicolas II and Mariâ Fedorovna, *Lettres de Nicolas II et de sa mère, l'impératrice douairière de Russie*, translation, introduction and notes by Paul L. Léon (Paris: S. Kra, 1928).

Noel, Lucie, *James Joyce and Paul L. Léon: The Story of a Friendship* (New York: Gotham Book Mart, 1950).

Noel, Lucie, 'Lucie Noel's Biographical Notes' (NLI MS 36,915).

Noel, Lucie, 'Case History' in *United States Congressional Serial Set*, Vol. 11904, for the 84th Congress, 2nd Session, House of Representatives (Report 2528), 28 June 1956.

The Paul and Lucie Léon/James Joyce Collection (Tulsa: University of Tulsa, 1985).

Prescott, Joseph, 'Two Manuscripts by Paul L. Léon Concerning James Joyce', *Modern Fiction Studies*, Vol. 2, No. ii (Spring 1958): 71–6.

Proust, Marcel, *The Past Recaptured*, translated by Frederick A. Blossom (New York: Albert & Charles Boni, 1932).

Quigley, Megan M., 'Justice for the "Illstarred punster": Samuel Beckett and Alfred Péron's Revisions of "Anna Lyvia Pluratself"", *James Joyce Quarterly*, Vol. 41, No. 3 (Spring 2004): 469–87.

Rowntree, Seebohm, *Poverty: A Study of Town Life* (London: Longmans, Green & Co., 1922).

Schatzmann, Benjamin, *Journal d'un interné: Compiègne-Drancy-Pithiviers: 12 décembre 1941–23 septembre 1942* (Paris: Fayard 2006).

Slocum, John J., and Herbert Cahoon, *A Bibliography of James Joyce, 1882–1941* (New Haven: Yale University Press, 1953).

Soupault, Philippe, *Souvenirs de James Joyce* (Algiers: Éditions Edmond Charlot, 1943).

Spielberg, Peter. *James Joyce's Manuscripts & Letters at the University of Buffalo: A Catalogue* (Buffalo: University of Buffalo, 1962).

Staël, Madame de, *Lettres de Madame de Staël à Benjamin Constant*, edited by Elisabeth de Nolde, baronne [1905], rev. edn by Paul L. Léon (Paris: Kra, 1928).

Stuart Gilbert. *Reflections on James Joyce: Stuart Gilbert's Paris Journal*, edited by Thomas F. Staley and Randolph Lewis (Austin: University of Texas Press, 1993).

Théolleyre, Jean-Marc, 'James Joyce à Saint-Germain-des-Prés', *Le Monde*, 26 October 1949.

Timašev, Nikolaj Sergeevi , *Introduction à la sociologie juridique, version française d'après le manuscrit anglais*, translated with Paul L. Léon (Paris: A. Pedone, 1939).

Van Hulle, Dirk, 'The Lost Word: Book IV', in *How Joyce Wrote 'Finnegans Wake': A Chapter-by-Chapter Genetic Guide*, edited by Luca Crispi and Sam Slote (Madison: University of Wisconsin Press, 2007), pp. 436–61.

Wahl, Barbara, 'Autour de Jean Wahl: textes, traces, témoignages', *Revista di Storia della Filosofia*, Vol. 66, No. 3 (2011): 517–38.

Wahl, Jean, *Poèmes de Jean Wahl, accompagnés de dessins d'André Masson*, edited by Marcel Raymond (Montréal: Éditions de l'Arbre, 1945).

Weller, Georges, *De Drancy à Auschwitz* (Paris: Éditions du Centre, 1946), republished as *Un juif sous Vichy* (Paris: Éditions Tiresias-Michel Reynaud, 1991).

Wievorka, Annette, and Michel Laffitte, *A l'intérieur du camp de Drancy* (Paris: Perrin, 2012).

Zuckermann Paul, *Berthe chérie*, edited by Michel Laffitte (Paris: Éditions du retour, 2014).

INDEX

www.ingramcontent.com/pod-product-compliance
Lightning Source LLC
Chambersburg PA
CBHW081356090726
47908CB00011B/2689

* 9 7 8 1 3 5 0 3 5 1 0 3 5 *